THE LGV LEARNER DRIVER'S GUIDE

D0610501

THE LGV LEARNER DRIVER'S GUIDE

A PRACTICAL GUIDE TO LGV LICENCES, THEORY AND DRIVING TESTS

JOHN MILLER

KOGAN
PAGE

Publisher's note

Every possible effort has been made to ensure that the information contained in this book is accurate at the time of going to press, and the publishers and authors cannot accept responsibility for any errors or omissions, however caused. No responsibility for loss or damage occasioned to any person acting, or refraining from action, as a result of the material in this publication can be accepted by the editor, the publisher or any of the authors.

First published in Great Britain in 2005

Apart from any fair dealing for the purposes of research or private study, or criticism or review, as permitted under the Copyright, Designs and Patents Act 1988, this publication may only be reproduced, stored or transmitted, in any form or by any means, with the prior permission in writing of the publishers, or in the case of reprographic reproduction in accordance with the terms of licences issued by the CLA. Enquiries concerning reproduction outside these terms should be sent to the publishers at the undermentioned address:

Kogan Page Limited
120 Pentonville Road
London N1 9JN
United Kingdom
www.kogan-page.co.uk

© John Miller, 2005

London Borough of Hackney

Askews		
629.2844	£14.99	
CLR	06/490	

The right of John Miller to be identified as the author of this work has been asserted by him in accordance with the Copyright, Designs and Patents Act 1988.

British Library Cataloguing in Publication Data

A CIP record for this book is available from the British Library.

ISBN 0 7494 3790 1

Typeset by Saxon Graphics Ltd, Derby
Printed and bound in Great Britain by Creative Print and Design (Wales), Ebbw Vale

Contents

About the Author

In over 30 years in the industry John Miller has been an instructor on both cars and lorries and for many years ran his own commercial driver training school in West Sussex. He has been a qualified tutor of instructors for a number of years and is now an independent training consultant.

John is also co-author (together with Margaret Stacey) of *The Driving Instructor's Handbook* and *Practical Teaching Skills for Driving Instructors*, both of which are published by Kogan Page and which are recommended by the Driving Standards Agency for the Approved Driving Instructors (ADI) exams and for the voluntary register of LGV instructors.

Introduction

The 2003 Road Haulage and Distribution Training Council survey has estimated that there is a shortage of more than 20,000 LGV drivers in the industry at the present time. Over the next few years this shortfall is likely to rise to about 60,000 as a result of new legislation for maximum working hours combined with an ageing workforce. The regulations will reduce the normal working week in the industry from the present average of about 60 hours to only 48 hours, which means that the workforce needs to increase proportionally. Clearly, there will be a continuing and increasing need for properly trained drivers and instructors. Looking further ahead, the new European Union (EU) directive on compulsory training and retraining of vocational drivers will have an even greater impact on the industry, with a shortage of instructors being a particular issue.

Learning to drive an LGV requires considerable input from the trainee in terms of time, effort and expertise. Just as importantly, there is a need for good-quality, professional instruction, with the trainee receiving plenty of time at the wheel as part of a structured programme of training. For these reasons, information about driver training as a career is included in Chapter 6.

The book does not attempt to teach you to drive; that can only be done in a practical way, with an effective instructor and with plenty of practical experience. It does, however, give an overview of all the requirements for obtaining a vocational licence, details of the theory and practical tests, a summary of the main points of law for the LGV driver and some of the areas of responsible driving.

Obtaining a driving licence is now more complex and demanding than previously, with higher standards for each of the theory, hazard perception and practical tests. There is also the requirement for separate testing on each of the different categories, from C1 to C and CE. The test requirements are covered in detail in Chapters 2 and 3.

Teaching driving can be a worthwhile and satisfying occupation, with a direct involvement with trainees from different backgrounds and with varying levels of aptitude, ability and motivation. To become an effective instructor you need much more than the ability to drive a large vehicle safely and competently. You also need special skills in communication and motivation as well as a complete understanding of the teaching/learning processes and methods.

It has already been shown that there is a demand for instructors at all levels in the industry and that this demand will increase over the next few years. To qualify as an instructor you need to have held a full, unrestricted licence for at least three years for the type of vehicle that you will be instructing on. To qualify as a DSA-approved instructor you must pass the exams for theory, own driving and instructional ability. These subjects are covered in Chapter 7, but for more detail on teaching and learning you should refer to *The Driving Instructor's Handbook* and *Practical Teaching Skills for Driving Instructors*, both of which are published by Kogan Page. Accredited centres for instructor training are listed at the end of the book.

1

LGV Driving Licences

Driving licences for all categories, including vocational licences, are issued by the Driver and Vehicle Licensing Authority (DVLA) at Swansea.

Only photo-card licences are now issued, as the old-style paper licences are being phased out. The photo-card shows details of the driver's full licence details, including those for LGVs and passenger-carrying vehicles (PCVs). On the reverse of the card any restrictions such as 'not for hire or reward' or 'restricted to vehicles with automatic transmission' are shown by means of a code. Details of the codes are given on page 11. Any provisional entitlements, together with any endorsements, are shown on the accompanying paper document, officially referred to as the 'counterpart'.

A fact sheet on photo-card licences (INF 61) is available from the DVLA by phoning them on 01792 792 792 or online at www.dvla.gov.uk. Fact sheets are also available from the DVLA for:

Minimum Test Vehicles	INF29
Towing Trailers	INF30
Driving Large Vehicles	INF52

LICENCE ENTITLEMENTS

Anyone passing the ordinary L test now receives full entitlement for goods vehicles up to 3.5 tonnes gross weight and for passenger vehicles with up to 8 passenger seats – that is, any category B vehicle. If your first full licence was issued before 1 January 1997 you will have additional entitlement for categories C1 and D1 vehicles (goods vehicles up to 7½ tonnes and passenger vehicles with up to 17 seats).

LGV DRIVING LICENCE CATEGORIES

The driving licence categories are shown in Table 1.1.

Table 1.1   LGV driving licence categories

Type of vehicle	Category	Minimum age
Goods vehicle with a maximum authorized mass (MAM) between 3.5 and 7.5 tonnes and a trailer of up to 750 kg	C1	18
Goods vehicle and trailer (category C1 vehicle with a trailer of more than 750 kg and a total weight of not more than 12,000 kg	C1 + E	21
Large goods vehicle with a MAM of more than 7.5 tonnes	C	21
LGV with drawbar trailer (rigid vehicle with a trailer of more than 750 kg)	C + E (restricted to drawbar trailers)	21
Articulated vehicle	C + E	21

For all other driving licence categories see Table 1.2 (page 5).

If you passed your car test before January 1997 you will have C1 entitlement on your licence. This allows you to drive rigid vehicles up to 7.5 tonnes. For a vehicle with a trailer you are restricted to a total weight of not more than 8,250 kg.

Even if you do not have C1 entitlement you are allowed to progress from B to C to CE, subject to the minimum age limit. However, an 18-year-old would need to take the category C1 theory and practical tests before moving on to category C at 21.

To obtain provisional entitlement for category C vehicles you need to be over 21, or over 18 for category C1. For details of the different categories, see Table 1.2 (page 5). The main categories of licence and the minimum driving ages for driving goods vehicles are shown in Table 1.1, but for full details refer to the DVLA booklet D100, which is available from most post offices or at www.dvla.gov.uk.

Your entitlement to drive particular types of vehicle and trailer combinations depends on various factors. These include your age, when you first obtained a licence, and the weight of the vehicle and/or trailer. Specialized and over-sized vehicles have separate regulations regarding age and eligibility.

There are special rules for minimum driving age for:

- drivers who receive Disability Living Allowance;
- members of the armed forces;
- trainees in the Young Driver Scheme;
- drivers of minibuses and PCVs in limited circumstances.

Passing your driving test for a particular category may entitle you to drive vehicles of other types, but there are some restrictions. For example, if you pass the test on a vehicle with automatic transmission you are not entitled to drive a vehicle with manual gears.

Table 1.2 shows the various driving licence categories.

Table 1.2   Driving licence categories for tests passed on or after 1 January 1997

Category	Type of vehicle	Additional categories covered
A	Motorcycle	B1, k, p
A1	Light motorcycle	p
B1	Three- or four-wheel light vehicle	k, p
B	Motor car	f, k, p
B + E	Car with trailer	
C1	Medium-sized goods vehicle	
C1 + E	Medium-sized goods vehicle with trailer	B + E
C	Large goods vehicle	
C + E	Large goods vehicle with trailer	B + E, C1 + E
D1	Minibus (up to 17 passenger seats)	
D1 + E	Minibus with trailer	B + E
D	Bus or coach	
D + E	Bus or coach with trailer	B + E, D1 + E
f	Agricultural tractor	
g	Road roller	
h	Tracked vehicle	
k	Mowing machine or pedestrian-controlled vehicle	
l	Electric vehicle	
p	Moped	

VOCATIONAL LICENCES

To drive a vehicle over 3½ tonnes, or with more than eight passenger seats, you need to apply for a provisional licence for that category of vehicle. To obtain a provisional LGV licence you first need to hold a full car licence, and a full rigid vehicle licence (for category C) is required before you can drive an articulated vehicle or a drawbar outfit.

There are also some restrictions on the type of trailer that can be towed. For example, a separate licence entitlement is needed to tow a large trailer behind a heavy car if the combined weight is more than 4,250 kg or if the gross weight of the trailer is more than the unladen weight of the towing vehicle.

Ordinary car licences are normally valid until the holder's 70th birthday, after which a new licence is issued for one, two or three years at a time depending on health and other factors. Vocational licences such as LGV and PCV are renewable at age 45 and then every five years up to age 60. After that age, vocational licences are renewed each year because of the more stringent health requirements. A renewal of the licence in these circumstances is free of charge.

LICENCE FEES

There are now no fees for vocational licences, or for a change of address. For other replacements, alterations, duplicates or additions to the licence a fee as shown in Table 1.3 is applicable.

If you were disqualified from driving you would normally have to pay £50 for a new licence (or £75 for certain drink-drive offences).

A duplicate or exchange licence is usually valid for the period of the original licence. If you are adding an extra licence category you will need to obtain an exchange licence. A duplicate licence is required to replace a licence that has been lost, stolen, defaced or destroyed.

HEALTH AND EYESIGHT

The health standards for drivers of large vehicles are much higher than they are for car drivers. This is mainly because the responsibilities of handling this type of vehicle are much greater. To obtain a licence, and for each renewal, you need to undergo a stringent

Table 1.3   Driving licence fees (as at May 2005)

Licence type	Fee
First provisional licence	
– car, motorcycle or moped	£38
– LGV or PCV	Free
Changing provisional for first full licence	
– first provisional issued before 1 March 2004	£9
– first provisional issued after 1 March 2004	Free
Duplicate licence	
– licence lost, stolen, defaced, destroyed	£19
Replacement	
– change of address	Free
Exchange – removing expired endorsements or exchanging an old-style licence for a new-style photo-licence	£19
Adding a test pass to a full licence	Free
New licence after revocation under the New Driver Act	£38
Renewing a licence	
– car licence at 70 or over	Free
– full licence for LGV or PCV	Free
– provisional for medium/large goods vehicle, minibus, bus	Free
– for medical reasons	Free
Exchanging a licence from other countries	
– full Northern Ireland licence	Free
– full EC/EAA or other foreign licence (including Channel Islands and Isle of Man)	£38
New licence after disqualification	
– car, motorcycle, LGV, PCV	£50
– if disqualified for some drink-drive offence	£75

medical examination and your doctor has to complete the medical certificate form D4. There is a charge for this, but the cost is normally allowed against tax as a legitimate expense.

The law does not allow a new LGV licence to be issued for someone who has a history of epileptic attacks, or to anyone who is being treated by insulin for diabetes.

The eyesight standard for driving large vehicles is also much more stringent than it is for other road users. For car drivers the requirement is simply the ability to read a car number plate in good daylight from a distance of 20 metres. To qualify for an LGV licence you must have visual acuity of at least 6/9 in the better eye and at least 6/12 in the weaker eye. If corrective lenses are worn, the uncorrected acuity must be no less than 3/60 in each eye.

Some of the other conditions that might make it unsafe to drive larger vehicles – and that might cause the DVLA to refuse to issue a licence – include heart problems, alcohol or drug dependency, and psychiatric illness. A complete list of the relevant medical conditions for LGV drivers is available from DVLA.

An applicant who declares a disability to the DVLA may be asked for permission to obtain a report from his or her doctor. In these circumstances the licence may be issued for a limited period so that the condition can be reviewed at regular intervals. Alternatively, the licence may be restricted to certain types of vehicle, or a vehicle with a particular modification (see Table 1.4).

When information about a disability is given, applicants may be asked to have a specific medical examination carried out either by their own doctor or by one nominated by the DVLA. If you are unsure about any aspect of your health in terms of your eligibility for an LGV licence, you should consult your doctor or discuss the details with the Drivers' Medical Group at the DVLA. They can be contacted on 0870 240 0009.

APPLICATION FOR A LICENCE

The application form (D2) is normally available from most post offices. To apply for an LGV licence you need to send the form (see page 9) to the DVLA together with:

- your original licence;
- photographs;
- form D750;
- your medical form;
- an identifying document such as a passport or your birth certificate;
- the appropriate fee (see Table 1.3).

If you do not have a passport, or you do not want to send it away, you will need to have your application form verified by a responsible person to confirm your identity. Alternatively, to avoid the need to send off your passport or birth certificate you can have the documents checked and verified at a main post office. There is an extra fee of £4 for this service in addition to the cost of the licence.

To apply for a provisional LGV licence you must first hold a full car licence (category B). You will receive a licence for rigid vehicles only, because you have to pass a test on this type of vehicle before moving on to vehicles with a trailer or an articulated vehicle. This system of 'staged testing' means that in order to eventually drive an articulated vehicle or a large vehicle with a trailer, you have to go through the following sequence:

- provisional licence for LGV category C;
- LGV Theory and Hazard Perception Test;
- LGV category C Practical Test;
- full category C licence (with provisional entitlement for trailers);
- artic or drawbar (category C + E) Practical Test.

As previously indicated, no fee is involved for LGV licences (see Table 1.3).

Application forms (D2) are normally available from main post offices or from commercial LGV driving schools. The form, together with the other documents, should be sent to DVLA at Swansea SA99 1AD. The DVLA will normally process your application within about 10 working days, but remember that you must not drive the larger vehicle until your licence has actually been issued.

An LGV licence is normally valid until the driver's 45th birthday. For drivers over 45 the licence lasts for five years but from the age of 65 it must be renewed annually. A medical report is required with each application.

PROVISIONAL LICENCE

When driving an LGV the learner must:

- hold a provisional licence for that category of vehicle;
- be supervised by a driver who has held a full, unrestricted licence for that type of vehicle for at least three years;
- display 'L' plates (or, alternatively, 'D' plates in Wales if preferred) on the front and back of the vehicle.

THE 'YOUNG DRIVER' SCHEME

The normal age for driving large vehicles with a gross weight of more than 7.5 tonnes is 21 (although there a few exceptions listed on page 5). However, under the Young Driver scheme it is possible to drive larger vehicles at an earlier age as part of a continuous programme of training.

The scheme, which is managed by the Road Haulage and Distribution Training Council on behalf of the Department for

Transport, is supported by the Road Haulage Association, the Freight Transport Association and by the main trade unions. Under the scheme, trainees between the ages of 16 and 21 receive a comprehensive programme of training (including driver training) leading to the National Vocational Qualification (NVQ) or the Scottish Vocational Qualification (SVQ). This enables the driver to gain experience and entitlement for the various categories of licence from category B through to category C + E from the age of 18 rather than the normal minimum age of 21.

The driver training elements of the course are carried out by a specially registered 'approved training organization' (ATO), using a structured programme that has been agreed between the trainee, the ATO and the trainee's employer.

Further details of the scheme are available from The Road Haulage and Distribution Training Council (RHDTC), 14 Warren Yard, Warren Farm Office Village, Stratford Road, Milton Keynes MK12 5NW (tel: 01908 313360; website: www.rhdtc.co.uk).

DRIVING LICENCE INFORMATION CODES

On British driving licences you will find certain information codes adjacent to the 'entitlement' section. These codes indicate any particular restrictions that might apply to an individual driver, or to the type of vehicle he or she is allowed to drive (see Table 1.4).

EXEMPTIONS FROM LGV LICENSING

An LGV driving licence is not required when driving the following types of vehicle:

- goods vehicles propelled by steam (for example, large vehicles with coal- or wood-burning engines);
- road construction vehicles used or kept on the road solely for the conveyance of built-in road construction machinery (with or without articles or materials used for the purpose of that machinery);
- engineering plant (vehicles designed or constructed for the purpose of engineering operations);
- works trucks (primarily designed for use in private premises or in the immediate vicinity, for example dumper trucks and forklift trucks);

Table 1.4   Driving licence information codes

Code	Description
01	Eyesight correction
02	Hearing or communication aid
10	Modified transmission
15	Modified clutch
20	Modified braking systems
25	Modified accelerator systems
30	Combined braking and accelerator systems
35	Modified controls layouts
40	Modified steering
42	Modified rear view mirror(s)
43	Modified driving seat
44	Modifications to motorcycle
45	Motorcycle only with sidecar
70	Exchange of licence
71	Duplicate of licence
78	Restricted to vehicles with automatic transmission
79	Restricted vehicles (details in brackets)
101	Not for hire or reward
102	Drawbar trailers only
103	Subject to certificate of competence
105	Not more than 5.5 m long
106	Restricted to vehicles with automatic transmission
107	Not more than 8,250 kg
108	Subject to minimum age limit
110	Limited to invalid carriages
111	Limited to 16 passenger seats
113	Limited to 16 passenger seats except for automatics
114	With special controls required for safe driving
115	Organ donor
118	Start date is for earliest entitlement
119	Weight limit does not apply
120	Complies with health standards for Category D1

- industrial tractors (tractors used mainly for haulage work off the public road. The vehicle must not have an unladen weight exceeding 7,370 kilograms and must have a design speed not exceeding 20 mph);
- agricultural motor vehicles that are not agricultural or forestry tractors (primarily used off the public road, for example crop sprayers or combine harvesters);

- digging machines (vehicles that are limited to travel on a public road only for the purpose of proceeding to or from sites – used for trench digging or any kind of excavating or shovelling work, for example vehicles with digging buckets or shovels);
- a goods vehicle that is not used on public roads or, if it is so used during any calendar week:
  - is used only in passing from land in the occupation of a person keeping the vehicle to other land in the occupation of that person; *and*
  - is not used on public roads for distances exceeding an aggregate of 9.7 kilometres in that calendar week;
- a goods vehicle, other than an agricultural motor vehicle, that:
  - is used only for purposes relating to agriculture, horticulture or forestry;
  - is used on roads only in passing between different areas of land occupied by the same person; *and*
  - in passing between any two such areas does not travel a distance exceeding 1.5 kilometres on roads;
- goods vehicles used for no purpose other than the haulage of lifeboats and the conveyance of the necessary gear of the lifeboats that are being hauled;
- goods vehicles manufactured before 1 January 1960, used unladen and not drawing a laden trailer;
- articulated goods vehicles not exceeding 3.05 tonnes unladen weight;
- goods vehicles in the service of a visiting force or headquarters as defined in the Visiting Forces and International Headquarters (Application of Law) Order 1965 (a);
- a goods vehicle driven by a constable for the purpose of removing or avoiding obstruction to other road users or other members of the public, for the purpose of protecting life or property (including the vehicle and its load) or for other similar purposes;
- a goods vehicle fitted with apparatus designed for raising a disabled vehicle partly from the ground and for drawing a disabled vehicle when so raised (whether by partial superimposition or otherwise) being a vehicle that:
  - is used solely for dealing with disabled vehicles,
  - is not used for the conveyance of any goods or load other than a disabled vehicle when so raised and water, fuel, accumulators and articles required for the operation of, or in connection

with, such apparatus or otherwise for dealing with disabled vehicles; *and*
- has an unladen weight not exceeding 3.05 tonnes;
- a mobile project vehicle having a maximum authorized mass exceeding 3.5 tonnes and constructed or adapted to carry not more than eight persons in addition to the driver and that carries principally goods or burden consisting of:
  - play or educational equipment and articles required in connection with the use of such equipment, or
  - articles required for the purposes of display or of an exhibition, and the primary purpose of which is used as a recreational, educational or instructional facility when stationary.

MINIMUM AGES FOR DRIVING EXEMPTED VEHICLES

The minimum age for driving an exempted goods vehicle is determined by its weight. Vehicles with a maximum authorized mass that exceeds 3.5 tonnes but not 7.5 tonnes may be driven at age 18 years. A vehicle that weighs more than 7.5 tonnes can be driven from the age of 21 years.

Mobile cranes

Up to December 1998, category B licence holders were allowed to drive mobile cranes. Since then a driver requires a category C1 driving licence to drive a mobile crane exceeding 3.5 tonnes but not over 7.5 tonnes, and a category C licence if the crane weighs more than 7.5 tonnes.

Driving buses

The holder of a full category C (LGV) driving licence is allowed to drive a large bus provided he or she has held the licence for at least two years and the vehicle is: 1) damaged or defective and being driven to a place of repair or being road-tested following repair; and 2) not used for the carriage of any person who is not connected with its repair or road testing.

Note: The above information is extracted from the official DLVA document 'Special Licensing Arrangements for Drivers of Large Goods Vehicles', but should be used as guidelines only.

DRIVING ABROAD

Visiting another country

To drive in any country belonging to the European Community (EC) or the European Economic Area (EEA) you are allowed to use your GB licence.

If you want to drive in a non-EC/EEA country you should check with one of the motoring organizations whether you need an International Driving Permit (IDP). The AA, the RAC, RSAC and Green Flag issue IDPs. To qualify for an IDP you must be resident in Great Britain, have passed a driving test and be over 18 years of age.

Moving to another country

If you move abroad you should check with the licensing authority of the country you move to for information about the exchange of licences. If you return to Great Britain from a non-EC/EEA country you may drive for up to 12 months on your foreign licence.

VISITORS TO AND NEW RESIDENTS OF GREAT BRITAIN

You normally have to be resident in Great Britain to qualify for a full driving licence. There are, however, special rules for exchange of foreign licences and for driving in this country as a visitor or new resident. These rules vary, depending on the country that issued the licence. There are also some variations for vocational licences, for example for lorries and buses.

Countries of the European Community and European Economic Area

A visitor to Great Britain from any of these countries can drive using his or her Community licence for as long as the licence remains valid. The licence will show the various types of vehicle that can be driven.

A person newly resident in Great Britain can exchange his or her Community licence for a GB one at any time. Alternatively, he or she may drive on their foreign licence up to the age of 70 or for three years, whichever is the longer. Vocational licence holders who do not exchange their licence for a GB one may drive:

- until they are aged 45 or for five years after becoming resident, whichever is the longer;
- if aged over 45 (but under 65), until reaching 66 or for five years, whichever is the longer;
- if aged 65 or over, for 12 months.

Northern Ireland

A licence from Northern Ireland can be used until it runs out. Alternatively, it can be exchanged for a full car, motorcycle or moped licence if the original licence has been valid since 1 January 1976. A lorry or bus licence can be exchanged if it was issued on or after 1 April 1986. A driving test pass certificate is acceptable for exchange.

Gibraltar and designated countries

The 'designated countries', other than Gibraltar, are Australia, Barbados, the British Virgin Islands, Canada, the Republic of Cyprus, the Falkland Islands, Hong Kong, Japan, the Republic of Korea, Malta, Monaco, New Zealand, Singapore, South Africa, Switzerland and Zimbabwe. Someone visiting Great Britain from one of these countries is allowed to drive vehicles of up to 7.5 tonnes and with up to 16 passenger seats for up to 12 months, whether or not the vehicle was brought into the country with that person.

Holders of licences for larger vehicles may only drive vehicles that have been brought into Great Britain from the designated country.

For new residents the rules are slightly different. Small vehicles may be driven for up to 12 months, during which time the foreign licence must be exchanged for a GB one. New residents must not drive medium or large goods vehicles or passenger-carrying vehicles until they have passed the relevant GB test.

Vocational licence holders from Gibraltar may drive for 12 months and can exchange the licence within five years of residency.

Jersey, Guernsey and the Isle of Man

Visitors with ordinary licences can drive any category of vehicle shown on the licence for up to 12 months. Vocational licence holders from Jersey or the Isle of Man can drive large vehicles for up to 12 months. If the vocational licence was issued in Guernsey, only vehicles that have been imported temporarily can be driven.

New residents from Jersey, Guernsey or the Isle of Man may drive for up to 12 months, but should exchange their licence during that period.

All other countries

Visitors from other countries are allowed to drive vehicles of up to 7.5 tonnes and with up to 16 passenger seats, provided that the original licence is still valid. With large vehicles, only those that have been registered outside Great Britain and that have been driven into the country may be used.

For new residents, provided that the full licence remains valid, any small vehicle shown on the licence may be driven for up to 12 months. During that time a GB licence must be obtained. New residents with vocational licences may not drive larger vehicles without passing the GB driving test for that type of vehicle.

Licences from these countries are not exchangeable.

Please note that these are guidelines *only. For precise details, go to the DVLA website at www.dvla.gov.uk, or contact DVLA Customer Services on 0870 240 0009.*

2

The LGV Theory Test

INTRODUCTION

You must take and pass the Theory Test before applying for the practical test. The Theory pass certificate is valid for two years, giving plenty of time in which to prepare for the practical part of the test.

The Theory Test involves both a multi-choice question paper and a 'hazard perception' test. Most of the questions in the multi-choice part are answered with one correct answer from four alternatives, but some questions require two or more answers from a selection of alternatives. You are allowed 40 minutes to complete the test and must achieve at least 30 correct answers out of a possible 35 to pass.

The DSA publication *The Official Theory Test for Drivers of Large Vehicles* should be used in conjunction with your training. This publication contains the complete question and answer bank, together with details of the syllabus and a list of all LGV theory test centres.

Although you will need to take the Theory Test when applying for a Category C or C1 licence, it is not required when upgrading from C1 to C, or from C to C + E.

For the Theory Test you need to make sure that you are familiar with the contents of *The Highway Code*, particularly with regard to the signs, signals and road markings that are applicable to driving large vehicles. You must also have a sound knowledge and understanding of the following subjects, all of which are part of the theory test for LGV drivers.

SYLLABUS

Vehicle weights and dimensions

- *Vehicle size:* the dimensions of your vehicle.
- *Stowage and loading:* the importance of a secure load.

- *Vehicle markings:* the requirement for clear markings showing vehicle size and dimensions.
- *Speed limiters:* rules concerning speed limiters.

Drivers' hours and rest periods

- *Driving limits:* the EC driving limits and UK hours rules.
- *Keeping records:* the records you keep, and how long to keep them.
- *Tachograph rules:* the rules concerning the use of tachographs in the United Kingdom and abroad.
- *Tiredness:* the reasons for not driving when tired.
- *Vehicle security:* your responsibility for your vehicle and load.

Braking systems and speed limiters

- *Types of brakes:* the different types of braking systems used on vehicles.
- *Maintenance and inspection:* the importance of ensuring that your brakes are in good working order.
- *Connection and proper use of brakes:* how to connect and use them;.
- *Tailgating:* why following too closely is dangerous and how to avoid it.
- *Freezing conditions:* the effects of freezing weather on the braking system.
- *Anti-lock brakes:* how the system works.

Attitude and alertness

- *Consideration: considering other road users.* Being positive and treating others as you would wish to be treated.
- *Courtesy:* not using the size of your vehicle to intimidate other road users.
- *Priority:* being aware that others break the rules or may not understand the position you need to take on the road.
- *Vehicle safety equipment:* correct use of vehicle safety equipment, including the use of seat belts and head restraints.
- *Tiredness:* not driving when you are tired, even if you are within your driver's hours.
- *Drugs and alcohol:* being aware of changes in driving behaviour due to alcohol or drugs.

Safety margins and hazard awareness

- *Anticipation:* planning ahead to prevent the need for last-second reactions.
- *Hazard awareness:* recognizing a hazard ahead and planning for it.
- *Attention:* looking out for problems ahead when you're driving.
- *Speed and distance:* travelling at the correct speed for the situation, leaving a safe distance to react if a problem arises.
- *Reaction time:* being aware that you need time to react.
- *Risk factors:* knowing how various road and weather conditions affect safety.

Accident handling

- *Reducing risk:* good planning and anticipation, to lessen the risk of an accident.
- *Injuries:* what to do if someone is injured.
- *Casualties:* treatment and reporting procedures.

Vehicle condition

- *Wheels and tyres:* taking precautions during the removal and replacement of wheels and the correct fitting, use and care of tyres.
- *Principles of construction and function of large vehicles:* the internal combustion engine and its fuel, lubrication, coolant and ignition systems, the vehicle's transmission, lubrication and electrical systems.
- *Vehicle coupling mechanisms:* maintenance and use of coupling systems.
- *Breakdowns:* preventive maintenance, running repairs and locating the cause of breakdowns.

Leaving the vehicle

- *The driver's cab:* your own safety, and that of others.

Vehicle loading

- *Loading:* loading and unloading goods; the use of loading equipment.
- *Safety:* stowing, fastening and controlling the load.
- *Types of load:* dealing with different types of load.

Restricted view

- *Mirrors:* using your mirrors effectively to help spot hazards around you.
- *Signals:* giving clear and well-timed signals to help other road users understand your intentions.
- *Parking:* understanding that thoughtless parking or unloading might cause a hazard.
- *Moving off:* taking effective all-round observation to ensure safety.
- *Blind spots:* Understanding that parts of your vehicle might restrict your vision. Extra effort should be taken to observe all round your vehicle.
- *Observation at junctions:* understanding that effective observation is essential to reduce the risk of an accident.

Vehicle and transport documents

- Documents required for national and international carriage of goods.
- Driver's responsibility when receiving, carrying and delivering goods in accordance with the agreed conditions.

Environmental issues

- *Vehicle noise:* using audible warning devices.
- *Wind resistance:* fitting a wind deflector to reduce fuel consumption.
- *Fuel consumption:* planning routes to reduce mileage.
- *Refuelling:* taking care when refuelling.

Other road users

- *Vulnerable road users:* children, pedestrians, cyclists, horse riders, the elderly and the disabled.
- *Other vehicles:* the difficulties faced by users of other vehicles and their fields of view.

Traffic signs

- *Road signs:* these tell you about the road ahead.
- *Speed limits:* signs showing speed limits.
- *Regulations:* these can be shown by means of a road sign.

Note: The above is an extract from the official DSA Theory Test syllabus. Full details are given in The Official Theory Test for Drivers of Large Vehicles.

APPLYING FOR THE THEORY TEST

The test can be taken at any one of about 150 centres throughout England, Scotland and Wales. All test centres in Wales, and some in England, are equipped to conduct the test in Welsh. Candidates who are not able to read or understand the English language, or who want to take the test in their first language, can listen to the test in one of 20 other languages. For candidates with special needs, a variety of different facilities are available.

The most efficient way to arrange your test is by booking online at www.driving-tests.co.uk. You will be able to get an immediate response and will be given a time and date straight away.

Alternatively, you can book by telephone using a credit or debit card. To do this you need your driving licence details and other personal information. Remember that the person making the telephone booking must be the cardholder (or the cardholder must be present). The central booking office number is 0870 01 01 372. For Welsh-speaking applicants the number is 0870 01 00 372.

Whichever method you prefer, you should keep a detailed record of the transaction in case of any queries at a later date.

To book by post you will need an application form (DLV26). Forms are normally available from any test centre, or from the DSA at Nottingham. When booking by this method you will probably not receive a response for about 10 days or so and you may not be offered the date requested. Make sure that you keep a photocopy of the application in case of any queries and as a means of reconciling the payments. The application form (with the appropriate fee) is sent to Driving Standards Agency, PO Box 148, Salford M5 3JY.

The cost of the theory test (at May 2005) is £20.50.

If you are taking lessons with a professional instructor, he or she will normally be able to deal with your application under the 'trainer booking' system.

Cancelling or postponing

If you need to cancel or postpone the test, you must contact the DSA booking office at least three clear working days before the date of the test. When applying the 'three-day' rule, remember that this does not include weekends, Bank Holidays, the day of the test and the day of cancellation. This means that a test for a Wednesday, for example, should be cancelled at the latest by the previous Thursday (and earlier if there is an intervening Bank Holiday).

Attending for the Test

When attending for the test you will need to take with you the signed photo-card licence and the paper counterpart. If you do not have a photo licence, some proof of visual identity, such as a passport, is required.

In preparing for the test make sure that you know and understand the format and procedures for both the multiple-choice and the hazard perception sections.

MULTIPLE-CHOICE SECTION OF THE TEST

A short period of time is allowed for you to familiarize yourself with the system before the test starts. Once the test starts, you will be shown one question at a time on-screen, with the option to look again at any individual question and to review the complete programme. The system allows you to move backwards and forwards through the questions with the facility to alter any of your answers.

The maximum time allowed for this part of the test is 40 minutes. Most people find that there is plenty of time available so long as they are adequately prepared with thorough, professional training.

You will find it helpful to have a copy of *The Official Theory Test CD ROM for Drivers of Large Vehicles* as this gives you the opportunity to test yourself against the official question bank. It should not be seen as an alternative to proper, professional training, but is an effective way of revising for the exam and is useful as an assessment of your level of knowledge.

Other learning aids that you might find useful include:

The Highway Code
Know your Traffic Signs
The Official DSA Guide to Driving: The essential skills
The Official DSA Guide to Driving Goods Vehicles
The Official Theory Test for Drivers of Large Vehicles

All these books are published by The Stationery Office and are available from DeskTop Driving Ltd, Unit 6, Gaugemaster Way, Ford, Arundel, West Sussex BN18 0RX (tel: 01903 882299; website: www.desktopdriving.co.uk).

SAMPLE QUESTIONS

1.   You are driving along a motorway in thick fog at night. The reflective studs are red on your left and white on your right. You are driving:

(Mark one answer)

  – on the hard shoulder;
  – in the middle lane;
  – in the right-hand lane;
  – in the left-hand lane.

2.   You are taking a weekly rest period away from your normal base. Under EC rules the minimum number of consecutive hours this rest period must be is:

(Mark one answer)

  – 18 hours;
  – 24 hours;
  – 36 hours;
  – 45 hours.

3.   An endurance brake (retarder) may work in which TWO of the following ways?

(Mark two answers)

  – increasing engine braking;
  – using an extra transmission device;
  – sensing wheel speed;
  – using the parking brake;
  – using the secondary brake.

4. You are driving an empty curtain-sided vehicle. Why might you consider tying the curtains open?

(Mark one answer)

- to use less fuel;
- because it is a legal requirement;
- to prevent the curtains tearing;
- to reduce the effect of crosswinds.

5. Which THREE of the following would make a tyre illegal for a large vehicle?

(Mark 3 answers)

- different makes of tyres on the same axle;
- a lump or bulge;
- a deep cut more than 25 millimetres (1 inch) long;
- an exposed ply or cord;
- recut tyres;
- a tread depth of 1.3 millimetres.

6. Before starting a journey you want to check your brake system warning lights. On some vehicles these are not operated by the ignition switch. What else can you do?

(Mark one answer)

- look for a 'check' switch on the dashboard;
- get someone behind to check your brake lights;
- check them at the end of your journey;
- pump the brake pedal a number of times.

7. How could you improve the fuel consumption of your lorry?

(Mark two answers)

- brake late as often as you can;
- fit a cab-mounted wind deflector;
- avoid sheeting any bulky loads;
- make regular checks on tyre pressures.

8. Some large vehicles with restricted vision to the rear may be fitted with an audible warning device for reversing. In areas with a 30 mph speed limit the device may be used:

(Mark one answer)

  - between 7 am and 11.30 pm only;
  - between 11.30 pm and 7 am only;
  - during hours of daylight only;
  - at any time.

9. You are driving a vehicle that is over 17 metres (55 feet) long. What should you do at a level crossing?

(Mark one answer)

  - cross over, using your horn and hazard warning lights;
  - stop before the crossing and phone the signal operator;
  - increase your speed to clear the crossing quickly;
  - stop before the crossing and look both ways before going on.

10. What is the maximum speed limit on a dual carriageway for a lorry carrying a load that is 4.5 metres (14 feet 9 inches) wide?

(Mark one answer)

  - 15 mph;
  - 25 mph;
  - 35 mph;
  - 45 mph.

11. Markings are required on the rear of lorries over 7.5 tonnes maximum authorized mass. What colour are these?

(Mark one answer)

  - red/white;
  - red/yellow;
  - black/yellow;
  - black/white.

12. The 'mode' switch on a tachograph is used to record:

(Mark three answers)

  - driving;
  - illness;
  - taking a weekly rest period;
  - other work;
  - resting.

13. After overtaking another large vehicle how would you know when it was safe to move back to the nearside lane?

(Mark one answer)

- by waiting for the driver you have just overtaken to flash the headlights;
- by checking your nearside mirror;
- by using your hazard warning lights as a signal;
- by moving over to the nearside in the hope that the other vehicle will slow down.

14. An attendant must accompany you when your load is wider than:

(Mark one answer)

- 2.6 metres (8 feet 5 inches);
- 3.0 metres (9 feet 9 inches);
- 3.3 metres (10 feet 9 inches);
- 3.5 metres (11 feet 5 inches).

The above questions are taken from the official DSA question bank, with acknowledgement to the DSA. The answers to these questions are on page 28. For the full bank of questions, see *The Official Theory Test for Drivers of Large Vehicles.*

After the multiple-choice part of the test, you are allowed a short break before moving on to the next part.

HAZARD PERCEPTION TEST

In this section of the test you are given a set of video clips depicting moving traffic situations. Hazard perception is included in the Theory Test to ensure that you have an extensive understanding of some of the risks involved in driving large goods vehicles.

This part of the test consists of 14 film clips shown on the computer screen. Each clip lasts about a minute. To respond to the hazard, you click on the 'mouse' as each hazard appears or develops. The earlier the response is made, the higher the score for that clip. On this part of the test you do not have the opportunity to review or check your responses; on the road you only get one chance. The hazards depicted are the types that would require some sort of response from the driver – such as changing speed or direction.

You would not be penalized for clicking on insignificant hazards; only the designated developing hazard is marked. However, if too many unnecessary responses are made in a very short space of time, there is a danger that the system will give a score of zero for that clip.

The pass mark for this part of the LGV theory test is currently (May 2005) 50 out of a possible 75.

AT THE END OF THE TEST

Candidates are given the result of both parts of the test within a few minutes of completing the Hazard Perception Test. Feedback is given on any incorrect answers.

Successful candidates are issued with a pass certificate that is valid for two years. The practical test must be taken within that time or a further theory test would need to be taken.

To prepare for both parts of the LGV theory test you will need to study the publications listed on page 22. You should have a thorough knowledge of the contents of all of these books. This is necessary not only to prepare yourself for the theory test, but also because you should have a detailed knowledge of the syllabus and topics so that you can prepare yourself for the practical test.

There are many books and CD ROMs on the market to help with theory training. Some of these materials contain the complete DSA question bank.

For more information about the LGV Theory Test, log on to the DSA website at www.dsa.gov.uk or telephone DSA on 0870 01 01 372.

THE LGV THEORY TEST: ANSWERS TO SAMPLE QUESTIONS ON PAGES 23–26

1. In the left-hand lane.
2. 24 hours.
3. Increasing engine braking; using an extra transmission device.
4. To reduce the effect of crosswinds.
5. A lump or bulge; a deep cut more than 25 millimetres (1 inch) long; an exposed ply or cord.
6. Look for a 'check' switch on the dashboard.
7. Fit a cab-mounted wind deflector; make regular checks on tyre pressures.
8. Between 7 am and 11.30 pm only.
9. Stop before the crossing and phone the signal operator.
10. 25 mph.
11. Red/yellow.
12. Driving; other work; resting.
13. By checking your near-side mirror.
14. 3.5 metres (11 feet 5 inches).

3

The LGV Practical Driving Test

APPLYING FOR THE TEST

Once you have passed the Theory Test, you can apply to take the practical test at a test centre that is most convenient to you and/or your instructor. A list of test centres is given on page 112.

You can book your test online at www.driving-tests.co.uk. Payment can be made by credit or debit card. You will need to have your licence details available, as well as details of your theory test pass certificate. Alterations, postponements and cancellations can also be made online.

Alternatively, you can book by phone. Again, payment can be made by credit or debit card. If you are not using your own card, the cardholder must be present at the time of booking. You will be offered an appointment straight away, with written confirmation following a few days later. The central booking office number is 0870 01 01 372.

To apply by post, you will need the application form DLV26. Forms are normally available from LGV test centres or from the DSA at Nottingham, as well as from your instructor. Payment can be made by cheque, postal order or credit/debit card. The form and fee should be sent to the DSA at PO Box 280, Newcastle upon Tyne NE99 1FP. You will normally receive a response after about a week or so, but you will not necessarily be given the date that you asked for.

Whichever method you choose to use, make sure that you keep an accurate record of the application and payment in case of any query or misunderstanding between you and the DSA.

If you are having professional training, your instructor will probably be able to deal with your application by means of a 'trainer booking'. This system of block booking allows the training organization to make a booking in its own name and then allocate the test to individual trainees at a later date. By using this system the instructor is in a better position to coordinate a programme of training with trainees' test dates.

The fees for a practical LGV test are currently (May 2005) £76 for mid-week tests and £94 for a Saturday test.

If you need to cancel or postpone a test, you need to give the DSA at least 10 clear working days notice. This period does not include the day of the test, the day the information was given to the DSA, or weekends and Bank Holidays.

ATTENDING FOR THE TEST

On the day of your test, make sure that you have both parts of your photo-licence and your Theory pass certificate with you. If you have an old-style paper licence with no photograph, you must take with you an additional means of visual identity. This could be a signed, valid passport, an employer's pass or a trade union card.

The test normally takes about 90 minutes and is in three parts:

- off-road manoeuvring exercises and safety questions;
- on-the-road driving;
- uncoupling and recoupling exercise.

TEST VEHICLE

You must provide a suitable vehicle for the test. In particular:

- The vehicle must be unladen.
- It must be of the correct category for the type of licence required.
- 'L' plates (or 'D' plates in Wales) must be displayed on the front and rear.
- It must have sufficient fuel for a test lasting up to 1½ hours.
- Secure seating must be provided for the examiner.
- The vehicle must be in roadworthy condition, with all stop lamps and direction indicators working properly.
- It must have an overall length of not more than 60 feet.
- A vehicle on trade licence plates cannot be used for the test.
- The vehicle must be capable of being driven at speeds of up to 80 kph (50 mph).
- It must conform to the following 'minimum test vehicle' require-ments.

The minimum test vehicle requirements for vehicles first registered before 1 October 2003 are as shown in Table 3.1.

Table 3.1 Minimum test vehicle requirements (for vehicles first registered before 1 October 2003)

Type of test	Min. vehicle wt (MAM)	Min. vehicle length	Min. trailer length/wt	Min. overall length	Min. overall wt
Category C1	4 tonnes	N/A	N/A	N/A	
Category C1 + E	4 tonnes	N/A	2 tonnes MAM	8 metres	
Category C	10 tonnes	7 metres	N/A	7 metres	
Category C + E (artic)	N/A	N/A	N/A	12 metres	18 tonnes
Category C + E (drawbar)	10 tonnes	7 metres	4 metres	12 metres	18 tonnes

Note: MAM = maximum authorized mass

The minimum test vehicle requirements for vehicles first registered on or after 1 October 2003 are as follows:

All vehicles presented for test must be fitted with a fully working tachograph and with an anti-lock braking system (ABS).

Category C1

- Rigid goods vehicle;
- Maximum authorized mass (MAM) of at least 4 tonnes;
- At least 5 metres long.
- A closed-box cargo compartment at least as wide and as high as the cab.

Category C1 + E

- Drawbar outfit comprising a category C1 vehicle:
  - Trailer of at least 2 tonnes MAM.
  - Closed-box trailer slightly less wide than the towing vehicle.
  - Rear view by external mirrors only.

Or

- Articulated lorry with a MAM of at least 6 tonnes:
  - Combined length of least 8 metres.
  - Closed-box trailer slightly less wide than the towing vehicle;
  - Rear view by external mirrors only.

Category C

- Rigid goods vehicle:
  - MAM of least 12 tonnes.
  - At least 8 metres in length.
  - At least 2.4 metres in width.
  - At least eight forward gears.
  - Closed-box cargo compartment at least as wide and as high as the cab.
  - Maximum length of 12 metres (39 ft 4 in).

Category C + E

- Drawbar outfit combining a Category C vehicle and trailer:
  - MAM of 20 tonnes.
  - Combined length of at least 14 metres.
  - Trailer at least 7.5 metres in length from coupling eye to extreme rear.
  - At least 2.4 metres in width.
  - At least eight forward gears.
  - Closed-box cargo compartment at least as wide and as high as the cab.
  - Maximum length of 18.75 metres (61 ft 5 in).

Or

- Articulated lorry with a MAM of at least 20 tonnes:
  - Minimum length 14 metres.
  - At least 2.4 metres in width.
  - At least eight forward gears.
  - Closed-box cargo compartment at least as wide and as high as the cab.
  - Maximum length 16.5 metres (or 18 metres for low-loader manufactured on or after 1 April 1991).

Acknowledgement: These minimum test vehicle requirements are taken from official DSA documents.

SYLLABUS

The test covers the following main topics:

- vehicle controls: accelerator, clutch, footbrake, handbrake, steering;

- precautions before starting;
- moving off safely and under control;
- use of mirrors: well before signalling, changing direction or changing speed;
- use of signals: when necessary, correctly and properly timed;
- reversing exercise: under control and with effective observations;
- controlled stop: promptly and under control;
- gear change exercise;
- uphill and downhill starts;
- clearance to obstructions;
- response to signs and signals: traffic signs, road markings, traffic lights, traffic controllers, other road users;
- use of speed;
- maintaining a safe following distance;
- maintaining progress: use of appropriate speed, without undue hesitation;
- junctions: speed on approach; observations; right and left turns; avoidance of cutting corners;
- judgement: overtaking, meeting, crossing the path of other vehicles;
- road positioning: in normal driving; lane discipline;
- pedestrian crossings;
- safe positioning for normal stops;
- awareness and planning;
- ancillary controls;
- uncoupling and recoupling.

The full syllabus is in the DSA publication *The Official DSA Guide to Driving Goods Vehicles*. You should have a copy of this to supplement your training. It should be used in conjunction with *The Official DSA Guide to Driving – the essential skills*.

MARKING SYSTEM

During the test the examiner uses the marking sheet DL25 (see page 39). You are continuously assessed, with any errors being recorded at the time and 'graded' by the examiner as 'dangerous faults', 'serious faults' or 'driving faults'. You will fail the test if any dangerous or serious faults are committed, or if you accumulate too many driving faults.

- *Dangerous fault:* recorded when a fault is assessed as having caused actual danger during the test. A single fault in this category will result in failure.
- *Serious fault:* recorded when a fault is assessed as potentially dangerous. A habitual driving fault can also be assessed as serious when it indicates a serious weakness in the candidate's driving. A single serious fault means an automatic failure.
- *Driving fault:* a less serious fault, which is assessed as such because of the circumstances at that particular time. Driving faults only amount to a failure when there is an accumulation of 15 or more.

Examples

- You are approaching a junction to turn right into a fairly wide road. Visibility into the road is good and, after checking that it is safe to turn and that the side road is clear of traffic, you turn into the side road, unnecessarily cutting the corner in doing so. No potential danger was caused to other road users because you had checked the situation before turning. On test this would be marked as a *driving* fault.
- You are approaching the same right turn. This time, visibility into the side road is restricted because of parked vehicles, making it difficult to see whether there is any traffic approaching in the side road. You cut the corner unnecessarily, but there was no actual danger because no other traffic appeared. However, this was purely by chance and, as the incident involved potential danger, the error would be marked as *serious*.
- In exactly the same circumstances you cut the corner. This time, another vehicle is approaching in the side road. That driver has to brake to avoid your vehicle. As the incident involves actual danger, the examiner would mark this as a *dangerous* fault.

MANOEUVRING

The manoeuvring exercises are of two kinds: 1) a reversing exercise; 2) a braking exercise. These manoeuvres are carried out on a special area at the test centre. Refer to the latest edition of *The Official DSA Guide to Driving Goods Vehicles* for full details of the layout of the manoeuvring area and for information on how the area is set up for your particular training vehicle.

Note that the examiner will be observing the reverse exercise from outside the vehicle. This is so that he or she can check on the accuracy of the manoeuvre as well as make correct observations of the candidate. On the braking exercise and for the rest of the test, the examiner travels in the cab.

Reversing

As part of the recent changes to the practical test, the reversing exercise now includes a simulated loading platform. You are expected to reverse so that the rear of the vehicle finishes on a black and yellow hatched marked area. At the back of the reversing bay is the simulated platform. Marking of this part of the exercise includes:

- hitting or dislodging the simulated loading/unloading platform – serious fault;
- stopping short of the marked stopping area – serious fault;
- stopping within the marked stopping area, but well short of the platform – driving fault;
- loss of control, causing danger to the driver, the examiner or other road users – dangerous fault.

Braking

For the braking exercise, you are expected to reach a speed of about 20 mph within a 200-foot distance and then apply the brakes on reaching a pair of marker cones. The exercise must be done under complete control. You should be able to stop safely and in a straight line without locking the wheels.

VEHICLE SAFETY QUESTIONS

Recent changes to the DSA syllabus mean that you are now asked several 'show me' and 'tell me' questions on the practical driving tests. This part of the test includes questions on:

- engine oil levels;
- engine coolant levels;
- windscreen wipers and washers;
- tyres, wheels and mudguards;
- brake lights, indicators, reflectors;
- headlamps, side lights and tail lights;
- windscreen and windows;
- vehicle suspension and power-assisted steering;

- loading mechanisms and safety factors;
- air pressure and leaks;
- cab locking mechanism;
- tachographs and discs;
- instrument checks;
- audible warning devices;
- vehicle body condition.

Typical questions

- *'Show me how you would check that the wheel nuts on this vehicle are secure.'*
- *'Tell me how you would check the condition of the suspension [or windscreen, wipers, reflector] on this vehicle.'*
- *'Show me how the cab locking mechanism is secured on this vehicle.'*
- *'Tell me how you would operate the tail lift mechanism on this vehicle.'*
- *'Show me how you would replace the tachometer disc on this vehicle.'*
- *'Tell me how you would check that the power-assisted steering is working.'*

You will be asked five questions on a rigid-vehicle category C or C1 test. Each incorrect answer will constitute a 'driving fault'. If all five questions were answered incorrectly, a 'serious fault' would be marked.

On the artic or drawbar test (category C + E or C1 + E), only two questions are asked. At this stage the candidate is expected to be a reasonably competent category C or C1 driver. As a result, if both questions are answered incorrectly, a 'serious fault' is recorded.

ON THE ROAD

At the start of the test the examiner will explain that you should 'follow the road ahead unless otherwise directed'. Any instructions to turn off to the left or right will be given in good time so that you are able to plan ahead.

The 'on-road' part of the test usually lasts about an hour and covers a route of about 25–30 miles. As well as normal driving in various different road and traffic conditions, several specific exercises are included:

- gear-changing exercise;
- uphill and downhill starts;

- moving off from behind a parked vehicle;
- selecting a safe place to stop.

You should properly prepare for all these test exercises, but without practising too much on test routes.

The *gear change exercise* involves using gears that you would probably not use during the normal driving part of the test. For example, you may not need to use first or second gear, or some of the intermediate gears.

The examiner will ask you to pull away using the lowest gear and to change up progressively through each gear. After reaching the highest gear (or the one nominated by the examiner), you are then expected to slow down and change down through each gear until the lowest one is selected. The vehicle should be driven for a short distance in each gear to demonstrate efficient control.

During this exercise you are not expected to use auxiliary systems such as a two-speed axle.

Uphill and downhill starts are included so as to test the candidate on all-round observations, use of signals where appropriate, and control of the clutch, handbrake, footbrake, accelerator and gears.

To move off uphill you need to coordinate the accelerator and clutch with the handbrake efficiently and smoothly. The manoeuvre should be carried out under complete control without any unnecessary engine noise and without the vehicle rolling back.

For moving off downhill:

- select an appropriate gear (possibly second or third);
- apply the footbrake;
- release the handbrake;
- look all round;
- signal if required;
- coordinate the release of the clutch and the footbrake.

Moving off at an angle. You will be asked to pull up in a particular place fairly close to a parked vehicle. Your ability to move off efficiently at an angle from behind the other vehicle is assessed. This manoeuvre involves good coordination combined with effective observation, timing of the manoeuvre, the use of signals as appropriate and efficient control of the vehicle in a confined space.

When you stop, make sure that you are leaving sufficient room to pull out. To move off, use all mirrors effectively, including a check in the left-hand mirror that you are clearing the parked vehicle.

Stopping in a safe place. You will be asked to 'pull up on the left at a convenient place'. This is to assess whether you select a stopping place that is safe, legal and not causing an unnecessary obstruction. It is also a way of checking on your proper use of mirrors and signals, and general awareness of other road users.

UNCOUPLING AND RECOUPLING PROCEDURES

The final part of the test for drivers of artics and drawbars (categories C + E and C1 + E) involves a practical test of uncoupling and recoupling the trailer. The candidate is asked to uncouple the trailer and then to park the vehicle alongside the trailer. After this, the towing vehicle is realigned with the trailer and recoupled.

During the exercise the driver is marked on any points relating to control, accuracy and all-round observations. Faults are assessed as 'dangerous', 'serious' or as 'driving faults' depending on the type and severity of the fault.

Uncoupling

- Trailer and vehicle brakes 'on'.
- Remove and stow number plate.
- Landing gear lowered – store handle.
- Air line taps 'off'.
- Disconnect and stow air lines.
- Disconnect and stow electric line.
- Remove safety clip on kingpin handle.
- Release locking bar.
- Move the tractive unit away.

Recoupling

- Trailer brake 'on'.
- Check height of trailer with fifth wheel.
- Replace number plate.
- Reverse up to trailer to lock kingpin mechanism.
- Pull forward to check locking mechanism.
- Vehicle brakes 'on'.
- Connect security clip to kingpin handle.
- Connect electrics and air lines.
- Turn on taps.
- Landing gear raised – stow handle.
- Trailer brakes 'off'.
- Start engine – check air pressures.

Figure 3.1 Driving test report (form DL25)

THE DRIVING TEST REPORT FORM (DL25D) EXPLAINED

The following is a direct extract from the DL25, using DSA terminology.

1(a) The eyesight test

At the start of the test, the examiner asked you to read a vehicle registration number. If you required glasses or contact lenses, you must wear them whenever you drive. If you had problems with the eyesight test, perhaps you should consider consulting an optician.

1(b) *Highway Code/safety*

If you didn't need to take a separate Theory Test, for example because you were obtaining a licence for a tractor or other specialist vehicle, you will have been asked questions on the *Highway Code* and other related motoring matters. You will also have been asked to identify some traffic signs. If you had difficulty with these questions, make sure that you study properly by reading as wide a range of publications as you can to increase your understanding. If you have already passed a Theory Test, you will not have been asked *Highway Code* questions at the practical test stage; but you should still have a thorough knowledge of it.

Safety questions (if applicable) – you should know the location of, and be able to operate, safety components such as the fire extinguisher, fuel cut-off switch and emergency door.

2 Controlled stop

You will need to be able to display a high level of skill in bringing your vehicle to a stop, safely, promptly and under full control, avoiding locking the wheels.

Remember that in wet weather it can take twice as long to stop safely.

3, 4 and 5 Reverse exercises

You will need to display the ability to control the vehicle safely whilst reversing to the left or right, or when parking on the road or into a parking bay.

You must take good, effective, all-round observation throughout the manoeuvre and show consideration to other road users.

6 Turn in the road

You will need to display the low-speed control and observation skills necessary to carry out this exercise safely with due regard for other road users and pedestrians.

7 Vehicle checks

You will need to display to the examiner a basic knowledge of the fundamental safety checks applicable to your vehicle – for example, safe fluid levels, and lighting and tyre checks.

8 Taxi manoeuvre

You must be able to display the ability to turn your car around by whatever means available, making sure you take effective, all-round observation showing consideration to other road users and pedestrians.

You should control your vehicle smoothly, making proper use of the clutch, accelerator, brakes and steering.

You should not use a driveway or allow your vehicle to mount the pavement as this could damage your vehicle.

9 Taxi wheelchair

You should be able to:

- securely erect wheelchair ramps;
- safely install the wheelchair and an imaginary occupant into your vehicle;
- ensure the wheelchair and occupant are secured in readiness for the journey; and
- reverse the entire process.

10 Vehicle and trailer combinations: uncoupling/recoupling

You will need to demonstrate the skills necessary when uncoupling and recoupling your vehicle, driving the towing vehicle to a designated position prior to recoupling safely.

11 Precautions

Before you start the engine, make sure that you are comfortably seated and all controls can be safely operated.

12 Control

This section covers, where appropriate, the safe and controlled use of accelerator, clutch, gears, footbrake, parking brake and steering.

Additional specific control elements apply to the drivers of different vehicle categories:

- Always try to use the vehicle controls as smoothly as possible. This means less wear and tear on your vehicle and a smoother ride for your passengers.
- Make proper use of your accelerator and clutch to make a smooth start.
- Always depress the clutch just before you stop.
- Select the correct gear to match the road and traffic conditions.
- Change gear in good time but not too soon before a hazard.
- Do not allow the vehicle to coast by running on in neutral or with the clutch depressed.
- There should be no need to look down at the gear lever when changing gear.
- Use the footbrake smoothly and progressively.
- Brake in plenty of time for any hazard.
- Make full use of the parking brake whenever it would help you to prevent the car from rolling backwards or forwards, and if you are parking.
- Steer the vehicle as smoothly as possible.
- Avoid harsh steering, or steering too early or too late as it may cause you to hit the kerb or swing out towards another road user.
- If you are riding a motorcycle slowly, maintain a straight line and do not allow the machine to wobble towards other vehicles.

13 Move off

You will need to demonstrate your ability to move off smoothly and safely on the level, on a gradient and at an angle, taking the correct precautionary observations.

14 Use of mirrors: rear observations

Use all the mirrors fitted to your vehicle safely and effectively.

You must always check carefully before signalling, changing direction or changing speed.

Use the mirrors–signal–manoeuvre (MSM) routine effectively.

15 Signals

You must signal clearly to let others know what you intend to do. You should only use the signals shown in the *Highway Code* if it would help other road users (including pedestrians).

Always signal in good time and ensure that the signal has been cancelled after the manoeuvre has been completed.

Do not beckon to pedestrians to cross the road.

16 Clearance to obstructions

Allow plenty of room to pass stationary vehicles or obstructions and be prepared to slow down or stop. A door may open, a child may run out or a vehicle may pull out without warning.

17 Response to signs and signals

You should understand and be able to react to all traffic signs and road markings.

You must act correctly at traffic lights, and check that the road is clear before proceeding when the green light shows.

Obey signals given by police officers, traffic wardens and school crossing patrols.

Look out for signals given by other road users, including people in charge of animals, and be ready to act accordingly.

18 Use of speed

You should make safe, reasonable progress along the road bearing in mind the road, traffic and weather conditions and the road signs and speed limits.

Make sure that you can stop safely, well within the distance you can see to be clear.

Do not speed. Remember that as a new driver, your licence will be revoked if you accrue six or more penalty points during the first two years, and you have to retake and pass both theory and practical tests.

19 Following distance

Always keep a safe distance between yourself and other vehicles.

Remember, on wet or slippery roads it takes much longer to stop.

When you stop in traffic queues, leave sufficient room to pull out if the vehicle in front has problems.

20 Maintain progress

In order to pass your test you must show that you can drive at a realistic speed appropriate to the road and traffic conditions.

You should approach all hazards at a safe, controlled speed, without being over-cautious or interfering with the progress of other traffic.

Always be ready to move away from junctions as soon as it is safe and correct to do so.

Driving excessively slowly can create dangers for yourself and other drivers.

21 Junctions (including roundabouts)

You should be able to judge the correct speed of approach so that you can enter a junction safely and stop if necessary.

Position your vehicle correctly.

Use the correct lane.

If you are turning right, keep as near to the centre of the road as is safe.

Avoid cutting the corner when turning right.

If turning left, keep over to the left and do not swing out.

Watch out for cyclists and motorcyclists coming up on your left and pedestrians who are crossing.

You must take effective observation before moving into a junction and make sure it is safe before proceeding.

22 Judgement

Only overtake when it is safe to do so.

Allow enough room when you are overtaking another vehicle.

Cyclists and motorcyclists need at least as much space as other vehicles. They can wobble or swerve suddenly.

Do not cut in too quickly after overtaking.

Take care when the width of the road is restricted or when the road narrows.

If there is an obstruction on your side or not enough room for two vehicles to pass safely, be prepared to wait and let the approaching vehicles through.

When you turn right across the path of an approaching vehicle, make sure you can do so safely. Other vehicles should not have to stop, slow down or swerve to allow you to complete your turn.

23 Positioning

You should position the vehicle sensibly, normally well to the left.

Keep clear of parked vehicles and position correctly for the direction that you intend to take.

Where lanes are marked, keep to the middle of the lane and avoid straddling lane markings.

Do not change lanes unnecessarily.

24 Pedestrian crossings

You should be able to recognize the different types of pedestrian crossings and show courtesy and consideration towards pedestrians.

At all crossings you should slow down and stop if there is anyone on the crossing.

At zebra crossings you should slow down and be prepared to stop if there is anyone waiting to cross.

Give way to any pedestrian on a pelican crossing when the amber lights are flashing.

You should give way to cyclists as well as pedestrians on a toucan crossing and act correctly at puffin crossings.

25 Position/normal stops

Choose a safe, legal and convenient place to stop, close to the edge of the road, where you will not obstruct the road and create a hazard.

You should know how and where to stop without causing danger to other road users.

26 Awareness/planning

You must be aware of other road users at all times.

You should always think and plan ahead so that you can:

- judge what other road users are going to do;
- predict how their actions will affect you; and
- react in good time.

Take particular care to consider the actions of the more vulnerable groups of road users such as pedestrians, cyclists, motorcyclists and horse riders.

Anticipate road and traffic conditions, and act in good time, rather than reacting to them at the last moment.

27 Ancillary controls

You should understand the function of all the controls and switches, especially those that have a bearing on road safety. These include:

- indicators;
- lights;
- windscreen wipers;
- demisters;
- heaters.

You should be able to find these controls and operate them correctly when necessary, without looking down.

28 Health declaration

You must declare any change to your health status since you last applied for a licence. It is a criminal offence for you (or anyone else) to make a false statement in order for you to obtain a driving licence, and can lead to prosecution.

Note that the above text is a direct extract from the DL25, using DSA terminology. The DL25 includes information that is only applicable to certain types of vehicle

AT THE END OF THE TEST

Successful candidates are given a pass certificate (D10V) and a copy of the examiner's driving test report (DLV25). The examiner also offers a brief verbal explanation of any driving faults that have been marked during the test.

The pass certificate together with your licence should be sent off to DVLA at Swansea SA99 1BR. This should be done as soon as possible but in any event must be done within two years, as the pass certificate would be invalid after that time. You should keep a photocopy of any documents before sending them away.

In the unlikely event that you are not successful, the examiner will give you a statement of failure (DL25A) showing details of all the faults marked during the test. The examiner will also offer a more detailed explanation. You should discuss the report form with your instructor and compare it with any previous training notes. Between you, it should be possible to formulate a short refresher programme before organizing a retest.

With an appropriate amount of structured training, combined with plenty of practice, you should be able to achieve a professional standard of driving and therefore a test pass.

AFTER THE TEST

Whether you have passed or failed, it is sensible for your instructor to drive you away from the test centre. This is because:

- You can vacate the parking space for the next test candidate.
- If you have passed, you will be feeling very elated and may not be able to concentrate properly on your driving.
- If you have failed, you may be feeling disappointed, angry or frustrated – none of which will be conducive to good driving.
- The test centre is not the best place for carrying out a 'post mortem'.

IF THINGS GO WRONG: THE DSA COMPLAINTS PROCEDURE

Full information about complaints is given in the DSA's 'Service Standards' leaflet, which is available from the DSA at Nottingham. If you have a genuine complaint about the conduct of the test, you need to write or phone the appropriate section at DSA.

This would apply to complaints regarding:

- test cancellations;
- compensation;
- lost applications;
- delays in providing a test;
- theory test results;
- conduct of a practical test.

Note that if you have a complaint about the conduct of a practical test, the result of the test cannot be overturned. However, if it can be shown that the test was not conducted properly according to the regulations, you can contact a magistrates' court (or a sheriff court in Scotland). It is possible for the court to order a retest.

4

The Law and the LGV Driver

As a professional LGV driver you need to have a thorough understanding and a good working knowledge of the regulations and procedures relating to your use of a large vehicle.

This chapter deals mainly with a summary of the legal responsibilities of the LGV driver and instructor in relation to:

- legal obligations and responsibilities;
- disqualification;
- penalty points;
- drivers' documents;
- driving offences;
- fixed penalties;
- driving licence endorsements;
- endorsement codes;
- motor vehicle insurance;
- supervising learner drivers;
- drivers' hours and tachographs.

LEGAL OBLIGATIONS

Most driving offences are included in the 1991 Road Traffic Act (RTA), although some offences are covered by civil or common law and by the requirements of the Construction and Use Regulations. Drivers are sometimes confused by the status of the *Highway Code*. Although the contents of the *Code* are approved by Parliament and are based on the requirements of the RTA, a breach of it does not necessarily constitute an offence. However, the *Highway Code* can be used as reference in a court when assessing the specific actions of a driver.

Some of the major offences that are covered by the RTA include:

- causing death by dangerous driving;
- dangerous driving;
- causing death by careless driving when under the influence of drink or drugs;
- causing danger to other road users.

In relation to these offences, the usual standard applied is that 'the driving falls far below that expected of a competent and careful driver'. For an offence to be committed, there must be evidence of actual or potential danger of physical injury or serious damage to property. The standard of driving does not take into account the age or inexperience of the driver. It is not intended that the driver who makes a careless mistake, of a kind that any driver might make from time to time, should be regarded as falling 'far below the standard expected'. The danger must be one that a careful and competent driver would have appreciated or observed.

Careless and inconsiderate driving is defined in relation to 'a person driving a mechanically propelled vehicle on a road or other public place'. This means that non-motorized vehicles and offences on private property to which the public have access may be included. The main constituents in this offence are referred to in terms of 'driving without due care and attention, or without reasonable consideration for other road users'.

Offences of driving without a licence, without 'L' plates, without supervision or under the age when a licence can be obtained are now dealt with under the offence of 'driving otherwise than in accordance with a licence'. Penalty points for this offence vary from three to six depending on the circumstances and seriousness of the offence.

Offences incurring disqualification

The following offences carry automatic disqualification:

- manslaughter caused by the driver of a motor vehicle;
- causing death by dangerous driving;
- causing death by careless driving when unfit through drink;
- dangerous driving;
- motor racing on the highway;
- driving, or attempting to drive, when under the influence of drink or drugs, or with more than the permitted blood/alcohol level;
- failure to provide a blood or urine sample.

The extended driving test

Courts have the power, for some of the more serious offences, to order disqualification until an 'appropriate' driving test is passed. These offences include motor manslaughter, causing death by dangerous driving and dangerous driving. The test is normally longer and more rigorous than the ordinary 'L' test. It therefore provides scope for the driver to be tested in a greater variety of road and traffic conditions.

In determining whether to make such an order, the court must have regard to the safety of road users. For offences involving oblig- atory disqualification, the 'appropriate' test is the extended driving test, and might therefore apply to the driver who has been disqualified under the 'totting up' procedure, and who has been ordered by the court to retake the test. For offences involving obligatory endorsement (as opposed to obligatory disqualification), the appro- priate test is the ordinary test of competence to drive.

PENALTY POINTS

Penalty points for some offences are graded according to the seri- ousness of the offence (Table 4.1). An accumulation of 12 points within three years means that the driver will automatically be disqual- ified from driving, although the courts are given powers not to disqualify in exceptional circumstances. The three-year period is measured backwards from the date of the latest offence.

The period of disqualification as a result of an accumulation of penalty points is:

- six months, if there has been no disqualification in the past three years;
- one year, if there has been one disqualification in the past three years;
- two years, if there has been more than one disqualification in the past three years.

Disqualification may be imposed for a single offence if the court feels that the offence is serious enough.

An endorsement with penalty points can be removed after four years from the date of the offence.

An endorsement or disqualification may be removed four years after the date of conviction (11 years for drinking and driving offences).

Table 4.1   Penalty points

Offence	Points
Being in charge of a vehicle when unfit to drive	10
Failing to stop after an accident	5–10
Failing to report or to give particulars	5–10
Careless and inconsiderate driving	3–9
Driving while uninsured	6–8
Driving while disqualified by a court	6
Driving other than in accordance with a licence	3–6
Exceeding a speed limit	
– in court proceedings	3–6
– by fixed penalty	3
Contravention of temporary prohibition or restriction	
– in court proceedings	3–6
– by fixed penalty	3
Contravention of motorway regulations	
– in court proceedings	3–6
– by fixed penalty	3
Failure to give identity of driver	3
Unlawful carriage of motorcycle passenger	3
Contravention or failure to comply with C & U Regs	3
Driving with defective eyesight	3

After a disqualification for a period of more than two years the driver can apply for the disqualification to be lifted after a period of:

- two years if the disqualification period is less than four years;
- half the period of disqualification if between 4 and 10 years;
- five years if the disqualification was for more than 10 years.

Fixed penalties

Traffic wardens and police officers are empowered to enforce the law in connection with various offences by use of the fixed penalty system. The relevant offences include waiting, parking, loading and obstruction as well as offences relating to vehicle tax, lights and reflectors. Driving offences such as making an unauthorized 'U' turn and driving the wrong way in a one-way street are also included.

The ticket is given to the driver or is fixed to the vehicle. Payment must be made within 28 days, or alternatively the offender may request a court hearing. If the driver who committed the offence cannot be identified or found, the registered owner of the vehicle is ultimately responsible for payment of the fine. However, in the case of hired vehicles, special rules apply and the person who hires the vehicle will become liable for any fines or excess charges.

The extended fixed penalty scheme covers various moving traffic offences including speeding, failure to comply with traffic directions and vehicle defect offences. The following categories are included in the scheme, and for these offences the issuing of the ticket is normally the responsibility of the police:

- contravening a traffic regulation order;
- breach of experimental traffic order;
- breach of experimental traffic scheme regulation in Greater London;
- using a vehicle in contravention of a temporary prohibition or restriction of traffic on a road, ie where a road is being repaired, etc;
- contravening motorway traffic regulations;
- driving a vehicle in contravention of order prohibiting or restricting driving vehicles on certain classes of roads;
- breach of pedestrian crossing regulations;
- contravention of a street playground order;
- breach of a parking place order on a road;
- breach of a provision of a parking place designation order and other offences committed in relation to it, except failing to pay an excess charge;
- contravening a parking place designation order;
- breach of a provision of a parking place designation order;
- contravention of minimum speed limits;
- speeding;
- driving or keeping a vehicle without displaying registration mark or hackney carriage sign;
- driving or keeping a vehicle with registration mark or hackney carriage sign obscured;
- failure to comply with traffic directions or signs;
- leaving vehicle in a dangerous position;
- failing to wear a seatbelt;
- breach of restrictions on carrying children in the front of vehicles;
- driving a vehicle elsewhere than on the road;
- parking a vehicle on the path or verge;
- breach of Construction and Use Regulations;
- contravention of lighting restrictions on vehicles;
- driving without a licence;

- breach of provisional licence provisions;
- failure to stop when required by constable in uniform;
- obstruction of highway with vehicle.

Penalty tickets for endorsable offences are handed to the driver, as the driving licence will have to be surrendered for possible endorsement with the appropriate penalty points. If the licence shows an accumulation of points that, together with the current offence, would bring the total to 12 points or more, then the fixed penalty ticket would not be issued. In those circumstances a prosecution for the offence would follow.

If the licence is not immediately available, it must be produced within seven days at a nominated police station. A receipt for the licence is then issued and this is an accepted document if for any reason the licence has to be produced at a later date.

The fixed penalty fines of £30 for non-endorsable and £60 for endorsable offences are payable within 28 days (or as specified in the notice). If payment is not received in time, the charge is increased by 50 per cent to £45 and £90 respectively. A driver may request a court hearing if he or she considers that the issue of the ticket was wrong or unfair.

DRIVER IMPROVEMENT SCHEME

Several police forces are now offering the Driver Improvement Scheme as an alternative to prosecution for drivers committing some less serious or less careless driving offences. Offenders are given the opportunity to attend a short (one- or two-day) course at their own expense. The aim is to address driver behaviour and to provide remedial instruction tailored to suit the individual driver's needs. The scheme is not normally used for more serious offences or where there is an element of dangerousness or deliberate recklessness.

DRIVER IDENTITY

The 1991 Act defines the circumstances in which a person can be required to give information about the identity of a driver who is alleged to be guilty of a road traffic offence. This is particularly important in connection with the identification of drivers involved in speeding or other offences detected by automatic devices, including cameras.

A photograph, showing the registration number, is taken of the offending vehicle. It is not intended that the registered keeper of the vehicle should bear responsibility for the offence detected by the device if someone else was driving at the time of the offence. It is, therefore, necessary to trace the driver through the registered keeper. The penalty for not providing the information has been increased to three penalty points to provide an incentive to do so.

The existing fixed penalty system requires the vehicle and the person committing the offence to be present at the time the fixed penalty ticket is issued. However, under the provisions of the RTA 1991, a conditional fixed penalty offer is available for all fixed penalty offences, including those detected by automatic cameras and other devices. These provisions allow for the police to issue a notice to the alleged offender by post.

The notice is first issued to the registered keeper of the vehicle, requiring information about the identity of the driver. The conditional offer of a fixed penalty will then be issued to the person identified as the driver of the vehicle when the offence was detected. If the information about the driver is not given, the 'keeper' of the vehicle will have committed an offence, which is now endorsable.

If the driver wishes to take up the offer of the fixed penalty, the driving licence and payment are sent to the Fixed Penalty Office and the payment is accepted, so long as the licence shows that the driver would not be subject to a 'totting up' disqualification. In those circumstances, the payment and licence would be returned and a court summons would then be issued.

DRIVING LICENCE ENDORSEMENTS

Endorsement offences appear on a driving licence in a coded version that includes details of the court, the offence, the fine and endorsement.

Code **Offence**
Accidents
AC10   Failing to stop and/or give particulars after an accident
AC20   Failing to report an accident within 24 hours
AC30   Undefined accident offence

Driver banned from driving (disqualified)
BA10   Driving while disqualified
BA20   Driving while disqualified by virtue of age

Careless driving
CD10   Driving without due care and attention
CD20   Driving without reasonable consideration for other road
          users
CD30   Driving without due care and attention or without
          reasonable consideration for other road users

Construction and Use offences
CU10   Using a vehicle with defective brakes
CU20   Causing or being likely to cause danger by reason of use
          of unsuitable vehicle, or using a vehicle with parts or
          accessories (excluding brakes, steering or tyres) in a
          dangerous condition
CU30   Using a vehicle with defective tyres
CU40   Using a vehicle with defective steering
CU50   Causing or likely to cause danger by reason of load or
          passengers
CU60   Undefined failure to comply with Construction and Use
          Regulations

Drink-drive offences
DR10   Driving or attempting to drive with blood alcohol level
          above limit
DR20   Driving or attempting to drive while unfit through drink or
          drugs
DR30   Driving or attempting to drive then refusing to supply a
          specimen of blood or urine for laboratory testing
DR40   In charge of a vehicle while blood alcohol level above limit
DR50   In charge of a vehicle while unfit through drink or drugs
DR60   In charge of a vehicle then refusing to supply a specimen
          of blood or urine for laboratory testing

Insurance offences
IN10   Using a vehicle uninsured against third party risks

Licence offences
LC10   Driving without a licence
LC20   Driving when under age

Miscellaneous offences
MS10   Leaving a vehicle in a dangerous position
MS20   Unlawful pillion riding
MS30   Play-street offences
MS40   Driving with uncorrected or defective eyesight or refusing
          to submit to an eyesight test

MS50   Motor racing on the highway
MS60   Offences not covered by other codes
MS70   Driving with uncorrected defective eyesight
MS80   Refusing to submit to an eyesight test

Motorway offences
MW10   Contravention of Special Roads Regulations (excluding speed limits)

Pedestrian crossing
PC10   Undefined contravention of Pedestrian Crossing Regulations
PC20   Contravention of Pedestrian Crossing Regulations with moving vehicle
PC30   Contravention of Pedestrian Crossing Regulations with stationary vehicle

Provisional licence offences
PL10   Driving without 'L' plates
PL20   Driving while not accompanied by a qualified person
PL30   Carrying a person not qualified
PL40   Drawing an unauthorized trailer
PL50   Undefined failure to comply with conditions of a provisional licence

Speed limits
SP10   Exceeding goods vehicle speed limit
SP20   Exceeding speed limit for type of vehicle (excluding goods or passenger vehicles)
SP30   Exceeding statutory speed limit on a public road
SP40   Exceeding passenger vehicle speed limit
SP50   Exceeding speed limit on a motorway
SP60   Undefined speed limit offence

Traffic directions and signs
TS10   Failing to comply with traffic light signals
TS20   Failing to comply with double white lines
TS30   Failing to comply with a 'Stop' sign
TS40   Failing to comply with directions of a traffic constable
TS50   Failing to comply with a traffic sign (excluding 'Stop' signs, traffic lights or double white lines)
TS60   Failing to comply with a school crossing patrol sign
TS70   Undefined failure to comply with a traffic direction or sign

Theft or the unauthorized taking of vehicle

UT10	Taking and driving away a vehicle without consent (or attempting to)
UT20	Stealing or attempting to steal a vehicle
UT30	Going equipped for stealing or taking a vehicle
UT40	Taking or attempting to take a vehicle without consent; driving or attempting to drive a vehicle knowing it to have been taken without consent; allowing oneself to be carried in or on a vehicle knowing it to have been taken without consent

Special code

XX99	Signifies a disqualification under the 'totting-up' procedure

Notes: Aiding and abetting offences are as listed above, but with the 0 changed to 2 (eg UT20 becomes UT22).

Causing or permitting are as listed, but with the 0 changed to 4 (eg PL20 becomes PL24).

Inciting offences are as listed, but with the 0 changed to 6 (eg DR10 becomes DR16).

MOTOR VEHICLE INSURANCE

Compulsory motor vehicle insurance was introduced in 1930. At that time it was decided that insurance was necessary to make sure that people who were injured in a road accident were not left uncompensated. Property damage should be included within the minimum insurance and this cover is required by the Road Traffic Act 1988.

Other types of insurance policies have been in operation for many years, as it is recognized that there is a need for more cover than the minimum requirements of the Road Traffic Act.

Types of insurance

Compulsory insurance

Users of motor vehicles must be insured with an authorized insurer against third party risks. The cover must include compensation in respect of death, injury to another person and also the cost of any emergency medical treatment. All passengers must be covered and no 'own risks' agreements are allowed between passengers and the user of the vehicle. This type of insurance policy (which is very rare) is sometimes known as a 'road traffic only' policy, and leaves the user with a vast amount of risk. As an alternative to insurance, application may be made to the Secretary of State at the Department for Transport for a warrant to enable a deposit of £500,000 in cash or securities to be made with the Accountant-General.

Third party property damage is a compulsory requirement under the Road Traffic Act 1988.

Third party insurance only

A 'third party' insurance policy usually requires at least the minimum cover as described above. This type of policy would normally cover:

- liability for injuries to other people (including passengers in your vehicle);
- liability in respect of accidents caused by them (for example, causing injury to a passer-by, or damaging their property by opening a cab door);
- liability for damage to other people's property (for example, damage to another vehicle may be paid in full or in part by your insurance company).

For an additional fee, the policy may be extended to include the risks of fire and theft. A 'third party, fire and theft' policy offers slightly more than the bare minimum but still leaves a lot of risk with the driver/owner/operator.

Comprehensive insurance

In view of the heavy cost of repairs, most owners these days take out a 'comprehensive' insurance policy. However, there is no such thing as fully comprehensive insurance and care should be taken in reading the small print. The term 'comprehensive' as applied to motor insurance means that a variety and a great deal of protection is provided under one policy document, but does not mean that cover is provided against every conceivable contingency of whatever nature.

Most owners (two out of three) use this type of insurance cover, which will normally include the risks for third party, fire and theft, together with cover for accidental damage to your own car, medical expenses, and loss or damage to personal effects in the car.

The policy will specify the uses to which the vehicle may be put. For instance, a policy restricting use to social, domestic and pleasure purposes will not provide cover for any business use. There may also be a restriction to cover driving by specified drivers only, or it may exclude driving by certain persons.

Other restrictions will vary from one insurance company to another, but it is normal practice for the company to specify an 'excess' when a learner or young, inexperienced driver is driving the vehicle. The excess is the amount that you would normally have to pay towards the cost of repairing your vehicle in the event of a blame-worthy accident. If the accident was the fault of another driver, you may need to recover this amount from that person.

Driver's responsibilities

As a driver, you must provide details of your insurance to the person who holds you responsible for an accident that results in damage to his or her property. The law also requires you to give insurance details following an injury accident. For your own convenience, you should be prepared to give your insurance details following an accident, or to a police officer, who can ask to see evidence of your insurance at any time.

Even with the new insurance requirements, drivers and other road users can find themselves without a source of compensation. This can happen where the accident is nobody's fault, or where you yourself are in some measure to blame. It is for you, as a driver, to consider whether you take out additional insurance cover against such risks as injury to yourself in these circumstances.

SUPERVISING A LEARNER DRIVER

Anyone supervising a learner driver must be over 21 years of age and have held a full, unrestricted GB licence for that particular type of vehicle for at least three years. It is the learner's responsibility to check that anyone supervising his or her practice is covered by these regulations. An offence against the regulations carries a penalty of a £400 fine, discretionary disqualification or two penalty points.

The vehicle being used for instruction must display regulation-size 'L' plates (or 'D' plates in Wales, if preferred) that are clearly visible within a reasonable distance from the front and rear of the vehicle. 'L' plates should be removed from the vehicle when a full licence holder is driving it, except in the case of instruction vehicles.

In addition to the responsibilities as driver, already covered in this chapter, the instructor has further responsibilities. Where a supervisor sees that the 'L' driver is about to commit an unlawful act, whether through ignorance or lack of skill, and takes no verbal or physical action to prevent it, a prosecution for aiding and abetting could ensue. For example, if a learner was about to ignore a red traffic light and the instructor allowed the vehicle to be stopped after passing the solid line, an offence would have been committed by both the driver and the instructor.

DRIVERS' HOURS AND TACHOGRAPHS

Drivers of all goods vehicles for commercial or business use have restrictions on the number of hours spent driving. There are also special rules about rest periods and minimum breaks to be taken. Additionally, goods vehicles over 3.5 tonnes maximum authorized mass must be fitted with a tachograph to record details of the movement of the vehicle as well as the driver's working and driving hours.

Different rules apply for:

● travel within the European Union (EU);
● international journeys outside the EU;
● UK domestic journeys.

From September 2004 the existing mechanical tachographs are being phased out and replaced by a new digital system that incorporates a driver's identification and record card, together with the vehicle unit. This system will reform the way that operators and drivers currently use the system.

Full details of the requirements for drivers' hours and the use of tachographs can be found in David Lowe's excellent publication *The Pocket Guide to LGV Drivers' Hours and Tachograph Law,* published by Kogan Page.

5

Responsible Driving

SPEED LIMITS

A speed limit of 30 mph normally applies where there is regular street lighting. If there is a higher limit on this type of road, there will be repeater signs showing the maximum speed. Where there are no streetlights but a speed limit exists, there will be repeater signs showing the limit.

Unless otherwise indicated, the national speed limit on single carriageways is 60 mph. On dual carriageways and motorways the limit is 70 mph. These limits apply to cars and car-derived vans up to 2 tonnes maximum laden weight.

If you tow a trailer behind your vehicle, the speed limit on single-carriageway roads is 50 mph and on dual carriageways and motorways it is 60 mph. You are not allowed to use the third lane of a three-lane motorway with this combination because of the lower speed.

When driving goods vehicles, the maximum speeds are as shown in Table 5.1.

Speed limits are imposed on residential and urban areas to make the roads safer for all road users, particularly pedestrians. Because stopping distances are much greater at higher speeds, driving at a speed that is too fast for the conditions is potentially dangerous.

Remember to reduce your speed where there are potential hazards and in poor weather conditions and at night.

Table 5.1 Maximum speeds for goods vehicles in the United Kingdom (mph)

Type of goods vehicle	Single carriageway	Dual carriageway	Motorway
Up to 7.5 tonnes	50	60	70
with trailer	50	60	60
LGV (over 7.5 tonnes or artic)	40	50	60

STOPPING DISTANCES

'Stopping distance' is measured from when you first realized that you have to brake to the point where your vehicle eventually stops. This overall distance depends on a number of factors, including the speed at which you are travelling, the condition of your vehicle, the weather and road conditions, and your reaction time in response to developing conditions.

The stopping distance is the total of thinking distance and braking distance (Table 5.2).

Thinking distance is based on the reaction time of the driver. This varies from one person to another, but is generally about two-thirds of a second. In this time, at 30 mph you will travel about 9 metres. The distance increases proportionally with speed, so at 60 mph the distance will be about 18 metres. If you are travelling at 70 mph on a motorway you will cover about 21 metres (about five to six car lengths) before you even start braking. If you are tired, or are not fully concentrating, your reaction time will be slower and the distance covered will be greater.

Braking distance depends on the speed at which you are travelling. At 20 mph the braking distance is about 6 metres, but this increases to 24 metres at 40 mph. In other words, doubling your speed makes the braking distance four times greater. At 70 mph the braking distance for a car in normal driving conditions will be about 75 metres. On wet or slippery roads these distances will be much longer.

Separation distance is the distance you should keep between yourself and the vehicle in front. Ideally, this distance should be the same as the overall stopping distance – that is, about 96 metres when travelling at 70 mph. In busy traffic conditions this is not always practicable, but the gap should always be at least the thinking distance.

Table 5.2   Stopping distances

Speed			Thinking distance		Braking distance		Overall stopping distance	
mph	Metres/s	Feet/s	Metres	Feet	Metres	Feet	Metres	Feet
20	9	30	6	20	6	20	12	40
30	14	45	9	30	14	45	23	75
40	18	60	12	40	24	80	36	120
50	23	75	15	50	38	125	53	175
60	27	90	18	60	55	180	73	240
70	32	105	22	70	75	245	96	315

A lot of drivers use the 'two-second' rule to judge the appropriate gap. This involves checking when the vehicle in front passes a particular reference point and then counting two seconds before you pass that same point. In poor weather conditions this distance should be increased to four seconds.

If someone behind is travelling much too close, you should leave more of a gap from the vehicle in front. This is to ensure that the total gap between the three vehicles is sufficient.

Anti-lock braking systems

Anti-lock braking systems are designed to make sure that maximum braking is applied, but that the wheels do not lose their grip in normal conditions. They allow you to steer at the same time as braking firmly, so are much safer in controlling the vehicle in an emergency situation. They do not necessarily mean that you can stop in a shorter distance.

DRINK-DRIVING

Driving with alcohol in your blood is potentially dangerous. Without your necessarily realizing it, your ability to drive safely will be reduced. Alcohol has the effect of slowing down your reactions and can affect your judgement of speed and distance. At the same time, it tends to give a false sense of confidence.

You will be committing a serious offence if you drive with a breath alcohol level of more than 35 micrograms per 100 millilitres. This is the equivalent of 80 milligrams to 100 millilitres in terms of blood alcohol.

Alcohol takes some time to leave the body. Some alcohol may be left in the bloodstream a considerable time after drinking, such as the morning after consuming alcohol the previous evening.

For a drink-drive offence a court must disqualify you from driving for a minimum of one year. If there was a high reading, or for a repeated offence, the disqualification would be much longer. For a second offence within a 10-year period the court must disqualify for a minimum of three years.

As well as the disqualification there will be a heavy financial penalty and you will find that insurance at the end of the disqualification period may be difficult. At best you can expect to pay much more and at worst the insurance company may refuse to cover you.

After a conviction for a drink-driving offence the court can offer the offender the opportunity to attend an approved rehabilitation course. If the offender takes the course, the period of disqualification may be reduced by up to one quarter. Fees for the course (currently about £150) have to be paid by the offender.

Courses normally require attendance for two or three hours each week for six to eight weeks.

ACCIDENTS

If you are involved in an accident that causes damage to someone else's property or to another vehicle you must stop – even if you think that it is only minor. Any vehicles that are directly involved in the accident should not be moved until all the formalities have been completed, and any casualties dealt with.

If you are one of the first at the scene of an accident you will need to warn other traffic of the obstruction by switching on hazard warning lights and by displaying an advance warning. You might need to arrange other means of controlling approaching traffic.

Call the emergency services, making sure that you give accurate details of the location. On a motorway, refer to the emergency telephone reference number as well as the nearest junction number.

Move any uninjured people away from the vehicles. On a motorway this means well away from the road, the hard shoulder and the central reservation.

The legal definition of an 'accident' is an incident that causes injury to another person or animal, or one that causes damage to another person's vehicle or property.

If you are involved in an accident you must give your name, address and vehicle details. If there is personal injury, your insurance details must be given to anyone who has reasonable cause to see them. You must also give information about the ownership of the vehicle.

If it is not possible to exchange these details at the time, the accident must be reported to the police as soon as possible, and in any case within 24 hours. These responsibilities apply regardless of who is to blame for the accident. Even if you feel that the accident is relatively trivial, or that it was not your fault, you still need to follow the procedure outlined in Figure 5.1.

Note:
The chart shows the *minimum* legal requirements

Accident procedure – notes

1. An 'animal' is regarded as horse, cattle, ass, mule, sheep, goat, pig or dog.
2. You must exchange details not only with the other driver, but also with any person who has reasonable grounds for asking for them.
3. 'Damage' includes roadside furniture, for example lamp posts and other fixtures.
4. You must report an accident as soon as possible, and at least within 24 hours. Your insurance certificate must be produced at the time of reporting or within seven days.
5. Your details must be given to the owner of a vehicle, property or animal.

Figure 5.1   Accident Procedure Flowchart

'SAFE AND FUEL EFFICIENT DRIVING'

'Safe and Fuel Efficient Driving' (SAFED) is a driving training programme that has been developed as a result of a government initiative with the aim of promoting safe and fuel-efficient driving. According to government figures, LGVs are using in excess of 1.6 billion gallons of fuel each year. One of the objectives of the scheme is to reduce this figure by at least 5 per cent, giving an annual cost saving of about £300 million as well as a significant reduction in carbon dioxide emissions.

As part of an individual training programme a specially trained instructor assesses the person's driving and then gives guidance on safe and fuel-efficient driving procedures and techniques. A further assessment is then carried out, usually over the same route as previously.

The SAFED programme is usually carried out as a one-day course for two drivers. The training includes practical assessments and in-class presentations covering the main themes of: 1) accident prevention and reduction; 2) fuel-efficient driving.

The main elements involved in achieving safe driving combined with fuel economy are normally discussed during the training. For each element of driving a set of criteria have been identified:

- acceleration and cruise control:
  - steady and progressive acceleration whenever possible;
  - avoid speed peaks;
  - use of smooth acceleration;
  - use of cruise control where appropriate;
- braking (including engine/exhaust brake):
  - smooth and positive braking with tapering on and off;
  - handbrake used when required;
  - effective use of engine/exhaust brake when possible;
- clutch control:
  - efficient and controlled use of the clutch;
- driving position/seat belt:
  - maintaining an alert posture;
  - seat belt to be used where fitted;
- road and weather conditions:
  - awareness of the conditions;
  - consideration of visibility and braking distances;
- steering:
  - correct and appropriate use of steering techniques;

- gear selection and use:
  - accurate gear selection;
  - use of block/skip changes;
- hazard perception and prioritization:
  - forward observations;
- speed:
  - legal speed limits;
  - adjustment of speed for varying road and traffic conditions;
  - planning ahead for potential changes of speed;
- lane discipline and positioning:
  - lane markings;
  - correct positioning to maximize visibility/safety/progress;
  - correct braking distances;
- making progress and planning:
  - maintain safe progress;
  - take advantage of safe gaps in traffic;
- use of mirrors and blind spots:
  - effective use of all mirrors;
  - check of blind spots when required;
- use of signals:
  - correct use of signals when needed;
  - information to other road users;
- overtaking:
  - safely and positively;
- vehicle sympathy:
  - low engine speeds where possible;
  - high power when necessary;
  - smooth control;
- driver attitude/technique:
  - positive attitude;
  - good concentration;
  - consideration and courtesy towards other road users;
- reaction to road markings and signs:
  - observation;
  - safe and efficient reaction.

Note: the above 'elements' are reproduced by kind permission of SAFED. For full details of the SAFED programme – for drivers and instructors – contact:

SAFED Programme Co-ordinator
AEA Technology plc
329 Harwell
Didcot
Oxfordshire OX11 0QJ
Tel: 0870 190 6354
Fax: 0870 190 6320
e-mail: enquirics@safed.org.uk
www.safed.org.uk

6

The LGV Instructor

The professional LGV driver needs to be someone who can control and manage a large, complex vehicle and its load – often with a total value of more than £100,000. As a qualified LGV licence holder you will have demonstrated that you have the skill to control and manoeuvre a vehicle of up to 44 tonnes on Britain's congested roads and in a UK road system that is less than perfect. You will also have a high level of knowledge about a variety of subjects, including drivers' hours, tachographs, road transport law, load stability and security as well as customer care.

Recent changes to both the LGV licensing scheme and the driving test system have meant that it is increasingly difficult and time-consuming for a new driver to obtain the appropriate vocational licence.

The enhanced Theory Test now includes a section on hazard perception and has a revised and enlarged question bank covering a wide variety of subjects. These include vehicle weights and dimensions, drivers' hours and rest periods, braking systems, vehicle safety equipment, drugs and alcohol, accident handling, vehicle condition, types of load and load stability, driving documents, and road signs and markings.

The Practical Test now includes a more stringent set of manoeuvring exercises as well as the introduction of questions relating to technical and safety matters. This part of the test involves 'show me, tell me' questions. The standard of driving required is as high as ever, with just one serious driving error resulting in a failed test.

New proposals by the European Union (EU) will mean that the standards of professionalism for drivers of large vehicles will be raised to an even higher level. It will not be sufficient simply to pass the driving test, as at present. The new driver will have to undergo a lengthy period of study and training; and the Theory and Practical tests will be much more stringent. The likelihood and expectation is that these new proposals will lead to a certificate of professional competence for drivers of large vehicles.

Under the scheme, training for new drivers will consist of attendance on a course of between 140 and 280 hours, followed by a series of more stringent tests. It is proposed to follow the initial training with periodic refresher courses of 35 hours every five years. The main objectives of the new proposals are not only improved road safety, but also the raising of professional standards in the industry.

It has been estimated that as a result of these initiatives there will be a severe shortage of LGV drivers; some experts have suggested that the shortfall may be as much as 80,000 by 2010. When the changes are combined with new legislation on maximum working hours and other working time directives, it can be seen that the market for training new drivers will expand enormously over the next few years. The need for a greater number of properly qualified professional instructors and trainers is clearly urgent.

ROLE OF THE LGV INSTRUCTOR

Driving tests for LGV drivers were introduced some 30 or so years ago. Since that time the size and complexity of vehicles have changed significantly; road and traffic conditions are dramatically different; and the methods of teaching and learning are somewhat different. The range of services required nowadays by the customer and offered by the training industry has expanded considerably compared with the 1970s. At that time, the LGV instructor might only have been involved in very basic driver training on relatively small training vehicles. The range of skills required in today's market might include:

- basic driver training to DSA test standards;
- assessments and refresher training for full licence holders;
- fuel efficiency training;
- carriage of dangerous goods;
- lorry-mounted crane operation;
- lift truck training;
- tachograph courses for drivers and supervisors.

The instructor today needs, therefore, to be an all-round trainer in the industry, and not just a basic driver instructor.

Large goods vehicles are involved in a sizeable proportion of road traffic accidents – in Great Britain over 3,000 people are killed or seriously injured each year in accidents involving this type of vehicle. In today's increasingly complex driving situations, and with traffic speeds increasing, the LGV instructor needs to be much more than a good driver. He or she needs to have a serious interest in upgrading the standards of professionalism in the industry.

Instructors must have a thorough understanding of the rules and principles of safe driving and the ability to put them into practice thoughtfully and efficiently. The need is to teach your drivers how to apply these principles and to instil safe attitudes and habits. You must be able to manage the learning process of your trainees – both individually and in a group situation. This is particularly important as the LGV driver is professionally trained and should therefore be in a position to make allowances for the mistakes of other untrained road users such as cyclists, pedestrians, the elderly and the very young. Your drivers should be taught to accept and to compensate for these mistakes and to be tolerant to the less skilled driver.

The role of the instructor is very satisfying, but at the same time can be very demanding. When you qualify as an LGV instructor you will have demonstrated that you have the necessary qualities to become a professional in your field.

QUALITIES OF A GOOD DRIVER

To be able to maximize your own personal driving and instructional skills you need to be aware of the qualities of a good driver. These include the following.

Responsibility

You should always show proper concern for other road users, your passengers and yourself.

Concentration

You need to concentrate at all times. When you are driving a large, heavy vehicle, any distraction – even a momentary one – can have a disastrous effect, particularly in today's traffic conditions and congested roads.

Anticipation

A major part of your skill as an LGV driver is the ability to predict what might happen and to identify potential hazards at an early stage.

Patience

Be patient and show restraint when dealing with the mistakes and inefficiencies of other road users. Not everyone is as effectively trained and tested to high standards as is the LGV driver. With your own name, or that of your company, on the vehicle, it is good public relations to avoid confrontational situations.

Confidence

Conscientious drivers display confidence at all times. This confidence stems from being totally 'at one' with the vehicle; travelling at a speed that is suitable for the road, traffic and weather conditions; driving with the appropriate gear selected; and driving in the correct road position. Planning well ahead and anticipating any possible changes in the traffic scene, the confident LGV driver will be able to avoid the need for last-minute, rushed or potentially unsafe decisions.

Knowledge

As an efficient LGV driver you will have a thorough knowledge of, and the ability to apply correctly, the rules, regulations and procedures from the *The Official DSA Guide to Driving* and *The Official DSA Guide to Driving Goods Vehicles*.

Communication

When you are driving a large, bulky vehicle, your communication with other drivers and road users is vital. In particular, you need to show your intentions by effective and appropriate use of:

- direction indicators (and arm signals where necessary);
- brake lights;
- reversing lights and audible warning;
- horn and flashing headlights;
- hazard warning flashers;
- eye contact;
- by early positioning of your vehicle in the most appropriate road position.

Instructional qualities

You then need to think of instructional qualities in terms of your own instructional ability and skills.

Responsibility

Always be conscious of the safety and well-being of your trainees, particularly in the early stages of their training. Avoid getting into traffic situations that they are not able to cope with. Remember that you are responsible for their safety (as well as your own!).

Concentration

The concentration that is required when you are accompanying an inexperienced driver in a large vehicle is even more demanding than with your own driving. You need to read the road much further ahead than your trainee is doing. Any developing situations need to be assessed and taken into account so that your trainee feels capable of dealing with them safely.

Anticipation

Anticipation is even more important for an instructor than for a driver – particularly in a large vehicle with a novice driver. You have to understand the needs of individual trainees and anticipate how they might respond or fail to respond to any changing traffic situations. Your observations and anticipation have to be focused much further ahead than the trainee's; you need to anticipate any potential problems so that you can either give positive instructions or prompt the trainee in good time to take any appropriate action.

Patience

Your trainees will normally be aware of any mistakes that they make. Losing patience will only make the situation worse. Be ready to deal with the error in a different way and to offer more help, even if you have explained the point previously. Showing patience and helping your trainees to learn and improve their skills will assist in building up their confidence. Your own attitude, showing patience and tolerance, will have a beneficial effect on their own attitude.

Confidence

To be an effective instructor you have to be confident in yourself, and in your own ability. This will, in turn, help the trainees' own confidence. Make sure that each topic of your training syllabus, and the routes you select, are suitable for the trainees' level of ability. By doing this, and by avoiding situations that they are not ready for, you will build up their confidence.

Knowledge

Passing on your knowledge of the subject to the new LGV drivers you train will enable them to apply the correct principles for safe driving. As an instructor, you need to keep yourself up to date with any changes in the law, regulations and procedures so that you are able:

- to handle various types of vehicle legally and safely;
- to apply modern teaching techniques;
- to maintain a safe teaching/learning environment;
- to offer advice to trainees on licensing requirements, basic mechanical principles and on the rules and regulations for safe driving;
- to answer questions from your trainees accurately and with confidence.

Sound knowledge forms the basis of your skill as an LGV instructor. It is tested in the theory element of the LGV instructor's exam; how to apply it is assessed in the driving ability test; and how you pass the knowledge on to trainees is checked as part of the instructional ability test.

Communication

You will need to develop ways in which to communicate with the wide variety of trainees you will be dealing with. The terminology you use will be adapted so that each individual trainee understands exactly what you mean and what is required of him or her. You need to be able to teach not only how to apply the relevant procedures and techniques, but also why these procedures should be followed.

There are many ways of communicating with your trainees. They include:

- establishing the level of understanding of the trainee so as to determine the appropriate way of communicating with him or her;
- explaining new principles in a clear and straightforward manner;
- using visual aids where appropriate so that the trainee has a clear picture of what you mean;

- giving practical demonstrations for any complicated procedures;
- giving directional instructions early enough for the trainee to respond safely and in good time for the hazard;
- giving encouragement to the trainee through positive feedback and praise where appropriate;
- finding out whether trainees have fully understood by asking questions;
- encouraging trainees to ask questions.

ROAD SAFETY ISSUES

Driving large vehicles these days has been made much easier by modern developments in vehicle design and efficiency. However, road and traffic conditions are becoming increasingly more complex and demanding. As a responsible LGV instructor, you need to be aware, and to make your trainees aware, of some of the major causes of road traffic accidents. They include:

- ignorance of, or disregard for, the basic rules of the road;
- lack of concentration and attention to developing situations;
- carelessness;
- driving while under the influence of drink or drugs;
- driving while tired or unwell;
- driving with defective eyesight;
- using a vehicle that is not in a roadworthy condition;
- driving while under the stress of having to be in a particular place at a particular time;
- using mobile phones while on the move.

Because of ever-changing road and traffic conditions and the constant modifications to rules and regulations, driving procedures have to be continually adapted to suit the new conditions. Your new drivers have to be taught to a far higher standard than was previously the case, with hazard perception playing a major role in their development as professional drivers.

It is your responsibility as an instructor to ensure that your trainees at all levels are taught:

- to handle their vehicle sympathetically and economically;
- to drive with courtesy and consideration;
- to look and plan well ahead, anticipating what might happen;
- to make allowances and compensate for the mistakes of others;
- to understand what they are doing and why they need to do it.

To be able to do all this, you must be prepared to keep yourself up to date with changes that are relevant to the driver training industry and to the teaching of driving generally.

The Driving Standards Agency sends out a copy of its magazine *Despatch* to approved driving instructors and to LGV instructors who are on the voluntary register. The magazine contains most of the latest information and current changes to legislation and test procedures. You should make sure that you are on the mailing list.

Another way to ensure that you are up to date is by joining one of the trade associations that are available for LGV instructors, such as:

Institute of Large Goods Vehicle Driving Instructors (ILGVDI)
57 St Margaret's Road
Lowestoft
Suffolk NR32 4HR
Tel: 01502 515379

Additionally, if you or your firm is eligible, join one of the trade organizations for the transport industry:

Road Haulage Association
Roadway House
35 Monument Hill
Weybridge
Surrey KT13 8RN
Tel: 01932 841515

Freight Transport Association
Hermes House
St Johns Road
Tunbridge Wells
Kent TN4 9UZ
Tel: 01892 526171

More information about training facilities and qualifications can be obtained from:

Road Haulage and Distribution Training Council (RHDTC)
14 Warren Road
Warren Farm Office Village
Stratford Road
Milton Keynes MK12 5NW

THE DRIVING STANDARDS AGENCY REGISTER OF LGV INSTRUCTORS

The Driving Standards Agency (DSA) introduced the Voluntary Register of LGV instructors in 1997 with the original aim of raising the standards of training for drivers of large goods vehicles. The Register was developed in close cooperation with various organizations, including:

- the Freight Transport Association;
- the Road Haulage Association;
- the Road Haulage and Distribution Training Council;
- the National Training Federation;
- the Institute of LGV Driving Instructors;
- the Association of Vocational Driver Training Providers;
- RTITB Services Ltd.

DSA examiners who have previous experience on LGVs carry out the initial testing of candidates. The overall monitoring of the Register is the responsibility of the Registrar at the DSA.

Qualification

To qualify for the Register you must have held a full LGV licence for at least three years. This fits in with the driving regulations, which require an 'accompanying driver' of a learner to have held a full licence for that category of vehicle for that period of time. You can take the exam in any category of LGV, but will be registered according to the type of vehicle used.

Qualification for the Register is dependent on your passing a three-part entrance exam: a theory test, followed by a test of your own driving ability and then a further test of your instructional ability. The theory test must be taken and passed before you can apply for the practical part. The two practical tests may be taken on the same occasion, but if you were not successful in the driving part of the test you would not be allowed to proceed to the instructional ability test and your fee would be lost. In this situation you would not be allowed to use the time to take the driving part of the exam again.

To qualify for registration you also need to be able to comply with certain conduct considerations and criteria, including various driving and other offences relating to drink, drugs, theft or sexual offences.

You are allowed a maximum of three attempts for each test, and all three parts have to be passed within a one-year period. The current pass rate for each test is around 80 per cent. After you qualify, your registration lasts for four years, after which you have to re-sit the exams. If you are not successful within the 12-month period, you are not allowed to reapply for at least one year, starting from the date of the last failed exam. The fees are currently (May 2005) £58.75 for the theory part and £82.75 for each practical element.

It is anticipated that qualification for the Register will become compulsory within the next few years. It is probable at that stage that the DSA will introduce a system of regular check-testing as an alternative to compulsory requalifying every four years.

TRAINING AS AN INSTRUCTOR

To train to become an LGV instructor you can decide on the method of training that suits your particular circumstances. Most people find that they do not have too much difficulty with the first two parts, but that the instructional ability part is more difficult.

When you are considering how to deal with your training, bear in mind that not all instructors are necessarily good trainers – in the same way that a good driver would not automatically be an efficient instructor.

A list of DSA-accredited LGV instructor training centres is given below. These centres are spread around the United Kingdom from Inverness to Sussex. Remember, though, that the fact that an organization is not listed does not necessarily mean that it is not efficient; it may be that it simply has not registered with the DSA.

A1 Motoring School	Bristol
British Airways	London
Crystal Commercial Training Services Ltd.	Cumbria
Highlands and Islands Fire Brigade	Highlands
The Page Group	West Sussex
Stockport LGV Training Centre	Greater Manchester
Rollright School of Transport	Oxfordshire
Tyneside Training Service Ltd	Tyne and Wear
Wallace School of Transport	Middlesex

Full contact details of these organizations are shown on page 115. Details of preparing for the exams are given in the following chapter.

7

The LGV Instructor Exams

This chapter is divided into three main sections covering each of the three parts of the exams, followed by final sections dealing with registration and with training for the exams:

- Part 1 – Theory and Hazard Perception Test;
- Part 2 – the Driving Test;
- Part 3 – the Instructional Ability Test;
- Registration;
- Training for the exams.

Pre-entry qualifications

To qualify for the exams you must have held a full, unrestricted licence for at least three years for the type of vehicle you use for the exam. You must not have been disqualified from driving at any time in the previous four years.

Applying for the exams

To apply for the examinations, you need to send the form LGV1 to the Driving Standards Agency (LGV Register) at Stanley House, 56 Talbot Street, Nottingham NG1 5GU, together with the fee for the Theory Test. You will be asked to supply details about any motoring and some non-motoring offences, and these will be taken into account by the DSA staff when they consider your suitability as a qualified LGV instructor.

If your application is rejected for any reason, you can apply for a full refund of the fees. If you have any doubts or queries about your eligibility, you can contact the DSA on 0115 901 2625 for further information.

PART 1 – THE THEORY TEST

There are more than 150 test centres throughout England, Scotland and Wales. They are the same centres as those at which the ordinary L-driver and LGV theory tests are taken. You can decide which is the most convenient centre for you. When you attend for the test you will be asked to provide some form of visual identity such as a photo-card licence or your passport.

The Theory Test is in two parts: a multiple-choice, screen-based test followed by a hazard perception test.

Multiple-choice question paper

Each test paper is grouped into topic areas or 'bands':

- road procedure and driving technique;
- instructional techniques;
- mechanics; vehicle condition; drivers' hours and rest periods; loading, unloading and load security;
- driving test; environmental issues; accident handling.

You are allowed up to 90 minutes to complete the test, the overall pass mark being 85 per cent, with at least 80 per cent correct in each band.

All the questions in the exam are selected from publications that are readily available. Although the complete question bank is published by the DSA, there is no substitute for learning the subject properly and thoroughly, rather than simply memorizing the answers to individual questions.

You are strongly recommended by the DSA to use the following publications as source material in preparation for your exam. You will also find them useful as reference books for the practical parts of the exam and later in your regular day-to-day work with trainees.

- *The Highway Code*. £1.49. Published by The Stationery Office.
- *The Official DSA Guide to Driving Goods Vehicles*. £14.99. The Stationery Office.
- *The Official Theory Test for Drivers of Large Vehicles*. £14.99. The Stationery Office.
- *The Driving Instructor's Handbook* (13th edition), by John Miller and Margaret Stacey. £19.50. Kogan Page.
- *Practical Teaching Skills for Driving Instructors* (4th edition), by John Miller and Margaret Stacey. £17.99. Kogan Page.

- *Instructional Techniques and Practices for Driving Instructors* (2nd edition), by L Walklin. £17.99. Stanley Thornes.

The examination questions are based on your knowledge of:

- the principles of road safety generally, and their application in particular circumstances;
- techniques of driving an LGV correctly, courteously and safely, including control of the vehicle; road procedures; recognition of hazards and taking proper action;
- dealing properly with pedestrians and other road users; the use of safety equipment;
- the theory and practice of learning, teaching and assessment;
- the tuition required to instruct a trainee driving an LGV, including the techniques set out above; the correction of trainees' errors; the manner of the instructor;
- *The Highway Code*;
- *The Official DSA Guide to Driving Goods Vehicles;*
- interpretation of the reasons for failure given in the form DLV25.

Examples of teaching/learning questions

1. Initial assessment of trainees before commencing instruction would normally be carried out in order to determine:

(Mark one answer)

- the range of general intelligence;
- the length of instruction required to complete the course;
- the level at which instruction should begin.

2. From the trainee's point of view a major advantage of being given learning objectives is that they:

(Mark one answer)

- will have no need to ask questions of the instructor;
- can drive a vehicle with responsibility, concentration and patience;
- will know exactly what is expected of them and can evaluate their own progress.

3. In order to produce the maximum amount of learning when using a demonstration as a teaching method, it should be followed by:

(Mark one answer)

- consolidation of the skill by means of practice;
- detailed analysis of the manoeuvre carried out;
- discussion with the trainee of possible faults that may occur.

4. If a trainee under instruction fails to make satisfactory progress, the instructor should:

(Mark one answer)

- be patient and continue with the well-tried methods that are working with other trainees;
- vary the methods of instruction being used;
- allow the trainee to go to another instructor.

5. As an aid to progressive learning, a trainee's progress on a course should be measured:

(Mark one answer)

- as an ongoing assessment;
- at the end of the course;
- only when an improvement has been made.

6. The preparation of instruction in short, progressive steps is likely to lead to:

(Mark one answer)

- a sense of boredom by the trainee;
- sustained interest from the trainee;
- a lack of coordination in driving the vehicle.

7. When teaching a trainee to drive an LGV in a smooth and coordinated manner, the area of activity where learning will take place will be:

(Mark one answer)

- psychomotor;
- emotional;
- intellectual.

8. What is the purpose of an introduction to a lesson?

(Mark one answer)

- to promote interest and motivate the trainee;
- to clearly state the objectives of the lesson;
- to confirm the trainee's prior knowledge or skill.

9.   At the end of each lesson the most important task is to:

(Mark one answer)

- arrange the next lesson;
- go over all the mistakes that have been made;
- recapitulate on the main points covered in the lesson.

10.   When a trainee gives only a partially correct answer to a question, the instructor should:

(Mark one answer)

- stop the trainee responding to prevent him or her acquiring bad habits;
- give praise for the correct response made;
- ignore the correct part without comment; ensure that the response is corrected.

Answers to these teaching/learning questions are given on pages 100–01.

Hazard Perception Test

Following the multiple-choice section, you are allowed a short break before starting the 'HPT' part of the exam. This part consists of a series of short video clips of moving traffic situations. The clips each feature a specific developing hazard that you should recognize and respond to as soon as you can. The earlier you respond, the better the score you achieve.

There are normally 14 separate clips, with one clip showing two hazards. The maximum score possible is 75 – that is, 15 hazards with a possible maximum of five points each. The current pass mark for this part of the test is 57, compared with 50 out of 75 on the LGV 'L' test. Full details of the HPT procedure are given in Chapter 3, 'The LGV Practical Driving Test'.

The result of your test is given to you shortly after completing it. The current fee (May 2005) is £58.75 (£50 plus VAT).

PART 2 – THE PRACTICAL TEST OF DRIVING ABILITY

Practical tests are conducted at more than 30 test centres throughout the United Kingdom. These centres are listed on page 112. You can decide which one is most suitable for you. The current fee (May 2005) is £82.25 (£70 plus VAT).

The routes used for this part of the test are similar to those used for the practical LGV driving test, but are longer and more demanding. The test usually takes about 1½ hours. You should appreciate that a high standard of professional competence is required at an advanced level.

Syllabus

Manoeuvring exercises carried out on the area at the test centre:

- a braking exercise that is carried out at the start of the test;
- a reversing exercise – normally at the start of the test;
- an uncoupling and recoupling exercise – at the end of the test;
- a drive of about one hour or so, which includes a wide variety of road and traffic conditions on a route that takes in, where possible, dual carriageways, motorways, heavy traffic and one-way systems;
- a gear change exercise, normally carried out at a convenient location during the on-road phase;
- moving off safely and smoothly on the level, uphill, downhill and at an angle;
- the ability to:
  - meet and overtake other vehicles safely;
  - cross the path of other vehicles;
  - maintain a safe separation distance;
  - negotiate various types of roundabouts;
  - exercise correct lane discipline;
- display courtesy and consideration to other road users, especially:
  - pedestrians;
  - riders on horseback;
  - cyclists;
  - motorcyclists;
- apply correct procedures at:
  - pedestrian crossings;
  - level crossings (including tramways where appropriate);
  - road junctions;
- demonstrate:
  - effective use of mirrors;
  - correct use of all signals;
  - alertness and anticipation;
  - observation of speed limits;
  - vehicle sympathy.

During the test, the examiner will monitor and assess your ability in all the elements in the above syllabus. You need to show that you have a sound knowledge of the principles of driving a large vehicle; and you must have the skill to apply these principles in a wide variety of road and traffic conditions.

Test vehicles

The vehicle that you provide for the test can be any one of the following:

- category C1: medium-sized goods vehicle;
- category C1 + E: category C1 vehicle with trailer;
- category C: large goods vehicle over 7.5 tonnes;
- category C + E: LGV with trailer, or articulated.

If you take the test on a C + E vehicle, you will be registered for all the other categories, but if you take it on a smaller vehicle you will only be registered for that category.

Whatever type of vehicle you choose, it must meet the minimum test vehicle requirements (as shown in Chapter 3) and must be completely legal and roadworthy. In addition, the vehicle should:

- not have 'L' plates displayed;
- have manual transmission and right-hand steering;
- be unladen and be capable of normal performance;
- have a forward-facing seat for a passenger.

If the vehicle does not meet these standards, the examiner will not be able to conduct the test and your application fee will be lost.

If you want your trainer to be with you during the test, you should ask the examiner at the start.

Occasionally, a supervising examiner may wish to sit in on a test. If this happens, remember that the supervisor is monitoring the performance of the DSA examiner and not double-checking on your ability.

Marking system

The marking system used by the examiner is similar to that of the LGV 'L' test, with faults recorded as 'dangerous' ('D'), 'serious' ('X') or 'driving faults' ('/') on the marking sheet.

- *'Dangerous'* faults are those that cause *actual* danger to the examiner, the candidate, the general public or to property.

- *'Serious'* faults involve a potentially dangerous situation for examiner, the candidate, the general public or property.
- A *'driving'* fault is one that is less serious, but which you would not expect an experienced LGV driver to commit.

You will pass the test as long as you have no serious or dangerous faults, and not more than six driving faults.

During the test, try to drive as you normally would, making sure that you are driving safely and within legal limits. Examiners are not impressed if you try to put on an act for their benefit, as this inevitably affects your concentration and, ultimately, your driving performance.

PART 3 – THE TEST OF INSTRUCTIONAL ABILITY

The test is conducted at the same centres as the driving ability part of the exam and you may, if you wish, take the two parts consecutively. However, if you were not successful with the driving part you would not be allowed to take the instructional ability part. You would not be allowed to use the time for a retake of the driving part. In these circumstances, you would have wasted the fee for the instructional ability test.

As with the driving part of the test, you are allowed a maximum of three attempts and you must pass both parts within six months. If not, you will have to wait a further 12 months before starting again.

The current fee for this part of the test (May 2005) is £82.25 (£70 plus VAT).

The vehicle

You have to provide a suitable vehicle that conforms to the following requirements:

- It must be an LGV that is legal, roadworthy, properly taxed and insured.
- It can be a category C, C + E, C1 or C1 + E vehicle that meets the 'minimum test vehicle' requirements.
- It should have right-hand steering and manual transmission.
- There should be a readily adjustable driving seat and also a forward-facing seat for a passenger.
- You must provide and display 'L' plates to the front and rear of the vehicle.

- The vehicle must be capable of a normal performance for a vehicle of its type.

Insurance

Your insurance must cover, for the time the examiner is driving, any liability the examiner may have for all third party and damage risks, and for any liability to any passengers, including any official passenger. You should make sure that the insurance covers any DSA examiner and not name a particular one, as it cannot be guaranteed that a specific examiner will be conducting the test.

Role play

During the test, the examiner takes the role of a trainee driver and will assess your ability to give instruction to that 'trainee'. The role adopted will be that of a trainee at an early stage of learning to drive an LGV, a trainee upgrading to an articulated vehicle or vehicle with trailer, or a trainee who needs remedial instruction following a test failure.

The precise 'role play' situation will be described by the examiner by use of a detailed word picture of the 'trainee' and may be supplemented by production of a test failure sheet. The examiner then drives the vehicle and will simulate the type of faults regarded as appropriate to the described situation.

Test syllabus

To achieve the objectives of the test, the syllabus has been arranged into a series of nine preset test exercises. At the start of the test the examiner will explain in detail which of these is to be dealt with during your test:

- safety precautions; main controls of the vehicle; moving off and stopping;
- signs, signals and road markings; braking exercise;
- general driving; gear change exercise; reversing;
- use of mirrors; uncoupling and recoupling the trailer;
- judgement of speed; road positioning;
- turning into and emerging from junctions, roundabouts and crossroads;
- approaching and turning at crossroads, roundabouts and junctions;

- meeting approaching traffic; overtaking other traffic; anticipation of the actions of other road users;
- remedial instruction after failing an LGV test.

You should listen very carefully to the briefing by the examiner, making notes if appropriate. If you are not sure of what is required, you should say so. This will enable the examiner to repeat the explanation or to elaborate on what is required.

Once the exercise is under way, remember that the examiner is acting the part of your trainee and you should deal with the situation accordingly, treating the examiner exactly as you would a real trainee. Your instruction needs to be tailored to the standard of the trainee being portrayed and to the available time.

As in the 'real-life' situation, you will need to establish the 'trainee's' prior knowledge by asking a series of appropriate questions and responding effectively to the answers given. (More detail on question and answer techniques is given in *The Driving Instructor's Handbook* and *Practical Teaching Skills for Driving Instructors*.) Having established the trainee's prior knowledge, you should then be able to structure the lesson to the needs of the trainee even though you have not taught him or her previously.

During the test you are allowed to use any lesson plans or training aids that are appropriate to the situation, and you might want to refer to brief notes. However, you should not be reading direct from the notes; you should be using them only as reminders. Make sure that you have an outline lesson plan for each topic or the preset test exercises.

Always make sure that you give your 'trainee' plenty of opportunities to put into practice what you have explained. Any errors should be corrected either on the move (in the case of very minor errors) or by stopping for a discussion followed by a repeat, where required, of the particular topic.

Your question and answer technique should be used effectively during, and at the end of each part of, the lesson. The trainee must be encouraged to ask questions and should be given the opportunity to ask them at appropriate times during the lesson.

Assessment

During the test you will be assessed for your ability to identify and analyse any faults of the 'trainee' and to take the appropriate remedial action. The examiner will be checking on all the following elements of your instruction and lesson planning:

- *The level of instruction given:*
  - Have you established their level of ability accurately?
  - Are you pitching the instruction appropriately for the ability of the trainee?
- *Planning the lesson:*
  - Did you clearly define the main objectives at the start?
  - Have you done a recap on the trainee's previous learning?
  - Were you able to establish the appropriate starting point for today's lesson?
- *Control of the lesson:*
  - Were your directional instructions given clearly?
  - Is the trainee able to follow your instructions and explanations effectively?
  - Are you controlling the content of the lesson and the level of instruction given?
- *Communication:*
  - Are you using clear and easily understood wording?
  - Do you avoid using unnecessary jargon and technical expressions?
- *Questions and answers:*
  - Do you ask appropriate questions?
  - Do you encourage the trainee to ask questions?
  - Do you respond accurately and effectively to the trainee's questions?
- *Feedback and encouragement:*
  - Do you respond correctly to the trainee's performance and his or her questions?
  - Are you using feedback from the trainee to assess his or her progress?
  - Is your summary at the end of each section effective?
- *Use of vehicle controls:*
  - Are you avoiding unnecessary and indiscriminate use of the controls?
  - Do you keep the trainee informed on why you are using them?
  - Do you use a demonstration as an effective teaching tool?

The examiner will be assessing you on your personal instructional characteristics – in particular, whether you are:

- articulate;
- enthusiastic;

- encouraging;
- friendly;
- patient;
- confident

in your approach to dealing with the 'trainee' in all situations during the test.

The assessment by the examiner will cover:

- the method, clarity, adequacy and correctness of your instruction to the trainee;
- your observation and correction of the trainee's driving errors;
- your general manner and attitude when dealing with the trainee.

As in all teaching/learning situations, be patient and tactful, giving encouragement where deserved as well as criticism when appropriate. You need to show the examiner that you are flexible in your approach and that you are dealing with the examiner in his or her role as a trainee in the same way as in the normal training environment.

More detail about instructional techniques and training for the exams is covered later in this chapter. You will also find it helpful to refer to *The Driving Instructor's Handbook* and *Practical Teaching Skills for Driving Instructors* – both of which are recommended by the Driving Standards Agency for the approved driving instructor (ADI) and LGV exams.

REGISTRATION

After passing all three parts of the qualifying exam within the prescribed time limits, you can apply to become a 'DSA Registered LGV Instructor'.

The fee for a four-year period of registration is currently (May 2005) £58.75. You will receive a 'Certificate of Registration', which should be displayed on the windscreen of the training vehicle.

At the end of the four years you can apply for re-registration, but will have to take the practical exams again. If your registration lapses and you do not renew it within 12 months, you will need to retake all three parts of the exam again.

Full details of the Register and the examinations can be obtained from:
LGV Register Manager
Driving Standards Agency
Stanley House
56 Talbot Street
Nottingham NG1 5GU
Tel: 0115 901 2625
www.dsa.gov.uk

TRAINING FOR THE EXAMS

As we have seen, the LGV instructor's exam is in three parts:

- Theory Test and Hazard Perception;
- Driving Ability;
- Instructional Ability.

Part 1 – the Theory Test

To prepare yourself properly for the exams you will need the following items, all of which are recommended by the DSA:

- *The Official DSA Guide to Driving Goods Vehicles*, published by The Stationery Office;
- *The Highway Code*;
- *The Driving Instructor's Handbook*, by John Miller and Margaret Stacey, published by Kogan Page;
- *The Official Theory Test for Drivers of Large Vehicles*, published by The Stationery Office;
- *Know your Traffic Signs*, published by The Stationery Office;
- Driving Test Report and notes (DL25A/B/C) – Your Driving Test Report Explained, available from the DSA;
- *Practical Teaching Skills for Driving Instructors*, by John Miller and Margaret Stacey, published by Kogan Page;
- *Instructional Techniques and Practices for Driving Instructors*, by L Walklin, published by Stanley Thornes.

These books will be useful to you not only in preparation for the Theory Test, but also for the Part 3 exam and for future reference in your everyday work with your trainees.

The DSA question bank for the Theory Test consists of more than 800 questions and there are about a dozen different set question papers. The computer will randomly select one of these papers for your exam. Although there are different 'bands' of questions – as described earlier in this chapter – the questions do not necessarily appear on the question paper in those bands. Do not think, therefore, that you will simply be able to memorize all the questions and answers. Bear in mind that some questions are worded negatively or obliquely, while others require two or three correct answers from a set of five alternatives. Since the pass mark is 85 per cent, you need to have a thorough knowledge and understanding of the principles and topics covering a very wide range of subjects.

Don't forget that you will also need to be able to apply those principles effectively and professionally if you are going to be successful in the practical parts of the exam as well as in your role as an instructor.

Failing any part of the exams can be expensive. You must be prepared to exercise self-discipline in your preparation and to set aside sufficient time for your studies.

There are several ways in which you can study for this part of the exam – by working with an experienced instructor tutor, for example. Whatever you decide to do, make sure that you have all the appropriate recommended books and that you structure your learning to cover all the topics and subjects thoroughly.

For the Hazard Perception part of the exam, a very effective CD ROM is available from the DSA.

Apply for the test only when you are confident that you have a thorough knowledge and understanding of all the subjects. It is better to delay taking the test than to waste your time and the exam fee if you are not ready.

Part 2 – Driving Ability

To drive an LGV skilfully and safely you need a thorough working knowledge of *The Highway Code*, *The Official DSA Guide to Driving* and *The Official DSA Guide to Driving Goods Vehicles*. It is not sufficient to know what the rules are; you must be able to apply them sensibly and efficiently.

The Part 2 exam is not just a slightly more difficult L-driver test; it is of an advanced nature, and a very high standard of competence is required. You must show that you have a thorough understanding of the principles of good driving and road safety, and that you can apply these principles in practice in a wide variety of situations.

To prepare for the test you should obtain guidance from a recognized and experienced trainer. He or she will know what the examiner will be looking for and will be skilled at assessing your driving and advising on any adjustments needed to improve your efficiency.

A list of DSA-accredited training centres is given on page 115.

Even if you have been driving LGVs for some years, you may need to make some modifications to your methods or procedures. We all get into bad or sloppy habits with our driving – often without realizing it. A good trainer will be able to guide you and prepare you for the test procedure.

When you take the test, remember that you are not expected to be driving like a good learner; the examiner wants to see you drive with skill and confidence. Don't try to 'put on an act' for the benefit of the examiner. This can be counter-productive and can lead to errors such as not making proper progress. In any case, you would find it almost impossible to maintain an 'act' for the length of the test.

To prepare properly for the test, you should:

- take advice from your tutor on aspects of your driving that need improvement;
- continue referring to your study books;
- get as much practice as possible on different types of road and in differing conditions;
- try to maintain progress in relation to the road conditions, the law and the type of vehicle that you are driving;
- practise giving a running commentary as you are driving along.

As well as making progress, you should take into account vehicle sympathy and passenger comfort. To do this you should:

- use the controls smoothly and progressively;
- use the steering properly and smoothly;
- be selective with gear changes in conjunction with braking;
- plan well ahead to avoid excessive and harsh use of the brakes;
- maximize fuel economy by maintaining engine revs at an appropriate level.

To maintain progress and to demonstrate your personal skills, you should:

- look and plan well ahead;
- prepare for hazards well before you reach them;
- adjust your speed to avoid unnecessary stops;
- start looking early at road junctions so as to take advantage of safe opportunities to proceed;

- be aware of speed limits for your particular vehicle and make progress according to the conditions.

To protect yourself, your passengers and other road users you should:

- be aware of what is happening all around at all times by using all mirrors regularly;
- respond appropriately to what you see in your mirrors;
- anticipate and make allowances for other road users' mistakes;
- exercise self-discipline and avoid being provoked;
- show courtesy and consideration to all other road users – particularly the old and very young;
- be prepared to give way, even if you feel that you have a priority.

Show that you can handle your vehicle in all the manoeuvring exercises by:

- maintaining absolute control on gradients, using the handbrake where appropriate;
- making effective observations throughout;
- demonstrating accurate steering skills during the exercise;
- keeping full control of the vehicle in the braking exercise, avoiding skidding.

Try not to be influenced or put off by the examiner sitting next to you. If you are putting into practice the principles of safe driving that you have previously learnt, then your decisions should be influenced only by what is happening around you. The examiner is specially trained and will understand what you are basing your decisions on.

In preparation for Part 2, it is worthwhile having one or two 'mock tests' with your trainer/tutor, just in case there are any doubts or queries about the test procedures.

Part 3 – Instructional Ability

While you were studying for Part 1 – Theory Test you will have gained a lot of the background knowledge that you will need for training your learners. Similarly, while you were preparing for Part 2 – Driving Test your tutor will have demonstrated many of the teaching skills that you will be putting into practice as an instructor.

The Part 3 test combines these two elements of knowledge and skill in the teaching/learning situation. A good tutor will teach you how to:

- establish the trainee's prior knowledge by use of question and answer techniques;

- break down each subject into its key elements;
- adopt the basic teaching principle of explanation/demonstration/practice;
- use question and answer techniques to maximize the trainee's understanding and to obtain feedback;
- give full 'talk-through' instruction;
- give more responsibility to the trainee by gradually reducing the level of instruction at appropriate times;
- improve the trainee's awareness and understanding by encouraging commentaries;
- supervise and assess the more experienced trainee;
- use visual aids to assist the trainee's understanding;
- identify, analyse and correct driving errors;
- make appropriate use of verbal intervention to avoid potential problems.

Training and practice

Practice with genuine learners can be beneficial during your training, but it should not be attempted until you have had a reasonable amount of training with your tutor acting the part of a trainee. It is essential, therefore, that your training is properly structured and controlled.

To teach instructors, a good trainer needs the ability to realistically role-play drivers with differing needs and aptitudes so that you can learn in a safe and controlled environment. Your tutor should teach you how to:

- set the baseline for each lesson by establishing the trainee's prior knowledge;
- plan your instruction to suit the level of ability of each individual trainee;
- organize appropriate training routes that are suitable for the trainee's abilities and that are not excessively demanding;
- avoid inconveniencing other road users;
- maintain safety for your trainees, for yourself and for other road users.

What the examiner will be looking for

The Part 3 exam is not a test of your knowledge; that has been assessed in the Theory Test. Neither does it test driving ability; those skills are dealt with in Part 2. It is a test of your *practical ability to give driving instruction*. The examiner will be assessing whether you can transmit your knowledge and skills effectively, in a way that will result in the trainee's understanding and in good driving practices being learnt by the trainee.

At the start of the test the examiner will give a brief description of the 'trainee' to be portrayed and an outline of the current standard of his or her standard of driving. At this stage you need:

- to listen very carefully to the description (and make notes if necessary);
- to ask the examiner to repeat anything that you are not sure about;
- to structure your tuition at an appropriate level to suit the trainee described.

You should make every effort to add realism to the lesson. You can do this by:

- trying to treat the examiner like a real trainee;
- getting into your 'instructor' role by asking appropriate questions to establish the 'trainee's' prior knowledge of the subject;
- listening very carefully to the responses, as these will give you extra useful information about the trainee.

The examiner will select one subject out of the list of preset tests on page 106.

Your lesson should be tailored to suit the standard of the trainee and the time available. How much instruction you give while stationary will be governed by the trainee's prior knowledge. Remember, though, that this is not a test of your knowledge; it is more a test of your ability to *teach*. Try to focus on the key elements of the topic and avoid too much unnecessary talk.

You are allowed to use brief notes or subject headings, but be careful that you do not simply read from a text. Training aids should be used where appropriate, particularly if the subject matter is new to the trainee and where a visual aid would be helpful.

Keep your trainee involved by asking questions where appropriate. Make sure that your questions are pitched at the right level for the trainee's level of ability.

Do not assume that your 'trainee' will always follow your instructions, or carry out the correct procedures – even if he or she has covered the topic previously. Remember also that mistakes and errors may not necessarily be related to the subject being dealt with.

Fault identification and giving advice on faults is an important part of the exam. Even minor faults, particularly if they are repeated, are worth mentioning to the trainee and may be dealt with on the move. For more serious errors it will probably be necessary to stop in order to have a detailed discussion about them.

During the test you will be assessed on:

- core competencies:
  - identification of faults;
  - fault analysis;
  - remedial action;
- instructional techniques:
  - level of instruction;
  - planning;
  - control of the lesson;
  - communication;
  - question and answer techniques;
  - feedback and encouragement;
  - instructor's use of controls;
- instructor characteristics:
  - attitude;
  - approach to trainee.

Note that where the word 'trainee' appears, this refers to the examiner playing that role. When the 'trainee' has been explained to you, and the examiner has assumed the role, you must treat the examiner as a 'real-life' trainee throughout the rest of the exam.

Because of the time constraints, you may not be able to cover every detail of the topics to be taught. However, you must ensure that you include all the key elements, as well as the basic routines and procedures. This may be done either during your explanation at the start of the lesson, or during the time when the trainee is driving.

During the test you should demonstrate your ability:

- to explain clearly the key elements of the topic;
- to give the necessary help and talk-through instruction to develop and improve the trainee's skill;

- to use questions and answers to help the trainee to understand why certain rules and procedures must be followed.
- to develop the trainee's confidence by transferring responsibility as his or her skills improve;
- to identify, analyse and correct errors by explaining how to deal with situations more effectively;
- to give feedback and encouragement when any improvements take place.

More detail on fault identification and analysis is given in *The Driving Instructor's Handbook*.

ANSWERS TO THE TEACHING/LEARNING QUESTIONS ON PAGES 82–84

1. An initial assessment before you start on a programme of training will determine the level of skill and knowledge of the trainee. From this you will be able to establish a base from which to start the training.

2. The aims and objectives of course of lessons, or an individual lesson, need to be clearly stated. By knowing these aims and objectives, your trainee will be able to know exactly what is required of him or her and will be able to judge his or her own progress.

3. A demonstration should follow an explanation of the topic or manoeuvre. It is important to consolidate the demonstration by giving the trainee plenty of practice under controlled conditions.

4. If your trainee is not making satisfactory progress, you should consider changing your approach by applying a different teaching method. This might involve a different way of explaining the point; a demonstration; a question and answer session; or a full talk-through. You will often have to adapt your style of teaching to suit the ability and aptitude of individual trainees.

5. Continuous assessment of your trainee's performance is necessary to monitor his or her progress. The assessment should take into account the level of ability of the trainee. Make sure that you are judging the reasons why faults are occurring, rather than the result of the error.

6. Preparing your instruction in short, progressive steps is more likely to promote an ongoing and sustained level of interest on the part of your trainee. Setting intermediate targets will provide evidence of progress through each phase of learning.

7. Physical skills are involved in controlling a motor vehicle in a smooth and coordinated manner. These practical skills are referred to as the psychomotor domain. The 'emotional' and 'intellectual' domains are more concerned with knowledge-related skills and attitudes.

8. Part of your introduction should include a statement of the aims and objectives of the lesson so that the trainee knows and understands the purpose of the lesson and what is expected of him or her.

9. An important part of your summary at the end of the lesson will be to recap on the main points that were covered in the lesson. This would include some of the good points as well as some of the areas where improvement is needed.

10. If a trainee gives only a partially correct answer you should at least give him or her some praise for the correct part of the response. After more questions, or further explanation, the trainee may then be able to understand and answer the original question more completely.

All these subjects and other teaching/learning topics are covered in more detail in both *The Driving Instructor's Handbook* and *Instructional Techniques and Practice*. The complete question bank for the LGV instructor exam is available from the DSA.

8

LGV Driver Training

Most training for new LGV drivers is carried out by commercial driving schools or by 'in-house' trainers; very few trainees attempt to learn privately. LGV instructors are usually qualified by way of the DSA voluntary register, by the Road Transport Industry Training Board or by the various qualifications from the armed forces. All of these qualifications are, at the present time, voluntary. The only legal requirement is that the supervisor of a learner driver should have held a full, unrestricted licence for the particular type of vehicle for at least three years. However, the DSA voluntary register is likely to become compulsory within the next few years and would then be organized and managed along similar lines to the existing Approved Driving Instructor qualification for car driving instructors. For details of the LGV Register exams, see Chapter 7.

Training as an LGV driver normally consists of a concentrated period of instruction both in class and on the road for about 5 to 10 days depending on the type and category of vehicle being used. Training should also include periods of instruction at an 'off-road' area to cover the basics of vehicle control, steering, braking and manoeuvring.

An effective instructor can cover the complete syllabus in a structured way, minimizing the total amount of training needed. There is, however, a real need to have as much 'at the wheel' time as possible. As it is not usually possible to get private practice on a large vehicle, make sure that your training involves plenty of 'on the road' mileage so that you have experience of driving over a wide variety of different roads and in various traffic conditions.

DRIVER TRAINING SYLLABUS

To give you the most effective training, your instructor should be able:

- to start your training with what you already know (or can do) and build on this knowledge and skill;
- to structure your learning in short, progressive steps;
- to be consistent with instructions and terminology, making sure that you have fully understood (details of this are given on page 104);
- to keep any explanations brief and straightforward;
- to emphasize the important key points for each topic;
- to give you positive instructions and advice;
- to allow you plenty of practice – you will learn much more quickly by doing rather than just listening;
- to give continuous feedback on your progress;
- to correct your errors before they become habits;
- to set intermediate, achievable targets;
- to give you a varied programme of training;
- to select training routes for you that are appropriate to your level of ability and training needs.

Your training should cover the complete driving syllabus, including:

- vehicle controls: accelerator, clutch, footbrake, handbrake, steering;
- precautions before starting;
- moving off safely and under control;
- use of mirrors: well before signalling, changing speed or direction;
- use of signals: when necessary, correctly; properly timed;
- reversing exercise: under control; with proper observations;
- controlled stop: promptly and under control;
- gear change exercise;
- uphill and downhill starts;
- clearance to obstructions;
- response to signs and signals: traffic signs, road markings, traffic lights, traffic controllers, other road users;
- use of speed;
- maintaining a safe following distance;
- maintaining progress: use of appropriate speed, without undue hesitation;
- junctions: speed on approach, observations, right and left turns, avoidance of cutting corners unnecessarily;
- judgement: overtaking, meeting, crossing the path of other vehicles;
- road positioning: in normal driving, lane discipline;

- pedestrian crossings;
- safe position for normal stops;
- awareness and planning;
- ancillary controls;
- uncoupling and recoupling.

INSTRUCTIONS

During your training your instructor will use a consistent method for giving directional instructions. A few examples of these are:

- *'I want you to follow the road ahead unless otherwise directed by road signs or markings – when I want you to turn, I will ask you in good time.'*
- *'Would you take the next road on the left; it's just past the parked vehicles.'*
- *'I'd like you to take the second road on the right – this one being the first.'*
- *'At the roundabout, would you take the road leading off to the right; that is, the third exit.'*
- *'I want you to pull in and park on the left when convenient.'*
- *'I'd like you to take the road ahead at the roundabout – it's signed "Brighton".'*

By having the instructions given to you in this way, you will be more prepared for the type of terminology used by the examiner on your practical test.

LORRY-MOUNTED CRANES

At the present time there is no legal requirement for drivers to have a special licence or certificate for using lorry-mounted equipment, including cranes. There are, however, various voluntary schemes run by commercial organizations and by Centrex (previously known as the Road Transport Industry Training Board). Under health and safety requirements, anyone involved in an incident with this type of equipment would need to show that they had received proper training. For this reason, most employers would expect the driver to have the appropriate certificate.

DANGEROUS GOODS

Drivers of vehicles that carry any dangerous goods are required to hold a Vocational Training Certificate (VTC) issued by DVLA. This requirement covers vehicles that carry dangerous goods either in packages or in tankers carrying liquids. To obtain a certificate you need to attend an approved course and pass an exam set by the City and Guilds organization. A VTC is valid for five years and must be renewed by taking a refresher course and exam.

The regulations apply generally to:

- tankers with a capacity of more than 1,000 litres;
- tank containers with a capacity in excess of 300 litres;
- vehicles of more than 3.5 tonnes maximum authorized mass carrying specified dangerous goods in packages.

COMPULSORY TRAINING

Looking to the future, there may well be requirements for the training and retraining of all large vehicle drivers. As a result of an EU directive, the government is committed to a programme of improving the skills and professional expertise of drivers in the industry.

The draft EU directive contains proposals for compulsory initial training and periodic refresher training for professional LGV drivers. On successful completion of the training and test, the driver would be awarded a 'Certificate of Professional Competence' (CPC).

The proposals include:

- a recognized training syllabus;
- a minimum number of hours of intensive training – either 140 hours or 280 hours, depending on the type of vehicle being used;
- periodic (refresher) training of 35 hours every five years;
- training to be carried out only by recognized and approved training centres.

Although the law is due to be introduced in 2006, it is likely that it will not actually be implemented for LGV drivers in the United Kingdom until 2009.

One of the advantages of the CPC as described in the EU regulations is that it allows for larger vehicles to be driven at age 18 under certain circumstances.

Under the rules, the need for compulsory training would not apply to the drivers of vehicles that have a maximum authorized speed not exceeding 45 kph. Additionally, any driver who had previously held a full, unrestricted licence would be exempt from the training requirements.

INSTRUCTOR TRAINING

As an experienced LGV driver, you may be considering moving on to training other drivers. The job of the instructor is a rewarding one, but one that requires much more than the ability to drive a large vehicle safely and competently. To become a professional and effective trainer you also need:

- to have a thorough understanding of the rules and principles involved in safe driving;
- to be able to put these principles into practice by driving thoughtfully and efficiently;
- to have a clear understanding of how people learn and of different teaching methods;
- to be able to patiently teach drivers how to apply the principles of safe driving;
- to instil safe attitudes in your trainees.

The qualifying exams for the Register of LGV Instructors are explained in Chapter 7 and the exam syllabus is given on page 88.

On the instructor's exams the syllabus is set out in the form of 'preset tests' (PSTs). For each one you need to have a clear lesson plan that should include an introduction, your explanation and a summary. You also need to have a brief checklist of the key points to include for each topic in the PSTs.

PST 1   *Safety precautions/controls*
Accelerator, clutch, footbrake, handbrake, steering, gears

Move off and stop
On level, uphill, downhill, angled
Mirrors, observations, control

PST 2   *Signs, signals and road markings*
Road signs, markings, traffic lights, controllers, other road users
Recognition, appropriate action

Braking exercise
Safely, full control, quickly, distance

PST 3   *General driving*
Faults – identification, analysis, remedial

Gear change exercise
Control, observations, signals

PST 4   *Use of mirrors*
Moving off, signalling, changing direction/lanes,
turning, overtaking, increasing speed, slowing down,
leaving vehicle, parked vehicles

Uncouple/recouple
Safe place, brakes, landing gear, taps, air lines,
coupling mechanism, number plates

PST 5   *Judgement of speed*
Road, traffic, weather, vehicle speed limits, hazards

Road positioning
Keep left, parked vehicles, weaving, lanes, one-way,
road markings

PST 6   *Junctions (turning in and emerging)*
Position, speed, observations, priorities

Roundabouts and crossroads
Mirrors/signal/manoeuvre (MSM),
position/speed/look (PSL), gears, observations,
lanes, position through, exit

PST 7   *Approaching or turning at crossroads, roundabouts or
junctions*
MSM, PSL, gears, observations

PST 8   *Meet approaching traffic*
Mirrors, signal, speed, gears, position, observation

Overtaking/anticipating the actions of other road users
View, speed, limits, bends, junctions, gradients
Mirrors, signals

PST 9   *Remedial lesson after test failure*
DLV25, assess, faults

Remember that effective teaching involves much more than simply giving explanations. The whole process of teaching/learning should include:

- methods of learning;
- structured training;
- terminology and route selection;
- assessing progress;
- fault identification, analysis and remedial instruction;
- question and answer techniques;
- communication skill.

Full details of these subjects and the principles of the teaching/learning process are given in *The Driving Instructor's Handbook* and in *Practical Teaching Skills for Driving Instructors*, both of which are published by Kogan Page and which are recommended by the Driving Standards Agency for the LGV instructor exams.

To train as an LGV instructor you will need to find an effective training course that will suit you. A list of DSA-accredited centres is given on page 115.

Useful Addresses

Theory tests

Driving Theory Test
PO Box 148
Salford M5 3SY
Tel: 0870 01 01 372

Practical tests

Driving Standards Agency
PO Box 280
Newcastle upon Tyne NE99 1FP
Tel: 0870 01 01 372
Welsh-speakers, tel: 0870 01 00 372
Fax: 0870 01 02 372

LGV Instructors Register

Driving Standards Agency
Stanley House
56 Talbot Street
Nottingham NG1 5GU
Tel: 0115 901 2625

DSA Customer Services

DSA
Stanley House
56 Talbot Street
Nottingham NG1 5GU
Tel: 0115 901 2500
Fax: 0115 901 2940

Driving licences

Driver and Vehicle Licensing Authority
Swansea SA6 7JL
Tel: 0870 240 0009

Books and training supplies

The Stationery Office
PO Box 276
London SW8 5DT
Enquiries, tel: 0171 873 0011
Orders, tel: 0171 873 9090
Fax: 0171 873 8200

Desk Top Driving Ltd
Unit 6
Gaugemaster Way
Ford
Arundel
West Sussex BN18 1HD
Tel: 01903 882299
Fax: 01903 885599

RCM Marketing Ltd
20 Newtown Business Park
Albion Close
Poole
Dorset BH12 3LL
Tel: 01202 737999
Fax: 01202 737909

Instructor and training organizations

Driving Instructors Association (DIA)
Safety House
Beddington Farm Road
Croydon
Surrey CR1 4XZ
Tel: 020 8665 5151
Fax: 020 8665 5565
www.driving.org

Motor Schools Association GB Ltd
101 Wellington Road North
Stockport
Cheshire SK4 2LP
Tel: 0161 429 9669
Fax: 0161 429 9779
www.msagb.co.uk

Road Haulage and Distribution Training Council (RHTDC)
14 Warren Yard
Warren Farm Office Village
Stratford Road
Milton Keynes MK12 5NW
Tel: 01908 313360

National Training Federation (NTF)
c/o West Herts Training Ltd
Ver House
Frogmore
St Albans
Hertfordshire AL2 2WH
Tel: 01727 873878

Institute of LGV Driving Instructors (ILGVDI)
57 St Margaret's Road
Lowestoft
Suffolk NR32 4HR
Tel: 01502 515379

Motoring organizations

The Automobile Association
Fanum House
Basingstoke
Hants RG21 2EA
Tel: 0990 448866

The Royal Automobile Club
RAC House
1 Forest Road
Feltham
Middlesex TW13 7RR
Tel: 020 8917 2500

Transport and haulage organizations

Freight Transport Association
Hermes House
St John's Road
Tunbridge Wells
Kent TN4 9UZ
Tel: 01892 526171

Road Haulage Association
Roadway House
35 Monument Hill
Weybridge
Surrey KT13 8RN
Tel: 01932 841515

Driving Standards Agency Test Centres

Theory Test centres

England

Aldershot, Barnstaple, Barrow, Basildon, Basingstoke, Bath, Berwick-upon-Tweed, Birkenhead, Birmingham, Blackpool, Bolton, Boston, Bournemouth, Bradford, Brighton, Bristol, Bury St Edmunds, Cambridge, Canterbury, Carlisle, Chelmsford, Cheltenham, Chester, Chesterfield, Colchester, Coventry, Crawley, Derby, Doncaster, Dudley, Durham, Eastbourne, Exeter, Fareham, Gillingham, Gloucester, Grantham, Grimsby, Guildford, Harlow, Harrogate, Hastings, Hereford, Huddersfield, Hull, Ipswich, Isle of Wight, Isles of Scilly, King's Lynn, Leeds, Leicester, Lincoln, Liverpool, London (Croydon, Ilford, Kingston, Palmers Green, Southwark, Staines, Uxbridge), Lowestoft, Luton, Manchester, Mansfield, Middlesbrough, Milton Keynes, Morpeth, Newcastle, Northampton, Norwich, Nottingham, Oldham, Oxford, Penzance, Peterborough, Plymouth, Portsmouth, Preston, Reading, Redditch, Runcorn, St Helens, Salford, Salisbury, Scarborough, Scunthorpe, Sheffield, Shrewsbury, Sidcup, Slough, Solihull, Southampton, Southend-on-Sea, Southport, Stevenage, Stockport, Stoke-on-Trent, Stratford-upon-Avon, Sunderland, Sutton Coldfield, Swindon, Taunton, Torquay, Truro, Watford, Weymouth, Wigan, Wolverhampton, Worcester, Workington, Worthing, Yeovil, York

Scotland

Aberdeen, Ayr, Dumfries, Dundee, Dunfermline, Edinburgh, Elgin, Fort William, Gairloch, Galashiels, Glasgow Central, Glasgow Northwest, Greenock, Helmsdale, Huntly, Inverness, Isle of Arran,

Isle of Barra, Isle of Benbecula, Isle of Islay (Bowmore), Isle of Mull (Salen), Isle of Tiree, Kirkwall, Kyle of Lochalsh, Lerwick, Motherwell, Oban, Pitlochry, Portree, Stirling, Stornoway, Stranraer, Tarbert (Aberdeenshire), Tongue, Ullapool, Wick

Wales

Aberystwyth, Bangor, Builth Wells, Cardiff, Haverfordwest, Merthyr Tydfil, Newport, Rhyl, Swansea

Northern Ireland

Ballymena, Belfast, Londonderry, Newry, Omagh, Portadown

LGV Practical Test centres

Northern

Berwick-upon-Tweed, Beverley, Bredbury (Manchester), Carlisle, Darlington, Gosforth (Newcastle), Grimsby, Kirkham (Preston), Patrick Green (Leeds), Sheffield, Simonswood, Steeton (Keighley), Walton (York)

Wales and Western

Bristol, Caernarfon, Camborne, Chiseldon (Swindon), Exeter, Gloucester, Haverfordwest (Withybush), Llantrisant, Neath, Plymouth, Pontypool, Poole, Reading, Rookley (Isle of Wight), Southampton, Taunton, Wrexham

Midlands and Eastern

Alvaston (Derby), Chelmsford, Culham, Featherstone (Wolverhampton), Garretts Green (Birmingham), Harlescott (Shrewsbury), Ipswich, Leicester, Leighton Buzzard, Norwich, Peterborough, Swynnerton (Stoke-on-Trent), Watnall (Nottingham), Weedon (Northampton)

London and South-East

Canterbury, Croydon, Enfield, Gillingham, Guildford, Hastings, Lancing, Purfleet, Yeading

Scotland

Aberdeen, Benbecula, Bishopbriggs (Glasgow), Dumfries, Elgin, Galashiels, Inverness, Kilmarnock, Kirkwall, Lerwick, Livingstone (Edinburgh), Machrihanish (Kintyre), Perth, Port Ellen, Portree, Stornoway, Wick

LGV Instructors Register Practical Test Centres

London and South-East

Enfield, Croydon, Guildford, Gillingham, Hastings (Ore), Lancing, Purfleet, Reading, Southampton, Yeading

Midlands and Eastern

Featherstone, Garretts Green, Leicester, Leighton Buzzard, Norwich, Peterborough, Shrewsbury, Watnall, Weedon

Northern

Bredbury, Carlisle, Darlington, Grimsby, Kirkham, Newcastle, Sheffield, Simonswood

Wales and Western

Bristol, Llantrisant, Neath, Plymouth, Poole, Wrexham

Scotland

Aberdeen, Bishopbriggs, Inverness, Kilmarnock, Livingston, Perth

DSA-Accredited LGV Instructor Training Centres

British Airways
Airport Operation Centre
Cranebank Training Centre
Block D (S588)
PO Box 10
Hounslow
Middlesex TW6 2JA
Tel: 020 85133 866
Contact: Christopher Willis

Crystal Commercial Training
c/o Stalkers Transport
Townfoot Industrial Estate
Brampton
Carlisle CA8 1SW
Tel: 016977 42071
Fax: 01228 562413
Contact: Kevin Watson

Driver Training Centre
2 Alexander Parade
Park Avenue
Hastings
East Sussex TN23 2PQ
Tel: 01424 432200
Contact: Gary Curtis

Highland and Islands Fire
Brigade
16 Harbour Road
Longman West
Inverness IV1 1TB
Tel: 01463 227000
Contact: William Stewart

The Page Group
Robert House
Rudford Industrial Estate
Ford
Arundel
West Sussex BN18 0BD
Tel: 01903 736300
Fax: 01903 736335
Contact: Alan Summers
e-mail: alansummers@
pagegroup.co.uk

Roadtrain
Truckworld
Oliver Road
West Thurrock
Essex RM20 3ED
Tel: 01708 890953
Contact: Nick Smith
e-mail:
roadtrain@btconnect.com

Rollright School of Transport
Enstone Airfield Complex
Enstone
Oxon OX7 4NP
Tel: 01608 677618
Contact: Mike Middleton

Tyneside Training Services
Beaminster Way East
Airport Industrial Estate
Kingston Park
Newcastle upon Tyne NE3 2ER
Tel: 0192 862919
Contact: Alan MacNaught

Wallace School of Transport
Unit 5, Pop In Building
South Way
Wembley HA9 0HF
Tel: 0845 602 9498
Contact: Neil Wallace

Index

D0680470

GLOBAL
PARADOX

Books by the Author

Global Paradox
Megatrends

With Patricia Aburdene
Reinventing the Corporation
Megatrends 2000
Megatrends for Women

With Shosaburo Kimura
Japan's Identity Crisis

GLOBAL PARADOX

*The Bigger the World
Economy, the More Powerful
Its Smallest Players*

John Naisbitt

NICHOLAS BREALEY
PUBLISHING

LONDON

First published in Great Britain by
Nicholas Brealey Publishing Limited in 1994
156 Cloudesley Road,
London N1 OEA

Reprinted 1994

© 1994 by John Naisbitt

ISBN 1 85788 051 X

British Library Cataloguing-in-Publication Data
A catalogue record for this book is available from the British Library

All rights reserved. No part of this publication may be reproduced, stored in a
retrieval system, or transmitted, in any form or by any means, electronic,
mechanical, photocopying, recording and/or otherwise without the prior written
permission of the publishers. This book may not be lent, resold, hired out or
otherwise disposed of by way of trade in any form, binding or cover other than that in
which it is published, without the prior consent of the publishers.

Printed in Finland by Werner Söderstöm Oy

Contents

GLOBAL
PARADOX

1

Global Paradox

On the 14th of March, 1993, the people of Andorra, perched high in the Pyrenees between France and Spain and numbering 47,000, overwhelmingly passed a referendum granting themselves sovereignty. Now the new country of Andorra—about one-tenth the size of Delaware—can have its own international dialing code, Olympic team, stamps, currency, and a seat at the U.N. (which it got in July 1993, to become the 184th member).

But didn't this assertion of independence occur at a time when European countries were marching toward greater union? When Europe was on the verge of adopting a single new currency? When the Maastricht Treaty called for the establishment of a common currency for the 12 countries that make up the European Community?

Actually, Andorra is much more in the direction the world is going than European union.

Freddie Heineken, the brewery baron in Holland, has caused something of a stir by proposing an alliance of Europe with 75 countries, each with a population of five to 10 million—a very manageable size for governance—and each with reference to its ethnic and linguistic history.

Iceland, Norway, Sweden, Finland, and Denmark would stay the same. Scotland and Wales would become independent countries. In Spain, Catalonia and the Basque region would become independent. Paris and the area around it would become Ile-de-France, with a population of about 10 million. Switzerland and Italy would be divided into nine different countries. And so on.

Some would call it Utopian. And it is hard to imagine how the details of such an arrangement could be worked out. But the fact of the matter is that preposterous as the idea seems, it is much more in tune with the trends shaping today's world than is European union.

That is why I feel confident in asserting that the Maastricht Treaty, which seeks to go beyond trade and bind countries politically—moving toward a common foreign policy and defense, as well as a common currency—is doomed to failure. There are many who disagree with me—vociferously. But that is because they do not understand that although people want to come together to *trade* much more freely, they want to be *independent* politically and culturally. There will be no real union of Europe. It is in name only. The very watered-down version that was ratified in the fall of 1993 will never be implemented. The more people are bound together economically, the more they want to otherwise be free to assert their own distinctiveness. The EC will not adopt a common currency—not in this century and beyond—because our money, both paper and coin, which we imprint with national symbols and national heroes, is one of the things that distinguishes us from others. Further, with the multiplication of countries, the world is going to have many more currencies, not fewer.

Besides, a common currency already exists: electronics. There is no need for another one. We know instantly how many Italian lire make up an English pound, how many French francs constitute a German Mark.

Peter T. White, writing in the January 1993 *National Geographic* magazine, gives us a personal illustration of electronic currency.

"I'm in Paris, it's late evening, and I need money, quickly. The bank I go to is closed, of course, but outside sits an ATM, an automated teller machine—and look what can be made to happen, thanks to computers and high-speed telecommunications.

"I insert my ATM card from my bank in Washington, D.C., and punch in my identification number and the amount of 1,500 francs, roughly equivalent to $300. The French bank's computers detect that it's not their card, so my request goes to the CIRRUS system's inter-European switching center in Belgium, which detects that it's not a European card. The electronic message is then transmitted to the global switching center in Detroit, which recognizes that it's from my bank in Washington. The request goes there, and my bank verifies that there's more than $300 in my account and deducts $300 plus a fee of $1.50. Then it's back to Detroit, to Belgium, and to the Paris bank and its ATM—and out comes $300 in French francs. Total elapsed time: 16 seconds."

Maastricht will not become a reality because it is so out of tune with the times. There will be no union of Europe. Free trade, yes. Union, no.

The world's trends point overwhelmingly toward *political* independence and self-rule on the one hand, and the formation of *economic* alliances on the other.

Freddie Heineken's interest in the shape of Europe led him early on to meet with the British historian Professor Cyril Northcote Parkinson (of Parkinson's Law fame). Parkinson talked about his ideas regarding European union. Parkinson said he doubted one united Europe would work, partly because of the many differences in size, population, and economic muscle. For balance, he thought it would be a good idea to break up the countries into many smaller states of more equal size and importance.

Heineken went on to identify the 75 parts of Europe that he thought could sensibly become the 75 countries of Europe. Heineken points out that the present nations of Europe are artificial and in many cases of quite recent invention: "The present setup of nations," he says, "is in many ways just as arbitrary as my ideas may seem."

All over the world people are agreeing to trade more freely with each other. And all over the world people are asserting their independence, their sovereignty, their distinctiveness.

THE GLOBAL PARADOX

There are many paradoxes in this dramatically changing world. I have identified the one I think embraces much of today's change and is the main focus of this book:

The bigger the world economy, the more powerful its smallest players.

I am dealing here with paradox as it is generally understood: a statement or formulation that seems contradictory or absurd but is actually valid or true. A famous paradox in architecture that has served the profession well is "Less is more," meaning that the less you clutter a building with embellishments, the more elegant it can be, the greater a work of architecture it can be.

In business we have to deal with paradoxes all the time: the tensions between the need to both decentralize and centralize; the desirability of being simultaneously a leader and a follower, an individual and a team player.

Some get carried away with the lore of paradox. That melancholy Dane, Søren Kierkegaard, once said that "the paradox is the source of the thinker's passion, and the thinker without a paradox is like a lover without feeling; a paltry mediocrity."

At least one purpose of a paradox is to provoke fresh thinking. That is certainly part of my purpose. But more than that, a paradox can be a powerful tool for understanding. In this book I mean to show that the paradox I have formulated is key to understanding the new era we are entering. "The bigger the world economy, the more powerful its smallest players" is, like all paradoxes, an *apparent* contradiction, but when understood it becomes a sturdy framework for understanding the world.

Timothy Ferris in his book *Coming of Age in the Milky Way* says, "The late twentieth century may be remembered in the history of science as the time when particle physics, the study of the smallest structures in nature, joined forces with cosmology, the study of the universe as a whole."

A similar phenomenon occurs in the worlds of politics and economics: the Global Paradox.

The study of the smallest economic player, the entrepreneur, will merge with the study of how the big bang global economy works.

The entrepreneur is also the most important player in the building of the global economy. So much so that big companies are decentralizing and reconstituting themselves as networks of entrepreneurs.

Networks of Entrepreneurs

The principle of the global paradox—the bigger the world economy, the more powerful its smallest players—applies especially to business. Huge companies like IBM, Philips, and GM must break up to become confederations of small, autonomous, entrepreneurial companies if they are to survive.

Big companies and "economies of scale" succeeded in the comparatively slow-moving world of the four decades to the mid-1980s. But now, only small and medium-sized companies—or big companies that have restyled themselves as networks of entrepreneurs—will survive to be viable when we turn the corner of the next century. Already 50 percent of U.S. exports are created by companies with 19 or fewer employees; the same is true of Germany.

Only 7 percent of U.S. exports are created by companies with 500 or more employees. The Fortune 500 now account for only 10 percent of the American economy, down from 20 percent in 1970. Ninety percent of the U.S. economy is elsewhere: small and medium-sized companies. Entrepreneurs—individuals—are creating the huge global economy.

To survive, big companies today—ABB, AT&T, GE, Grand Metropolitan, Coca-Cola, Benetton, Johnson & Johnson, British Petroleum, Honda, Alcoa, Xerox—are deconstructing themselves and creating new structures, many as networks of autonomous units. Deconstruction is now in fashion, because it is the best way to search for survival.

Philip M. Burgess, president of the Center for a New West, calls what is going on in American corporations today the "ODD effect'': outsourcing, delayering, and deconstruction. The result is radical downsizing.

Downsizing, reengineering, creating networking organizations, or the latest, the virtual corporation, whatever it is called, it comes down to the same thing. Companies have to dismantle bureaucracies to survive. Economies of scale are giving way to economies of scope, finding the right size for synergy, market flexibility, and above all, speed.

The most deconstructed of the large global companies is ABB Asea Brown Boveri, the world's largest power-engineering group. Annual revenues exceed $30 billion from 1,200 companies. Each company averages only 200 people. CEO Percy Barnevik says, ''We grow all the time, but we also shrink all the time.'' In the process of deconstructing, the headquarters staff in Zurich was reduced from 4,000 to fewer than 200. No less than 90 percent of the sales of this Swiss-Swedish company are from outside the host countries.

''We are not a global business,'' Barnevik says. ''We are a collection of local businesses with intense global coordination.''

That's it. Perfect.

Jack Welch of GE, whose corporate message for the 1990s is ''Think small,'' says, ''What we are trying relentlessly to do is to get that small-company soul—and small-company speed—inside our big company body.'' Welch is also making his company smaller—to make it more efficient. Employment has been reduced by 100,000 in 11 years to 268,000 in 1992. In those 11 years annual sales have gone from $27 billion to $62 billion in 1992, and net income from $1.5 billion to $4.7 billion.

Similarly, Paul Allaire, the chairman of Xerox, says of his radical redesign of what he calls his company's ''organizational architecture,'' ''We are trying to get the small-company benefits of quickness in time to market, decision-making and the elimination of bureaucratic activities.''

John Bryan, the CEO at Sara Lee, says that ''entrepreneurial management'' is the ''defining attribute'' of Sara Lee: many entrepreneurs acting swiftly throughout the company.

Subsidiarity is a word not much used by Americans but one that is heard throughout Europe (particularly recently, as Europe talks about union). It means that power should belong to the lowest possible point in the organization. Used in a political and economic context, it should mean the EC should not do what the individual nation can do better (though that won't stop the Brussels bureaucrats from trying). In companies it means decisions are made at the lowest appropriate level, and that is what Robert Galvin means when he tells Motorola's sales force that "they have all the authority of the chairman when they are with customers."

The result in all these areas is smaller and stronger units.

A rather bizarre example is Aeroflot. Once the world's largest airline, and surely the world's worst, it is now 80 different airlines (Azerbaijan Airlines out of Baku, Byelorussia Airlines out of Minsk, Uzbeki Airlines out of Tashkent), and before long will be more than 200 carriers in Russia alone. Who would doubt that in time, flying one of these smaller carriers will be a better experience than flying the old bureaucratic Aeroflot? Aeroflot itself, once the mother of all airlines and now what is left of it, known as Aeroflot Russian International Airlines, has been reduced to relatively few international routes.

Louis Gerstner, the new CEO of IBM, is also thinking deconstruction. "The Challenge for us at IBM is how to incorporate small-company attributes—nimbleness, speed and customer responsiveness—with the advantages of size, like breadth of investment in research and development." But he would probably be the first to admit that the challenge is whether he can act on it.

Part of that answer may come from IBM UK. In mid-1993 IBM's London headquarters announced that the UK sales operation was being divided into 30 separate businesses, each of which on its own authority could fix prices and costs and be totally responsible to its customers. Some will have only 50 people. The center will exercise no control unless the business starts to fall apart. The IBM announcement said, "The creation of a business federation will give more ownership and accountability to business managers, enabling the company to return to profit more quickly." Two years ago there were 2,500 employed at the staff headquarters. That number will be reduced to 100 or fewer people who will manage the new central holding company. In an echo of Timothy Ferris's description of the uniting of particle physics and cosmology in *Coming of Age in the Milky Way*, IBM's code name for the plan is "Galaxy." Andy Williams, assistant to IBM UK chief executive Nick Temple, who created the plan, said their idea was to "reach for the stars."

As the world integrates economically, the component parts are becoming more numerous and smaller and more important. At once, the global economy is growing while the size of the parts are shrinking.

AT&T, once the very definition of a monopolistic oligarchy, is being reconfigured under the leadership of its chairman, Robert Allen. The company has been reorganized into 20 separate product areas. For the first time, each product area is responsible for its own pricing, marketing, product development, and profits. AT&T is shedding its monolithic structure and reorganizing itself into a network of independent organizations.

"As new computer systems decentralize control and empower people all along the information chain, they dissolve conventions of ownership, design, manufacturing, executive style, and national identity," writes George Gilder, in the *Harvard Business Review*. To illustrate his point, Gilder describes the Brooktree company, inventor of RAM-DAC and related devices that convert digital video information for analog display or analog images for digital manipulation, windowing, panning, editing, and zooming.

Brooktree is one-third owned by its 450 employees, half of whom are engineers. The company generated revenues in 1993 of more than $100 million. Explains Gilder, "Brooktree is not a hierarchy but an information heterarchy, with multiple centers of power and hundreds of on-line workstations around the globe. The company has no one factory of its own but links its process technology with any number of major chip fabs [fabricators] around the world. Its devices are made in Japan or the United States, packaged in Korea, and burned in and tested in San Diego."

The company also is growing at the rate of 50 percent a year, as its RAM-DACs are now critical to the image-processing performance of nearly every workstation, multimedia system, and electronic-imaging device in the United States and Japan.

Gilder also describes the decentralized structure of Cypress Semiconductor, an organization of six separate companies with a network of on-line workstations. Cypress combines the unity of computer networks with greater autonomy and personal freedom for its executives, engineers, and workers. Similarly, Microsoft is essentially a peer network of software programmers who communicate directly with CEO Bill Gates.

This is the direction in which all companies are headed, as the advantages of doing business anywhere, anytime, through any medium will be possible for the individual entrepreneur and small companies as well. They will compete on a stronger footing in the global marketplace. Information is, indeed, power, and as more and more information becomes available to the individual through telecommunications systems, individuals will be empowered as never before.

Simstar Inc.'s president, David Reim, exemplifies the entrepreneur of the '90s. With four Macintosh computers installed in the bedroom of his Sunnyvale, California, home, Reim is building a company that makes interactive multimedia software for health-care patients. As the company's only employee, he teams up with independent partners. Reim describes himself as a general contractor who manages subcontractors over a computer network. The ultimate in deconstruction is the solo performer.

In the years ahead all big companies will find it increasingly difficult to compete with—and in general will perform more poorly than—smaller, speedier, more innovative companies.

The mindset that in a huge global economy the multinationals dominate world business couldn't have been more wrong.

The bigger and more open the world economy becomes, the more small and middle-sized companies will dominate.

In one of the major turnarounds in my lifetime, we have moved from "economies of scale" to "diseconomies of scale"; from bigger is better to bigger is inefficient, costly, wastefully bureaucratic, inflexible, and, now, disastrous. And the paradox is that that has occurred as we move to a global context: The smaller and speedier players will prevail on a much expanded field.

In the center of Europe, in Belgium, sits European Telecom, a company that allows customers to dial their international calls by remote control by way of California, using American carriers. This saves customers one third against the stiff European rates. European Telecom has only three employees and only $50,000 worth of equipment.

Strategic Alliances

The other big trend in the global business community is strategic alliances, many examples of which appear in the discussion of telecommunications in Chapter 2. Mergers and cross-border takeovers are, if not out, very much on the wane.

Competition and cooperation have become the yin and yang of the global marketplace. Like yin and yang they are always seeking balance and always changing. Competition we know about. One thrust of the new cooperation, the new strategic alliances, is to carve out a piece of your world in which you agree to cooperate with your strongest competitor who very much remains your competitor. In mid-1993, Japan's second-largest automaker, Nissan, took the unheard-of step of agreeing to buy parts from a supplier affiliated with its arch rival, Toyota, Japan's largest car company.

In the United States about the same time, U.S. West invested $2.5 billion in Time-Warner's cable and entertainment operations in a strategic alliance to jointly take on the opportunities promised by the revolution in interactive telecommunications.

Most of the strategic alliances are international. British Telecom agreed to pay America's MCI $4.3 billion in cash for a 20 percent stake in the United States' number-two carrier, part of a strategic alliance to act globally.

Telecommunications and automobile companies are in the forefront of global alliances. Indeed, it is almost impossible to buy a car today that is not the product of a network of strategic alliances.

Pharmaceutical companies, long ago globalized, also now seek safety in alliances. In the first half of 1993, there was a spate of joint ventures, mergers, and alliances. Two British firms, Wellcome and Glaxo, each made separate deals with America's Warner-Lambert. Wellcome and Warner-Lambert are combining their over-the-counter (OTC) businesses, creating a new group: Warner-Wellcome Consumer Health Care Products. It is expected to become the world's third-largest OTC firm with annual sales of $1.6 billion. Meanwhile, Glaxo formed a separate OTC alliance with Warner-Lambert to market its prescription drugs. In fact, Glaxo's products, like all Warner-Lambert's other OTC products, will be sold through the new Warner-Wellcome alliance.

Strategic alliances are being created daily as part of the process of moving to a single-market world, where it is getting harder to tell the nationality of a product or company. Milton Friedman recently made the point that it is now "possible to produce a product anywhere, using resources from anywhere, by a company located anywhere, to be sold anywhere." Increasingly this is being done through webs of strategic alliances.

One of the unarticulated reasons for the growth of strategic alliances is companies avoiding getting bigger.

Forming an alliance rather than merging or making an acquisition means that you gain added muscle without getting any bigger.

Big companies will of course not disappear overnight, and some, like commercial aircraft makers, will by the nature of their product have to remain large. But all the trends clearly favor small and medium-sized companies—or big companies that reconstitute themselves as networks of entrepreneurs.

Summarizing the reasons:

- The removal of trade barriers all over the world initially looked like a great opportunity for big companies. But it actually opened the way for small companies. They now have easy access to markets that in the past only large companies could operate in—they were the only ones who could afford the cost of navigating through legal and bureaucratic problems and roadblocks.
- Computers and telecommunications have turned out to be formidable weapons for small companies to get an edge on big companies. In the past, only big firms could afford new technology. Now, any microbusiness can

have the same state-of-the-art technology as IBM or
AT&T. But small firms are not burdened with layers of
bureaucracy and the leaden weight of bigness. Small
companies can deconstruct and reorganize much faster
than large companies. As a result, they can innovate
faster, not just in products but in internal operations, to
take advantage of the new technologies. No wonder
small companies are making many of the breakthroughs
in software and biotechnology.

• The deregulation and globalization of financial markets have given small and medium-sized companies
access to capital that they never had before. Now
small companies borrow capital from all over the
globe. And the much maligned Junk Bonds have had
the effect of liberating small and medium businesses
from banks and have given them access to vast
amounts of capital.

• Consumer tastes have converged across borders all over
the world. Global Television channels display more and
more life-style products and options. The more choice,
the more discrimination in choice, and the more appetite
for additional options. The more we integrate, the more
we differentiate. This explodes markets and market
niches.

• Quality can today be found and replicated everywhere
and anywhere (this is killing name brands). The game
now is speed to market and innovation, further handi-
capping bigness.

• Smaller firms have the advantage when it comes to personnel, too. Working for a big company no longer carries the prestige it once did. It is exciting and satisfying
to work for a small company, where a person has more
responsibility and control, and is much more engaged
in the mission of the organization. The small company
can more easily comply with all the personnel regulations without tying itself in knots, and it is exempted
from some. The very best people are increasingly sign-

ing up with small companies—or starting their own businesses.

As the global economy gets larger, the component parts get smaller.

It is a little like the paradox in research in physics: Bigger and bigger machines are being built to study tinier and tinier things. Now a Supercollider is needed to study protons and particles.

We are making business units smaller and smaller so we can more efficiently globalize our economies.

The more global mutual funds become, the smaller the companies listed.

In the huge global economy there will be smaller and smaller market niches. A Mexican company saw a market niche for small refrigerators for hotel rooms, dormitory rooms, and offices. That company now sells more refrigerators to the United States than any other company in the world.

There is now much talk about having 500 TV channels. So now to replace the Bruce Springsteen song "57 Channels and Nothing On," we could have "500 Channels and Still Nothing On." But, actually, those 500 channels will probably mean you have a much better chance of finding a show to your liking. This will mean much, much smaller market segments for the individual channels.

But we will be globalizing at the same time. While the market segment for an Opera Channel may not be large enough to sustain it in an individual country, a Global Opera Channel broadcasting to all countries certainly could be a great success.

The almost perfect metaphor for the movement from bureaucracies of every kind to small, autonomous units is the shift from the mainframe to PCs, with PCs networked together.

THE NEW TRIBALISM

"Tribalism" reentered the world's vocabulary in 1993, mostly with horrifically negative connotations growing out of the brutality, rapes and killings, and other forms of "ethnic cleansing" in the former Yugoslavia.

The Economist, seriously alarmed early on, said that the "virus of tribalism . . . risks becoming the AIDS of international politics— lying dormant for years, then flaring up to destroy countries."

There is developing a mindset that says: "Yes, the Cold War is over, but now we have Yugoslavia."

Yes, we do have the tragedy of Yugoslavia. But we also have witnessed more peaceful, successful examples of the creation of new countries, the "velvet divorce" that created two countries out of Czechoslovakia, for one. The Eritreans declared their independence from Ethiopia and in the spring of 1993 became the 183rd member of the United Nations. The Israelis and Palestinians have an agreement and handshake to seek a peaceful accord. The old Soviet Union more or less peacefully split into 15 independent countries, although the jury is still out in some of those regions.

And now in the early '90s the 11 countries of the so-called Commonwealth of Independent States have begun splitting up, none more extensively than the Russian Federation itself.

Balancing Tribal with Universal

The desire for balance between the tribal and the universal has always been with us. Now democracy and the revolution in telecommunications (which spreads word about democracy and gives it urgency) have brought this need for balance between tribal and universal to a new level.

The tribes have returned. And the anguished drama of their return is most pronounced where they were repressed the most brutally.

Democracy greatly magnifies and multiplies the assertiveness of tribes; repression does the reverse.

Indeed, it could be argued that separate states are necessary if democracy is to flourish.

After all, it has been hundreds of years since the southern parts of Sweden were returned from Denmark, and a very long time since Norway became free of Sweden.

But tribalism should not be confused with nationalism, as it so often is in the media. Nationalism, which flourished from the 18th century until the end of World War II, is a belief that one's nation-state is more important than international principles or individual considerations. World War II put an end to the nationalism of Italy and Germany and greatly diluted the force of nationalism for the West.

Tribalism is the belief in fidelity to one's own kind, defined by ethnicity, language, culture, religion, or, in this late 20th century, profession. And this belief is flourishing.

The bonding commonality of human beings is our distinctiveness.

Also in this late 20th century, each of us—absent a threat to our core identity—can identify with a number of tribal manifestations. One person can, with the freedom that comes with security, be simultaneously a Houstonian, a Texan, an American, an accountant, and Chinese. But if you are a Muslim in dangerous Bosnia, you are overwhelmingly a Muslim.

Virtual Tribes?

Also, there will be "virtual tribes" or "electronic tribes." For example, particle physicists bond through computers, cellular phones, and face-to-face meetings. They certainly speak another language. And it won't be long before they and we all have a lifelong personal phone number and all calls will be local. More bonding.

E-mail is a tribe-maker. Electronics makes us more tribal at the same time it globalizes us.

From particle physicists to accountants, associations of professionals take on symbolic and tribal-like rituals. Yes, even accountants. Some accountants are pushing to have the inventor of double-entry bookkeeping acknowledged as the father or patron saint of accounting. In 1494 in Sansepolcro, Italy, Luca Pacioli, a priest and member of the Franciscan Order, came up with this basic idea of accounting. A marble statue of Pacioli is to be installed in Sansepolcro's town square and a 500th-year celebration is planned for 1994. A video of Pacioli's life, financed by four of the Big Six accounting firms, has been made. The group tried to get the U.S. Postal Service to issue a commemorative stamp of Luca Pacioli but was turned down because a stamp celebrating the 100th anniversary of accounting in the United States, issued in 1987, "didn't sell very well."

With the new emphasis on what is tribal in a world increasingly global, the New Age mantra "Think Globally, Act Locally" is turned on its head. It is now:

Think Locally, Act Globally.

One modern nation and economic superpower functions much like a tribe. The Japanese. This most homogeneous of cultures has been doing extraordinarily well thinking locally and acting globally for many years.

A U.S. company that has excelled at thinking locally and acting globally is Motorola. Former CEO Robert Galvin even designated a "tribal storyteller" to tell new employees and remind old ones of the triumphs and setbacks of Motorola's road to global success.

Hot Spots

The new urge for tribalism has resulted in an escalation of conflicts in many parts of the world. There are many places where ethnic or religious groups are being suppressed rather than celebrated. Some of those places, in addition to Bosnia-Herzegovina, are:

- Iran. The Islamic government is trying to do away with the Baha'i minority by denying them education and jobs.
- Sudan. The Muslim government in the north is brutally fighting rebellious black animists and Christians of the south rather than deal with their grievances. About 40,000 killed.
- Tibet. 40 years of military occupation by the Chinese.
- Iraq. Baghdad government's massive human-rights violations against Kurds.

And here are some we don't read about in the newspapers every day:

- Papua New Guinea: The separatist movement on the island of Bougainville wants independence. As many as 5,000 killed.
- Bangladesh. Buddhist Chakmas have fought for separation from this officially Islamic country for almost 20 years.
- Fiji. Ethnic Indians vs. ethnic Fijians.
- Burundi. Thousands have been killed as a result of ethnic clashes between the majority Hutus and the formally politically dominant Tutsis.

Some people insist that the forces that are making the world into a single economy have separated people from longstanding identities and have, at the same time, weakened the nation-state. Hence the violence in these troubled "hot spots." And that in the future, most armed conflict will be ethnically or tribally motived, rather than politically or economically motivated.

In fact, these economic and technological forces of change have weakened the nation-state, but they have strengthened, not separated people from, longstanding identities. Language, culture, religion, and ethnic heritage reinforce people's sense of belonging. These are the bonds out of which will be created new communities. At the same time, the global community has embraced, at least in concept, the notion that there are certain basic human rights—although the East and West may well continue to argue over just exactly what those rights are—that must be protected.

There also is evolving a new global code of conduct to protect those rights spread by the extraordinary reach of communications technology, which will in time ensure that all communities are held to the same standards of behavior. Those that do not will be held to account by the rest of the international community. War and other forms of aggression against fellow citizens will become, if not obsolete, at least increasingly intolerable. When the world is watching, a community's behavior is influenced by the anticipated reaction of its economic allies.

UNIVERSAL VS. TRIBAL

Also, as we globalize the world's economies, many things will become universal. What remains tribal will become more important and more powerful—another paradox that is an important aspect of the Global Paradox:

The more universal we become, the more tribal we act.

Which in the Global Paradox also means more and smaller parts.

Language

Take language. English is becoming the universal language of the world.

As English becomes everyone's second language, their first language, their mother tongue, becomes more important and more passionately held.

Look at Quebec, and its language fight with the rest of Canada.

That English is becoming universal there is little doubt.

There are, in the world today, more than one billion English speakers—people who speak English as a mother tongue, as a second language, or as a foreign language.

60 percent of the world's radio broadcasts are in English.

70 percent of the world's mail is addressed in English.

85 percent of all international telephone conversations are in English.

80 percent of all the data in the several 100 million computers in the world is in English.

English is a strategic asset in the global marketplace.

The universal is English. The tribal is one's mother tongue.

And some go to great lengths to protect their own language. None more so than the people of Iceland. Everyone in Iceland speaks English as a second language, and most speak other languages as well. But they fiercely protect the purity of the Icelandic language. If a new word comes along, like *software,* or *nanosecond,* a committee decides which Icelandic words and sounds should be put together to stand for the new thing or idea. There are no non-

Icelandic sounds in the language of these people who number only about 250,000. It is worth noting that Iceland also has the world's oldest extant democratic (parliamentary) government and highest literacy rate.

Moscow authorities have begun to worry about losing their Russianness. In 1993 they created a law that requires all stores and businesses to display signs in Russian. So now McDonald's, Pizza Hut, Benetton, and other English-language businesses have to have signs in Russian also, and the Russian signs must be bigger and more prominent.

This is reminiscent of Quebec, where there is a French-only sign law and so-called language police to make sure there are no signs in English. The Quebec law was recently challenged—in the United Nations.

Gordon McIntyre, who operates a funeral parlor in the town of Huntingdon, got mad when the government refused to let him write FUNERAL HOME on a sign in front of his business, and told him he would have to use the term SALON FUNÉRAIRE. McIntyre appealed to the UN's Commission on Human Rights in Geneva. The commission (after debating McIntyre's case for three years) handed down a verdict in March 1993 saying that the Quebec French-only law governing commercial signs violated freedom of expression. Although the UN cannot force Quebec to comply, it has been a matter of some embarrassment. The Quebec parliament is now debating a new law that would modify the French-only rule, permitting non-French words—but only if the French words are at least twice as big.

In newly independent Ukraine, a country of more than 50 million people, 95 percent of all the place names were changed from the ones created during the Communist period.

In Lithuania every Russian sign is now gone. The government is creating a new state language commission, changing all official paperwork into the Lithuanian language. Estonia passed a law that requires a language test for Estonian citizenship. Russians, most of whom do not speak Estonian, make up 40 percent of the population.

In 1993 Indonesian authorities started cracking down on the use of English in advertising. This was largely in response to a recent increase in the pace of "Westernization," which has "raised concerns about the erosion of local cultural identity." There have been rules since 1959 banning the use of English in favor of the local Bahasa Indonesia, but there has been little enforcement until now. Authorities announced fines and jail terms for those who continue to flout the rules. (Bahasa Indonesia itself is a modern synthetic lingua franca, based primarily on Malay, which was promulgated specifically to reduce cultural and ethnic differences among the hundreds of ethnic groups that make up the Indonesian population.)

With English spreading so rapidly on the European continent, the French government has decided that France's regional languages are suddenly contributing to the country's heritage rather than subtracting from its identity. For more than 400 years Paris strove to impose a standard French on the whole country, while repressing the eight regional languages and many dialects. Now the government has a big plan—announced in January 1993—to have schools and teachers in those eight regions begin to create bilingual education. It also wants local governments to promote regional language and culture through music, theater, and film.

But not in English. Longtime French minister of culture Jack Lang used both restrictive legislation and incentives to limit English language material in France, especially U.S. equipment and software. As *Le Monde* reporter Michel Colonna d'Istria asked, "What will our collective consciousness be tomorrow if the horizon of our Gameboy is conceived in Tokyo, if the games are played in English in a McDonald's?"

Minority languages all over Western Europe are achieving a new status as people hold more tightly to their heritage as ballast to the creation of a larger, more economically homogenous Europe.

Currencies

Currencies—the language of commerce—are cherished as symbols of heritage and tradition—and replaced if they have been imposed.

In Western Europe there is great resistance to a common currency; people want to keep their own. English Archbishop Dr. George Carey says: "I want the Queen's head on the banknotes. The point about national identity is a very important one. For me being British is deeply important. I don't want to become French or German."

The most widespread examples of replacing currencies come of course from what was the Soviet Union. Before 1994 is over, most of the former republics—including Russia itself—will have created their own currency.

The three Baltic states—Estonia, Latvia, and Lithuania, the first to break away from the USSR—were also the first to introduce new currencies and coupons, which they did in 1992.

While it was initially and widely thought that the Commonwealth of Independent States would be well served by having a common ruble, by the spring of 1993 the ruble zone turned out to be what *The Wall Street Journal* called "a sort of monetary Chernobyl." Inflation was well over 2,000 percent in 1992, and continued to rise sharply in 1993. By summer Ukraine had joined the Baltic states in abandoning the ruble. Moldova, Armenia, Georgia, and several other republics were getting ready. Turkmenistan in Central Asia said it would introduce its own currencies in the fall of 1993. Since the beginning of 1993 the ruble has been printed with "Bank of Russia" rather than "USSR," and Lenin's face has been removed.

In May 1993 the small and very poor republic of Kyrgyzstan dropped the ruble and introduced its own currency—the som—with its own heroes printed on the notes. After the introduction, Boris Fyodorov, Russia's finance minister, welcomed the change. "I hail this decision," he said. "The sooner all the republics of the former Soviet Union introduce their own currencies, the sooner they will become real states." This small republic, along with the others, is switching to its own currencies partly because leaving the ruble zone and establishing its own currency helps get support from the International Monetary Fund and the World Bank.

Response to the som in Kyrgyzstan, which is located in the mountains near China, depended somewhat on your ethnic point of view. About half the population of the country is ethnic Kyrgyz, and they welcomed it as a symbol of independence. Russians, about a fifth of the population, were mostly unhappy. "To us this isn't even a serious word, 'som.' In Russian it means a kind of fish," as one Russian businessman put it. Word from the central bank is that in Turkic, *som* means a solid unit of currency.

We hold on to our language and our currencies even as, or because, we are becoming universal in so many other ways.

UNIVERSAL

Many things are in the process of being globalized, of being made universal.

Bar codes—they are even called Universal Product Codes.

Free market mechanisms have become the universal way to organize economic life.

The decline of the nation-state is becoming a universal phenomenon. At once, we are witnessing the receding of the importance of the nation-state, and, paradoxically, the creation of many more countries.

As the importance of the nation-state recedes, more of them are being created.

We have globalized our concern for the environment. Indeed, it appears that preoccupation with the Cold War is being replaced by a global preoccupation with attending to our environment.

There is no flagging in the globalization of travel and tourism. Tourism, the second industry to be globalized after financial services, is and will continue to be the world's largest industry. Today, one out of every nine people working on this planet is in travel and tourism (204 million).

Jeans are certainly becoming universal, and Levi Strauss in 1992 became the first apparel company to exceed $5 billion in annual sales.

Also becoming universal are chopsticks, karaoke bars, soccer—with the World Cup matches being held in the United States in 1994—the Western business suit, and wearing baseball caps backward (I saw it even in Hanoi).

With an increasingly affluent world, luxury goods will experience strong if not spectacular growth.

Many luxury-goods makers, like Dunhill, for decades had no market outside the city—in this case, London—where they began. (And why, by the way, are almost all luxury-goods makers European?) Home-city–bound was true until sometime in the 1970s. The global boom for luxury goods really got under way in the 1980s because of globalization and democratization—selling to the newly rich in the middle class, and yuppies.

Asians are learning how to be affluent. A global Asian affluent looks something like this: He wears Ferragamo-designed shirts and ties, sports a Rolex or Cartier watch, has a Louis Vuitton attaché case, signs his signature with a Montblanc pen, goes to work in his flashy BMW, endlessly talks on a mobile Motorola cellular phone, puts all his charges on the American Express card, travels Singapore Airlines, maintains a city apartment, and keeps a country home. He uses Giorgio Armani aftershave and buys Poison for his girlfriend. The rising group of affluent Asian career women have wardrobes filled with Christian Dior and Nina Ricci, dressing tables congested with makeup and skin care from Guerlain, YSL, and Estée Lauder, shoes from Bruno Magli, wear Chanel No. 5 and jewelry from Tiffany. They both listen to Beethoven's Ninth Symphony from their Sony compact disc player either in the car, at home, or in the office.

Paris-based Cartier, which has just opened its first China outlet in Shanghai, is one of the most successful companies in the luxury-goods business. Annual sales are around $1.5 billion. Tiffany, Cartier's biggest rival, sells only one third of that. Cartier's leading markets, in order, are Italy, Hong Kong, the Far East, France, the United States, and Japan.

Like Dunhill, Cartier for almost all of its 146 years was a small shop serving an elite clientele. Now that it is global and very successful, there have been rumors that the company might be floated on international stock exchanges. Alain Perrin, Cartier's longtime president, shudders at the thought. "Just the idea of being listed beside a company with the name Caterpillar would break the Cartier magic," he says.

And with luxury goods here is the paradox: Exclusivity is the name of the game, and if these goods become common and less costly they lose their exclusivity—and their market, as overexposed Pierre Cardin discovered. In any case, globally, the luxury class is growing and must spend its money on something.

America's Pop Culture

America's popular culture is overwhelmingly dominant in the global life-style department.

American music and television and books and magazines, and especially movies, seem to stick out of every corner and nook and cranny of the world, becoming universal. American basketball is about to become the world's most popular sport. The National Basketball Association finals in Phoenix and Chicago in June 1993 were broadcast in 109 countries in 20 languages. American basketball is now played in 192 countries.

Everyone in Europe can now watch *Oprah Winfrey* subtitled or dubbed in his or her own language.

Vietnam's most popular band sings Bruce Springsteen songs.

American movies have no competition to speak of. At any given time the top 10 films showing in almost any major city in the world are American made. The American movie industry has a $4 billion trade balance, and earns more than 40 percent of its revenues from abroad.

Terminator 2 has sold more than $500 million in tickets, mostly overseas. Michael Jackson's latest album, *Dangerous,* sold 15 million copies, two thirds outside the United States.

Many people say to me, "Isn't it terrible that we invented the VCR in the United States but now the Japanese are making all of them?" No, I don't think it is terrible at all. The profit margins in this hardware are very thin. The money is in the software and the United States makes 90 percent of the software.

It's the software, Stupid.

People want genuinely authentic American stuff. Americans may not know what that would be, but others seem to.

The Euro Disney people discovered that Europeans wanted a dis-

tinctively American theme park. Philippe Bourguignon, the French-
man who has been running Euro Disney since January, said, "Each
time we tried to Europeanize the product we found it didn't work.
Europeans want America and they want Disney, whether the French
intellectuals like it or not." Too bad for Disney that the European
recession rather than the French intellectuals has put a damper on
business.

The Daily Planet

Also, we are simultaneously creating global and local (tribal)
publications.

In Telluride, Colorado, where I live, I read *The Financial Times*
every day. I also read *The European, China Daily, The Asian Wall
Street Journal, Nihon Keizai Shimbun,* and so on.

But I read the Telluride *Times-Journal* first, our weekly local
newspaper. Now you would think that in a town of only 1,400
permanent residents, the Telluride *Times-Journal* would not be
challenged by a new weekly. But earlier this year a new *daily*
newspaper was born: *The Daily Planet*. (Excuse me while I step
into this telephone booth.) It used to be that it cost almost as much
to start a newspaper as to start a steel plant. But with today's desktop publishing, a newspaper can be started overnight at very little
cost. The Telluride *Daily Planet* is entirely digitized, including the
use of digitized cameras whose images feed directly into a computer.

Now the first thing I read every day is *The Daily Planet*.

With the help of increasingly inexpensive technology and with
the need to be increasingly grounded in community, expect many
new local publications, fiercely focusing on local—tribal—interests
as we globalize our economies and our life-styles.

**The riddle of the '90s is: What will become universal? What
will remain tribal?**

THE MORE DEMOCRACY, THE MORE COUNTRIES

The more democracy, the greater the number of countries in the
world. In Barcelona there were teams representing 172 countries.

For the Olympics in Atlanta in 1996, planners expect the participation of well over 200 countries. By the beginning of the next century we should have at least 300 countries in this world.

The United Nations was founded with 51 countries in 1945. By 1960 there were 100 UN countries, and by the year 1984 when Brunei Darussalam joined, 159. There were no new member states added between 1985 and 1989. Only Namibia and Liechtenstein joined in 1990. But in the two and a half years from the beginning of 1991 to mid-1993, 25 countries were added—including Estonia, Latvia, and Lithuania, and Azerbaijan, Kyrgyzstan, Tajikistan, Uzbekistan, Georgia, and Andorra—to bring the total number of countries in the United Nations to 184.

In the spring of 1993 even a country without a name was admitted to the UN. The former Yugoslav republic of Macedonia was allowed to join on the condition that Greece and the new member would work out what the country's name would be. Greeks objected to "Macedonia" because it had the same name as the northern Greek province and somehow implied a territorial claim. Until the problem is worked out, the country is just descriptively referred to as the "Former Yugoslav Republic of Macedonia."

Name That Country

On the other hand, we are beginning to have contests to name new countries. President Vaclav Havel of the new Czech Republic has let it be known that a search is on for a new name for his country, partly because the very word *republic* is still associated with communism. The president is looking for something distinctive but traditional. So the helpful London *Sunday Times* invited readers to suggest names. There had been talk of Czechlands but that sounded a little too close to Gracelands. Czechia was discussed, but that seemed an echo of Cheka, an early version of the KGB. The *Sunday Times* offered a bottle of champagne for the best entry. More than 1,000 came in.

The old name, Bohemia, got the most votes with 66 entries. "The new name should be Bohemia. Please bite the bullet on this one," said Faith Bryars of Osterley, Middlesex. But as several writers pointed out, the Czech Republic is made up of Bohemia *and* Moravia *and* Silesia, all partners.

The great and widespread respect for President Havel was much in evidence. The third-most votes, after second-place Czechovia, was for Vaclavia. "It links the old with the new—the traditional history with the Velvet Revolution," said Nicky Stanton of Henley-on-Thames, Oxon. "President Havel should not be inhibited from using his own name. He, after all, has been a powerful influence in bringing into existence a new country."

There were 17 votes for Czechslovia and 16 writers wanted to honor former Czechoslovak leader Alexander Dubček. A little awkward, because Dubcek was born in Slovakia. M. J. Barnsley of Clehonger, Hereford, suggested Elberia "because so much of the land contains the course or tributaries of the river Elbe. Avoid the titles of any previous tribal inhabitants and you will not provoke any ethnic animosity. Furthermore, the word is easy to pronounce and spell."

Some readers were of course a little flip. From Dorset came this entry: "The new name should be Amoebia because Czechoslovakia has split into two—both swimming alone."

The bottle of champagne went to one A. J. Sinclair of Dundee for Vaclavia, pulled from the other entries of the same name. All the entries were sent to the Czech embassy in London where spokesperson Jan Vymetal would not state his preferred choice. "There is still a lot of debate," he said. "I don't know the exact way forward—perhaps a referendum or public opinion poll. It is still not clear and far from easy."

One of the contestants, Helen Corscadden of Cawthrone, suggested: Germolatria, Cripettel, Linomanlopogeria, and Elbegerma. The *Sunday Times* thought their connection to the Czech Republic not immediately apparent, but "they are obviously names crying out for a country to which to attach themselves."

A WORLD OF 1,000 COUNTRIES

With the extraordinary spreading of democracy in the world, people—tribes—see an opportunity for self-rule. And surely self-rule is a pillar of democracy. People all over the world are beginning to seize that opportunity. This mounting tribalism must be connected with the revolution in telecommunications because it makes everything transparent, that is, everyone can see what is happening everywhere. We can all monitor the process of a massive move to self-rule, and check the excesses—if we want to. At this writing we still hadn't done so in Bosnia.

Most reference books report that there are 4,000 to 5,000 languages being spoken in the world today. Some say as many as 10,000.

The old Soviet Union was made up of 104 officially recognized ethnic groups. What was once one country already is now 15 countries and is on its way to eventually becoming perhaps as many as 60 or 70 countries.

China has 56 different nationalities. Five of China's 30 provinces are autonomous. It is not hard to imagine that sometime in the next century China could become a confederation of dozens of regions or countries held together by economic self-interest.

Some version of Freddie Heineken's alliance of Europe is eventually possible, perhaps with a couple of hundred independent countries and cities.

Kenichi Ohmae, managing director of McKinsey in Tokyo and well-known author and speaker, has proposed breaking up homogeneous Japan into nine or 10 autonomous regions. Ichiro Ozawa, former secretary-general of the Liberal Democratic party and now one of the forces behind the new coalition that is in power in Japan, is advocating breaking up Japan into 300 autonomous regions in order to radically decentralize power and authority. He wants each region to govern itself. He outlines all the details in his big 1993 best-seller, *Plans to Rebuild Japan.*

In South America there are more than 100 different language groups.

More languages are spoken in Africa than on any other continent. There are, for example, 40 different ethnic groups in Kenya, each with its own language and culture. Uganda and Gabon also each have about 40 ethnic groups. More than 200 languages are spoken in Zaire.

There are 300 ethnic groups living on 3,000 of Indonesia's islands, artificially rounded up by the Dutch.

Only about 10 percent of the countries of the world are ethnically homogeneous.

We see that big companies work best, now that we have the telecommunications, if divided up into autonomous small units. Countries, too, will work best that way. And now that we are becoming one world—the smaller the pieces, the better it will work. Computers allow us to organize and keep track of complexity, the complexity of having many small units—for companies and for the world.

The breakup of countries (artificially put together) into national or tribal entities is surely as beneficial as the breakup of companies. It eliminates duplication and waste, reduces bureaucracy and promotes motivation and accountability, and results in self-rule (subsidiarity) at the most basic level—just like in companies.

If we are going to make the world a single-market world, the parts have to be smaller.

It is not that all countries will break up. The key is that there will be tens of thousands of different crisscrossing communities co-located on the same territories. Territory as a defining concept will become increasingly meaningless.

A world of 1,000 countries is a metaphor for moving beyond the nation-state. Countries will become more and more irrelevant. The shift will be from 200 or 600 countries to a million "hosts" of networks that are all tied together. The people we network with will become more important as the country we happen to operate out of becomes less important.

The Unbundling of Russia

The world's attention during much of 1993 was focused on the fight in Moscow between the president and the Congress. But the provinces and cities of Russia are becoming increasingly autonomous. One province, oil-rich Chechenya, formerly Chechen-Ingushetia, has declared full independence, entirely withdrawing from Russia (yet another country trying to be born). The big oil

producer, Tatarstan, in Russia's heartland, has approved a constitution that says that ''the Republic of Tatarstan will build its relations with the Russian Federation on the basis of a bilateral
treaty,'' thus asserting itself as an independent republic.

Now all of Russia's 21 republics have claimed autonomy and, to
one degree or another, control over their natural resources. Russia's
67 smaller jurisdictions are beginning to push for similar independence.

The 88 republics and regions in Russia are already ''semi-
autonomous,'' and most are headed in the direction of full
autonomy.

In his 1993 call for a new vote of confidence from the people of
the Russian Republic, Boris Yeltsin promised more and more autonomy for the republics and regions. The republic of Yakutia, now
calling itself Sakha, which has huge diamond resources and wants
to control its own wealth, has made noises about declaring itself
independent. As of mid-1993, 15 of Russia's 21 republics warned
they might not sign the post-Soviet constitution being hammered
out in Moscow.

In July 1993 Sverdlovsk, Yeltsin's home territory, and one of
Russia's richest and most industrialized regions, declared itself a
republic and renamed itself the ''Urals Republic.'' The capital,
also known as Sverdlovsk, the fourth-largest city in Russia and on
its way to embracing a free market, was renamed Ekaterinburg.
Ten days later the Russian Far East region, with its capital in
Vladivostok (5,000 miles east of Moscow), declared itself a republic.

The republic of Karelia, adjacent to Finland, now has its own
parliament and laws and economic policy, and more often than not
simply ignores laws coming out of Moscow.

**This is typical of many of the republics of Russia. It is leading
to either the disintegration of the Russian Federation or the real
beginnings of a federated democracy and free markets.**

During the election campaign, Yeltsin, eager for Karelia's support
in his fight with the Russian parliament, signed a decree that now
allows Karelia to keep 90 percent of the tax revenue that had been
going to Moscow.

Little Georgia (population 5.5 million), which along with the three Baltic states chose not to join the C.I.S., is struggling with Abkhazia (population 93,000) and South Ossetia (population 65,000), each of which wants to secede from Georgia and form its own independent country.

New Era of Self-rule

Democracy is sweeping the world and the world is learning about it through the global telecommunications system. The new era is an era of self-rule for peoples around the world all connected with each other, a network of PCs. Adding another paradox:

Several decades from now it will be easier to keep track of 1,000 countries and thousands of global networks than it was to keep track of 100 countries two decades ago.

It may be a long time before there are 1,000 countries in this world, but by the middle of the next century we should be close to that number; that is the direction we are going.

Will the United States be splitting up? Probably not anytime soon. Compared to centrally run European countries, the federation of the United States is very decentralized, with people in states and cities and towns exercising a great deal of self-rule.

Even so, a measure of the times is the serious debate in California to split the state three ways. In the summer of 1993 the State Assembly voted 46 to 26 to ask voters to express their opinion on creating three separate states of Southern California (from Los Angeles to San Diego), Central California (from Santa Barbara to San Francisco), and Northern California (from the wine country of Sonoma up through the forests to the northern border). In 1992, 27 out of 31 northern counties voted in favor of splitting up the state.

In Hawaii in 1993, Governor John Waihee, the first governor of native ancestry, sought federal recognition of a "Hawaiian Nation." It would co-exist with the state, have its own island, and allow native Hawaiians to elect their own representatives. About 20 percent of Hawaiians are natives.

The year 1993 marked the 100th anniversary of the overthrow of Queen Liliuokalani by a group of white businessmen and sugar

planters in the name of U.S. annexation of the islands. Governor
Waihee removed U.S. flags from state buildings during the com-
memoration of the event. "My friends," he said, "we are on a
razor's edge. We are an island community, and it is impossible to
turn our backs on the injustices visited to our host culture, who are
now one in five among us."

1,000 Countries

We are moving toward a world of 1,000 countries because:

- Many people of the new tribalism want self-rule and
  every day they see others getting self-rule, or moving
  toward it.
- The nation-state is dead. Not because nation-states were
  subsumed by super-states, but because they are breaking
  up to smaller, more efficient parts—just like big companies.
- The revolution in telecommunications not only informs
  this tremendous move to democratic self-rule but monitors and makes transparent the character and nature of
  the process. Modern telecommunications also allow and
  encourage extraordinary cooperation among people,
  companies, and countries.

And so we see part of the global paradox being played out.

**As the global economy gets larger, the component nation
players get smaller and smaller.**

LEADERSHIP VACUUM

The old leadership in Europe does not understand. And the leaders of the G-7 are being knocked off one by one.

It is as if citizens feel that with the end of the Cold War it is
safe to entertain alternative brands of leadership. And today, domestic issues far outweigh foreign-policy issues.

In the nine months between November 1992 and July 1993 when

the Group of Seven had its economic summit meeting in Tokyo, four of the seven leaders were thrown out and the remaining three were political cripples. First Bush was beaten in November, then Mulroney resigned in the spring, departing as the least popular Canadian prime minister in history. Amato in Italy resigned amid huge scandal. Miyazawa was voted out in June 1993 (the lame-duck host at the Tokyo summit was not even a member of the Diet, it having been dissolved two weeks before in preparation for a new parliamentary election). Of the three left, perhaps the most pathetic was poor old Mitterrand. After his Socialist party got a dismal 17 percent of the vote in the spring and lost almost all of its seats in parliament (one of the last nails in the coffin of socialism), he will have to resign or be totally ineffectual. Kohl is not long for this political world. His approval rating back home at the time of the summit was 38 percent. And Prime Minister Major of Britain was down to a 21 percent approval, the most unpopular P.M. since polling began. President Clinton was lower in the polls than any previous U.S. president so early in his term. What's going on?

First of all the G-7 summit is a relic of the Cold War and the energy crisis of the 1970s.

Second, the kind of leadership that was appropriate during the Cold War and before the great revolution in telecommunications is obsolete.

The G-7 Tokyo economic summit had all the appearances of a bunch of mainframes talking to each other in a PC world.

Where Are the Churchills?

We didn't sufficiently understand the extent to which fear of the Soviet Union was the glue that held the Western Alliance together.

The Western world has been weakened by no longer having a strong enemy.

Nor did the West sufficiently understand that we for so long defined ourselves by what we were not. We mostly were not Communists. That was what we were working against. With the fall of communism, we in the West have to define and perhaps agree to what we are. Or do we? As we move toward a borderless world and a single global economy, is the East-West distinction any longer valid? I think not.

Today, the external stimulus that created the Western Alliance is gone. Leadership and vision will have to make the difference. This is giving Europe and the West a very large identity crisis. And to one degree or other—with the Cold War pulled out from under us—we are all experiencing some kind of identity crisis. This is the opportunity for new ideas and new leadership.

People plead, "Where are the Churchills?" "Where are the de Gaulles?" But would they be just as irrelevant today as the current pretenders? As great as they were for their time, their brand of leadership would not necessarily work today.

The fall of G-7 leaders was mirrored in the extraordinary oustings of CEOs in recent months: Robert Stempel of GM, John Akers of IBM, James Robinson of American Express, Kay Whitmore of Kodak, among others.

Whether prime minister or CEO, if you are an old mainframe thinker you are no longer relevant.

THE END OF POLITICS

We live in a time of great change, a time of new beginnings. We live in a time when many things are coming to an end.

In the evolution of democracy we are coming to the end of that phase of democracy that we think of as representative democracy. For centuries we have elected people to represent us, to give us voice in far-off forums, and then we judged how well they represented us. Representative democracy began before electricity, before the telegraph and the telephone, before the pony express, and, of course, before television, airplanes, computers, E-mail, Federal Express, and fax machines.

The crisis in political leadership we are witnessing today is the crisis of an earlier invented arrangement that has become irrelevant. Because we are now in a position to know all we have to know as soon as everyone else knows it—including those who represent us—we do not have to have that kind of *representativeness* anymore. We don't have to have people on the scene who have the knowledge and information to make judgments for us. We have the same information and knowledge and we are also on the scene. The only thing the representative on the scene has that the citizen at home doesn't have is knowledge of the culture of the institutions of government—and most of that culture is antidemocratic and maladaptive.

The idea that the central government—one huge mainframe—is the most important part of governance is obsolete.

Democracy developed as representative democracy because of scale and the distance between an event and the time people found out about it—the information float. Now with the electronics revolution both representative democracy and economies of scale are obsolete. Now everyone can have efficient direct democracy.

What I think we are moving toward, following the long period of representative democracy, is the ultimate in direct democracy, a "free-market democracy." (By this I do not mean "market democracy," a shorthand phrase much used these days to mean a society that has *both* a free-market economy system and representative democracy.) What would free-market democracy look like? Suppose that after all that incredible amount of debate we witnessed on the merits of NAFTA, all of the American people had an opportunity to vote it up or down. Suppose we all had a chance to vote on whether or not to spend $2 billion to build a supercollider. This is direct democracy, rather than representative democracy. People are given an opportunity to vote on the things that directly impact on their lives.

I am suggesting that the next stage will be a free-market-of-ideas democracy, a consumer-driven democracy, that directly resolves issues, eliminating representatives. It has been working in science, a real free market of ideas, for many years. Someone makes a proposition, and then the individuals in the scientific community—if interested—say they think the idea is good, bad, or irrelevant; that is, the marketplace decides. This has been made all the more efficient by the revolution in telecommunications. The ideas marketplace decides and it decides efficiently. Free-market democracy would be just that, a free market of ideas and opinions, with votes taken when appropriate.

The only place I know that has a more free-market and direct democracy than Switzerland is my own hometown of Telluride. We, the voters, decide almost everything. It seems that on most Tuesdays we are voting on something. Several years ago we voted on whether to allow the Grateful Dead to put on a concert in the town park (which would have meant 15,000 "Deadheads" invading our little town of 1,400 permanent residents). The referendum passed by a margin of three to one. In November 1993 Telluride residents voted to set aside 20 percent of the town's budget for the acquisition of property to be held as open space.

Any voter can get a question on the ballot with signatures of only 15 percent of the people who voted in the last election. That is how the 20 percent for open space got on the ballot. Also on the ballot is a referendum to allow the school board to float bonds to pay for a first-rate performing-arts facility. And we were the first place in America to ban smoking in all public places.

The scale of Telluride is such that this marketplace democracy can take place and has for years. Now, with the new electronic technologies (see the description of Internet later in this chapter), post-representative, free-market democracy can expand greatly, and I believe it will to a surprising level.

We are, all over the Western world, in a "political crisis" because political leaders have ceased to be very important.

It is almost a universal condition in the West. But take away politics and there is no crisis.

The 40 years of standing against communism have been replaced with boredom and apathy, and the political leaders have nothing to do except worry about their economies, which they can do very little about.

The people know it. Most are not even bothering to vote for someone to represent them.

In the most technologically and economically sophisticated countries in the world—the United States and Japan—only half the people vote.

In France in the spring of 1993, we witnessed the biggest political defeat of a sitting government in this century. The Socialist party of President François Mitterrand lost 210 of its 270 seats in the

French parliament. Then came an even greater defeat for a government in power when, in late October 1993 in Canada, the Progress Conservative party lost an astonishing 155 out of the 157 seats it held.

We also saw it in Japan. In July 1993, the LDP lost its outright majority of Diet members for the first time in 40 years, and the Socialist Labor party went from 135 seats to 70.

Political parties are dead. Haven't their leaders noticed?

No one joins a political party anymore (at least in a tribal sense). Tribal affiliations—cultural and professional—are much more important.

The world today is about the individual, not the state. It is about self-organization, just as business has experienced the shift to self-management. Bill Gates is the leadership model today, Bill Gates and the millions of entrepreneurs we haven't heard of. The world is being run by the collective judgments and actions of individuals.

Countries don't decide the value of their currency anymore. Individuals do. Sovereign states decided the value of their money and often printed as much as they liked. Now the approximately 22,000 currency traders with their computer screens make individual judgments about the relative value of a country's currency, and buy or sell millions of dollars with their clients' money and their money. These decisions are made largely on the basis of judgments about the economic viability of each country involved. And because they are backed up by very large bets and are not just casual opinions, they constitute a pretty good index of economic health. That is, the constantly shifting collective judgments of 22,000 individuals, with a large stake in the outcome, about the value of a country's currency against other currencies can probably be trusted more than most other judgments.

Politicians seem oblivious to change. They understand neither globalization nor the triumph of the individual.

It has to do with the deployment of power and that is shifting from the state to the individual. From vertical to horizontal. From hierarchy to networking.

Politics are less and less important in people's lives as they get more and more control over their lives.

Power is flowing in all directions—unpredictable, a little chaotic, certainly messy—not well-ordered like hierarchical, top-down arrangements.

In post-representative democracy, people represent themselves, and ultimately everyone becomes a politician.

1,000 Countries in Cyberspace

A world with 1,000 countries. Picture 1,000—or 2,000!—Andorras, all connected to global computer networks, all cooperating and competing. Not the countries connecting, but individuals in the 1,000 countries connecting. You have just had a glimpse of the 21st century.

It is already happening. Computer networks are being created every day. Internet is the world's largest. Initially created by the Pentagon in the late 1970s, it was divested in 1986 to other agencies in the United States and around the world for educational research and commercial purposes. By 1990 it became largely commercial. Internet now links several million people around the world through close to 1,000,000 "hosts."

Individual computers are usually linked to a host through local area networks which use wires owned by companies, universities, or some other organization. Hosts are linked together by long-distance, high-capacity lines leased from telephone companies.

Begun as a data-sharing mechanism using remote computers, and for the exchange of electronic mail between academic and corporate researchers and government officials, Internet now contains large and small, commercial and nonprofit networks that offer an astonishing array of services.

Nobody really knows how many hosts there are in the Internet system. Every few months a computer at Stanford Research Institute asks all the hosts that can receive it to tell Stanford who they are. Each time the system receives 20 percent to 30 percent more replies than the time before. Most recently, the new voices have come from hosts overseas and from companies that have grown up around the heart of Internet.

Another way of thinking about Internet: It is a network of 11,000 networks. It has 1.7 million computers interconnected as of the summer of 1993, with an estimated 15 million people all over the world using those 1.7 million computers. An individual can send a message to all 1.7 million computers, to one of the 11,000 networks, or address any one of the computers, or any single user of any such computer. Each user, computer, network, or host has a unique address.

On a per capita growth basis, Norway has more Internet hosts than any other country: almost 5 per 1,000 persons. The United States is next with 3.8 per 1,000, followed by Australia (3.7), Switzerland (3.4), Finland (3.2), Iceland (3.0), and Sweden (2.9). Germany has 1.4; Japan .2, about 1/20th as many hosts per capita as the United States.

If the present rate of growth of Internet users continues, there will be 300 million by 1999, 750 million by 2000, and 1.5 billion by 2001.

Theoretically all 5.5 billion people on the planet could be hooked up with each other on Internet, but only theoretically. In practice, hundreds of millions of people could in time be on the same network of networks. And just after the century turns, all those PCs could have the power of today's supercomputers.

Community Computer Networks

We are already seeing the development of community networks, which have been unfolding during the last three years, following the development of thousands of electronic bulletin boards in the 1980s. The best known of the community computer networks are Hawaii FYI (which is being partly used for cultural preservation and language instruction); a community network model called Freenet, used in many areas including Seattle, Santa Barbara, Denver, Buffalo, and Peoria; Wellington, New Zealand (65 percent of New Zealand households have computers); and Big Sky, Montana.

Essentially the community networks offer electronic mail and discussion groups for local users. They also provide a vast array of information, a few categories of which are job opportunities, health information, lifelong-learning schedules, bus schedules, calendars of events, local regulations, drafts of strategic plans for local development, reports from the local member of Congress.

The next stage is to start to link up local computer network communities with other such communities, in the direction of a web of networking communities in each country, and then global interconnection of all communities (local spiders, global web).

One country, Costa Rica, has begun the development of a nationwide computer network that will be linked with Internet.

Beyond Left and Right

Politically, the world has shifted from left vs. right to local vs. global, or universal vs. tribal. What will become universal? What will remain tribal? That cuts across the old political left and right and gives new leaders something to do. New leaders will help us balance the tribal and universal.

In the old world you had to choose between left and right. In the new world you choose global and tribal—both/and rather than either/or.

New leaders will facilitate—or at least not get in the way of—strategic alliances, not among governments but among individuals and companies. Just as in big business, strategic alliances are being formed among individuals, private institutions, and small companies.

The nature of leadership is changing because the power base is now spreading dramatically.

The new leadership will deal with many more issues as we go from ideology to pragmatism. The new leadership will be younger; there will be more women, and certainly more constituencies.

Paul Valéry, the French poet and critic, said, "Politics is the art of preventing people from taking part in affairs which properly concern them." That is what the old mainframe central governments used to practice. The new leadership will facilitate an extraordinary amount of free-market democracy in the new era of the personal computer.

As we need national leaders less, we hold them to higher standards.

That is because economic considerations, rather than political, are shaping leaders today, and we have better access to information against which to judge them.

What we are witnessing in the world today is not a chaotic bunch of isolated events but a process, a process of moving toward **the spread of governance without government.**

The grand vision aims to have all the individuals on earth eventually interconnected with interactive voice, data, image, and video capabilities. We have already come a considerable distance to make that a reality, as the next chapter explains.

ABB's Percy Barnevik describes his huge company as "a collection of local businesses with intense global coordination." Picture 1,000 autonomous countries around the world "with intense global coordination." Further, picture millions of individuals all over the world initiating projects and ventures with intense global coordination on a network of networks like Internet. This is linking citizens to citizens, and with prices continuing to come down, more and more people can participate. Today an inexpensive computer that will allow you to be on Internet costs $200; a state-of-the-art modem is $100, and prices will continue to drop.

The role of the new leadership in the world is to allow this to happen, to facilitate its realization. The role of the new political leadership is to clear the path for the increasingly smaller and more powerful parts.

We can now judge a country's economic viability by the extent to which the leadership of that country allows or facilitates the move from mainframe to collections of PCs.

Politics will reemerge as the engine of individualism.

Explosive growth follows when millions of people are liberated to contribute ideas and energy, rather than have everything come from a mainframe government.

IN SUMMARY

The world's trends point overwhelmingly toward political independence and self-rule on the one hand, and the formation of economic alliances on the other.

The bigger the world economy, the more powerful its smallest players, and all the big players are getting smaller.

The study of the smallest economic player, the entrepreneur, is merging with the study of how the global economy works.

Big companies are breaking up and becoming confederations of small, entrepreneurial companies in order to survive.

The result in all these areas is smaller and stronger units of the global economy. At once the global economy is growing while the size of the parts is shrinking.

In the years ahead all big companies will find it increasingly difficult to compete with smaller, speedier, more innovative companies.

The mindset that in a huge global economy the multinationals dominate world business couldn't have been more wrong. The bigger and more open the world economy becomes, the more small and middle-sized companies will dominate.

Competition and cooperation have become the yin and yang of the global marketplace. Cooperation is taking the form of a vast array of economic strategic alliances. Products can be produced anywhere, using resources from anywhere, by a company located anywhere, to a quality found anywhere, to be sold anywhere. This is being done through webs of strategic alliances. One of the reasons for the growth of strategic alliances is companies avoiding getting bigger.

Removal of trade barriers has opened the way for small companies to have easy access to markets. We are making business units smaller and smaller so we can more efficiently globalize our economies.

The almost perfect metaphor for the movement from bureaucracies of every kind to small, autonomous units is the shift from the mainframe to PCs, with PCs networked together.

The more universal we become, the more tribal we act, which in the Global Paradox also means more and smaller parts. The desire for balance between the tribal and the universal always has been with us. Now democracy and the revolution in telecommunications have brought this need for balance between tribal and universal to a more intense level. The new age mantra ''Think Globally, Act

Locally" is therefore turned on its head. It is now: Think Locally, Act Globally. Think Tribally, Act Universally.

Minority languages all over the world are achieving a new status as people hold more tightly to their heritage as ballast to the creation of a larger, more economically homogeneous world. Currencies—the language of commerce—are being both held on to as symbols of heritage and tradition and replaced if they have been imposed. We hold on to our language and our currencies even as, or because, we are becoming universal in so many other ways.

The more democracy, the greater the number of countries in the world. As the importance of the nation-state recedes, more of them are being created as we move toward a world of 1,000 countries. As the global economy gets larger, the component nation players get smaller and smaller. This will be a middle stage. As we move toward linking up millions of host computer networks, countries will become irrelevant and begin to fade away.

The idea that the central government—one huge mainframe—is the most important part of governance is obsolete, which means the end of politics as we have known it, as we shift from representative democracy to free-market democracy.

The deployment of power is shifting from the state to the individual. From vertical to horizontal. From hierarchy to networking. Power is flowing in all directions—unpredictable, a little chaotic, certainly messy—not well ordered like hierarchical, top-down arrangements.

Politically, the world has shifted from left vs. right to local vs. global, or universal vs. tribal. New leadership must help us sort this out as politics begins to reemerge as the engine of individualism.

It is a global shift from the state to the importance of the individual, and riding on the wave of the telecommunications revolution, the opportunities for individual freedom and enterprise are totally unprecedented.

2

Powering the Paradox: The Telecommunications Revolution

Powering the Global Paradox is the revolution in telecommunications.

Telecommunications is the driving force that is simultaneously creating the huge global economy and making its parts smaller and more powerful.

Telecommunications will provide the infrastructure every industry and every company will need to compete in a truly cosmopolitan marketplace. The telecommunications business will double and redouble as we drive toward global interconnectivity.

In the process, the telecommunications industry—which encompasses telephones, televisions, computers, and consumer electronics—has moved into a period of thrashing, creative chaos.

Essentially, four big ideas are struggling to be realized:

1. The blending of technologies. As computers, telephones, and televisions each are endowed with the capabilities of the others, there will evolve a splendid array of telephone/television/computer hybrids. The introduction

53

to the marketplace of these personal communication systems will be accompanied by a shift in focus for the telecommunications industry from solving the problems of business with technology to empowering individuals by greatly enhancing their ability to communicate with one another. The shift will be from business-driven to individual-driven. This is part of the Global Paradox. The bigger the world economy, the more important its smallest players. Companies that endure over the next few decades will exist to meet the communications needs of individuals.

2. Strategic alliances. Already, many strategic alliances have been formed to meet the needs of what will be the consumer-driven information age. The industry establishment and entrepreneurial upstarts alike are partnering at a dizzying pace, fully aware that no single company—and no single country—can alone be a successful player in the new global game.

3. Creating a global network. As the direction of the telecommunications revolution becomes increasingly clear, efforts are under way to create a seamless, global telecommunications network of networks that will allow everyone in the world to be connected with everyone else. This (mostly) digital global web of networks* will make it possible for individuals to communicate with anyone anywhere on the planet in real time, forever altering the way we work, the way we play, the way we move about, and the way we view our fellow citizens of the global network.

4. Personal telecomputers for everyone. Eventually,

---

*This network of networks is often referred to these days as an "information superhighway." This is not a good analogy. What is being put together now is a patchwork of local networks. It is being built from the bottom up in the marketplace. *Superhighway* has echoes of large-scale command and control systems (like the old Interstate system that had federal plans and standards and 90/10 matching grants and federal overseers). The networks are emerging; no one is in charge. The superhighway metaphor is a huge step backward just as we are entering the age of distributed systems. In time it will come to stand for what is really happening. In the meantime, it is not a helpful analogy.

everyone in an office or home or en route will be able to have telecomputers (maybe located in your purse or pocket) from which to send and receive communications by voice, data, image, and video. Telecomputing will become thoroughly decentralized, completely individualized, and will, among other things, further erode the centralized character of corporate giants that grew out of the industrial era as they give way to loose federations of small entrepreneurial-like companies. **Early in the information age of the twenty-first century all the communications capabilities we could possibly need will fit on our desk, in our car, or in the palm of our hand.**

This, too, then is a corollary of the global paradox. **As the power and reach of the communications infrastructure expands, the tools needed to harness that capability shrink.** They will become smaller, cheaper, lighter, and more portable. As we all become part of the greater global economy, the most efficient and effective economic unit becomes the individual.

The new revolution in telecommunications was announced on October 13, 1993, when Bell Atlantic and Tele-Communications, Inc. (TCI) said they would merge, a $30 billion telephone and cable marriage. It was like a thunderclap, at least to the media. On that day it seems that everybody "got it." The announced merger embodied a revolution that would change the world. And so it will.

Millions of Companies Created; Thousands Survive

Ever since the first modern electronic computer went on-line in 1944, there has been an underlying fear that machines endowed with the ability to analyze, to reason, and to interpret information would usurp control from people. Alarmists said that someday we would all be slaves to machines—big brother would have humanlike qualities, without the humanity.

The reverse has happened: The greater the power of technology, the more empowered its individual user has become.

The greater the capacity of computers to handle the complexities of modern life, the freer the individual to think of creative ways to exploit complexities.

The less we have to think about the mechanics of communication, the greater our ability to learn and to profit through the effortless sharing of information worldwide.

Information is power, but unlike earlier times, concentrating information in the hands of a few is no longer possible. That makes life, commerce, and economics even more complex than most of us can possibly imagine.

In the global economic network of the 21st century, information technology will drive change just as surely as manufacturing drove change in the industrial era.

We know that telecommunications is the force that is creating the global economy, but where is it taking us and what will the world be like when we get there? A look back at a similar period at the beginning of the automobile industry in the United States is instructive.

When we started to build cars, it was not clear what the automobile industry was: What would fuel it? What would it look like? What would be its capacity and speed? Who would buy it? What would it take for consumers to purchase a replacement?

During the first several decades of experimentation and growth, no fewer than 2,300 automobile companies were established in the United States. Now there are only three, plus, recently, Honda.

The telecommunications industry is in a similar period. The nature and character of the communications industry—which encompasses telephones, televisions, computers, and consumer electronics—is such that we will end up with hundreds of thousands of hardware and software companies rather than just a handful, but globally we will go through millions of companies to get there. And millions more companies will emerge to serve and support the new world economy.

These companies will be manufacturing the communications units (certain to be computer/television/telephone hybrids), building and maintaining the communications infrastructure, refining the technology that allows the effortless transport of information from point

A to point B, devising new applications for communications technologies and the information it carries, and untold other activities we haven't even thought of yet.

1. THE BLENDING OF TECHNOLOGIES. COMPUTERS, TELEPHONES, TELEVISIONS MERGE INTO ONE TELECOMMUNICATIONS INDUSTRY

The information age we are now creating will be based on all communications technologies and the networks that interconnect them. John Sculley describes it as a "post-industrial promised land where four giant industries—computers, consumer electronics, communications, and information—will converge."

Sculley believes that the convergence of these industries will give birth to, among other things, an affordable hand-held electronic personal assistant that works anywhere. This device will not only function like a computer—calculating, word processing, and tapping into databases anywhere in the world—but also will serve as a television, telephone, notetaker (using pen and voice), fax machine, mailbox, appointment calendar, and even a sketch pad.

John Sculley is convinced that today's junior video-game aficionados will be tomorrow's personal-technology consumers. And he's not alone.

Putting Your Office in the Palm of Your Hand

Personal intelligent communicators, personal digital assistants (PDA), personal communications devices (PCD), or picocomputers. Call them what you will, the world's communication-industry leaders call them big business. And best of all, there is no confusing computer lingo to master. Many of these devices will let you write on the screen in plain English; microprocessors do the rest.

Apple Computers is making a lot of noise about its personal digital assistant and has even set up a whole new division to market it. It's called Apple Personal Interactive Electronics—Apple PIE.

Apple PIE developed Newton, a hand-held machine that can understand handwriting and act as a sort of electronic assistant. Scrawl "lunch with Jane" on its screen and Newton will translate your handwriting into clean computer text, figure out who Jane is, schedule the lunch on your calendar, and send you a reminder of the appointment the day before. Not only that, it can fax a letter to Jane confirming the appointment. It is somewhat crude, but it is a beginning

Not a telephone, exactly, and not really a computer, the personal intelligent communicator will be to a generation raised on Nintendo, Game Boy, Sega, and Game Gear what videocassette recorders are to the television generation—a logical step in the journey toward greater personal freedom.

AT&T's first entry into the personal communicator systems sweepstakes is the Personal Communicator 440. Using a special AT&T microprocessor, the pen-based device was designed by EO Inc. of Foster City, California, developed by Go Corp. of Foster City, California, which is 50 percent owned by AT&T, and funded, in part, by two Japanese companies.

A host of other companies want to be players. IBM developed the IBM PC Radio. It resembles a notebook computer with an optional cellular telephone, and users can communicate by voice and fax and also tap into a central data base. Meanwhile, chipmaker Intel Corp. is working with Swedish phone-equipment maker Ericsson to produce a personal communicator system for sending and receiving E-mail that is interchangeably wireless and land-based. And Motorola developed Dragon, a PDA similar to Newton.

Several companies have either introduced or are about to introduce tiny hand-held personal computers called picocomputers. Computer giants like Sharp Electronics, the Sony Corporation, and Hewlett Packard, as well as start-ups like EO Computers, are feverishly working to put computers in the palm of your hand.

Picocomputers will be sold in stores like Kmart and Toys "R" Us and are expected to greatly increase the number of computer users. People who never learned to type don't have to take it up. The new machines will be operated by pen-type electronic styluses. Wireless radio and digital cellular technologies will make it possible to send and receive data.

Coming Together to Create Magic

Apple Computer, AT&T, Matsushita Electric Industrial, Motorola, Philips, and Sony are betting millions that a company with the rather fanciful name of General Magic can create and corner the market for the software for the next-generation communication device. Magic hopes its Telescript will become the "lingua franca" of mobile computing.

The company uses a rabbit jumping out of a magician's hat as its logo, so who could take it seriously? Everyone.

Remember ... it's the software!

Based in Mountain View, California, General Magic evolved out of Apple Computer's Advanced Technology Group. Denise Caruso, editor of *Digital Media,* explains the company's mission: "To develop the technologies that transform communication into a fundamental activity—the technological equivalent of breathing and paying taxes—for networks, information services, classical application software and electronic devices ranging from computers to hand-held organizers to telephones and other gadgets that haven't been invented yet.

"These technologies will be licensed to hardware manufacturers, software publishers and service providers, thus (hopefully) providing a ubiquitous platform for an even broader range of developers and information providers to create even more new services, communicating applications and hardware products."

Essentially, General Magic is working on two communications standards. The first, Magic Cap—CAP stands for Communication Application Platform—is an independent operating system that can be customized to interface with any existing computer application or information service. The second, Telescript, is a programming language, which will provide sophisticated communication functions wherever it resides. One example cited of how Telescript can enhance existing communications functions is the integration of Telescript with a traditional E-mail system.

Today's E-mail is passive and dumb. Send an E-mail and if the intended recipient is not available that message will sit there until someone retrieves it. Add Telescript and that same message will arrive with instructions as to what to do with the message if it is not retrieved. A message might be, "If she doesn't see this within two hours, send it to her secretary. If he doesn't get it, send it to her pager, and on to her cellular phone or to her home computer." On the flip side, the recipient who also has a Telescripted E-mail system can tell her system to simply ignore all messages coming from another system.

While the Magic Cap and Telescript can be used together, one does not require the other to perform. That's what all the excitement is about. And that's why six of the most powerful players in the telecommunications industry came together to make it happen. Each will undoubtedly take away from the partnership some piece of Magic Cap and/or Telescript and use it for the purpose of competing head-to-head with one of its General Magic partners. Welcome to a brave new world of telecommunications.

Certainly, being party to the development of state-of-the-art technology is intriguing to the partners, but the expectation of creating an industry worth billions (maybe trillions) of dollars contributes to their eagerness to cooperate with rivals toward a common goal. Of equal or greater importance is the partnership itself.

"Ten years ago, we were in our 20s and the industry was very different. We never gave a thought to cooperation. We were going to take over the world. We felt so strongly that we were in control of our destiny," says Joanna Hoffman, now vice president of marketing at General Magic, formerly a principal member of Apple's design team.

"Today, the industry is far more complex. There is a web of relationships in which companies cooperate and compete at the same time."

That six of the world's leading players would come together to develop the standards for the next generation computer technology is noteworthy. Not just for what it says about the market potential for these devices, but for what it tells us about future cooperation in the highly competitive, consumer-driven telecommunications industry.

Unplugging an Industry, Communications Goes Wireless

A decade ago, cellular telephones seemed little more than expensive gadgets for executives on the go. Market researchers at AT&T predicted that no more than 900,000 cellular phones would be in use in the United States by the year 2000. Still six years away from that date, that prediction has been eclipsed twelve times over, creating a $15 billion industry.

This market explosion is being repeated around the world. In Eastern Europe and other areas, wireless technology is being used to update phone services quickly—bypassing the need to install costly land-based, fixed-wire systems, which also take many times longer to install and are much more expensive.

Alone or in partnership, many companies are scrambling to create the units that will send and receive data. They also are working to ensure access to the pathways that will carry the data, to provide information services that will be accessed by these new communications units, and to ensure that wireless technology can be networked to ordinary phone systems.

In the United States more than 100 companies and groups—including cable TV operators—have petitioned the FCC to operate personal communication network systems. These systems will have twenty times the capacity of conventional cellular systems because hundreds of microcell transmitters will blanket a calling area.

In software, General Magic has signed AT&T and others to back its Telescript program as the language of wireless networks.

Today, all the big guns in the telecommunications industry are working on the next-generation wireless communications devices. Robert M. Kavner, a group executive with AT&T, likens the shift from fixed-wire systems to wireless networks to the shift from gaslight to electric bulbs, trains to airplanes, mainframes to PCs. Says Thomas E. Wheeler, president of the Cellular Telecommunications Industry Association, "We have just embarked on the wireless century." Yes, but a mix of pathways is the most likely.

Enthusiasm is high, but tempered by some marketplace realities, including considerations about space on networks, health, and costs. The Federal Communications Commission (FCC) has yet to allocate the radio spectrum needed for personal-communication network systems. Once allocated, it could still take years for the telecommunications infrastructure to catch up to the capabilities of the technology. Rumors linking cellular phones and brain cancer have not yet been laid to rest. Consumer concern for privacy might inhibit use of the technology.

Equally significant is cost. Most believe that such wireless devices will be accepted by the marketplace only if the accompanying price tag is $500 or less. At present, prototype units and those with limited capabilities already in the marketplace are priced considerably higher, upwards of $2,000. AT&T's Personal Communicator 440 carries a $3,000 price tag.

Nevertheless, true converts remain convinced that the market exists, that the technology soon will, and that the $500 price limitation will be met and thus will not be an issue by the time products are ready for mass marketing. What's more, the industry is counting on people's desire for greater independence, including the freedom to live and work anywhere. Observes Craig O. McCaw, chairman of McCaw Cellular Communications Inc.: ''Man started out as nomadic, it may be the most natural state for human beings.''

There is a ready-made market for these wireless gadgets among the executives and professionals who snapped up cellular phones when they became available. An even bigger and more technologically sophisticated market is the generation raised on Nintendo and Sega Genesis.

Wireless productivity

Even before the computer television telephone becomes available—at whatever price—simple wireless terminals are already changing the way service personnel and production workers do their jobs.

At Pitney Bowes technicians carry wireless terminals connected to the wireless Ardis network, a joint venture of Motorola and IBM. The setup tells technicians where their next service call is and provides them with information about the last date of service for the equipment they will be working on. If parts are needed, reps can order them over the Ardis system and have them delivered. Murray D. Martin, president of Pitney Bowes Copier Systems, credits the system with improved customer satisfaction and an increase in productivity of 12 to 15 percent.

According to George M. C. Fisher, former chairman of Motorola, "There's a very clearcut productivity argument." Corporate America seems to agree. Deloitte & Touche conducted a survey of 3,500 top executives: "more than 90 percent said that they expected wireless communications to boost productivity by the mid-1990s."

Once the price comes down, "these devices are really going to blow open the volume markets," said Brian P. Dougherty, chairman of Geoworks, a small Berkeley, California, company that is writing software for these small machines. "Each time you come down a factor of 10 in computer price you get more than a factor of 10 in growth of the market."

The Ultimate Personal Assistant Speaks Any Language

Of course, the ideal hand-held device would combine elements of all of these devices. It would be a wireless video phone with a fast notebook computer that recognizes human scribbles. Or take it one step further, a device that can do all the above and translate the spoken word from one language into another.

In January 1993, Toshiyuki Takezawa, a researcher with Japan's Advanced Telecommunications Research (ATR) Institute International in Tokyo, sat down at a bank of computers and spoke into a microphone, saying, "Moshimoshi." Twelve seconds later a computer in Pittsburgh conveyed Dr. Takezawa's message in English, "Hello."

Engineers call it automatic interpreting telephony; many others call it amazing. While the ability to dial anyone in the world and chat freely without language barriers is probably two decades away, by the end of this decade it is likely that the technology of interpreter telephones will be advanced enough to complete simple transactions like booking hotel rooms or airline reservations.

Meanwhile, there is much to be done and many players vying for
first place in the high-tech sweepstakes that will carry us into the
21st century. "The '90s are going to be a very confusing period
with a lot of silly, distracting, important products being introduced," says Paul L. Saffo, research fellow at the Institute for the
Future, a research foundation. "It may be that the winning industries at the end of the 1990s are none of the ones that dominate
today."

He's right. While most of the major players will likely still be
around, they won't look, or act, anything like the huge corporations
that have become household names in the past few decades. The
convergence of telephones, computers, and televisions is forcing
companies to look outside themselves for the expertise they lack.
Mergers, joint ventures, and creative alliances of all kinds are occurring at a dizzying rate as the three legs of the communications
industry move to become supporting players in the single telecommunications industry that will evolve.

2. STRATEGIC ALLIANCES ARE CREATING THE TELECOMMUNICATIONS INDUSTRY FOR THE 21ST CENTURY

The mating ritual has begun.

**Events unfolding today in the field of consumer electronics
will have an immediate, dramatic impact on how all of us receive and disseminate information.**

The first wave of strategic alliances is well under way. By 2000,
the lines between cable, telephone, and computer companies will
be completely blurred.

We are looking at a world in which the ordinary television set
allows viewers to select movies, TV programs, video games, educational programs, home shopping, banking, bill paying services,
reservations of all kinds, and counseling across the board. We are
looking at a world of information, communicating, learning, planning, and collaborating, and all of it accessed as easily as calling
your best friend.

Factor into this mix wireless technology—which includes satellite delivery, cellular phones, microwave, and new kinds of messaging units—and personal telecomputers, which can be programmed to receive television and radio signals as well as telephone transmission, and you have the blueprint for a revolution.

A dramatic benchmark for preeminence in the delivery to the home of communications services of all kinds came in early 1993 when Southwestern Bell Corporation announced its intent to buy two cable television systems in the Washington, D.C., area. While phone companies are not permitted to own cable companies where they operate phone systems, they can do so in markets outside their home territories.

"Everybody has been waiting for the first move by a telephone company," said Dennis Leibowitz, who tracks both the cable and the cellular telephone industry for Donaldson, Lufkin & Jenrette. "They want to get the experience of being in the cable business, and they want to offset the defensive risks that cable will offer competition in the phone business."

Stage Is Set for Alliances—and Raids

The stage has now been set for telephone to invade one another's territories and to do so in partnership with cable companies. And we can be sure that they will because each industry has strength in areas the other needs. "Cable companies can transmit enormous amounts of data," as *The New York Times* recently put it, "but are limited in their ability to offer two-way interactive services. Meanwhile, telephone companies have the sophisticated switching capabilities required for interactive technologies, but their transmission lines have limited capacity."

Southwestern Bell, which already owns a cellular-telephone franchise, wants a cable system to exploit the emerging field of inexpensive low-power wireless pocket phones. Cable systems are much more efficient than telephone systems in linking together personal communications devices.

Video-on-demand, or "dial-a-movie," service made possible by the marriage of the telephone and the television (and the computer, too, but that's another part of the story) is already available in some areas, but barriers remain.

Today, under current federal law, phone companies cannot own cable systems within their service territory. Now the door has been opened a crack by the FCC, which, despite the service-area ban, agreed to allow phone companies to offer "video dial tone"—the "ability to transmit video signals for all program suppliers, just as they now transmit conversations and data for business and residential customers."

Prior to Bell Atlantic and TCI's, one of the biggest deals was announced in June 1993 when U.S. West Inc., one of the regional Bell operating companies, agreed to pay $2.5 billion for a 25.5 percent stake in an entertainment subsidiary of Time Warner Inc., with holdings in movies and cable TV.

Other phone companies also are pursuing big cable deals. GTE Corp., for example, has been testing interactive video technologies and the demand for video services on a fiber-optic phone network in California. Not too long ago the company teamed up with Daniels Cablevision in Carlsbad, California, to introduce GTE Main Street. For $9.95 a month, 50,000 cable customers can use remote-control devices to tap into dozens of interactive educational, financial, shopping, and travel services for display on their television screens.

Elsewhere, according to *The New York Times,* Ameritech is testing a large-scale video service, a computer used to deliver full-motion videos, illustrations, audio, or text to employees over desktop computers. In Michigan, Ameritech is testing the fiber-optic delivery of nature and geography videos, encyclopedias on computer, and interactive programs to 115 fourth-graders over their home TV sets. Using a computer mouse linked to a TV converter box, "a nine-year-old can order programs chosen by teachers to supplement classroom work."

Cable Companies Fight Back

Cable companies, like giant Time Warner, are not about to stand by and let the phone companies be the big innovators. Time Warner, already big in pay-per-view movies and sporting events, is gearing up to beat the baby Bells at their own game—phone calls. In a move that shook up a lot of phone companies, Time Warner Inc. announced it would "deliver subscribers' phone calls over the existing cable-TV network" and offer 150 channels to subscribers in Queens, New York. The company will offer viewers selections from an extraordinarily large menu of programs and movies.

Time Warner claims its system will provide an unprecedented number of two-way capabilities including video phone calls, transmission of cellular phone calls, televised teaching, interactive video shopping, and electronic game playing between players in different homes.

Not to be outdone, Tele-Communications Inc., the world's largest cable company, headquartered in Denver, recently announced plans to upgrade its system, enabling it to offer 500 channels.

Time Warner says, make a selection from our enormous library.

Tele-Communications says, we are going to broadcast 500 channels simultaneously for you to select from. Also, multiple channels will be used to download vast amounts of information, using, for example, 200 channels all at once to download *Chariots of Fire* in three minutes to a hard disk on top of your TV.

Selecting from a large library what you want to watch seems to make more sense, except for serendipity. On one of those 500 channels there might be something of great interest to you that you didn't have the information or wit to ask for.

500 Channels and Nothing On

One can almost hear the complaints now: "500 channels and nothing on!" But competition and cooperation between telephone and cable companies isn't about watching television. It isn't *really* about video-on-demand, although certainly the companies' market research indicates that that is one of the things consumers want. It's about creating the channels through which all sorts of not-yet-created information can flow. And it's about creating options that you and I can't even envision yet.

Nor is this a simple showdown between two industries. As noted, in many cases, cable and telephone companies are working together.

- Phone company U.S. West has teamed up with cable Tele-Communications and long-distance carrier AT&T to test a movies-on-demand system in Littleton, Colorado.
- New Jersey Bell, choosing a different road than its parent Bell Atlantic, has a joint-venture TV project with Samson Communications, a New Jersey cable franchise.

As technology enables TVs to act like phones and computers, and lets phone lines carry TV shows and PC information, cable and phone companies will compete more directly and, paradoxically, cooperate more closely.

Computers Are Part of the Interactive Mix, and Technology Now Makes Stranger Bedfellows Than Politics

Wheels are turning among computer companies as well. Microsoft is intent on inventing an operating system for future TVs. Bill Gates says that by 2000, TVs will have the power of personal computers. The flow also goes in the other direction. Microsoft's hottest new product is Video for Windows, which lets a PC retrieve, store, and edit TV broadcasts. Gates intends this product to be the first brick in a path to future TV software.

Taking its very popular Windows program beyond the computer is the motivation behind Gates's meetings with Time Warner, Tele-Communications, and Paramount Communications. All three companies are interested in turning television into a more powerful communications tool. This was underscored by cable company Viacom's bid for Paramount in the fall of 1993.

- IBM has had conversations with Time Warner about collaborating on advanced digital cable-TV technology and with Tele-Communications about developing a two-way information system.

- AT&T is scheduled to spend $3.8 billion for a one-third stake in McCaw Cellular Communications, America's biggest cellular telephone operator, showing the importance of wireless systems and putting AT&T back in the local telephone business.
- MCI is testing the waters to gain acceptance for the creation of a consortium to run a national digital personal-communication network.

Meanwhile, Apple Computer is collaborating with Sharp Electronics and Toshiba to build consumer electronic products. Among other things Apple has licensed Newton to Sharp. The Japanese need the digital-programming skills at which American firms excel, while American companies need the Japanese experience with consumer electronics.

Cross-Industry, Cross-Border Alliances: Strategy for Growth

The trend toward telecommunications alliances is paying little attention to national borders.

Digital Equipment Corp. (DEC), like many of its competitors, crossed the ocean in an effort to increase its market share. DEC is buying 10 percent of Italy's Ing. C. Olivetti & Co. The Olivetti purchase was DEC's third such arrangement to gain market position in Europe. DEC bought the computer division of Philips, the Dutch electronics firm, and also formed a computer company with Mannesmann AG, a German conglomerate.

Cross-border strategies are not the preserve of U.S. companies. Stymied by small, insular markets and ever-escalating research and development costs, European computer manufacturers have been pursuing strategic alliances since the 1980s. The UK's ICL found a deep-pockets parent in Fujitsu of Japan. Finland's Nokia Data was later purchased by ICL, and Group Bull of France (already in partnership with Honeywell) accepted $100 million from IBM in exchange for a "small stake" in the company.

- BCE Inc., the Canadian telecommunications giant situated in a smallish home market, announced a major alliance with Cable and Wireless PLC, a leading British telecommunications company.
- In one of 1993's biggest deals, British Telecommunications PLC paid $4.3 billion for a 20 percent stake in MCI Communications Corp., the U.S. long-distance carrier. The two companies also plan to pour $1 billion into the joint venture. Their objective is to make the new company one of a few global carriers in the fast-growing market for global corporate network services. They face some stiff competition. AT&T already has launched Worldsource in partnership with Kokusai Denshin Denwa of Japan and Singapore Telecom for the same purpose, and its purchase of McCaw Cellular puts it into wireless.

As computer, telephone, and cable TV companies come to realize that their markets ultimately will be one and the same, cross-border, cross-industry alliances will become the norm. Joint ventures, mergers, and creative co-marketing arrangements of all kinds will quickly turn the three legs of the telecommunications industry into a single, global industrial sector, albeit made up of thousands of companies. Governments everywhere are liberalizing, paving the way for the telecommunications revolution.

Deregulation, Liberalization, and Privatization Will Accelerate

The deregulation of AT&T in the early '80s, along with the privatization of British Telecom (BT), was a harbinger for telecommunications. Other countries took courage and the privatization of the world's cumbersome, bureaucratic telecommunications monopolies began. There really was no other choice.

Argentina's president Carlos Menem put a For Sale sign on Entel, the country's telephone system, in 1989. At the time the country's economy was in what has been described as "terminal decline" and "a restructuring of the public sector was urgently needed" if the country was ever to recover (which it now has). While cash to help pay for the country's deficit was part of his motive in selling off Entel, Menem knew that an efficient telephone system was "essential for any modern economy."

Singapore Telecom, already one of the most modern and sophisticated telephone networks in the world, was privatized by the Singapore government for the express purpose of bringing in private investors to "assist with its transition from a state utility to a dynamic multinational competing for business in both its own and overseas markets."

Reinventing National Economies Through Privatization of Telephone Systems

Governments all over the world are betting that the private sector can do what the public sector, in all its cumbersome bureaucracy, cannot—reinvent national economies by turning over the communications infrastructure to private hands.

Latin America has been the most aggressive privatizer. Argentina, Mexico, Chile, and Venezuela already have sold majority shares in their national telephone companies, and Brazil, Uruguay, and Costa Rica have plans under way. African countries are catching on. Kenya, Nigeria, and the Sudan are working with the World Bank on privatization programs.

Across Europe, efforts to privatize are well under way in Germany, Sweden, Finland, Portugal, Hungary, Ireland, and Czechoslovakia. Countries of the Pacific Rim, such as Indonesia, South Korea, and Taiwan, also are planning for privatization.

Countries everywhere will release their monopoly stranglehold over telecommunications. The march toward deregulation, liberalization, and privatization will continue in quickstep. State-run telephone companies will disappear in the next century. Private information companies will stand in their stead, offering more service and lower costs in a world of global competition. But deregulation and liberalization must accompany privatization. Often not much is gained by going from a state monopoly to a private monopoly. There must be competition.

Managing the Revolution

Technology—specifically wireless communications—is rendering most of the old rules obsolete. Radio-based systems such as cellular telephones are no longer the province of the privileged elite. Technology is trickling down and prices are following suit. And with "roaming agreements" allowing radio-based phone users to make calls beyond national borders, any remaining pretense of control is slipping away.

In countries still struggling with the transformation from a central economy to a free-market economy—and still trying to shake off leftover Marxist, Leninist, Stalinist, or Maoist ideology—the path is not clearly marked.

In Marxist dogma, telecommunications networks were not a source of production but a burden on the economy, in addition to the mischief that could be caused by a lot of people talking to each other. Now, of course, all these countries want a state-of-the-art telephone system, but they don't how how to go about it.

All transitioning Communist governments know that while keeping information flow to a trickle might have been effective in suppressing democratic impulses in the past, today the lack of efficient communications is one of the greatest barriers to the transition from centrally planned to market economies, which cannot function unless companies can exchange information freely and efficiently.

Unless Eastern Europe and China and other countries in the Pacific Rim take enormous leaps forward in telecommunications, companies will be reluctant to invest in those regions. It is both interesting and instructive to watch events unfold as these regions prepare for the onrushing millennium.

The Fall of the Wall. Now What?

Nowhere is the need to make telephone services available a more urgent priority in stimulating economic growth than in the former Soviet Union and other once-Communist Eastern European countries.

Until quite recently, there were only 18 telephone lines between the old Soviet Union and the United States. Imagine. At any one time only 18 simultaneous conversations could take place between those two superpowers. Of course, the governments of Eastern Europe realize there is much to be done, and have plans to double or treble the size of their networks between now and the year 2000. Expanding telecommunications links between East and West is obviously a top priority.

Not surprisingly, the Western world's telecommunications companies are eagerly stepping into these new and growing markets. West Germany's Siemens, France's Alcatel, Sweden's Ericsson, AT&T, US West, Bell South, and Nynex of the United States, and Canada's Northern Telecom all are in active negotiations to form joint ventures with local companies across Eastern Europe.

Hungary, which like other Eastern European countries is suffering as a result of the collapse of its major trading partner, the former Soviet Union, has embraced cellular telephones as a means of bypassing woefully inadequate land-based systems.

Over the past four years, Westel Radiotelefon, a joint venture between the state-owned operating company and U.S. West, a regional Bell company, has extended telephone service to Hungary. Demand is twice as much as expected, with 1,000 people signing on each month. Although the cellular phones are outrageously expensive by American standards ($2,500 to buy, $1,000 to activate), the company is providing a much-in-demand service for a country with only 1 million land-based telephones for 10.5 million people.

The Hungarian government plans to spend $1.7 billion in government funds and Western loans to upgrade its telephone system. Installing a cellular network makes it possible to take a giant step forward today while the rest of the system plays catch-up.

Pacific Rim Plays Catch-up with International Joint Ventures

Even the government of mainland China, which knows all too well from its experience during the Tiananmen Square incident the impact instantaneous worldwide communications can have on political events, is nonetheless concentrating its efforts on building a state-of-the-art telecommunications infrastructure.

The Chinese, however, have not given up the reins as far as national security considerations are concerned. China's premier Li Peng is not about to let telecommunications slip completely out of government control. Sole regulatory responsibility for its operation is in the hands of the Ministry of Post and Telecommunications (MPT).

At the same time, the State Council limited to three the number of Sino-foreign joint ventures allowed to manufacture stored-program control (telephone) exchanges (SPCs), which are the mainstay of China's telecommunications expansion.

To date, there are two big foreign-money winners. The first is France's Alcatel, with a 30 percent share of line capacity already secure. Much of this capacity was inherited when Alcatel purchased Belgium Bell, which had a controlling interest in Shanghai Bell. The second is the United States' AT&T with a $1.2 billion contract to install switching systems—almost certain to blossom into a multibillion-dollar deal by the year 2000.

Two other players are a Beijing joint venture with Siemens of Germany and one with Japan's NEC in Tianjin. While "long-term prospects look dim," reports *The Far Eastern Economic Review,* just now for the world's other major suppliers, including Fujitsu, Northern Telecom, and Ericsson, none has given up hope that China's relentless drive to develop an integrated-service digital network to handle voice, data, text, and image transmission will open up opportunities for all of them. Eventually it will. In many cases they will come in through the joint ventures China will make with other Asian countries—where these international companies already operate.

Especially considering that all of the world's major telecommunications-equipment manufacturers now have partnerships, joint ventures, or subsidiaries elsewhere in Asia. As China continues to shift from a central economy to a market economy, the number of joint ventures between mainland companies and Asian neighbors increases. This will be no less true for the telecommunications industry.

In most Asian countries the strategy is to serve local markets by making parts under licensing agreements or building entire systems. Ultimately, the plan is to create an export market for components, whole units, or entire systems.

Taiwan

Taiwan's Directorate General of Telecommunications (DGT) has drafted a Six-Year Plan (1991–1996) that includes a $5.7-billion expansion of telecommunications services. Many components of the government's huge controversial infrastructure plan are behind schedule, but its telecommunications timetable has been accelerated.

Taiwan's intent is to become a regional financial center. To meet that goal it must expand its telecommunications infrastructure, including fiber-optic lines and radio-based communications.

In this sector, competition among international telecommunications companies has been intense.

- Sweden's Ericsson won a $66-million contract to expand the island's cellular telephone network.
- Motorola's Taiwanese associate, Motorola Electronics Taiwan, Inc., will contribute $1 million in software toward the effort. Motorola also obtained a $3.4-million contract to install equipment and services for 1.2 million paging units using Chinese character displays.
- Britain's Cable and Wireless will provide $8 million worth of support services.

Meanwhile in the Philippines

The backlog in Manila for telephones is estimated at 300,000. The city already accounts for 69 percent of the country's telephone lines. Meanwhile, the booming tourist and export center of Cebu has only 7 percent of the country's lines.

Heated competition among telecommunications multinationals is slowly eroding the Philippine Long Distance Telephone Company's (PLDT) monopolistic hold on telecommunications. While the company is determined to hold its monopoly, so far with the government's blessing, it is nevertheless going overseas for technical know-how. PLDT's principal technical partner is AT&T, while it gets much of its equipment from Siemens of Germany.

While tiny steps have been taken in the form of government approval to allow Philippine Global Communications and Eastern Telecommunications Philippines Inc. to open their own international services, the government will have to take much bigger steps to fill the enormous demand for services.

The National Telecommunications Development Plan estimates it will take $8.8 billion to raise the number of telephones from 1.5 per 100 people to 3.5 by 2010. PLDT can't do it alone; the government will have to untangle a complicated web of policy and protectionism if it is ever to accomplish its goal.

It's Not Either/Or but Finding the Right Mix

The developing world has a distance still to travel to catch up with the United States, Canada, and Europe, both to match the sophistication of their infrastructure and to eventually become part of the global infrastructure. In many areas, development has slowed as decision makers debate the relative merits of the innumerable communications systems available. What they are finally learning is that building a telecommunications infrastructure is not an either/or proposition. What's important is to find the right mix and to keep the systems open to future upgrades.

Pakistan and Bangladesh have both gotten the message. With the goal of stimulating economic development through the improvement of their telecommunications infrastructure, both countries are using a mix of technologies to achieve their goals. Satellite, cellular, and fiber optics all are part of that mix, and even as they move toward a totally digitized system, neither has plans to abandon the analog, copper-wire, land-based systems just yet.

And finally, both seek to develop alliances with international telecommunications companies for the purpose of obtaining suppliers' credit and technology transfer.

This is, in fact, an area in which rich countries—both technologically rich and financially rich—can help poorer and less developed countries.

Along with privatization and education, nothing can contribute more to a developing country's economic well-being than a state-of-the-art telecommunications infrastructure.

With the help of companies from the developed world, many developing countries will replace their copper-wire systems with fiber optics, wireless, and satellite systems, where appropriate. They will benefit immensely from the lessons learned by others. They can do it right the first time. Indeed, it gives them a chance to leapfrog many developed countries into the 21st century.

Europe

In Europe the members of the European Commission (EC) are in heated debate over the role of telecommunications networks in the further development of a single European market. As discussed earlier, each member country is in a different stages of deregulation, liberalization, or privatization. As the pace of the market accelerates, the debate becomes more heated.

The European telecommunications industry, bound up by parochial interests and friendly to protectionism, may be forced by global competition to see what it may otherwise remain blind to forever: that total competition, both domestic and international, is necessary for economic union and long-term survival.

The decision of whether to press for full liberalization of "voice telephony" (voice traffic on the telephones) in the EC will be formally made by the 17 commissioners. The marketplace nevertheless has dictated the outcome. In an address delivered at a Telecommunications Conference, sponsored by Northern Telecom and *The Economist,* Vicenzo Morelli, senior vice president of Northern Telecom Europe, presented a persuasive argument for the rapid liberalization of the European telecommunications market.

Observed Morelli, ''As the largest business customers extend their reach around the world they are demanding increasingly global arrangements with suppliers. . . . We need radical innovation in the areas of regulation, finance and marketing to match the power of the technology we have available. . . .

''Behind all of these developments are customers who will set the pace of change in Europe and, if we follow our customers, many other borders will become artificial and obsolete, and maybe even disappear. The challenge for all of us—telephone operators, regulators and customers, new entrants and consumers alike—is to move forward faster than we have in the past, without further delay, to recognize and agree on the new common ground on which we can all stand.''

New Satellite Systems

Some of the more interesting developments in communications technology are occurring in the satellite arena. Already, STAR TV (which Rupert Murdoch recently ingested) is blanketing China with television. It is a short hop until satellites provide communications services to individuals or communities at competitive prices.

Hughes is scheduled to launch by the beginning of 1994 the first of its direct-broadcast satellite (DBS) transmitters. This satellite will be capable of covering the United States with about 150 simultaneous channels. These satellites offer breakthrough technology with implications for the future of information delivery and exchange: 1) Their signals are digital, rather than analog as in current satellites, implying nearly lossless transmission. 2) The digital signals are compressed so each satellite can handle about 10 times the channels of analog satellites. One satellite can carry all the programming currently carried on multiple satellites, eliminating the need to reposition antennas for each group of channels. 3) The satellite is oriented so that its solar panels are continuously in line with the sun. This allows the power output of each satellite transponder to be 12 times that of current models. With a strong signal, the receiving antenna need be only 18 inches across. 4) The ground antenna and decompression box will cost only $700.

This is an almost perfect platform for information delivery. Experience has shown that the $700 figure will be reduced $100 the first year and $10 the second. In the same way that STAR now covers China with channels of TV, these satellites could easily deliver vast quantities of data.

More Strategic Alliances

While EC officials and governments in Eastern Europe and the Pacific Rim debate the relative benefits of opening telecommunications markets, the newly liberated industry is moving forward. Rushing to catch up to other globalized sectors such as financial services, automobile manufacturers, and pharmaceutical companies, the world's telecommunications companies aren't waiting for their marriages to be blessed by the powers that be.

With the impetus of a multibillion-dollar global communications market growing bigger every day, the world's telecommunications companies are partnering at a frenetic pace. France Telecom, AT&T and MCI in the United States, the UK's BT, Japan's NTT, and Germany's Deutsche Telecom are all talking to one another and to one another's rivals in a mating ritual that would be comical if so much wasn't at stake.

Without a Telecommunications Infrastructure, Economies Will Fail

Here in the early 1990s, why all this fuss about telephones? Well, it isn't about telephones really, it's about information—the crude oil that will fuel the economic engines of the 21st century. Telephones or, more accurately, telecommunications equipment, which includes televisions and computers, and the systems that carry telecommunications traffic—including voice, text, data, and images—are the transportation networks without which economies will cease to function.

It's about a new global order shaped by information technologies. It's about profits and being competitive. It is about the world's telecommunications businesses merging and partnering at ever-increasing rates.

And it is about connecting smaller and smaller units as the global economy gets larger and larger.

Following today's pattern among global manufacturers, financial institutions, and merchandise retailers, more and more industries will operate in a single, worldwide marketplace.

3. CREATING A SEAMLESS, GLOBAL, DIGITAL NETWORK OF NETWORKS

To dramatize what the outcome will be when all the pieces are in place, Randall L. Tobias, former vice chairman of AT&T, told the following parable:

"A theologian asked the most powerful supercomputer, 'Is there a God?' The computer said it lacked the processing power to know. It asked to be connected to all the other supercomputers in the world. Still, it was not enough power. So the computer was hooked up to all the mainframes in the world, and then all the minicomputers, and to all the personal computers. And eventually it was connected to all the computers in cars, microwaves, VCRs, digital watches and so on. The theologian asked for the final time, 'Is there a God?' And the computer replied: 'There is now!'"

While we are some years away from that kind of interconnectivity, we are not so far away as you might think. Even so, once we achieve that degree of connectedness and the awesome power that will result, machines will not become more God-like. Quite the reverse, the greater the power of the machine, the greater the power of the individual. The machinery of the 21st century will exist in and accommodate our world, not the other way around.

Compounding of Capabilities Gives Information Its Speed and Power

According to Michael Dertouzos, director of the Laboratory for Computer Science at MIT, "Independent of each other, computing and communicating tools have been improving at the annual rate of some 25 percent for at least the past two decades. This relentless compounding of capabilities has transformed a faint promise of synergy into an immense and real potential."

We need more and better networks and computers because the amount of information that has to travel on them is growing exponentially.

Stephen Hall, down the road from Dertouzos, at Harvard, where he is director of the Office for Information Technology, says: "We are finding that in the worlds of networking, higher education, and research the annual rate of growth doubles every six or seven months." Hall points out that "this is an incredible rate of growth. There aren't many things today that experience that kind of growth. It's tremendously popular, because there is very good information contained in a network that people can access in their work."

Computers can be found nearly everywhere. They are powerful and they are inexpensive. Today, there are more microprocessors (computers on a chip) than there are people on earth, and their ability to process enormous amounts of information keeps expanding. By the year 2000, it will be possible to put as much computing power on a desktop as is currently available on a supercomputer.

In an effort to put that rate of progress in perspective for his audience, Tobias updated the automobile comparison, saying: "If we had had similar progress in automotive technology, today you could buy a Lexus for about $2. It would travel at the speed of sound, and go about 600 miles on a thimble of gas."

Of course, today's highways would be totally inadequate. The same could be said of today's information highways. Throughout most of the world, development of the information infrastructure has not kept pace with the development of technologies that propel information through the system.

This is not to say that great strides have not been made. In fact, the reach and speed of networks have taken enormous leaps forward.

Explains Dertouzos: "Millions of miles of glass fibers handle most long-haul communications and are capable of relaying data at speeds of up to a billion bits (gigabits) per second. Local area networks have become indispensable webs, wiring numerous buildings and neighborhoods. Cellular and other wireless networks reach people while they are driving or even walking. And now these two giants, computers and networks, can be fused to form an infrastructure even more promising than the individual technologies."

Today's companies utilizing the new technologies can efficiently manage far-flung operations. Mazda, for example, produced a sports car designed in California, financed in Tokyo, and assembled in Michigan and Mexico. Some of its advanced electronic components were invented in a lab in New Jersey but manufactured in Japan. Mazda is but one of *hundreds of thousands* of companies worldwide that conduct business courtesy of anytime, anything, anywhere communication capabilities.

70 Million Simultaneous Conversations

With fiber optics, each light pulse represents data—voice, text, or images. We can now transmit 3.4 billion bits a second, the equivalent of 50,000 simultaneous phone calls on a single pair of fibers. Soon it will be possible to transmit one trillion bits per second or about 70 million simultaneous conversations on a single pair of fibers. These speeds and volumes are possible because the messages are digitized, and hence the continuing debate over whether tomorrow's communication channels should be 100 percent digital. And if so, how are we going to finance the system, install it, and keep global communications channels open while we do it? The answer is we are not going to "do it"; it already is happening.

Fiber, satellite, cellular, microwave, and the old standby, analog, copper-wire systems (aided by new compression technology, but more on that later) will all be part of the interconnected network of networks.

Oh, What a Tangled Web We Weave . . .

Those who work in an office are probably passingly familiar with local area networks (LANs). LANs are the systems that connect a company's desktop computers to the server—either a mainframe or, increasingly, another personal computer—that manages the flow of information through the system.

Fewer of us are familiar with the much more sophisticated networks that link together multisite corporate offices, universities, research laboratories, and governments. But these are the networks now being developed that all of us will one day be connected to.

First to introduce networking to wide-ranging audiences were the on-line information services like Prodigy, Compuserve, and America Online. Although suited to their purpose—dispensing electronic information simultaneously to thousands of users connected to the system—they are based on the limited technologies of the minicomputers and mainframes of the 1960s and 1970s. Among other limitations, the systems could become congested and users were limited in their options.

In the first chapter I talked about Internet, the world's largest network. There are many more networks and "bulletin boards" that allow like-minded people to keep in touch with one another—electronic tribalism—or to enhance productivity.

Wireless Webs

Less ambitious than Internet in its outreach, but no less revolutionary in its own field, is the mobile data network being created by America's United Parcel Service. Called UPSNET, it will keep track of the one million or so packages picked up and delivered by the company each day. More than 50,000 UPS trucks are linked to UPSNET via mobile telephones; many are also automatically and continually located via Global Positioning System satellites. Federal Express Corp. also built its own private radio network to keep track of the millions of packages that pass through its hub. Customers can call a central number and within seconds a dispatcher can tell them exactly where their package is and when they can expect delivery. If checking on a delivery, the dispatcher can tell customers who signed for the package and when.

Airborne Express has a similar tracking service. For companies that need to keep track of mass mailings, Airborne's central computer can download to a company's system. Say you have a mailing of 50,000 or 100,000 packages and it is absolutely critical that you know when they are delivered. The data collected by Airborne's delivery team is fed directly into a central computer, including tracking number, address delivered to, time delivered, and a facsimile of the signature of the individual who signed for the package. Within 24 hours that data is sent to the customer's computer. When the shipping managers come to the office in the morning, they simply turn on their computers, select the appropriate file, and *voilà!*, they know exactly what happened with every one of those packages. For many users the concept of real-time determination of *physical* location is of paramount importance. UPS went so far as to acquire II Morrow, Inc., a leading manufacturer of aircraft navigation systems, so that a dispatcher knows at once where every truck is (as well as which packages are aboard).

The potential use of such systems for an array of service providers is obvious. Motorola's market research suggests that the market for two-way wireless setups will reach $5 billion by the year 2000, by which time it is estimated that as many as 20 million U.S. workers will be walking around with wireless data terminals. I expect the numbers will be higher.

Networks Meet Individuals' Need to Communicate

For the free-spirited computer users among us, there is USENET, an international network linking millions of people eager to debate politics, or technology, or any other point of common interest via their computers. All one needs to do to join USENET is to find a member who will forward messages to your machine and agree to forward mail and news to others.

USENET is just one of nearly 60,000 electronic bulletin boards used by technophiles to communicate with others of like mind. If you can think of a topic, there are others who share your interest and who have the equipment to chat with you about it anytime, day or night. Computers and the networks to which they are linked are changing how people interact with one another in fundamental ways.

Like virtually all innovations that ultimately become ubiquitous, data networking emerged from the bottom up, not the top down.

Stimulated not by high-speed data highways, but by local area networks that companies and laboratories built so that workers and researchers could more effectively collaborate and pool data, networks evolved to address a pressing need.

Larger networks evolve when small networks fuse. Vijay Gurbaxani of the University of California found that networks tend to grow exponentially. With the addition of each new LAN, the benefits of joining rise as each new network provides many more people to talk to, while at the same time the cost of joining declines.

In articulating the broad impact of networks on how we all communicate, Dertouzos explains: "In a world in which hundreds of millions of computers . . . easily plug into a global information infrastucture, business mail would routinely reach its destination in five seconds instead of five days. . . . Consumers would broadcast their needs to suppliers, creating a kind of reverse advertising. Many goods would be ordered and paid for electronically while purchasers take care of children at home.

"A retired engineer in Florida could teach algebra to high school students in New York City. And from a comfortable position in your easy chair, you could enjoy a drive through your next vacation spot, a trip through the Louvre, or a high-definition video rented electronically, chosen from the millions available."

Although few dispute that a seamless, global-information network of networks will eventually connect everyone on earth to everyone else, naysayers and skeptics, nonetheless, insist that such interconnectivity is decades away. It will be too expensive to rewire the world with fiber optics, they argue, and no industry can justify investments in the billions of dollars with no guarantee of a return. These same people are convinced that the status quo will remain in place for years to come. Meanwhile, network by network, it is already happening.

Hybrid Networks

The world doesn't have to have an intricate web of fiber to achieve the *level of interconnectivity* needed; we already have what we need. The information highways of the future will not be constructed with *either* fiber or copper wire, *either* satellite or microwave, *either* telephones or cable systems, computers or televisions. They will be made of all of those things. By finding the right mix of technology, by forming the right partnerships, and by moving the political and regulatory processes along, we already are building the global-information "superhighway."

What is evolving is a hybrid network. Mitchell Kapor, developer and founder of Lotus 1-2-3 and now chair and co-founder of Electronic Frontier Foundation, explains. "Networks that reach into the home will be hybrids of the fiber-optic cable and existing copper wire and coaxial cable used by telephone and cable television companies. Fiber-optic cables will be used in the major arteries and portions of the distribution system, while existing copper and coaxial cable will be used in the last hundred yards.

"To achieve a broadband network capable of delivering high-quality video, voice, and data, it is both unnecessary and too expensive to replace the last segment into the home with fiber optics."

For a while in the mid-1980s, people got so excited about fiber optics they forgot about everything else. **Today, telephone and cable companies are learning that skillful use of existing technologies in combination with intelligent application of new technologies can achieve almost the same degree of sophistication as could be achieved by using only state-of-the-art technology.** While there ultimately may exist a completely fiber-optic information infrastructure, for the foreseeable future the communications highway will be a hybrid system.

Essential to the creation of this hybrid system was the pioneering work of researchers at Bell Communications Research Corp. (Bellcore), the research and development arm of Bell Operating Companies, which is being tested by Bell Atlantic, one of the "baby Bells." Bellcore came up with a way to circumvent the need for a fully fiber-optic cabling by developing a technique to jam full-motion video through existing copper wires.

Compressed Video Pictures

It is called asynchronous digital subscriber line (ADSL). And it uses digital signal processing and electronic circuitry to send *compressed* video pictures through ordinary copper wiring. Amazingly, there is enough capacity left over to carry phone conversations as well. With the announcement of the development of compression technology, Lanny Smoot, a Bellcore researcher, exclaimed: "What we have is a complete, end-to-end system that lets people move a video store into their own homes."

Arthur Bushkin, president of Bell Atlantic Corp.'s information services company, was a bit more reserved, saying: "For now, we have a technology that allows us early market entry with services our customers want. But we believe fiber optics will be the technology of choice for the future."

Bushkin may have understated the potential of ADSL. It cannot yet replace cable systems, because it can send only one channel at a time. Furthermore, it cannot serve households with more than one television in use at a time. Still, these technical limitations are temporary. Within two years the technology will be sufficiently developed to carry live news and sports as well as to serve households using multiple televisions at the same time.

The "fiber-or-bust" mentality of the '80s and the early '90s is quickly giving way to a more practical, bottom-line–driven, "find ways to use what we have" philosophy.

ADSL is gaining converts as a means of transitioning to higher-capacity networks without losing customers in the meantime.

Nynex views ADSL as a critical transition technology. Says Bob Lawrence, technical director of the transmission and video systems laboratory at Nynex's Science and Technology subsidiary: "With 160 million miles of copper in place, Nynex definitely wants to mine the full potential of our copper." He adds that even once fiber is being deployed, it will take a long time to pull out that tremendous volume of copper. That's 1500 miles of copper per Nynex employee. I don't know how long it will take me to get my 1500 miles out, but it ain't going to be overnight.''

ADSL emerged from the same Bellcore research that produced ISDN—Integrated Services Digital Network. Designed for the public switched telephone network, ISDN allows low-cost communication in data, voice, graphics, and video. Like ADSL, it is designed to use the existing local copper loop that connects the telephone company's central office to homes and offices.

Through the National ISDN-1 program, the Bell companies, long-distance carriers, and information providers are agreeing to standards for hardware and software protocols. That is critical if ISDN is to be integrated into the information networks.

In Kapor's network scenario, hybrid networks will deliver a full range of interactive services to home and office at a fraction of the cost of a fully fiber network. He envisions a highway that includes the convergence of separate cable systems into regional hubs, which, in turn, will be interconnected to form a national network. High-capacity video file services capable of storing thousands of hours of programming will be attached at the regional level. Existing cable systems ultimately will be replaced by high-capacity, noiseless fiber-optic cable reaching from the system's head into each neighborhood. The last segment of the network, from the node to the home or office, will use existing coaxial cable. This is the arrangement that both Time Warner and TCI intend to use.

4. PERSONAL COMPUTERS FOR EVERYONE. AN EVOLUTION IN TELECOMMUNICATIONS TECHNOLOGY IS CREATING A REVOLUTION IN INFORMATION SHARING

What does all this mean to the average person? History is again instructive. Technologies introduced at critical junctures almost always generate a great leap in economic development. In the 19th century in the United States it was construction of the transcontinental railway. In the 20th century, three developments—electric power, the automobile, and the interstate highway system—gave birth to new industries and accelerated job production.

Completion of the interstate highway network (if indeed it could ever be called complete) made possible such industries as courier services, fast-food restaurants and hotel chains, and the efficient delivery of goods of all kinds. Building highways wasn't about mixing and pouring concrete; it was about efficiently transporting people and goods from place to place.

Similarly, the space program championed by John F. Kennedy wasn't about putting a man on the moon; it was about creating new technologies, expanding the country's economic horizons, and accepting and meeting challenges that would teach us how to do things differently.

And certainly technologies emerging out of the space program have been put to good use in the telecommunications industries.

Computer companies typically emphasize the benefits of people *working* with computers, but the real benefits, which will be increasingly realized over time, are quite the reverse. Telecommunications and its infrastructure put people in touch with one another. They will have an extraordinary impact on the social, political, and economic climate in the global community. The telecommunications revolution is really about enabling broader access to information.

All this telecommunications activity is leading us in the direction in which we have always been going since the beginning of time. Through the ages, humanity has demonstrated a yearning to enrich life by sharing information to increase knowledge. This as yet unsatisfied desire has triggered a revolution in global telecommunications that will make dramatic changes in the way we communicate tomorrow.

An evolution in telecommunications technology is creating a revolution in information sharing.

Just as we are globally moving to one economic marketplace, we are moving in telecommunications to a single worldwide network of information networks, with everything linked to everything else.

At present, there are some practical limitations to network

growth. Commercial and regulatory arrangements will have to be reached between companies and, equally important, within and between countries.

A number of elements integral to the creation of this global network have yet to fully evolve. Universal standards of information packaging need to be agreed to and the world's information-transportation system needs to be installed where there is none and upgraded where it is inadequate.

What will evolve from all of this is a very real global community that exists in what "techies" call cyberspace, a place that is, as Kapor writes, "more egalitarian than elitist, and more decentralized than hierarchical. . . . In fact, life in cyberspace seems to be shaping up exactly like Thomas Jefferson would have wanted: founded on the primacy of individual liberty and a commitment to pluralism, diversity, and community."

Digital Technology Will Impact Every Aspect of Our Lives

Digital technology is the key to the successful completion of the information infrastructure. It also is the technology that will reinvent the way people live, work, and entertain themselves. Bill Gates, Microsoft Corp.'s pioneering president, describes what is happening as the creation of a "new digital world order." It is a technological revolution that will enhance almost all of our previous technologies and our lives.

In December 1992, employees of Sun Microsystems got a small preview of what is to come in the form of a digitized global greeting card from Sun chairman Scott McNealy.

On December 15, 1992, at 10:00 A.M., any one of Sun's 13,000 employees in the United States, England, Scotland, Brazil, Japan, Germany, the Netherlands, France, and Hong Kong could open a 2.5-inch-square window on their computer screen and watch as Scott McNealy wished them holiday greetings from his office in Palo Alto, California.

Facsimile transmissions are possible because data can be translated into the 1's and 0's read by microprocessors, transported in packets over telephone wires, and reassembled in recognizable form at the other end. What's more, digital technology permits much greater fidelity and clarity than analog technology.

All communication—voice, text, image, and video—can be translated into the 1 and 0 language of the microprocessor, which means all four can be sent through the telephone lines and reassembled on the receiving end. Each bit of information, regardless of its original form, travels in an individualized packet. Each packet takes up the same amount of space on the system as every other, although some have to travel at a higher rate of speed than others in order for all to arrive at their destination in time to be reassembled.

However, information packets from any one communication do not have to travel together, so voice, video, and text can all be sent through the system at the same time in whatever order of priority microprocessors assign. Each information packet is appropriately labeled (a sort of computerized shipping tag) so that computers at the other end know which communication medium the packet belongs to.

Digitization Makes It Possible to Communicate in Real Time

Digitization will consummate the marriage among television, computers, and telephones, making it possible to communicate with anyone, anywhere, anytime. Scientists and researchers, although geographically separated by continents, will be able to work on the same project in real time, heightening their collaborative opportunities. Events, ideas, and innovations will be shared almost as soon as they occur, greatly accelerating the rate and perhaps even the acceptance of change.

Business problems that took months to solve as managers in far-flung offices awkwardly attempted to work together will soon be addressed by co-workers in separate locations tapping into the same database, pulling the same files up on their PC screens, and chatting via telephone or electronic mail about the best approaches and the most workable solutions. Situations that might once have required an overseas flight will now be resolved in cyberspace. Problems can theoretically be solved in one quarter of the time.

Corporations will save millions of dollars in needless travel as some meetings are held via satellite video conferencing. International relations could be revolutionized via digitized communications: Why couldn't world leaders meet via television—a sort of digital, high-tech negotiating table—for peace, for trade and commerce? Television channels in effect will become diplomatic channels. National boundaries will be only lines on the map as business and commerce flow freely in a borderless, digitized global economy.

In the very near future, anyone equipped with the right technology may choose to be a spectator at any world event as it occurs, from world soccer to the Paris spring collections to the elections in Paraguay, when the three legs of the telecommunications industry—television, computers, and telephones—merge to create a worldwide network connecting people to one another and to sources of information. Once the three merge, it will forever alter the political and cultural landscape in ways we can't yet imagine.

Individual Freedom Takes On New Meaning with Digitization

Perhaps the greatest benefit will be personal freedom. In a world of digital telecommunications, individuals will be free to work wherever on this planet they choose to live. Personal computers and wireless personal-communications devices will permit us to keep in touch with the office from wherever we are. Or, to look at it from a new perspective, wherever we are will be the office.

Individuals soon will be able to get lifelong personal telephone numbers, making it almost impossible to miss important phone calls. No longer will you have to be at a certain place to receive a call. Your computerized personal assistant will keep track of your whereabouts and forward calls to you wherever you happen to be. And, yes, you will be able to turn them off, reject calls, or forward calls to electronic message centers for later retrieval.

Language barriers will crumble: That critical call from your Japanese or European counterpart will come through to you in English.

Messages back to them will be translated into their language. Finally, telecommunications will overcome all the major barriers to
a truly global economy—time, distance, and language. (That leaves
the human high-touch side—peace and understanding—with still a
lot of work to do.)

Shaping Our Digital Future

Predictably, everyone is vying with everyone else to shape our
digital future. Consumer electronics and computer companies are
scrambling to create the magical boxes that will direct the digital
flow. At the same time, local phone companies, cable operators,
and even the water and gas utilities are each determined to win the
race to pave the digital highway that will carry all that data into
homes, schools, and offices.

Meanwhile, the media industry—publishers, movie studios, and
broadcasters—envision streams of dollar signs along with the
streams of 1's and 0's as they convert enormous libraries of books,
reference works, films, and video footage into digital "cash cows."

Observes Intel Corp. president Andrew S. Grove, "What's mo-
tivating all of us is greed." That's strong motivation. John Sculley
thinks the digital market will be worth more than $3 trillion by the
year 2000.

Market research firm Paul Kagan Associates predicts that by
1996, the U.S. market for digital cable converters will reach 4.5
million units annually, as cable companies upgrade the 65 million
converter boxes now in use. The new boxes will cost between $200
and $300 apiece, about twice as much as current cable boxes.

Everyone from chipmaker Intel Corp. to electronic gamemaker
Sega Enterprises is teaming up with cable companies. Every week
brings another announcement. PC industry leaders Intel and Microsoft are teaming up with General Instruments, today's leading supplier of converters. Time Warner is joining forces with
Scientific-Atlanta and Toshiba. And AT&T is working with General Instruments Corp. to provide boxes to Telecommunications Inc.
AT&T also has an alliance with 3DO Co., a California-based start-
up that is building an interactive game machine it hopes to convert

to a cable box sometime down the road. Other players exploring the market include Apple, IBM, and Nintendo Corp.

Everybody is looking for the pot of gold at the end of the rainbow, that place where consumers and businesses use digital technology to get information or entertainment at any time from anywhere. Will it happen? Will they find it? Yes, because eventually that information will be easily, instantly, and inexpensively accessed.

Multimedia—High Tech/High Touch for the 21st Century

Digital information is what will turn the new hybrid television, telephone, and computer electronic consumer product into an interactive medium.

Individualizing television viewing is just one piece of the interactivity pie. Home shopping, home banking, airline and hotel reservations, news, sports, two-player video games from remote locations, movies and MTV on demand, as well as libraries and encyclopedias, all will be available through something akin to the remote-control device consumers currently use to "channel surf."

Multimedia stands for a whole new generation of communications technologies with sophisticated audio and video capabilities.

"At its simplest, multimedia means the addition of sound and video to personal computers. At its grandest, it means the melding of technologies, such as PCs, TVs, and telephones, as well as the melding of the computer, consumer electronics, and telephone industries," writes Bradley Johnson in *Advertising Age*.

The enormous promise of multimedia is creating yet another wave of joint ventures, including some between arch rivals. IBM and Apple Computer have established a venture. NEC Technologies, Philips, Tandy Corp., Microsoft, and several other computer marketers are promoting the Multimedia Personal Computer, which incorporates compact discs that run sophisticated video games, call up an encyclopedia, and play music.

Meanwhile, Sony is teaming up with Apple Computer and Motorola to develop multimedia products. Sony brings expertise in audiovisual technology; Apple, experience in personal computing;

and Motorola, capabilities in digital cellular-phone technology.

While proponents insist multimedia portends a multibillion-dollar industry, skeptics question whether customers are eager to buy. Most emphatically, yes, say enthusiasts, extolling the product's many benefits. A journalist writing for *The Washington Post* summarized the attraction of multimedia as follows:

"Better entertainment as Americans dial up movies from distant electronic banks, or select the camera angle at football games. Better education as students browse electronically through the world's libraries. Better medical care as distant specialists view patients' symptoms over high-definition video links.

"Better products as information flashes effortlessly between office and factory. Better feelings about one another as far-flung families visit by home-to-home video links, and parents and children stay in touch with pocket phones."

And, declares Alan Kessler of 3Com Corp., a Santa Clara, California, computer network company, "The network of tomorrow will collapse time and space, erase cultural boundaries and move continents and people closer together."

If this sounds too good (or too fast) to be true, remember that a decade ago few of us had ever heard of a cellular telephone, a personal pager, or a facsimile machine. Go back a few more years and you can add the Sony Walkman, the compact disc, and the hand-held camcorder. Some of us can go back further still to a time when there were no television and no computers.

Technology is developing at an ever-accelerating rate of speed, with each new technology compounding the speed and capabilities of those that came before.

Will there be a market for multimedia? It seems certain. Consider the market for cellular phones and personal computers. But even more telling is the market for facsimile machines.

Fax and Ye Shall Receive

It was a facsimile transmission that changed the course of events during the uprising in China's Tiananmen Square, as students camping on the site faxed reports to media all over the world. That ubiquitous piece of office equipment has the power to change world events. Because it transmits information virtually instantaneously, recipients can respond immediately. There is almost no downtime between when people learn about, and when they respond to, events.

Furthermore, facsimile machines have been embraced because they foster the great potential for human interaction. We all know that what I call high tech/high touch is so much more successful than high tech alone. High touch is the reason the fax machine is much more successful than E-mail, for example. And, it has been accepted far more readily than the PC, the VCR, or any of the other technological innovations introduced in the past decade or so that force us to accept technology that is foreign to our nature (except for techies and persons under 15). When you receive a fax, you rip it off the machine and proceed to cut up, photocopy, mark up, and otherwise be physically engaged with it—high touch. Also you can write (or draw) something in longhand and send it back. With electronic mail there is no high touch, just high tech.

There are other reasons why fax has so far been more successful than E-mail. Fax is a plug and play solution. That is, you just plug it in, put in a sheet of paper, and send it to someone. You do not have to worry about whether your machine can communicate with my machine. Today, all fax machines communicate with each other. That is not true of electronic mail. If you are using Lotus and I am using Microsoft Mail, I have to figure out how to get the format of my message translated into the format of your mail system, and I have to figure out how to get routed to your mail system. Time and trouble. Also the fax represents an evolutionary development, a bridge between the old and new. Paper is slid into the fax machine much like being slid into an envelope. And the fax machine is dialed the same way the phone is. It is familiar and comfortable. Electronic mail, on the other hand, is revolutionary and does not relate to paper, only to electronics.

As people play more and more to E-mail's strength, it will start to gain on faxes. Consider a company and several of its major clients who do have their electronic-mail systems connected. Bill sits down to write a letter to Charlie. One choice Bill has is to write the letter on his word processor, print it out, and have his secretary take it to the fax room where it may have to be put in a queue to be sent out. On the other end, the fax arrives at Charlie's fax center which is around the corner from his office or 10 floors below it, where it waits to be delivered.

Let's say Bill decides instead to type his letter to Charlie on his PC, then sends it to his network's E-mail server instead of the printer. The message is routed within minutes to Charlie's E-mail server, which immediately forwards it to Charlie. At Charlie's workstation, a message pops up in the middle of his screen and a bell chimes to announce that he has new E-mail. He reads the letter, immediately types a reply without leaving his E-mail program, hits "reply" from his mail menu, and his message is sped back to Bill. Or how about that color chart that is needed across the country? Attach it to an E-mail message and it is there in minutes. Of course you can now also "broadcast" faxes and E-mail messages to 40 or 140 people, which gives more power to the individual.

As the office environment becomes more electronic and less paper, as our communications become more graphic and finally include sound and video, the fax machine will begin to fade away.

Data Transmissions Outpace Voice Transmissions

Telephone traffic increases at an annual rate of 10 to 15 percent. In 1992, international telephone traffic increased by 13 percent and has increased sixfold in the past decade. Frank Blount, former AT&T group president and current chief executive for Australian and Overseas Telecommunications Corp., believes the Asia Pacific telecommunications market alone will grow from $60 billion in 1990 to more than $200 billion by 2000. But increasingly, telephone traffic is data rather than voice.

Data transmissions account for more than half of all telephone traffic fueling the world's communication explosion. In 1991, for the first time, fax traffic between the United States and Europe exceeded voice traffic.

Until recently, talking accounted for about 80 percent of the traffic within the United States, but it is now less than half the traffic as the volume of digitized computer data on the networks has exploded by 50 percent. Worldwide, the number of installed facsimile machines is fast approaching 30 million units, and fax transmissions double every three years.

With as many fax machines as there are in offices today, and increasingly in the home, one might be tempted to think the market had reached saturation. Think again. Market researchers Frost & Sullivan estimate that the European market of $3.5 billion in sales in 1991 will rise to $7.6 billion by 1996 as changing work habits, and personal habits, create increased demand. Expected to grow dramatically is the market for home-based systems that combine "telephone, answering, fax, and PC-interface facilities," currently estimated at around $78 million. Frost & Sullivan anticipate $517 million in sales by 1996.

Big and small companies that engage in high-volume fax transmissions are ready to buy the most high-end fax equipment and services: Store-and-forward fax, pay-phone fax, networked fax, and integrated voice, fax, and electronic mail show strong growth.

In the United States, the stand-alone PC and network facsimile market is expected to grow from $63 million in 1991 to $185 million by 1996, with fax-network services growing tenfold, from $15 million in 1991 to $157 million by 1996, reports *The Financial Times*.

Thus far, manufacturers have only scratched the surface of the enhanced fax-service market for business. Services like optical character recognition for remote access to fax mailboxes and computer databases (already available from Konica and Xerox), voice annotation, and speech-to-text conversion are on the way and will only expand the market.

New features enhancing international communications, such as automatic fax-message redistribution via dual tone multiple frequency (DTMF) dialing, multilanguage greeting options for callers wanting to leave a fax/voice message, and direct dial, also will fuel the market, as will communications devices that integrate fax with cellular phone, modem, and pen-based computer technologies. The world's major communications players are vying for a piece of a market destined to be worth $20 billion by the year 2000.

Multimedia will be a lot more high tech than facsimile transmissions, but it will also be a lot more high touch, both in its content and its features, including touch-sensitive monitors and pen-based and voice-activated computer systems.

While the word *revolution* is much overused, there is no more appropriate word for the advent of truly interactive, multimedia telecommunications.

Instantaneous Global Communication Accelerates the Pace of Change

Since 1876, when Alexander Graham Bell told Watson to "come here, I want you," demonstrating that it was possible for the human voice to conquer distance, technology has propelled us in an evolution from the industrial age to the information age. Bell and his startled assistant probably never imagined what the telephone would become—a marvel of technological wizardry capable of transmitting information in any form at lightning speed to anywhere in the world.

Winners and losers in the 21st century will be defined not so much by technological wizardry but by the simple ability of technology to disseminate information where and when it is needed.

In the past four or five years, it is clear that global telecommunications have propelled dramatic world events. That trend is not lost on world leaders. Global information sharing has the power to shape world events by influencing perceptions and attitudes.

Observers and participants alike are firm in their conviction that telecommunications and the news media facilitated the end of the wars in Afghanistan, Angola, and Nicaragua, precipitated challenges to authoritarian governments in China and Eastern Europe, and contributed to the failure of the Soviet economy and the unification of Germany.

Indeed, the Cold War was brought to an end as much by the telecommunications revolution as by the failure of communism and central planning and the successful examples of capitalism and democracy. Both failure and success were magnified for all to see.

The Next Leap in Technology Will Be from Virtual Reality to Ubiquitous Computing

Already developed in a rudimentary form, "virtual reality" moves technology beyond sights and sounds to touch and even smell. Wearing special goggles that project images onto users' eyes, gloves and even body suits embedded with computer chips that sense users' motions and gestures so that they can move about and manipulate virtual objects, users can experience real situations like mountain climbing or white-water rafting without actually climbing a mountain or running a rapid.

While the technology might seem like a very expensive way to amuse oneself, there are practical and educational applications for virtual reality. It allows people to explore hidden realms: the inside of cells, or the surface of distant planets, even the information web of databases. Students could walk on the moon or along a battle sight in Gettysburg.

Architects can give home buyers the experience of walking through a house still in the blueprint stage. Engineers at Chrysler have been testing the dashboard and steering wheel of a 1997 model car—not yet off the drawing board—using a virtual-reality system.

The first generally recognized application of "virtual reality" was the so-called "Link Trainer" for instrument flying. Developed from amusement-park technology, it was in wide use by the late 1930s and remained in use until the mid-1960s. More advanced flight simulators have been in use since the 1950s. The state of the art was advanced significantly by the extensive use of simulation in the space program in the 1960s. Today, simulators for airliners and business jets are sufficiently advanced to be the primary means of training. They are so "real," and recognized as such by the FAA and its foreign counterparts, that in many cases, the first time a newly qualified 747 captain taxis away from the gate—with a full load of passengers—is very likely the first time he or she has ever flown the actual airplane instead of the simulator.

Back to Small-Town America

Ironically, the key attributes of our 21st century telecommunications system are as old as the telephone itself.

In small-town America, for example, Mrs. Jones could call the operator to say she needed to reach Dr. Brown. The operator knew Dr. Brown was making a house call across town and quickly connected the parties. Then, communicating was both highly personal and intuitive. We are at the dawn of a new age, when advanced technology will replicate the personal touch of yesteryear's small-town telephone operator.

During the next 20 years, the technologies of today, which most of us approach with baffled trepidation, will recede into the background, and become one with the environment. Computers and the next generation of information-processing technologies will do all the things discussed in this chapter and then some.

Machines Will Accommodate People, Rather Than the Other Way Around

Technology is taking us to a world some people call "ubiquitous computing" or "embodied virtuality." Mark Weiser, head of the Computer Science Laboratory at the Xerox Palo Alto Research Center, likens it to writing, which he refers to as the first information technology. He says: "The ability to represent spoken language symbolically for long-term storage freed information from the limits of individual memory. Today, this technology is ubiquitous in industrialized countries. . . . It is difficult to imagine modern life otherwise."

By contrast, computer-based information technology is far from becoming part of our environment. Millions of personal computers fill workstations at home and in the office, yet the computer still exists in a world all its own. Notes Weiser: "It is approachable only through complex jargon that has nothing to do with the tasks for which people use computers. The state of the art is perhaps analogous to the period when scribes had to know as much about making ink or baking clay as they did about writing.''

Weiser and his colleagues at the Computer Science Laboratory insist that the idea of a ''personal'' computer is misplaced, that the vision of laptop machines, dynabooks, and knowledge navigators is only a transitional step toward achieving the real potential of information technology: that it be so seamlessly, so invisibly, embedded in our daily lives that it delivers all the benefits described in this chapter without our even noticing it is there.

''We are therefore trying to conceive of a new way of thinking about computers, one that takes into account the human world and allows the computers themselves to vanish into the background. ... Only when things disappear in this way are we freed to use them without thinking and so to focus beyond them on new goals.''

That's the direction in which we are headed. Telecommunications are expanding individual freedoms, as example after example in this chapter illustrates. But technological change also influences us at the level of nationality and culture. The information revolution will erode old forms of power, while simultaneously creating new ones.

As technology empowers individuals, it creates greater opportunities for us all. The marketplace will become even more efficient because of the availability of timely, uncensored information. That will almost certainly put the bureaucracies—both in government and in commerce—out of business.

As more cultures become part of the global network, there will need to be a balance struck between the benefits of instantaneous worldwide communications and the value of preserving and protecting one's cultural heritage.

In the Global Paradox—the larger the world's economy, the more powerful its smallest players—it is virtually impossible to overestimate the role of global telecommunications.

3

Travel: Globalization of the World's Largest Industry

In the Global Paradox, the biggest industry is driven as no other by individuals' decisions. The smallest players decide. This situation also reflects the paradox of the more universal we become, the more tribal we act. The bigger and more competitive travel becomes, the more authentically distinctive to tourists we will make our cultures.

The more we integrate the world, the more we differentiate our experiences.

For many countries, tourism is by far the biggest money-maker and the strongest sector in funding the global economy.

The more exposure we have to other cultures, languages, and landscapes, the stronger our desire to experience them firsthand. These days everyone wants to reach out and touch someone; we are increasingly likely to do so by airplane as much as by telephone.

Travel, the world's biggest industry? What about energy, manufacturing, electronics, or agriculture? Well, what about them? A survey of 400 policy and opinion makers in 20 countries placed these and three other industries ahead of tourism in global economic contribution, but recently gathered statistics tell a different story. (In this chapter I use travel and tourism interchangeably: They mean all travel and tourism activities put together.)

As a contributor to the global economy tourism has no equal. Consider the following:

- Tourism employs 204 million people worldwide, or one in every nine workers, 10.6 percent of the global workforce.
- Tourism is the world's leading economic contributor, producing an incredible 10.2 percent of the world gross national product.
- Tourism is the leading producer of tax revenues at $655 billion.
- Tourism is the world's largest industry in terms of gross output, approaching $3.4 trillion.
- Tourism accounts for 10.9 percent of all consumer spending, 10.7 percent of all capital investment, and 6.9 percent of all government spending.

Furthermore, despite economically and politically induced setbacks, including wars in the Gulf region and Yugoslavia, threats of terrorism from a variety of global hot spots, recession in Europe, and economic upheaval in Japan and the once-Communist Eastern Bloc, the future of tourism is brighter than ever.

Expectations for growth in global tourism are 6.1 percent, 23 percent faster than the world economy. What's more, between 1990 and 1993, travel and tourism employment grew 50 percent faster than world employment. By the end of 1994, corporate, personal, and other taxes generated by tourism are expected to total $655 billion. The World Travel & Tourism Council forecasts:

Travel and tourism will create 144 million jobs worldwide between now and the year 2005—112 million in fast-growing Asia Pacific.

"In the 21st century," says Geoffrey Lipman, President of the World Travel & Tourism Council, "there will be a surge of Asian travelers in markets around the world, and Asian countries will be the premium visitor destinations.''

For the United States travel and tourism are now the number one source of foreign exchange earnings. In 1991 foreign revenues totaled $51 billion (including $11 billion spent on U.S. airplanes, cruise ships, and other carriers). This total surpassed agriculture ($39 billion) for the first time as the country's primary export industry.

If tourism is such a major contributor to the world's economic well-being, then the question arises: Why has tourism received so little attention from domestic policymakers and crafters of international trade agreements? Until very recently, trade in services was barely mentioned in General Agreement on Tariffs and Trade (GATT) negotiations, and in the Maastricht Treaty tourism is simply ignored.

A Multicomponent Industry

There is no one obvious answer. One explanation is that tourism is a multicomponent industry, many parts of which are inextricably linked to another economic sector, such as airlines to transportation; souvenir shops, concession stands, and restaurants to retail or service; and hotels and other accommodations to commercial development.

"Broadening the Mind: A Survey of World Travel and Tourism," published in *The Economist,* offers the following rationale:

> *The size of the travel and tourism business is difficult to comprehend, for at least three reasons. First, there is no accepted definition of what constitutes the industry; any definition runs the risk of either overestimating or underestimating economic activity.... Second, tourism is a business many of whose activities (like tour guides and souvenir salespeople) and much of whose income (tips) are well suited to practitioners of the underground economy. In countries with foreign-exchange controls (which are always evaded) every official figure on expenditure*

*abroad will be wrong. Third, international travel is be-
devilled by astounding differences in the data of different
countries.*

While efforts are under way to bring uniformity to data collection
and analysis worldwide, it will likely be some time before a consensus is reached on the scope and impact of the tourism industry.
However, at least two organizations are dedicated to the task of
giving travel and tourism its due as the world's largest industry.

Data Gathering, Industry Support

The Brussels-based World Travel & Tourism Council (WTTC)
is a coalition of 65 chief executive officers from all sectors of the
industry. Its goal, as stated in WTTC reports, is "to convince governments of the enormous contribution of travel and tourism to
national and world economic development, to promote expansion
of travel and tourism markets in harmony with the environment,
and to eliminate barriers to growth of the industry."

The World Tourism Organization (WTO), on the other hand, is
an agency of the United Nations Development Program. WTO's
membership comprises 113 of the world's governments and boasts
over 170 affiliate members from the travel and tourism industry. It
is the only intergovernmental organization open to the operating
sector. Its mission is the promotion and development of travel and
tourism as a means of stimulating business and economic development, and fostering peace and understanding between nations.

While there are certainly other organizations devoted to the promotion of travel and tourism, including domestic, regional, and international agencies, these two enjoy the respect of the industry and
of world governments. Additionally, both organizations offer reliable, well-analyzed data from which to identify emerging issues
and predict future growth.

Travel Industry Courts Business Travelers

Although leisure travelers are the bread and butter of the travel
industry, airlines, hotels, car rental companies, and restaurants

nonetheless actively court the business traveler. They do so because business travelers pay top dollar. Taking up about 20 percent of capacity, business travelers account for 50 percent of the airline industry's profits. While most tourists plan trips months (or years) in advance and take the time to shop around for bargains, business travelers seldom have that luxury.

Finding ways to keep their "cash cows" content is a major preoccupation of the world's airlines. Business-travel surveys are eagerly pored over for that one nugget of information that will lure high-paying corporate executives from one airline to another. Repeated surveys by the International Air Transport Association revealed that the single most desired feature for a business person traveling by air is plenty of leg room. Consequently, most major airlines have introduced a much larger business class, ripping out whole sections of coach class; wider seats have been installed, accompanied by higher price tags.

Where short-haul services make business-class sections impractical, airlines are offering other amenities to attract business people. Slightly better food, bigger baggage allowances, in-air telephone and fax capabilities, and seat-back videos for personalized entertainment. But many industry analysts insist it is not what happens in the air that matters, but how easily travelers can get onto the plane that distinguishes one airline from another.

Total-Journey Concept

Introducing the "total journey concept," many airlines are going to great lengths to take the hassle out of business travel. Qantas, Cathay Pacific, Virgin Atlantic, and Continental all offer door-to-door limousine service. British Airways has plans to relieve passengers of their baggage at their hotel and deliver it to their final destination. BA also is testing a mobile check-in service, with flight attendants carrying portable computers to reduce waiting time.

State-of-the-art lounge facilities offered by a growing number of airlines now make it possible for busy executives to continue conducting business en route.

Once at their hotel, these same executives can continue apace, taking advantage of business centers designed to be offices away from the office. It wasn't all that long ago that making a long-distance telephone call from one's hotel room was a major investment in time and a test of one's patience. Today, hotel rooms offer faxes, computer workstations with modem hookups, and two-line telephone-conferencing capabilities.

While the travel industry concentrates its energies and resources on the lucrative business-travel market, even as corporate travel budgets are slashed and accountants quibble over frequent-flyer mileage (ours or theirs), it is the leisure-travel market that is putting the starch back in the travel industry.

THE GLOBALIZATION OF THE AIRLINE INDUSTRY

McKinley Conway says, "The early years of the onrushing 21st century will witness a global revolution in personal travel. The mystical appeal of flying will be discovered by the populations of the world. There will be a new sense of community, a new realization of vast opportunities yet to explore."

In his book *Airport Cities 21: The New Global Transportation Centers of the 21st Century,* Conway envisions a world in which the air-transportation needs of the traveling public are met by supersonic transports traveling three times the speed of sound with a range of 10,000 miles; transatmospheric vehicles, providing transportation at hypersonic speeds in the Mach 25 range; tiltrotor aircraft, which take off vertically and cruise horizontally; and "roadable aircraft," small passenger vehicles that can either fly or drive along the road, depending on weather and traffic.

The gains in aviation for the next couple of decades will be in capacity, not speed.

Impressive though Concorde is (particularly given its age), it is significant that it never proved to be enough of a money-maker to prompt construction of more than the original 16 aircraft. The three prototypes have long since been retired; British Airways and Air France now run 10 or 12, with the remainder used as "hangar queens" for parts.

Concorde's problem, of course, is that it is way too small (only

100 seats). Various manufacturers have successors on the drawing boards with passenger capacities up to 300 or so. Unfortunately, the laws of physics—particularly those of aerodynamics, which dictate how much energy you need to move a given object through the air at a given speed—ensure that supersonic transportation will always require extremely large expenditures of energy per seat-mile, and will consequently always be exceedingly expensive. The amount of power required to propel an airplane increases with the *cube* of its airspeed, which means that to go twice as fast as a 747, you would need eight times as much power. That's why current airline thinking is running in the direction of transports of subsonic speed, but extremely large passenger capacity.

Boeing is working on the next version of the 747, in which the "bulge" of the upper deck will run all the way back to the tail. It will fly only about as fast as current transports but will lug 800 to 1,000 or more hapless souls toward a truly degrading lost-luggage experience at the destination.

Accommodating the aircraft and the people they carry will be not airports as we think of them today but airport cities, each designed to meet the needs of a specific transport sector and all linked together and to other transport modes. A sort of global hub and spoke system.

Airline Mergers Make Room for Entrepreneurs

But before work can begin on the airports of the future, the airlines of today have to get their act together. Each of the world's three major airline markets—the United States, Europe, and Asia—is struggling to cope with economic realities. The United States is in the final throes of the shakeout of its domestic market. Carriers in Europe are jockeying to anticipate the effects of Europe's becoming a single market while having to deal with a serious recession. Asia, on the other hand, must deal with the problems of success, and its dynamic growth is drawing in a lot of players.

In 1990, airlines worldwide lost $2.7 billion on international service alone. By the end of the first quarter of 1993, the U.S. airline industry had lost more than twice the accumulated profit it had earned since it began commercial service in the 1920s. About 18 percent of the industry already is in bankruptcy, and more airlines are poised to file for Chapter 11 protection. It is only through heavy government subsidization that many of Europe's state-owned airlines still fly, and Japan Airlines (JAL), the Japanese flag carrier, is struggling to overcome losses of $51 million in 1991 caused by the country's economic downturn, an increasingly cutthroat international aviation market, and sloppy management.

What impact will all this turmoil ultimately have on the airline industry? Will the airline industry collapse under its own weight? Will the world be left with a handful of mega-carriers naming their price and limiting passenger options?

Positive. No, and no. Despite what critics may say, the Airline Deregulation Act of 1978 is not responsible for the current spate of business failures. Economics are responsible—the realities of a marketplace in which it is not possible to separate one domestic market from another. The U.S. airline industry was deregulated during a time when it was possible to differentiate between domestic markets in nation-states. Today, all airlines exist in a global economy; the international airline industry will simply have to adjust. And adjust it will.

The industry will not collapse, nor will we end up with a handful of mega-carriers calling the shots. The world's business and policy decision makers are far too creative for that. What will emerge is a host of mergers, joint ventures, and partnerships among carriers serving the major international markets, while smaller carriers fly solo or team up with other small carriers in regionally based markets feeding into the international markets. It will one day be possible to fly from anywhere in the world to anywhere else in the world on what appears to be one airline but is actually several airlines, serving consumers cooperatively.

Liberalization Leads to Policy Shifts and Partnerships

On Friday, January 1, 1993, the 12-nation European Community began a four-year plan to deregulate its airlines. Deregulation, under many different names, is spreading throughout international markets, following the same pattern of easier market entry, no capacity quotas, and market-based pricing. The same forces of competition evidenced in the United States and Europe are being found in Canada, Australia, Japan, and a host of other countries.

In 1990, some 30 international airlines, in all parts of the world, were in the process of privatization, "driven," as the *International Herald Tribune* put it, "by the twin forces of management seeking greater flexibility and government looking for less responsibility."

As a result, airlines are beginning to act like every other business, making marketing deals, trading shares, and forming strategic alliances. Within hours of its approval by the U.S. Department of Transportation in March 1993, a media blitz announced the code-sharing agreement between British Airways (BA) and USAir. Television commercials hammered home the "two airlines, one vision" message, promising the flying public a blissful air-transportation experience.

But what does it really mean? It means that on USAir's domestic routes and BA's United States to Britain routes passengers will find one ticketing point and one baggage check-in. The airlines will operate synchronized flights, sharing the same designator code in computer reservation systems and the cabin crews on some London-Baltimore and London-Pittsburgh flights will be USAir employees wearing BA uniforms on BA airplanes. Both airlines hope that this is just the first small step in a long-term partnership involving broad integration.

Media hype aside, the USAir-BA deal was not the first, nor will it be the last.

With considerably less fanfare, United Airlines and Lufthansa announced in September 1993 that they would join forces for travel between the United States and Germany. Made possible by the signing of a bilateral aviation agreement between the two countries, the alliance fuses together another major segment of the globalized airline industry.

Of the major U.S. air carriers, only American Airlines is without either a European partner or an intra-Europe network. Unlike the deals between USAir and BA, and Northwest Airlines and KLM in which the foreign carriers pumped large sums of money into the

U.S. carriers, the United-Lufthansa pact is a straightforward marketing arrangement. Known as a code-sharing arrangement, it is much like existing arrangements between American Airlines and Qantas, and American Airlines and Cathay Pacific.

The Australian carrier Qantas and Hong Kong–based Cathay Pacific both have code-sharing arrangements with American Airlines in which the Asia Pacific airlines tap into the rich U.S. domestic market and American gains access to a rapidly growing region. Cathay Pacific has also teamed up with Lufthansa on the Hong Kong–Frankfurt route, with Garuda on service between Hong Kong and Denpasar (Bali), and with Air Mauritius and Air New Zealand.

Thai International has had a joint marketing arrangement with Scandinavian Airlines Systems (SAS) for the past 12 years. Similarly, Japan Airlines and Delta promote one another's services. An even more complicated arrangement exists between Singapore Airlines and Swissair, which also is closely linked with SAS, which in turn owns 25 percent of Airlines of Britain.

KLM and BA are tied together in a joint venture with Sabena. Lufthansa, Air France, and Iberia have formed a large Europe-based group with hopes of exerting control in local markets and have equity links between the East and West German flag carriers. Eastern European airlines, meanwhile, are in search of joint-venture partners and there appear to be more than a sufficient number of interested parties.

Code-Sharing and Co-promotion Will Lead to Airline Mergers

As the industry moves steadily toward complete deregulation and privatization of state-owned airlines, code-sharing and co-promotions will evolve into mergers. SAS, KLM Royal Dutch Airlines, Swissair, and Austrian Airlines are eager to cement their relationship. The four airlines began talks in January 1993 to see if they could forge an alliance, which would strengthen their market position vis-à-vis the three major European players, BA, Air France, and Lufthansa. In late April the four companies announced that they had agreed to pursue a merger that would create Europe's largest international carrier. They said they would work to establish, by sometime in 1994, a jointly owned company with its own new brand name and a single balance sheet.

This multiple cross-border merger certainly seems like a harbinger of things to come. Any number of carriers in Europe and Asia would like to have closer ties to U.S. mega-carriers. However, until the United States lifts restrictions imposed in 1926 on foreign ownership of U.S. airlines, no such merger can take place. That law limits ownership of U.S. airlines by foreign investors to 25 percent of voting stock and requires that the head of an airline and at least two thirds of its board and key management officials be U.S. citizens. A more recent interpretation of the law by the Department of Transportation limits total equity, voting and nonvoting stock, to 49 percent.

A report issued by the General Accounting Office (GAO) further warned that foreign ownership could stifle airline competition in the United States. Nonetheless, Federico F. Pena, secretary of transportation, told a Senate committee that he would consider easing the restrictions. The Department of Transportation already has approved a proposal by Air Canada and a group of Dallas businessmen to invest $450 million in bankrupt Continental Airlines.

Air Canada will invest $235 million and acquire 27.5 percent of the total equity and 24 percent of the voting stock in the reorganized company. British Airways abandoned plans to invest $750 million for a 44 percent stake in USAir when discussions between the United States and Britain fell apart on how to encourage greater competition for their airlines.

In reporting on the climate for foreign investment, the GAO also noted that "international air service is still regulated through bilateral agreements negotiated with foreign governments that could be undermined by foreign ownership. . . . It is probably unrealistic to expect foreign airlines to invest significant amounts in financially weak U.S. airlines without allowing them to have some influence over what happens to their investment."

High Anxiety over Open Skies

Government policies will be influenced by the forces of global economics. In 1992, the United States reached its first "open skies" pact with a European government. The agreement with the Netherlands lifts government restrictions on the routes and frequencies that U.S. airlines and KLM Royal Dutch Airlines can fly between their countries. The United States is eager to reach such agreements with other countries.

The Dutch may be just a bit ahead of their counterparts in Europe. The agreement between the United States and France expires in 1993, and rather than opening its skies, France is calling for more restrictive policies. Germany, meanwhile, is watching carefully and making noises about rescinding its current bilateral treaty with the United States in favor of more restrictive policies as well.

Within the 12-nation European Community there is strong commitment to introducing the borderless country concept to the airline industry.

Meanwhile, industry executives, led by Bob Crandall, outspoken head of American Airlines, are pushing the government to scrap all bilateral agreements and work toward a single global deal. Officials in Washington dismiss this as impractical. Eventually, they will have to do it.

Deregulation of the U.S. airline industry in the 1980s has resulted in lower air fares and a surge in international air travel, much of it on U.S. carriers. Today, U.S. carriers fly 71 percent of the traffic between the United States and France, and 61 percent of the traffic between the United States and Germany. And while government officials in both countries make threatening noises about more restrictive bilateral agreements, the airlines are moving toward increased strategic alliances like the ones between United and Lufthansa, and BA and USAir. Even as Air France was pressing its government for increased restrictions, it was forging an alliance with Continental Airlines to tap into the vast U.S. market.

One might think that European governments would be eager to open access to their markets, considering the huge and growing market that would become available to them if they had free access to the United States. Already, European carriers count on the U.S. market for as much as a third of their revenues. By contrast, U.S. carriers collect only a fraction of their receipts from any one country in Europe. International travel is expected to increase 6 percent a year, every year between now and the year 2000. Some 73 million passengers is nothing to sneeze at.

East vs. West Aviation Competition

There is a continuing aviation trade battle between the United States and Japan. Three times a week throughout the summer of 1992, a Northwest Airlines carrier from New York landed at Osaka's Itami airport. There, approximately 300 to 400 passengers disembarked. Another 300 to 400 boarded the plane and flew to Sydney, Australia. Japan views the proceedings as a blatant violation of a 1952 accord, which barred airlines from replacing more than 50 percent of deplaning passengers with Japanese customers. The United States disagrees. Their differing interpretations of the "beyond" rights has sparked an East vs. West aviation trade battle.

At stake is the world's fastest-growing aviation market. While Japan may enjoy a trade surplus with the United States in virtually every other market, in air travel the scale is tipped in America's favor. What's more, a positive trade balance exists for the United States in air travel between the United States and other Asian countries. Thailand allowed its agreement with the United States to lapse in 1990. Flights between the two countries are now operating under a standstill arrangement, which freezes services at current levels pending the outcome of negotiations. Complaints about the U.S. share of the market also have come from Australia, Hong Kong, Indonesia, Taiwan, and South Korea.

"The number of American travelers in the Asian region is decreasing as a percentage of the total, and U.S. carriers cannot expect to develop their [beyond] traffic to support their primary traffic," Chatrachai Bunya-ananta, president of the Orient Airlines Association, said in early February. "It is time for the U.S. and European carriers to face the fact that the Asian carriers are well able to serve the needs of the Asian market, even with all its potential for huge expansion.''

That huge expansion is what has all the airlines scrambling for a piece of the market. Air travel in Asia and the Pacific is expected to experience double-digit growth throughout the '90s, with growth in some markets—Japan, Korea, and Taiwan—expected to reach 20 percent annually. "Tourism is the really big issue," says James Scott, vice president of Northwest Airlines' Pacific division. He notes that no alternatives are currently provided by Japanese or Australian carriers for travelers who want to fly from Osaka to Sydney. "If the end-to-end carriers won't provide direct services, others will. The customer wants it," Scott says.

What the customer wants, the customer will eventually get. By the year 2000, bilateral agreements will have been scrapped in favor of global air-service agreements. Deregulation and increased competition will give the United States, and every other country, the cheap and efficient services travelers want.

The Little Carriers That Scan

There may well be only a handful of international mega-carriers creating a seamless global air-traffic network. "But this is where freedom of entry comes in," says *The Economist*. "If they were allowed to compete everywhere, not just on routes involving their home country, eight mega-carriers would be enough for competition to do its job. Moreover, that sort of freedom would be less likely to produce just eight airlines in the first place; the giants would face competition from many new, much smaller airlines."

This theory already is evidenced in the fast-growing Asian market where 50 new airlines—not counting China—have been launched in the past five years, including Aseana Airlines of South Korea and Taiwan's Eva Airways Corp. Owned by the world's largest container-shipping company, Evergreen Marine Corp., Eva Airways currently operates five aircraft flying to 10 destinations in Asia, Europe, and North America. It is positioning itself for the day when direct air links are established between Taiwan and mainland China, hoping to capture some of the millions of passengers who now are forced to travel via Hong Kong.

Spotting opportunities where others see none, or where others see losses, is an attribute that has propelled Mesa Airlines, based in Farmington, New Mexico, from being a struggling air shuttle to being the largest of 150 regional airlines and 11th largest of all U.S. carriers, behind Alaska Airlines. Mesa's strategy has been to buy failing regional carriers, start up commuter operations where there was a need, and win lucrative feeder-to-hub partnerships with United Airlines and USAir.

Eyeing still more commuter lines and negotiating additional feeder-to-hub partnerships, Mesa Airlines, which enjoyed revenues of $300 million in 1992, sees its future as a cloudless sky.

As the mega-carriers continue their mating rituals, and governments argue over just how friendly the skies should be, entrepreneurs and others will continue to fill the air-travel gaps, creating a vast web of regional carriers that will ultimately lead to the seamless global air-travel network travelers will expect.

WORLD'S TRANSPORTATION INFRASTRUCTURE GETTING AN OVERHAUL

Getting from point A to point B is only half the battle for tourists and other travelers. Upon arrival, travelers first must cope with congested, poorly planned airports and then figure out how to get to their final destination. In many areas, both roadways and railways connecting airports to city centers or tourist attractions are overburdened and inadequate. If things are bad now, just imagine what they may be like when the number of people traveling by air has tripled.

In the United States, the Airport Operators Council International says that $50 billion is required by 1995 to support the infrastructure needs of 800 million-plus passengers who will be traveling on U.S. airlines in 2001. For some airports, money isn't the only problem; they're running out of room to grow. That is certainly true for the three New York City airports. "New runways are out, new terminals are out, and a new airport is out," says Bill Cahill of the Port Authority of New York and New Jersey.

Denver built a huge, brand-new airport, scheduled to open in early 1994. Fast-growing Dallas/Ft. Worth has room to grow but faces mounting public pressure to limit expansions and limit growth in number of aircraft due to concerns for the environment and noise pollution.

Nor is the congestion problem limited to the United States. "The main problem planners will face," predicts airport expert John Hoyt of the U.S.-based Ralph M. Parsons Company, "is finding the land on which to build the airports of the future. Virtually none is likely to be available near urban areas."

In Japan, Narita will be expanded, and a new international gateway, Kansai International Airport, will be built. With land at a premium engineers have turned to reclamation to solve their real estate problems. Narita Airport—built on reclaimed land on Tokyo Bay—will be expanded onto an offshore solid-waste-disposal site. Kansai International Airport in Osaka will actually be an artificial island based on land-reclamation and foundation-improvement technologies. The island will be connected to the mainland by a two-tiered bridge.

Land reclamation is just one solution to the problem of finding sufficient space to accommodate an anticipated threefold increase in air travel over the next few decades. Airport authorities increasingly will be confronted with the conflicting priorities of environmentalists, urban dwellers, business travelers, and the tourism industry, for whom preserving and protecting the landscape is paramount. As the value of tourism to local economies puts the industry on an equal footing with airport authorities and urban planners, pressure to keep intact that which visitors come to experience will force planners to rethink airport development strategies.

The superhubs of the future are not likely to be located near major metropolitan areas. In its report on airports of the future, *Asia Technology* magazine said, "At the core of a new world air transport system envisioned by some planners is a network of base airports, known as superhubs. Unlike today's airports they will probably not be all that close to major population centers. Instead, passengers will be whisked to and from them by fast-moving trains or by tilt-wing aircraft that can take off and land vertically."

Airport Expansion

Until then, and I have my doubts about utilizing tilt-wing aircraft and airports that are great distances from major cities, we will have to make do with the hubs we have, many of which are already undergoing expansion of services and facilities. Frankfurt, situated at the commercial and geographical epicenter of Europe, is undergoing a major expansion. Serving 30 million passengers a year, it is second only to London's Heathrow Airport in passenger volume.

By the fall of 1994, Frankfurt will have a second terminal capable of handling an additional 12 million passengers. Despite overcrowding at the 20-year-old airport, it is still popular. One reason for that is ease of access to the city. Trains leave every ten minutes from platforms directly below the terminal and take about 12 minutes to get to Frankfurt. There also are direct rail connections to several other German cities, including Cologne, Bonn, Dusseldorf, and Stuttgart. A second train station is planned, which will be capable of handling high-speed trains.

Vienna's airport also is undergoing major alterations in anticipation of increases in air traffic, and Britain's northern hub in Manchester, which has emerged as a major international traffic center with the completion of Terminal 2, is giving Heathrow a run for its money.

Around the globe, new airports are being constructed at a record pace. "In the next decade the investment in new facilities," says McKinley Conway, "will be greater than the combined total for all previous history."

A new $5.4-billion international airport opened in Munich in 1992. South Korea is planning a $5-billion airport, which will be built on a man-made island off Inchon. Construction of a $16-billion complex has begun in Hong Kong. When completed in the late 1990s, the project will accommodate 87 million passengers a year—far and away the biggest in the world—and will include a two-runway airport and a 55-mile railway from the airport to Kowloon to Hong Kong island, and the present airport will be closed.

Elsewhere around the globe, a new $8-billion international airport
will be built about 40 miles from Malaysia's capital city, Kuala
Lumpur. Besides Kansai, Japan plans to spend $25 billion on eight
new airports to be completed by the year 2000.

COSMIC EVENTS FUEL GROWTH IN TOURISM

A confluence of cosmic events is fueling growth in tourism. *The
Travel Industry World Yearbook* notes that as we move through the
decade of the '90s, "old geo-political problems of the past half-
century have suddenly become irrelevant. No longer must the world
devote so much of its resources to the arms race. We now face a
new era of greatly increased international communications, more
freedom to travel, more international trade, and more investing
across international borders.

"Suddenly, there are 430 million, mostly well-educated citizens
of Eastern Europe and the old Soviet Union who are now free to
travel after having been locked up for more than 50 years. It is a
population larger than all of Western Europe."

Other global events certain to have an enormous impact on international travel include the switch from centralized economies to
free-market economies in China and India, which account for 38
percent of the world's population; the removal of border controls
between the 12 nations of the European Community; the creation
of the world's largest free-trade area of Canada, Mexico, and the
United States, encompassing 370 million consumers and having a
total output of almost $7 trillion.

Additionally, after 40 years of official hostility, China and South
Korea now have diplomatic relations; Israel and the Arab states
have a peace agreement; the United States again permits travel to
Vietnam; travelers to Alaska may take side trips to Siberia; and
tens of thousands of Russians and East Europeans are taking shopping expeditions to China.

Knowing an opportunity when they see one, American Express
recently opened five new travel offices in the Slovak Republic,
bringing its number of offices in Eastern Europe to 30. Located in
Brastislava, Piestany, Zilina, Porad, and Kosice, the new offices

offer American Express travel and financial services to both local and visiting travel customers and card members.

American Express has been very aggressive lately. In May 1993, the company made its largest investment outside the United States when it agreed to buy Nyman & Schultz of Sweden, the leading business-travel agency in Scandinavia, for $115 million.

Perhaps the single greatest contributing factor making tourism the world's largest industry is a globally experienced shift in attitude toward travel and tourism. Where once travel was considered a privilege of the moneyed elite, now it is considered a basic human right. In the United States, as well as in other parts of the developed world, families and individuals spend as much on travel as they do on food, clothing, or health care.

THE DEMOCRATIZATION OF TRAVEL

Technological innovations brought the world to our doorstep, making it possible to "visit" any part of the globe from the comfort of our living room. Global communications capabilities make it possible for the business of the world to be conducted via telephone, computers, fax machines, and video conferencing—no one has to worry about leaving home without their credit card; they don't have to leave home anymore.

"Tom Paine once wrote: 'My country is the world. My countrymen are all mankind.' Today, tens of millions of people all around the world are trying to test this sentiment expressed by citizen Paine in the 18th century," says the *Travel Industry World Yearbook*.

Why now?

A number of reasons have already been put forth. Dramatic world events have made the borders of nation-states more porous. Old and newly democratized countries are declaring freedom to travel a basic human right. The global transportation infrastructure is rapidly becoming a seamless interconnected pathway to all parts of the world. And as air travel becomes more affordable and more accessible, travelers are no longer limited to the distance a train can cover in half a day.

Once travel was considered a worthy undertaking rather than an enjoyable one. The word travel comes from the French *travail* (meaning "work" or "torment"), which was derived from the Latin *tripalium,* a three-staked instrument of torture. Now technology has made travel safe and comfortable, and yes, for many —save the world-weary business traveler who has experienced airports, hotel check-ins, and late-night dinners one too many times—fun.

Baby Boomers and Retirees Contribute to Tourism's Rapid Growth

Perhaps an even more important reason for the explosion in tourism is the world's changing demographics. Across America's highways a bevy of recreational vehicles sport bumper stickers declaring GET EVEN, SPEND THEIR INHERITANCE! And spend they do. Blessed with good health, good pension plans, and newfound freedom, the over-55s of the world are taking to the highways, to the air, and to the sea. And it's a sizable population.

In the United States, the population of people over 55 will rise from 21 to 27 percent of the total population by 2010. Their impact on the travel industry will be even greater than their numbers. By that time, 47 percent of the over-55 population will be from the *first half* of the baby-boom generation (born between 1946 and 1954); they are well educated and already well traveled, and as they are relatively prosperous they will be looking for ever greater travel experiences. The same is even more dramatically evidenced in Japan and Germany.

Meanwhile, the second half of the baby-boom generation in the United States and elsewhere is reaching its peak earning years. Two-income households have more discretionary income, fewer children to feed and educate, and having worked hard to earn their money, believe they are entitled to enjoy it. Also in this cohort is an unprecedented group of DINKs (dual income, no kids), who travel frequently for business and return for pleasure.

High school and college-age young people are traveling in record numbers. In Europe it is called "social tourism" (which also includes special programs for the economically disadvantaged), in the

United States, "foreign exchange," but whatever it is called it is introducing the youth of the world to the pleasure, excitement, and adventure of tourism. Similar programs put in place in Third World countries, where children represent the highest percentage of the population. Most important, rising living standards, new transportation technology, and our innate curiosity will ensure a viable tourism industry into the 21st century and beyond.

FROM MASS MARKETS TO NICHE TRAVEL

Changing demographics have fueled two important trends that are having a dramatic impact on the travel industry. First, in the United States at least, all those two-income households are making a startling discovery—they have less, not more, time for leisure activities. Hence, traditional two-week vacations by the seashore have given way to more frequent trips of shorter duration. This is apparently true in Europe and Asia as well, although it is not fueled by a lack of planned vacation time.

And second, today's travelers are more likely to have traveled before. As a result they are much more sophisticated consumers. They know where they want to go, how they want to get there, and what they want to do once at their destination. Travel agents can no longer herd eager masses of travelers onto a chartered air carrier, bus them from one site to another, and tell them what restaurants to patronize.

Pictures of mom, dad, and the kids in front of a tour bus are out. Pictures of seascapes, landscapes, natural attractions, local culture, and historic landmarks are in. Experienced travelers seek to fulfill specific desires rather than take a country or region by storm and absorb as much as possible as quickly as possible.

Statistics seem to bear this out. Between 1985 and 1990, travel from America to Europe grew 25 percent, yet the numbers of travelers going to each of the main European destinations (Britain, France, Germany, Italy, and Switzerland) fell during those years. Fewer of them were seeing Europe for the first time; consequently, fewer felt a need to stay a long time or to see more than one country. In 1990, Americans stayed on average two days less than they did in 1985. Also in 1985, 27 percent of American travelers visited more than three European countries. By contrast, in 1990 that percentage was 16 percent.

In a presentation to the 41st Annual Conference of the Pacific Asia Travel Association, on The Future of Tourism, Joseph Coates acknowledged the impact of demographics on the travel industry as well as the increasing desire of travelers for new and different experiences.

Commented Coates: "Perhaps more important [than demographics], present and new travelers are increasingly experienced. They want each new experience to exceed the previous one. They also come with a diversity of values. The tourist and the traveler are by no means homogeneous. The tourist or the traveler might be visiting the place for a score of different reasons, as noted earlier. And yet most travel today is homogeneous in the sense that it is a product prepared for a center cut of the world's middle-class population. The future lies in differentiating the travel market in order to satisfy the scores of different reasons why people go anyplace."

The growing demands of the experienced traveler for all things cultural, exotic, and untrammeled by fellow tourists has created enormous demand for specialty trips and tours. The industry has responded.

Adventure Travel—Having Fun Can Be Serious Business

"Nobody is sure exactly how many people have gone into the adventure-travel business in the last decade. We do know that the market has grown tremendously," says *Travel & Leisure* magazine. "Once the domain of a small group of hard-core athletic eccentrics, adventure travel has now gone mainstream. These days, it can mean anything from houseboating to horseback riding, from gourmet to gorp."

Some industry analysts estimate that adventure travel now accounts for 10 percent of the total domestic travel market in the United States. Major tour operators offer everything from rafting trips through Utah's Canyonlands to biking tours in Natchez, Mississippi, or a tour designed to teach travelers about Alaska's natural history.

In 1992, an estimated 1.5 million Americans spent close to $100 million to plunge from an extended crane or a bridge overhang only to bounce back into the air courtesy of a bungee cord. Another 2 million made trips down Class-3 white-water passageways, which are rivers with enough raft-tossing capability to be considered slightly dangerous. Yet another 2.75 million daredevils jumped from airplanes to satisfy their primal need to overcome fear.

Nor is this phenomenon unique to the United States. In Canada, adventure seekers can go wild-country skiing or river rafting, whale watching or salmon fishing. Peter Williams, director of the Centre for Tourism Policy and Research at Simon Fraser University in Burnaby, B.C., observes: "Previously, natural beauty was seen only as a backdrop to tourism. Now, it is seen as part of the infrastructure of the industry."

Adventure travel offers ample opportunities for entrepreneurs like Dave Loeks who parlayed years of experience as a guide and skier and a master's degree in business administration into Arctic Edge Ltd. For $1,000 to more than $2,500, nature lovers can take a canoe trip on the Snake, Upper Laird, or South Macmillan rivers in the Yukon or on the Keele or Mountain rivers in the Northwest Territories. The well-conditioned traveler also can backpack through the Donjek Valley or the Duke River Pass in Yukon's Kluane National Park.

Running Around the World

The truly energetic adventure lover can run around the world. Several travel agencies arrange tours around marathons. Exotic Marathons, Marie Frances de France Travel Agency, Sport Travel International, Ltd., the Association of International Marathons, and Marathon Tours, to name a few, will transport you to Bermuda, Mombasa, Berlin, Leningrad, Helsinki, Tahiti, or Reykjavik, where you can soak up the scenery while you run.

For many, adventure simply means going somewhere they've never been. With the lifting of the Iron Curtain more tourists are discovering Hungary, Poland, and parts of the former USSR. There is growing demand for individual trips across China in a rented car with a guide. According to a number of travel agents, "Thulagiri atoll in the Indian Ocean is 'in,' " says the *International Herald Tribune,* "as is the Sultanate of Omán, where Club Med is building a facility; an oasis is thrown in as a bonus. The Himalayas offer different kinds of natural attractions . . . there is an upswing in tourism to South Africa . . . and trekking in Nepal, [and] swings through Peru and other South American countries are becoming increasingly popular."

Risk Recreation

If there's an emerging phenomenon, you can bet attempts will be made to define it and to explain it to those who wouldn't dream of risking life and limb or go anywhere that didn't include a hot shower and electrical outlets. And there have been numerous attempts to explain adventure travel, or risk recreation, as some prefer to call it.

An article in *Parks and Recreation,* for example, contained the following definition of adventure recreation: "A variety of self-initiated activities utilizing an interaction with the natural environment that contain elements of real or apparent danger, in which the outcome, while uncertain, can be influenced by the participant and circumstance."

As to why people feel compelled to take risks at all, Bill Danner, a partner with Leisure Trends, a consumer research firm in Glastonbury, Connecticut, explains it this way: "Many people feel their lives are out of control, and they turn to recreation because it is something they can exert control over. Their recreational choices are a way for them to make statements about who they are. If a person is underemployed and bored on the job, he or she may have a greater tendency to engage in reckless activities as a way to compensate for what they are not achieving professionally."

Or it could be that people just want to have fun.

Culture and Natural Environments Attract
Growing Numbers

Cultural tourism and ecotourism are two other rapidly growing segments of the travel industry. According to a survey commissioned by the Irish Tourist Board, one quarter of all people visiting the EC countries in 1990 were attracted there by the continent's art, architecture, and ambience.

In that same year, the world's primary travel trade fair centered around its "Megatrend Culture" series of symposia in an effort to assess the opportunities and risks for the industry of a surge in cultural travel. The results of a survey of travel industry experts conducted in February 1993 by *USA Today* suggested that Mexico is emerging as a cultural tour center:

"The ruins of Mitla and Monte Albán (ceremonial centers of the Mixtec and Zapotec Indian civilizations), the baroque churches and cathedrals of San Cristóbal de las Casas, and craft centers like Cuernavaca, Taxco ('silver center of the world'), and Oaxaca are becoming meccas for culture-seeking travelers."

"There is increasing demand for tourism in which visitors are permitted to observe and participate in local events and life-styles in a nonartificial manner," says *World Travel & Tourism Review*. "Supporting this are efforts to move away from a mass tourism approach to one in which more specialized tourism experiences are developed and offered in a more personal and culturally sensitive manner."

The advent of world travel, international trade, and instantaneous global communications threatens a global homogenization of products, life-styles, architecture, food, and entertainment. A widespread fear is that the world will become "Americanized" as Disney builds theme parks in Europe, American television programs are broadcast worldwide, and a growing number of countries, including China, Japan, Russia, and Hungary, embrace McDonald's, Kentucky Fried Chicken, and the like.

In fact, the two will coexist quite nicely in the 21st century. Greater efforts will be made to foster and support cultural diversity which, rather than be subverted, will thrive in a sea of homogenization.

The Call of the Wild—Getting "Back to Nature" Goes Global

Coinciding with the entry of environmental issues into mainstream politics is the emergence of ecotourism. Concern for the environment is no longer a "special interest," it is everyone's interest, and with it has come a strong desire to see the world in all its natural splendor before it isn't there to be seen.

Travelers looking for the extraordinary, like a hike in an Ecuadoran cloud forest, a glimpse of Indonesia's last "dragons," or a visit with Kenya's nomads, can take their pick of travel packages. Officials of the Galápagos Islands project say that tourism will have increased eightfold from 1965 to 1995.

Ecotourism is defined in the Audubon Society's recent book, *Rebirth of Nature,* as "purposeful travel to natural areas to understand the cultural and natural history of the environment while (maintaining) the integrity of the ecosystem and providing economic opportunities that make the conservation of natural resources financially beneficial to the inhabitants of the host region."

In the United States alone, the market potential for ecotourism is considerable. According to Donald Hawkins, a professor at George Washington University, the most popular special-interest tours are related to nature-oriented outdoor activities. "Between 4 and 6 million Americans travel overseas each year for nature-related trips. About 30 million Americans in the U.S. belong to environmental organizations."

Some of the advantages of ecotourism:

- **Ecotourism saves habitat.** In Rwanda, the government was under strong pressure to cut the forest habitat of the mountain gorillas (biologist Dian Fossey's *Gorillas in the Mist*) to make way for crops and cattle. Instead, the Varunga Volcanoes were opened to ecotourists, who were charged $170 an hour to see the gorillas. These fees generated more than $1 million in gate receipts and the influx of visitors provides strong incentives for people living around the area to protect the gorillas, which are now their primary source of income.

A World Bank study for Kenya showed that an average elephant herd generates about $610,000 a year in tourist income, which makes an individual elephant worth about $1 million over a 60-year life span. Using elephant habitat for agriculture would return about 33 cents per acre, but using it for grazing elephant herds to draw tourists generates about $17 per acre. As the Kenyans say, "Wildlife pays, so wildlife stays"—and so does the Amboseli National Park to protect income-generating wildlife areas.

- **Ecotourism saves rain forests.** From Thailand to Costa Rica and the Caribbean island of Dominica, increasing numbers of tourists want to see tropical rain forests. People don't come to see burned-out lands or rusty chain saws. They come to see a living forest. So, sustainable ecotourism provides an alternative to unsustainable farming. According to Luis Manuel Chacon, the head of Costa Rica's tourism board, local people "will be the worst enemy of the parks if they can't make a living off them." Today in Costa Rica, tourism is more important than cattle as a source of income and is exceeded only by coffee and bananas.

- **Ecotourism employs people.** Remember the bloody Gulf of St. Lawrence seal hunts that made headlines in the late 1970s as newborn seals were bludgeoned to death? Worldwide publicity had two results: It led the Canadian government to ban the killing in 1987, but it also spurred interest in the seals. Today, income from tourists coming to watch the seals is three times greater than the income sealers once earned by selling the hides of dead seals to make trendy garments. Sealers have learned they can make a better living by protecting the environment than by destroying it.

In other areas, there are aggressive policies to make sure that local interests own the lodges and facilities, that local people are trained for jobs as guards and guides, and that food and other goods and services are purchased from the local economy.

- **Ecotourism is a way to earn foreign exchange.** In many countries—including Rwanda, Kenya, Costa Rica, Ecuador, and Nepal—ecotourism is the leading source of foreign exchange.

Rising interest in adventure travel and ecotourism has many downsides: Too many people overrunning vulnerable natural and cultural areas and too much pollution, especially by autos that bring too many people to national parks. But in a world where political leaders must deal with growing pressures of hunger and poverty, the market creates a will to conserve when wild places and ancient ruins can be turned into sources of revenue for local people and their governments.

Earthwatch

For those who want not just to see the world's natural beauty but to help restore it, there are opportunities to work side by side with conservationists. Volunteers will each be contributing $1,395 (tax deductible) to join Earthwatch's 1993 Fresh Water Initiative. Some will be taking a biological inventory in watershed areas around Seattle, Washington, while elsewhere teams will be working in national parks and forests, measuring the diversity of species found in rivers and streams, and thus helping to determine water quality. Another five teams will examine the freshwater ecosytem of the Alaskan taiga.

The Earthwatch effort highlights a growing concern around the globe. "Even ecotourism, the low-impact offshoot of the adventure travel industry, represents the best intentions of an educated and affluent middle class to travel without despoiling," says Hether P.

Kurent, writing in *World Travel & Tourism Review.* "However, the very presence of tourists, regardless of their mission to only watch wild animals, can threaten the ecology of such areas as the Antarctic."

A growing number of countries are recognizing that the world's appetite for experiencing environments and cultures other than their own is a golden economic opportunity.

For example, the Brazilian government and American Express Brazil began spending half a million dollars in 1992 to convince Americans that Brazil is more than samba dancers, women in string bikinis, and soccer.

The "Natureland Brazil" campaign includes an advertising blitz and the use of Brazilian musicians as "ambassadors." Aimed at the travel industry and individual tourists, the intent of the campaign is to portray Brazil as "a haven for ecotourists."

In recognition of the growing demand by tourists to see and do things that relate to Asian history and culture, Singapore has set aside $1 billion to preserve the city's architectural heritage and culture. The biggest single restoration project is the conversion of 60 warehouses and godowns at Clarke quay on the Singapore River into an integrated shopping, entertainment, and cultural center. The most important cultural development is the signing of a five-year agreement with China under which different exhibitions of Chinese art and artifacts will come to Singapore each year.

Tourism as Economic Development

In Third World countries and the newly democratized but cash-poor Eastern European countries, tourism, and ecotourism specifically, is seen as a way to accelerate economic development efforts. In 1991 tourism earned developing countries $312 billion in foreign currency, second only to oil revenues.

Tourists bring with them a ready supply of foreign currency and a taste for all things representative of local culture. As areas become increasingly popular international travel destinations, they also become increasingly attractive investment opportunities for multinational developers of hotels, theme parks, special events coordinators, and resort communities.

Tourism is a self-perpetuating industry. The evolution of the tourism industry in the Caribbean, which has shown steady growth in the last 15 years, illustrates the positive impact tourism can have on an area or country with otherwise limited opportunities for economic growth. Tourism is the leading industry of each of the 30 states in the region, accounting for from 50 to 70 percent of an individual state's economy. Through its linkages to other economic sectors such as fishing, agriculture, and manufacturing, tourism contributes an even higher percentage to a state's bottom line.

Tourism in the Caribbean also has encouraged interstate cooperation, discouraging growth-compromising competition. Strong regional marketing efforts have created a common purpose for states with diverse cultures and languages. One in six jobs in the Caribbean is related to travel and tourism, 15.8 percent of all jobs. By 1994, the WTTC reports that travel and tourism are expected to contribute 24.5 percent to the economies of the Caribbean. Area governments also are now working cooperatively to address tourism-related issues and to meet the challenges of an industry that is growing from 6 to 8 percent a year.

Fostering growth in tourism also is a means by which developed countries can assist Third World countries. For example, during 1989 and 1990, the United Kingdom offered technical assistance, through the Overseas Development Administration, to a number of areas, Kenya, Zimbabwe, and Turks and Caicos Islands among them.

As national borders open up, as the population matures and becomes more prosperous, and as governments, educators, and private industry continue to promote tourism as a basic human right, people will travel as never before. The tourism industry is responding with travel arrangements to meet every budget and every situation. Special deals for seniors, for families with children, for singles and singles with children, for people with disabilities, for women over 40—you name the differentiating characteristic and there is a package, program, or tour to meet the need.

Cruising on the High Seas, the Pleasure of Going Nowhere Fast

If the oft-repeated sentiment that cruises are for the "newly wed and nearly dead" is true, then there are an awful lot of people fitting that description. In 1991, "the cruise industry was the only segment of the U.S. travel industry to show increases in both number of passengers and volume of sales," noted Philip Davidoff, president of the American Society of Travel Agents.

And, belying part of the above, "the fastest-growing passenger segment is between the ages of 25 and 40. The median age has dropped from 58 years old in 1985 to just under 43 today. Families with children booked 28 percent of all cruise vacations, and there are lines catering to kids, with youth counselors to supervise activities ranging from treasure hunts to computer classes. Premier, the official cruise line of Walt Disney World, sails with Mickey Mouse and other Disney characters on board."

While the Caribbean remains the most popular cruise destination, with 55 percent of American passengers heading for sun and sea from ports in Florida, Mexico and Alaska run a close second. There are ships that follow the voyage of Christopher Columbus, and others that travel to the once-closed ports in eastern Russia, including Vladivostok. Based in the Far East, Pearl Cruise's *Ocean Pearl* carries passengers to Malaysia, Borneo, Brunei, Manila, and Corregidor in the Philippines and to Quandong Province, China. Other Pearl programs visit China and the Soviet Far East, Africa, Australia, the Spice Islands, and Japan.

Salen Lindblad Cruising's *Frontier Spirit* is "the first true expedition vessel to be built in 16 years." Its ice-hardened hull and shallow draft allow it to travel anywhere, and special features make it "environmentally friendly" in fragile ecosystems such as the Northwest Passage and Antarctica. *Frontier Spirit* carries passengers to explore the nature, wildlife, and culture off the coasts of Brazil, Uruguay, the Falkland Islands, and Cape Horn.

If going nowhere fast is your pleasure, there are any number of cruise lines that will take you there. There is a cruise ship for

virtually every taste and pocketbook and many more ships are being
readied to meet growing demand. According to the Cruise Lines
International Association, by the year 2000, 10 million people will
cruise annually. Having already doubled in size to 160 ships in the
last decade, the world's cruise fleet continues to grow.

Carnival Cruise Line recently launched its new superliner, *Ecstasy,* a 2,040-passenger vessel designed to be a "floating city."
Princess Cruises added the 1,590-passenger *Regal Princess* to its
fleet, a sister ship to the *Crown Princess,* which launched in 1990.
Royal Caribbean Cruise Line's new *Monarch of the Seas* boasts
capacity for 2,354 passengers with a 1,000-passenger main lounge
and two shopping promenades.

Singapore Wants to Become the Gateway to Southeast Asia

Recognizing a good thing when they see it, the Port of Singapore
Authority (PSA) and the Singapore Tourism Promotion Board
(STPB) are joining forces to become the "Miami of the Far East."
Singapore is investing $28 million to build a cruise center as part
of a commitment to its goal of becoming the cruise gateway to
Southeast Asia.

To be truly successful, other port cities in the area will have to
support the effort because cruising is a multiport destination.
Toward that end, the PSA and STPB are working with their neighbors—Indonesia, Malaysia, and Thailand—to develop the necessary infrastructure, while the Association of Southeast Asian
Nations busies itself promoting the region's mix of history, culture,
art, developing cities, and more than 21,000 islands in an effort to
generate interest among consumers and the trade.

To date, Windstar Cruises is the only major cruise operator to
make the commitment to base a ship in Southeast Asia on a year-round basis, but others like Royal Caribbean Cruise Lines are
studying the market.

It is a market that is certain to grow. As with all other travel,
many who take cruises will be repeat customers; eventually they
will be looking for the new and the exotic even if they never leave

the ship. ''The tide is rising for the Cruise industry,'' asserts Bob
Dickinson, chairman of the 34-member Cruise Lines International
Association. ''Cruising is hot!''

RAILS AND ROADS GET THEIR SHARE OF THE FUNDS

Rails and roads, along with ships and airplanes, will continue to
be important parts of the transportation infrastructure. Already,
plans are under way to make major improvements at the cost of
billions and billions of dollars. Landmark legislation passed in the
United States in 1991 earmarking $151 billion over a six-year pe-
riod to improve the infrastructure of America's surface-
transportation system.

Essentially, the legislation tells state and local governments to
make better use of road and mass-transit systems already in place.
It is more liberal than in the past about allowing state and local
authorities flexibility in deciding how to spend the money. For the
first time, it mandates that consideration be given to the general
needs of ''recreational travel and tourism'' in the transportation
planning process.

Around the world, congestion in the air has led to investment in
ground transportation. Important technical advances resulting in impressive speed increases in trains will make rail competitive for
longer trips. The Channel Tunnel between Britain and France, and
bridges and tunnels that will link Scandinavia to the rest of Europe,
are changing the face of transportation.

In Spain, an expressway now links Madrid to Seville. Another
new highway connects Seville, via Granada, to the Mediterranean
motorway, which in turn connects with the European freeway system. Additionally, Spain will invest $5.5 billion to bring its national
railway, Renfe, up to the high-speed standards of other European
carriers. A bullet train linking Seville and Madrid reduces travel
time between those two cities from 5 hours and 40 minutes to 3
hours.

In 1991, West Germany opened a 155-mph link between Mann-
heim and Stuttgart, almost matching the 186-mph high-speed train
that now connects Paris to Brittany, Bordeaux, and Spain. Else-

where, Switzerland, Sweden, and Italy are spending hundreds of millions of dollars to upgrade the quality of their railways. Japan continues to improve and expand its "bullet trains," while Australia offers a 2,376-mile, 65-hour rail trip between Sydney and Perth.

Even in the United States, where rail service gave way to the private automobile or to air travel, new rail links are in progress. In 1992, Amtrak announced the creation of the company's first transcontinental train linking Los Angeles with Miami, and business and leisure travelers in the Northeast now enjoy high-speed rail service that connects Boston, New York City, and Washington, D.C.

In Portugal, where tourism receipts have constantly covered a negative trade balance by as much as 41 percent, a government initiative created a new land-transport network that will carry the economic advantages of tourism to inland areas. In Australia, where tourism accounts for 12.5 percent of the country's employment— 987,000 workers—and $11.6 billion in tax revenues, the Australian Centennial Roads Development Program will spend $6 billion to fund construction and improvement of roads of "national economic importance" in both rural and urban areas.

Slowly but surely, the world's governments are recognizing the enormous impact travel and tourism have on their economic growth. Billion-dollar transportation-development projects are now seen as investments in the future.

GOVERNMENTS ACKNOWLEDGE EMERGING TOURISM ISSUES

There is growing worldwide recognition of the contribution made by tourism to every country's economy. Steps are now being taken to coordinate public and private tourism-related activities to facilitate growth into the 21st century.

In recognition of the growing economic importance of the tourism industry, Australia established a separate Ministry for Tourism, giving it Cabinet status. Also in progress is the development of a National Tourism Strategy. Released in September 1991, "Towards a National Tourism Strategy" put forth the following goals:

- to provide all levels of government, the industry and other interest groups with a clear statement of the Commonwealth Government's objectives for the future development of the tourism industry;
- to provide a sound basis for the formulation of government tourism policy and industry planning over the next decade; and,
- to enhance community awareness of the economic, environmental, and cultural significance of the tourism industry.

Similar position papers have been undertaken by the governments of Austria, which published "Guidelines for Tourism Policy up to the Year 2000"; Canada, which adopted its first-ever Federal Tourism Policy in September 1990; and the Netherlands, whose "Enterprise in Tourism" set forth six action points for future tourism development: creation of a policy on national and international cooperation; improvement in the management of the tourism and leisure industry; creation of tourism policies aimed at consumers; infrastructure improvements; policy on tourism information and promotion; and the expansion of the knowledge of the tourism industry through research and statistics.

These action steps could be the action steps of any country and, in fact, echo those set forth by others. Canada's policy statements sounded much the same: to increase international tourism revenues to Canada; to ensure that Canada has the products demanded by the customer; and to facilitate the industry's ability to undertake more information-based advocacy and decision making. Straightforward, perhaps, but easier said than done.

Tourism 2000

Virtually every country is giving new attention to tourism as a growth industry. Sweden created the Swedish Travel Federation in 1989 as a common organization for the different branches of the travel trade. In 1991, an Act of Parliament abolished the former New Zealand Tourism Department and replaced it with two sepa-

rate agencies reporting to the minister of tourism. They are the
Ministry of Tourism and the New Zealand Tourism Board. In Finland, the Finnish Tourism Board was reorganized in 1989 to reflect
the role of the board as a marketing organization. Meanwhile, the
new Finnish government, installed in April 1991, created a development plan called "Tourism 2000."

What is likely to evolve as governments recognize the value of
tourism to their national economies? To be sure, greater attention
will be paid to the institutional and infrastructural limits to growth.
Critical issues will be identified and attempts will be made to resolve those issues. For example, labor-force issues already have
emerged as critical to the industry's growth, and virtually every
government around the globe is focusing on employment training
and the professionalism of tourism employees who are de facto
"goodwill" ambassadors.

While all of these government efforts may push tourism along,
the industry is mostly still driven by private choices and by the
private sector. Most of what governments are doing is following
markets, not creating markets.

Education and Training

Tourism courses have been in development for many years in
such countries as Switzerland, where tourism accounts for 12.2 percent of the gross domestic product, France, for which tourism contributes $43.8 billion in tax revenues, and Italy, where 14 percent
of the population is employed in the tourism industry. The European Community's Social Fund subsidizes training for tourism in
less-favored regions and exchange programs designed to improve
the linguistic and cultural knowledge of young workers. And the
European Centre for Vocational Training evaluates the level of professional training needed for hotels and restaurants in Community
countries.

In the United States, tourism management-training programs
(Cornell, Northwestern, and UNLV), are now superior to those in
Europe. Cornell University in Ithaca, New York, developed a pro-
gram that is now being franchised elsewhere, while in Canada the

Tourism Industry Standards and Certification Committee, chaired by Tourism Canada, was established to coordinate the development of occupational standards and nationally recognized industry-based certification programs. And the Greek Ministry of Education created the first professional lyceums (high schools) of touristic orientation, a three-year course of study. Greece also is cooperating with all the other members of the EEC, with respect to the Centre de Formation Professionnelle, establishing equivalency standards for all schools of tourist professions. Already, the job profiles for eight tourism professions have been written.

Safety

Other issues in tourism include health, security, and safety. The worldwide AIDS epidemic has evidenced ways in which rising health concerns impact tourism. Fear of AIDS has reduced tourism to such African countries as Kenya and The Gambia, where AIDS reached epidemic proportions some years ago. Conversely, countries with a low incidence of this devastating disease are increasingly reluctant to admit travelers from countries where it is prevalent.

Concern for personal safety and the security of one's possessions when traveling abroad has a definite impact on decisions about where or if to travel. In the United States, perceptions of certain cities, including Los Angeles, Washington, D.C., New York City, and Miami as high-crime areas dampened enthusiasm among domestic and international travelers. The bombing of the World Trade Center in February 1993 didn't help matters. Rio de Janeiro has certainly suffered from an international reputation for street violence against tourists.

Escalation of armed conflict in certain regions around the globe can have a negative impact on worldwide tourism. The Gulf War demonstrated just how much of an impact armed conflict can have. More generally, the problems in the Middle East over the past 20 years, and political instability in Asia, substantially restrained tourism growth in those areas. And random acts of terrorism—inflated by the media—have led people to believe that it really can happen to them.

While issues involving labor, transportation, health, security, and safety are critical, probably the single greatest concern for every country is the impact tourism will have on its environment.

Already a recipient of considerable government attention, environmental issues will become more critical as countries realize that destruction of that which attracts tourists in the first place is simply not good business.

The Rio Earth Summit in June 1992 brought together the greatest number of world leaders ever gathered. Joining them were representatives of hundreds of private environmental organizations. Coinciding with the Earth Summit was the release of the first yearly review by the World Travel & Tourism Environment Research Centre (WTTERC). The Centre is a key component in the WTTC's comprehensive program to achieve lasting environmental improvement.

In 1991, New Zealand passed the Resource Management Act, which requires all aspects of air, land, or water to be managed in a more integrated manner. The focus of the act is on the environmental effects of activities, rather than the activities themselves. In France, developing nature tourism has been the main policy thrust for protecting rural and coastal areas from uncontrolled building or other development. New facilities in Belgium are authorized only after an environmental-impact study has been conducted and approved, and in Austria, a study of an "Integrated Alpine Protection Plan" was compiled, while the Austrian Association of Communities organized a campaign on "Maintenance of Environment, Culture and Village Style in Austrian Communities."

Clearly, environmental issues will continue to be the focus of national policy and international tourism organizations. At the 1990 Tourism Policy Forum's First International Assembly of Tourism Policy Experts it became clear that concern for the environment was the number-one issue of the decade.

Writes J. R. Brent Ritchie, professor at the University of Calgary: "Clearly, this concern reflects a much broader societal alarm about the degradation of our physical environment. Tourism, however, is perhaps even more sensitive and more dependent upon a high-quality environment for its long-term success than are many other sectors. In this regard, participants noted the decline in the quality of our land and water resources and the rising tension between protection of, and use of, the physical environment.

"They noted the increasing competition for physical resource use. In essence, participants pointed out that tourism development must, in the future, be compatible with the environment. They also noted that tourism is among the better alternatives for land use."

FROM BORDER PATROLS TO GLOBAL VILLAGE

In the 21st century there will be few barriers to international travel. Tourists will be courted by developed and Third World countries alike for the enormous infusion of capital that comes with tourism and for the benefits realized from a heightened awareness and appreciation of global cultural diversity.

Already a global industry by virtue of the sheer numbers of people traveling internationally, by cooperative arrangements between international air carriers, and by foreign investments in hotels and tourist attractions, it will become increasingly so. Deregulation of the airline industries in every country will be followed by more liberal policies on foreign investment in all travel and travel-related industries.

Tourism is the force that will make the global village truly one world. Already, regional partnerships are forming around the globe in recognition of tourism's enormous economic potential and the need to remove barriers to growth. The Tourism Annex, part of the Canada/U.S. Free Trade Agreement, eliminates barriers to trade in goods and services; facilitates conditions of fair competition; liberalizes fair competition; establishes a dispute mechanism to resolve problems; and lays a foundation for future cooperation. In 1990, Canada also signed a tourism cooperation agreement with Mexico in recognition of the benefits of removing obstacles affecting the movement of people and the operation of tourism and tourism-related businesses.

In 1986, the United States introduced the Visa Waiver Pilot Program to waive nonimmigrant-visitor visa requirements for the nationals of eight countries. By the end of 1989, the program was in effect in the United Kingdom, Japan, Germany, France, Sweden, Switzerland, Italy, and the Netherlands. Among the 12 nations of the European Community there is free movement of people, goods, and services from one country to another.

The Nordic Tourist Board initiates and funds projects promoting tourism in the Nordic region and is a forum for the coordination for tourism policy and for Nordic cooperation in international organizations. France is increasing the number of countries with which it has bilateral cooperative agreements, as are Germany and Greece. In the Pacific Basin, New Zealand is closely associated with the Pacific Asia Travel Association and the Asia-Pacific Economic Council, while Japan has extensive ties and cooperative arrangements with a number of other Asian countries.

Special Events Designed to Bring the World to Their Doorstep

Clearly, governments everywhere recognize tourism's contribution to their economy and the benefits of encouraging access. Organizing special events, or hosting internationally sanctioned events, has become a way for countries to promote goodwill, to introduce themselves to the world, and to generate enormous profits for the host city/country.

The eyes of the world were focused on Spain in 1992 as the country hosted the Summer Olympics in Barcelona and the World's Fair in Seville. By all accounts, both events were extraordinarily successful. Hungary is gearing up for the expected 10 to 12 million visitors who will attend the 1996 World's Fair in Budapest. Some 1.5 million visitors are expected to flock to the nine U.S. cities that will host soccer's World Cup in 1994.

In the years ahead, expect an explosion of festivals—music, film, art, ideas—sporting events, historic commemorations, fairs—anything that will promote tourism.

TOURISM ENTERS THE INFORMATION AGE

In the 21st century it will be possible for anyone to book airline, car rental, and hotel reservations from their home computer as the world's computerized reservation systems converge, creating a seamless global tourism-information network. Already, two of the world's biggest airline reservation companies have merged.

Galileo International, based in Chicago and with offices in Swindon, England, and Denver, Colorado, combines the European Galileo network with the U.S. Covia-Apollo reservations system. Shareholders will include British Airways, United Airlines, USAir, KLM, Swissair, Alitalia, Aer Lingus, Air Canada, Olympic Airways, TAP Air Portugal, and Austrian Airlines.

In what is to be the first global reservation system, the new company will be 50 percent owned by European carriers and 50 percent owned by U.S. airlines. Its main competitors will be the Sabre network owned by American Airlines and the Asian airlines system, Abacus.

With explosive growth in tourism, and with travelers' increasing sophistication, the demand for information will encourage the growth in consortia, which will lead to ever-greater interconnectivity. To remain competitive, independent operators and international companies alike will have to be linked to one or more reservation systems. Ultimately, these systems will be linked to one another, creating a complete information network and truly global industry.

Hand-Geometry Screening

Technology will soon be changing the travel experience in a number of other ways as well. Border crossing, always a major impediment to the free flow of travel, and an irritant to the traveling public, will soon be improved through technology. Pilot programs in Frankfurt, Montreal, New York, and Newark airports are testing a hand-geometry screening device called FAST (Future Automated Screening of Travelers) to expedite the immigration process.

FAST uses "biometric characteristics unique to each individ-

ual—in the form of hand-geometry data—to conclusively verify a
traveler's identity. After one-time-only voluntary enrollment, the
data, together with passport details, are placed in a machine-
readable travel document which can be quickly scanned at international borders.''

The German pilot program will allow passengers to bypass normal immigration procedures completely once their "FAST Card"
is issued. Upon arrival at Frankfurt Airport, card carriers will put
their card in one scanner and their hand in another. If the hand
images match, a gate will automatically open and the immigration
process is completed.

FAST was developed through a cooperative effort between the
WTTC, the International Association of Travel Agents, and a number of major airlines. The governments of the Netherlands, the UK,
and the United States also are involved in the development of a
system all hope will one day become universal.

Lost at Sea

Although years behind schedule, millions of dollars over budget,
and plagued by a host of problems that threaten further delay, there
is still hope that the Oceanic Display and Planning System
(ODAPS) will one day improve the safety of transoceanic flights.
Unlike domestic flights, overseas flights operate without radar cov-
erage for most of the time they are in the air.

For decades, controllers have relied on pilots to report their positions to a radio operator every 45 minutes or so when flying over
the ocean. The operator then sends the information by Teletype to
controllers, who record the data on strips of paper. This tedious,
low-tech procedure leaves lots of room for human error, and as the
number of transoceanic flights increases, it is a disaster waiting to
happen. ODAPS, which represents "the first step in a long-term
plan to improve oceanic flight control, provides controllers with a
computer-generated display of aircraft position based on flight plans
filed before departure, radio contact with a pilot during flight, and
wind reports received from the pilot." A related project will use

communications satellites to provide more acurate information about an aircraft's position.

Virtual Travel

Technology also will have an impact on how travelers experience their trip from picking a destination to recording the events of their journey. Interactive videos already allow people to "experience" a place before they ever leave home; virtual reality will make it possible for people to go rock climbing, hang gliding, or trekking through the Himalayas courtesy of technology, not air transport. Chances are if you don't like the virtual-reality experience of rock climbing, you won't be any happier hanging from a rope on a real cliff.

No more boring your neighbors with fuzzy photos of far-off places; tomorrow's cameras, camcorders, and compact discs will record all the sights and sounds and store them neatly for ready retrieval. What's more, you'll be able to fast-forward through the stuff nobody cares to remember, or zoom in for a closer look at the architecture of a building you can't remember seeing the first time around.

This suggests a new application for photo and digital-image storage technology: "Travel Salons," where you could go—singly or in groups—to be photographed in front of digitally stored pyramids, waterfalls, beaches, and so forth. The rental of appropriate outfits would be an important auxiliary profit center. Digital retouching would allow "trips" to be condensed by combining attractions. For example, think how impressive the Sphinx would be on an island in Lake Erie.

Travel is and will continue to be the world's largest industry. No matter how sophisticated the telecommunications infrastructure becomes, or how many of our business or leisure activities can be conducted from the comfort of our living rooms, most of us will continue to get up out of our easy chairs because there is no substitute for the real thing.

People have levels of identity, which make them both unique individuals and members of a group as defined by their language, religion, history, ethnic heritage, and even geography. Identification with a group is critical to one's sense of self. As the world economy integrates and the global society becomes increasingly homogeneous, the needs of individuals to retain a sense of self in a sea of homogenization grows stronger. Consequently, people are more likely, not less likely, to travel as they seek to maintain a sense of continuity and belonging.

4

New Rules: A Universal Code of Conduct for the 21st Century

New rules of conduct for the Global Paradox condition are beginning to emerge.

These new rules are grounded in the expectations we have of individual conduct and behavior. Again we are drawing from the smallest players in the world to create the new rules for the expanding global economic order.

In his 1993 book, *The Moral Sense,* sociologist James Q. Wilson says that *universally* important moral qualities derive from and are sustained by local practices and relationships, mostly "families, friends and intimate groupings."

Despite what cynics and pessimists might have us believe, the world is on no more or less shaky moral ground than it ever was. The difference between the latter half of the 20th century, particularly the last two decades, and all previous periods in history is that today when ethical or moral standards are compromised anywhere, we learn about it everywhere.

Instantaneous global communications have given all of us a window on the world through which can be seen both the wonder of it all and the things that make us wonder about it all. Throughout history there have been those who have taken the moral high road and those who have pushed the walls of the ethical envelope to the breaking point. Persecution, "ethnic cleansing," bribery, swindles, and scandals are hardly unique to this century.

In the past, however, when unethical conduct was revealed, citizens of the aggrieved community imposed sanctions and instituted systems to ensure that others were discouraged from similar actions. For the most part, knowledge of such situations was contained by the limits of communication technologies. Ignorance was bliss, or at least a viable excuse for not taking action. By the middle of the 20th century, news of events around the world reached our doorstep in a matter of days. Today, we watch events unfold in real time. It is far more difficult to ignore known situations in which ethical or moral standards are compromised.

Over time societies develop laws, regulations, and unwritten codes of conduct in an effort to maintain social harmony. When violations occur, it is the community's moral obligation to right the wrong. A fairly simple, and effective, system of governance when the community consists of one's neighborhood, city, or state. A more complicated proposition when the community is the entirety of the globe.

With the activities of the world being replayed for us in our living rooms each night, none of us can feign ignorance about affronts to society's ethical standards. We have all become our brother's keeper—at least in this sense. Communications technology has empowered individuals and communities through instant access to information of all kinds. With that access comes responsibility. Are we up to the task?

Fortunately, yes. Increasingly, individuals and organizations are voicing concern for and taking action against behavior that compromises the integrity of our fellow global citizens and the environment that supports us all. And there is emerging a new corporate player who believes that corporate responsibility is not limited to meeting shareholders' anticipated return on investment, that there are many stakeholders in any single company and success is contingent upon honoring an organization's ethical and moral obligations to all stakeholders.

This evolving code of conduct is also being embraced by politicians as global politics becomes increasingly driven by economics rather than sovereignty.

NEW ACCOUNTABILITY FOR POLITICIANS

Politicians and political activity around the globe are being scrutinized, and where respect for standards of decency and ethical conduct are found wanting, the public is demanding retribution.

Witness the events over the last few years in Brazil, Venezuela, Japan, Italy, China, and the former Yugoslavia. Revelations of corruption, in the form of bribes, kickbacks, and connections to organized crime, and human-rights violations, including forced prison labor and "ethnic cleansing," have become daily media fare. Flashed around the globe in a matter of seconds, information about each new atrocity fuels citizen outrage and escalates demands for redress.

Brazil: Television Can Make You, and It Can Break You

Who hasn't heard of Fernando Collor de Mello, who rode a rising tide of anticorruption sentiment straight into Brazil's presidential office, only to be found two years later to have illegally accumulated millions of dollars. While steadfastly maintaining his innocence, Collor abruptly resigned as Brazil's Senate was about to begin trying him on corruption charges.

All those who shook their heads and lamented the state of Latin American governance, long afflicted by arbitrary misrule and military coups, missed the point. Collor resigned because the people of Brazil, encouraged by support from the global community, would accept nothing less. Politics as usual, like business as usual, is no longer acceptable. Collor's threatened impeachment and his resignation signal a wholly new period in the political history of Latin America, where heads of state for years have enriched themselves with impunity.

Fernando Collor de Mello got only part of it right. As an almost totally unknown leader in a very poor province of Brazil, he realized that with television and the growing number of people in Brazil who had TV sets, a new politics was possible. Television in Brazil had reached critical mass. On TV he spoke directly to the people of Brazil, promising to clean up corruption, promising honesty in government. He came out of nowhere (a little like running for president from the state of Arkansas), the people responded, and he was elected president of Brazil. The part he didn't get right was that inappropriate conduct on his part would be magnified by the same TV that got him elected.

Venezuela

Venezuela's president, Carlos Andrés Pérez, can certainly attest to Latin America's political, and ethical, awakening. Pérez and two former cabinet ministers have been accused of misappropriating and embezzling $17 million in public funds. Maintaining his innocence, Perez stepped down as president when the Supreme Court ruled that he should be tried on both counts.

As demonstrators gathered outside the legislature shortly after the Supreme Court's announcement, carrying posters with pictures of Pérez behind bars, and the national guard positioned themselves to thwart riots, many voiced satisfaction that Venezuela had at last embraced democracy and the concept of "people power."

Venezuela's 35-year democracy, it seems, was a democracy in name only. According to Ruth Capriles, co-editor of *The Dictionary of Corruption,* before the international oil market collapsed and the export earnings dried up, "corruption was not only tolerated, it was expected. Nobody minded what [leaders] did as long as we all benefitted. That was our ethic."

Other observers say it goes beyond the current state of Venezuela's economy, insisting that citizens are at last gaining a sense of their own power to change the way their elected officials behave. Ramón Escovar Salom, the independent prosecutor who brought the accusations against Pérez and his ministers, believes that a combination of factors are converging to "awaken Latin Americans politically."

Factors cited include "the peaceful transition of power [in the wake of Collor's resignation], the dawn of democracy after decades of dictatorship in Paraguay and the end of Central America's internecine civil wars, but also the people's access to information from the rest of the world through satellite broadcasts, fax machines, and much more independent and probing Latin American news media."

Where Honesty Means Sharing Your Bribes

What is true for the people of Venezuela is becoming true for people everywhere. Would the godfather of Japanese politics have been forced to resign from the Diet, and later face criminal indictment, if the Japanese people had not seen on television the resignation and disgrace of Collor? How sweeping would Italy's criminal probe of political corruption have been if the public was not privy to events unfolding halfway around the globe?

It's hard to say whether this rising tide of "people power" is an example of spontaneous combustion coincidentally occurring in pockets around the globe, or whether each event as it occurs, and public reaction to it witnessed by others, doesn't provoke, encourage, and support similar public responses. Perhaps what is emerging is a global ethical standard to which all politicians and political activity will be held. People seem to be willing to accept economic hardship in exchange for greater freedom, but only if the burden is equally shared by those in public and in private life. Democracy and austerity are acceptable; democracy and corruption are not.

In Italy, what began as a routine investigation of alleged kickbacks at a nursing home in Milan turned into Operation Clean Hands. Some 2,500 prominent Italian politicians and businesspeople (including 200 members of parliament) have been arrested and are facing trial for taking kickbacks. Among them are Fiat financial director Francesco Mattioli, the auto firm's third-highest-ranking official, and Enzo Carra, the Christian Democrats' former press secretary. Sitting in prison are a veritable who's who of Italy's political and business elite.

"Though petty bribery has long been a way of life in Italy, many were shocked by the sheer scale of the corruption uncovered by Clean Hands." As *The Financial Times* put it in a headline, Italy has become a country "where honesty means sharing your bribes." For a country accustomed to scandal, the corruption probe and the political crisis it has sparked are draining an already weak economy and having a potentially disastrous impact on international investments.

Emboldened by Italy's hardline approach to corruption, voters elsewhere in Europe are pressing for similar action at home. In Germany, Social Democratic leader Björn Engholm, slated to challenge Chancellor Helmut Kohl in the '94 elections, resigned amid allegations that he gave false testimony in a six-year-old political scandal. At a press conference in Bonn, Engholm said he was stepping down, "to protect my party from being identified with my political mistakes."

Also in Germany, Kohl's economics minister, Jürgen Möllemann, resigned after admitting that he had promoted goods manufactured by a relative. Mollemann was the fourth minister in nine months to depart prematurely under a cloud of suspicion. "The political discussion here is rapidly moving away from policy toward an emphasis on corruption—a personalization of politics that we have not had before," said Stephan Russ-Mohl, a communications professor at Berlin's Free University.

Throughout Europe, voters are making it clear that they are fed up with "overly familiar faces," and with politics as usual. As a *Newsweek* reporter explained it, "In a gathering recession, with unemployment rising into double digits, Western Europeans are not, as might be expected, voting their pocketbooks. They are opting for strong (if incompatible) ideological positions. They are telling mainstream leaders that they want an end to corruption, a reordering of priorities and a new political order that speaks directly to their current hopes and fears."

Japan

This is an attitude that politicians in Japan are becoming uncomfortably familiar with. In the fall of 1992, Shin Kanemaru, the godfather of Japanese politics, was forced to resign his seat in the national legislature when it was revealed that he accepted $4 million in "contributions" from a trucking company. In doing so, Kanemaru broke one of Japan's few campaign finance laws: accepting more than $15,000 from a single source in a single year.

This most recent scandal in Japanese politics also included connections to Japan's most prominent organized-crime bosses and a long history of taking kickbacks from construction companies. According to many reports, it was neither the contributions nor the kickbacks nor even connections to organized crime that undid Kanemaru. It was arrogance. After the charges were made he returned to work as if nothing had happened, and that was more than the Japanese people were willing to tolerate, especially since they had seen on television that in other countries even powerful people were held accountable for their conduct.

Scandals are not new in Japan. Three years ago Kiichi Miyazawa, then finance minister, resigned in disgrace when it was discovered that his aides had accepted stock in a newly listed Tokyo company. Miyazawa later became prime minister. Similarly, Ryutaro Hashimoto resigned as finance minister in the wake of a stock-compensation scandal.

So why are the Japanese people now expressing outrage at what Westerners would consider unethical behavior? Because they have witnessed the downfall of politicians around the globe for similar infractions. And because they intuitively understand that to be citizens of the global community they will have to adapt their behavior to new standards. Observes Thomas W. Whitson, a partner and auditor at KPMG Peat Marwick in Tokyo, "If morality is important to do business in the United States, then I think they would go along with it—not because it's right, but because it's good business."

Why Now?

A cynical observation to be sure, and it isn't quite that simple. Fairness is not a uniquely Western quality. The United States has certainly experienced its share of political scandal. Many U.S. companies have paid bribes as the cost of doing business, not only in foreign companies but within the United States as well. Exposés on graft, influence peddling, and political contributions for special legislative considerations play themselves out in the U.S. media on a regular basis.

The question, why now?, is one that could be asked in any of the situations described. The answer is quite simple. A universal code of conduct is emerging. While some would argue that corruption in less economically advanced countries, like Latin America and the newly formed countries of the former USSR, is part of the evolutionary process and inevitable, others would insist that as we continue to move toward a single global economy, everyone will have to play by a new set of rules.

In the 21st century, citizens of the global community will be much less tolerant of perceived injustice in any form. This is certainly proving to be the case in the area of human rights.

WE ARE ALL OUR BROTHERS' KEEPERS

Even as President Clinton announced intentions to extend for one year China's "most favored nation" status, which allows Chinese products to enter the U.S. market at favorable tariff rates, there were reports of human-rights violations by Chinese police against Tibetan protesters in Lhasa opposed to Chinese rule.

Members of the U.S. Senate are insisting that China release political prisoners, prevent export of goods made by prison labor, and adhere to international guidelines on the transfer of missiles and weapons of mass destruction. Chinese officials in Beijing insist that if Washington imposes sanctions, they will have no choice but to retaliate. Retaliation could jeopardize U.S. exports and jobs, and would have a tremendous impact on Hong Kong, whose economy is inextricably tied to that of booming southern China.

Here's the dilemma. China's economy is the fastest growing in the world. There has been a surge of interest by American companies eager to take advantage of cheap labor and tap into a cash-rich consumer market. By early 1993, direct U.S. investment in China totaled $6 billion. How then should the United States deal with a country that is becoming more prosperous and open as its market economy expands while at the same time political repression remains strong?

Human Rights and Economics

Which takes priority, investments or human rights? And whose responsibility is it to monitor another country's behavior? And isn't a market economy the surest avenue to political liberation? While the United States struggles with the question in relationship to its trade policies with China, the question is being answered elsewhere around the globe. Human rights are everyone's responsibility.

A report issued by the State Department early in 1993 concluded that "the human rights observance trend line was, on balance, positive," said Patricia Diaz Dennis, assistant secretary of state for human rights. Yet the report went on to enumerate gross human-rights violations, including atrocities "bordering on genocide" in Bosnia-Herzegovina, bloody ethnic conflicts in Africa and in the former Soviet republics, the continuing "abysmal record on human rights" in Iraq, and deplorable conditions in Haiti.

The good news is that human-rights violations are being exposed wherever they occur, and the international community, not any single country, is assuming the role of enforcer and peacekeeper. For example, the U.N. Security Council recently adopted a resolution creating an international tribunal to prosecute those responsible for war crimes in Bosnia and other former Yugoslav republics. The tribunal is the first international court empowered to try crimes against humanity since the Nuremberg trials of Nazis after World War II.

Approved by the United States, Russia, France, Britain, and Spain, the establishment of a tribunal was the first item in an in-

ternational "joint action program" on the Bosnian war. The court's
11 judges will be selected from as many countries by the U.N.
General Assembly. The U.N. resolution also obligates all U.N.
members to assist the court by arresting and handing over to the
court persons accused of atrocities and lesser war crimes. The Security Council can impose sanctions on countries unwilling to cooperate.

U.N. peacekeeping forces in Cambodia were determined to ensure "free and fair elections" in the face of real and feared violence
and intimidation by both the Phnom Penh government and its
Khmer Rouge enemies. Yasushi Akashi, the Japanese head of the
U.N. Transitional Authority in Cambodia, warned that the 22,000-
member mission known as UNTAC could and would disqualify
even "highly placed" candidates linked to political violence. It also
threatened tough international response to attacks on voters or polling stations. The threats, or being in the international spotlight, had
"the desired effect."

In Sri Lanka, where reports of "extra-judicial executions and dis-
appearances" put the number of people killed at anywhere from
12,000 to 60,000, pressure from Western aid donors forced the
government to allow human-rights groups to visit. The government
has since adopted many of the group's recommendations. "It was
essential that the government worry about its image," says Deepika
Udagama, director of the Centre for the Study of Human Rights at
the University of Colombo.

Global "Hot Spots" Escalate Human Rights Debate

To be sure, some would assert that for every "hot spot" that
cools as a result of international sanctions, others continue to blaze
unchecked, and that the 21st century will witness an explosion of
violence fueled by ethnic, religious, cultural, or territorial disputes.
Kenneth Ross, acting executive director of Human Rights Watch,
a global monitoring group based in New York City, insists that
communal violence is the most pressing issue facing the human
rights movement today and that our foremost challenge well into

the future will be the containment of abuses committed in the name of ethnic or religious groups.

Mahbub ul Haq, a special U.N. Development Program adviser and former Pakistani minister of finance and planning, concurs. He believes that future conflicts around the globe will be "between people rather than states over issues related to culture, ethnicity, or religion."

Meanwhile, at the World Conference on Human Rights, held in Vienna in June of 1993, the old world mantra "East is East and West is West and never the twain shall meet" was the repeated refrain. The West—with the United States leading the parade— declared the "universality of human rights," and the East—led by China, Syria, and Iran—declaimed "cultural relativism," insisting that non-Western cultures should not be held to Western standards. Each accused the other of disguising political and economic agendas behind a veil of concern for human rights.

The West vowed to impose sanctions against any country found in violation of yet-to-be-defined universal rights, and the East vowed to retaliate. Needless to say, the debate remains unresolved.

What none of these points of view takes into account, however, is the continued integration of world economies. As described in the first chapter, there is and will continue to be a resurgence of tribalism. Explains Allen Kassof, director of the Project on Ethnic Relations in Princeton, New Jersey: "The forces of modernization have given many people a sense that they don't belong anywhere, or that there's nothing permanent or stable in ther lives. It's quite understandable that they then seek something that seems eternal and can't be taken away from them. One is membership in a group. Another is a belief system or religion."

Tribalism, however, is not synonymous with brutality and domination. Will there be "tribal" conflicts in the future? Certainly. Will they occur with greater frequency than in the past? No. In fact, as the world becomes more economically integrated and the developed world increasingly dependent on the developing world, "tribal" conflicts (for lack of a better word) will become less frequent. In some cases, international human rights organizations will impose economic sanctions, and in others, "bottom-line" realities will preclude countries or subgroups from incursion or other efforts at ethnically or religiously motivated "cleansing."

Whether worried about their image or about future business prospects or because it is the right thing to do, countries exposed by international human-rights organizations will in future act decisively to end abuses lest the global community impose sanctions. In the 21st century, tribal law will be imposed universally.

A CONSENSUS IS EMERGING ON GLOBAL ENVIRONMENTAL ISSUES

While "doing the right thing" in socially responsible behavior may engender global debates as to how best to achieve a balance among social, cultural, economic, and political objectives, "doing the right thing" environmentally does not. A global consensus is emerging that if we all do not act now to protect and preserve Mother Earth, social responsibility could be a moot point.

This is not to suggest that there are no debatable environmental issues on the global agenda—there most certainly are, for example, whether the earth is or is not warming to an intolerable level courtesy of the greenhouse effect—but only to say that protecting and preserving the earth is now seen everywhere as both politically correct and economically expedient.

That many attendees of the international Rio Earth Summit walked away with no clear sense of a common environmental strategy is testimony to the conflicting needs and values of developed and developing countries. In a perfect world, preserving any country's natural resources would be supported globally for the greater good. But this is not a perfect world. All too often, protecting natural resources means sacrificing jobs, economic opportunity, and local customs.

There is emerging a constituency that believes in approaching global environmental issues by appropriately managing resources at the local level.

It is virtually certain that this approach will not please all the people all the time, and in fact some of the people will never be pleased, but it does factor in the cost benefits of preservation and economic growth in both the short and long term.

Having grown up being warned about the coming ice age, I think one caveat worth contemplating comes from Ronald Bailey's book *Eco-Scam:* "Freeze or Fry, the problem is always industrial capitalism, and the solution is always international socialism." This sounds right regarding the West. The irony is that whatever is deplorable in the environmental record of the industrial capitalists, the record pales in comparison to what was considered standard operating procedure by industry in the erstwhile Soviet Union and its former satellites. Compared to, say, the steel mills and coal mines of Copsa-Mica in Romania, U.S. Steel is a veritable Sierra Club.

While the debate among world leaders and international environmental organizations rages on, business is taking a more practical, bottom-line–oriented position.

Observes Stephen Viederman, president of the Jessie Smith Noyes Foundation, a philanthropic organization supporting environmental and reproductive rights in North and South America: "We have never learned, or we have forgotten, that the environment is the basis for all life and for all production. Rather than being an interest competing with other interests for attention, it is in reality the playing field on which all interests compete. . . . We have consistently failed to recognize that the economic system is an open system in a closed and finite ecosystem."

In a presentation to the Eighth National Conference on Business Ethics, sponsored by the Center for Business Ethics at Bentley College, Norman Bowie, Elmer L. Andersen Chair of Corporate Responsibility, University of Minnesota, put forth the following argument: "Environmentalists frequently argue that business has special obligations to protect the environment. Although I agree with the environmentalists on this point, I do not agree with them as to where the obligations lie.

"Business does not have an obligation to protect the environment over and above what is required by law; however, business does have a moral obligation to avoid intervening in the political arena in order to defeat or weaken environmental legislation."

Many business leaders and keepers of the corporate conscience believe otherwise. Richard J. Mahoney, Monsanto CEO, is, as a reporter with *Business Ethics* magazine wrote, "an unlikely revolutionary." This fiftysomething business executive isn't likely to be found at an Earth Day rally or distributing pamphlets for Greenpeace, but he is a standard-bearer for environmental issues and it isn't all talk.

Two years ago, Mahoney issued a call to action that evidences a profound change in the way corporate leaders view their stewardship of the planet. "Our commitment is to achieve sustainable development for those aspects of the environment where we have an impact. Our commitment is to achieve sustainable development for the good of all people in both developed and less-developed nations."

But, he insisted, it is not enough just to "unpollute" the world; "companies need to rectify the past and provide the technology necessary to serve the people of the world in the future without leaving behind a mess."

Business Leadership

Business taking the lead in the environmental movement? *Business Ethics* magazine cites the following examples:

- Union Carbide CEO Bob Kennedy [no doubt driven by the disaster at Bhopal] and Dow Chemical vice president David Buzzelli were among those instrumental in pursuading the Chemical Manufacturers Association to adopt its Responsible Care Initiative.
- Robert Bringer, 3M vice president for environmental engineering and pollution control, is running what may be the nation's most effective waste-reduction program.
- Pacific Gas and Electric CEO Richard Clark is showing the way in the utilities industry.
- DuPont chairman Edgar S. Woolard, Jr., was largely responsible for drafting a Business Charter for Sustainable Development, which has been endorsed by more than 200 major corporations worldwide.

When Richard Swart moved from South Africa to Britain to manage Berger Aus Berg, manufacturers of metal-drum closures, he quickly gained an appreciation for environmental issues and the impact of sound energy-conservation practices on a company's bottom line. Hiring an outside consultant, Swart authorized an environmental review to assess the company's energy use, waste management, legal compliance, recycling, and potential cost savings.

Having implemented many of the consultant's recommendations, Swart anticipates his electricity bills will be reduced by 50 percent and that within eight months he will recoup his investment for changes made as a result of the review.

What Swart and others have learned is that relatively minor changes can result in enormous cost savings and that environmentally correct behavior is good public relations, particularly when voluntary rather than through legislative fiat.

There is mounting evidence that corporations are moving away from simple compliance to a stewardship philosophy. For example, L'Eggs is losing its egg. Embracing the green movement, the hosiery company is replacing its plastic egg-shaped package with a recycled-cardboard package. Its new packaging uses 38 percent less material and is more easily recycled.

Whirlpool Corporation has managed to devise a simple, easy-to-comply-with recycling program and to create jobs for handicapped adults at the same time. Whirlpool contracts with Gateway Sheltered Workshop to collect and process its recyclables. "We didn't have to change much to do this," explains Carol Sizer, manager of media and community relations for the Benton Harbor, Michigan, appliance manufacturer. "No new wastebaskets or bins or anything. Gateway picks up the paper for a modest charge. It was so simple."

The program has been good for Gateway as well. When the program started, the organization employed 18 people. Today, it employs about 70.

And from the "now I've heard everything" page: Wellman Inc., a plastics recycler and polyester maker, and Dyersburg Fabrics Inc., producer of fleece fabrics, have produced what they claim is the first commercial textile fabric made from used plastic beverage bottles. Eighty percent of the fiber in Dyersburg's DyerSport E.C.O. fleece fabric is made by Wellman from plastic bottles. The fleece, say company executives, has the feel, strength, colorfastness, and shrinkage of other fleece fabrics made from polyester.

While wearing recycled cola bottles may not be the fashion statement—or even the political statement—you want to make, taking a stand on environmental issues is a statement everyone is making and multinational corporations are listening. "The new era is all about public accountability," says Jerry Martin, Dow Chemical's environmental affairs chief. "The reality is that the way we're going to survive as companies and as an industry is with public acceptance. If we don't have that, we won't be here twenty years from now."

New Standards

Not all environmentally correct behavior is so simple to achieve. A report released by the Committee for Economic Development, an independent research and educational organization composed of business leaders, sets forth environmental standards the group would like to see adopted by U.S. industry.

According to an article in *Business Week*, "The group endorses cost-benefit analysis as the basis for establishing environmental standards. It also supports market-based mechanisms, such as taxes on polluting emissions, as preferable to command-and-control methods of regulation—such as those that mandate pollution-control technology and set emissions levels. The group also recommends including the social costs of pollution, such as the degradation of natural resources, in the costs and prices of goods and services."

Write Craig Cox, managing editor of *Business Ethics*, and Sally Power of the University of St. Thomas in St. Paul, "You can look at it as an imperative for business survival; you can look at it as a way to build a competitive edge. But ultimately, corporate environmentalists need to flex their considerable muscles for one fundamental reason: because they're the most powerful allies our planet has.

"And when they come down on the side of sustainability, when they integrate a broad commitment to the environment into their corporate mission, they're becoming part of something larger than their company, larger than their industry. They've become part of a movement that will change the world."

Integrity and the Bottom Line

"Many organizations believe there is no correlation between integrity and bottom-line performance," *Industry Week* told its readers in April 1992. "They are wrong. Integrity and performance are not at the opposite ends of a continuum. When people work for an organization that they believe is fair, where everyone is willing to give of themselves to get the job done, where traditions of loyalty and caring are hallmarks, people work to a higher level. The values around them become a part of them, and they think of the customer as someone whom they owe the finest possible product and service."

Paul O'Neill, CEO of Pittsburgh-based Aluminum Company of America (ALCOA), spearheaded a corporate restructuring and designed a corporate strategy that resulted in cost reductions of $400 million in two years. In 1991, O'Neill looked around him and saw that while ALCOA was in pretty good shape, it lagged behind world benchmarks. His challenge to ALCOA's 22 business units worldwide was to "close the gap between current practice and world benchmarks by a minimum of 80 percent in two years."

In little more than a year, business units around the world had made or exceeded 31 of 190 targets that represented the core of the company's program. How did he accomplish such an extraordinary feat? He didn't. Employees did. What O'Neill did was empower individuals through routine distribution of information previously given only to management, by revamping performance appraisals, and by encouraging flexibility and personal initiative by employees at all levels.

Empowering individuals and sharing information, however, is only half the story. The other half is values. O'Neill believes ALCOA's value system, which includes "integrity, the importance of people, and safety,'' is what allows people throughout the organization to ''exercise the individual leadership that is so critical to the company's success. I'm not willing to look the other way when somebody is off base with regard to integrity on the grounds that they're making such a wonderful technical or professional contribution that we can't afford to live without them. To me it's an easy choice.''

The Gray Areas

Perhaps an easy choice in situations that are clear examples of right vs. wrong, but when one is talking about integrity, values, and ethical standards, there are few black-and-white situations. Most day-to-day moral or ethical dilemmas fall into a vast gray area requiring the wisdom of Solomon to resolve. Who among us is so wise? *Industry Week* made an effort to find out. What they discovered is enlightening.

In a survey of 1,300 middle managers in medium-sized and large companies (companies with at least 500 employees), ''middle managers' responses to straightforward ethical questions reflect a pure and steadfast virtue usually reserved for Boy Scouts and clerics. When pushed into gray areas where loyalties, goals, and the desire to be honest don't coincide, however, rationalizations for shady behavior begin working their way into decisions.''

Ironically, when respondents were asked if they had lied in answering any of the survey questions, 5 percent admitted that they had. This despite the fact that the survey was both voluntary and anonymous. ''When asked if they had ever taken anything worth more than $25 from their company, 4 percent said that they had done so once and an additional 4 percent that they had done so repeatedly.'' Answers to other survey questions suggested that telling ''little white lies'' was ''ethically tolerable'' as was ''borrowing'' company materials or ''fudging on one's expense account.''

On the flip side, fully 98 percent of survey respondents said that they would not steal $100,000 from their company even given ''absolute certainty'' that they would not be caught. ''So, even though 5 percent admitted that they lied on the questionnaire, only 2 percent would commit a fail-safe theft. One possible explanation is that managers' ethical standards are higher when the gains of deception are enormous (and one's conscience comes into play).''

Respondents also were presented with the following scenario: While in the process of bidding on a contract for the U.S. Navy, they learn that although their prices are competitive, it would take their firm several months longer to develop and manufacture the product than their competitor. Managers were then asked how they would respond if asked about their development schedule.

About one fourth (26 percent) said they would describe the benefits of their product and avoid answering direct questions about scheduling. Another 13 percent responded that they would tell the Navy they could match their competitor's schedule and worry about how to do it later. A slight majority, 58 percent, said they would tell the Navy the truth.

Bias in the Hiring Process

On the subject of bias in the hiring process, 10 percent of the managers questioned admitted that they would prefer to hire a white male over a female and 34 percent said that they would not hire an admitted homosexual. Fully 52 percent said they would not hire a homosexual for a sales or management position. Although 90 percent of respondents said that they would not discriminate against females in the hiring process, 92 percent admitted that they would rather work for a man than for a woman.

Michael Josephson, a prominent Los Angeles ethicist who consults for some of America's largest public corporations, says his polls reveal that between 20 and 30 percent of middle managers have written deceptive internal reports.

Are we to believe, then, that the world's business organizations are populated by liars, thieves, and bigots? To be sure, increasing pressure from within the organization to maintain profitability and increasing competition between organizations in the global business community have created situations in which doing the most expedient thing rather than the right thing is tempting, but we shouldn't be too hasty in concluding that companies will always do what is most expedient.

Companies Introduce Codes of Conduct

Recent surveys suggest that more than three quarters of America's major corporations are endeavoring to build ethics into their organizations and a growing number of companies are installing ethics officers. Five years ago, very few companies had ethics officers. Today, 15 to 20 percent of big companies have them. Ethics officers typically hold the title of director or vice president and usually report directly to the CEO.

According to Michael Hoffman, director of the Center for Business Ethics at Bentley College in Waltham, Massachusetts, ethics officers "tend to be confessors, corporate conscience, enforcers and teachers rolled into one."

A survey conducted by the Institute of Business Ethics in Britain revealed that 30 percent of large corporations already have in place a code of ethics and that many more European companies are considering drafting standards of behavior. National Westminster Bank (NatWest) may be unwittingly setting a standard for other major companies to follow.

All 90,000 NatWest employees recently received a 10-page document that laid out the details of one of the most ambitious codes of conduct ever written by a British company. In summary, the booklet informs employees that the company's priorities are "integrity in dealings, delivery of customer satisfaction and creating opportunities for staff. It touches on conflicts of interest, criminal activities and accepting entertainment."

To ensure that its code of ethics was comprehensive and user friendly, NatWest hired a consultant who worked with people at every level of the company.

Throughout Europe, there is growing awareness of the impact unethical conduct has on employees, shareholders, and customers. Publication of a code of conduct by Spain's Banco Bilbao Vizcaya (BBV) was considered an "unusual step for any Spanish company," but commended as a means of seeking public amends for allegedly corrupt dealings with the government.

Disseminated to its senior executives, BBV's code of conduct insists that they refrain from any action involving the bank group in which, directly or indirectly, they might have particular interests. While a preoccupation with ethics may be new to business in Spain, it is not new to Scandinavian companies. Swedish businesspeople have long taken the problem seriously.

The Institute Against Corruption, a coalition of business representatives, has been in existence since 1923. Backed by organizations including the Stockholm Chamber of Commerce and the Swedish Federation of Industries, the institute keeps companies up to date about codes of practice and legislative changes.

Growing evidence of some unholy alliances between businesses and politicians in Germany has focused the nation's attention on a "moral crisis" in the country and has intensified a national debate on ethics. It is interesting that where corruption has been substantiated in Germany, it has been the politician, not the business executive, who has paid the price. This also has been the case in France, where when bribery has been revealed, it is the politician who is blamed for taking the bribe, not the businessperson for offering it.

Despite the fact that bribery is common practice in France, few French business owners express a need for greater sanctions against such activities. For example, Bouygues, France's biggest contractor, said it had no code of conduct. Observed one spokesperson: "The idea of voluntary rules going beyond what is in the law is very Anglo-Saxon. We regard state control as sufficiently tough for companies not to have to make any special effort to sensitize their employees to it."

Companies Tell Employees, "Let Our Conscience Be Your Guide"

Drafting codes of conduct to help guide employees and managers through troublesome ethical waters may well be an Anglo-Saxon ideal, but it has worked for many companies. Evidence is strong in

U.S. companies that establishing guidelines pays off in greater commitment and in better customer relations.

In existence for more than 50 years, Johnson & Johnson's statement of values, known as "the Credo," is seen as a model and is credited with helping to guide the company through its product-tampering crises with Tylenol in 1982 and 1986. In 1975, then J&J CEO James Burke held a series of challenge meetings with top managers to ensure that the company's 30-year-old statement was still valid.

For three years, Burke or J&J president David R. Clare met with 1,200 managers in two-day seminars of 25 people to challenge the Credo. Since then, there have been two major follows-ups, and challenge meetings continue to be held twice a year for new top managers. The Credo works because it strikes a "balance between centralized management controls and giving employees enough autonomy to build mutual trust critical to maintaining a values system."

J&J emphasizes individual autonomy and initiative, yet sees its value statement as "an exception to decentralization." Says Burke: "The Credo is a unifying force that keeps the individual units marching together."

Textron's Bell Helicopter started an ethics program in 1987. Introducing first an ombudsman whose job was to handle ethics infractions and employee complaints, Bell Helicopter now has an ethics officer and a far more comprehensive program. In addition to hearing employee complaints and "questions on issues from expense accounts to possible misconduct by colleagues," Bell's ethics officer also helps "coordinate meetings for senior management's ethics committee and monitors broader corporate ethics issues."

It is virtually certain that other companies will join ranks with J&J and Bell Helicopter as new federal regulations encourage companies to form ethics programs. Effective in November 1992, new sentencing guidelines permit penalty reductions for companies fined for ethical breaches if the company has an ethics program or office.

Ethics Officers Are a Terrible Idea

Some industry consultants see a downside. Peter J. Neary, a senior program associate for the Center for Creative Leadership in Colorado Springs, Colorado, says ethics officers are "a terrible idea" because "you're giving ownership of the corporate conscience to one person, and it becomes that person's responsibility to catch ethics violations."

He has a point. Besides, the mere fact that an ethics program or value statement exists doesn't ensure that all members of the organization will abide by it. Hertz Corp. has an ethics code and employees are required to sign a compliance statement, but that didn't prevent people within the company from overcharging motorists and insurers $13 million for repairs.

"As much as 80 percent of the $13 million in overcharges" resulted from charging the retail cost of fixing cars, even though Hertz received volume discounts on repairs. Senior managers approved this practice on the advice of in-house legal counsel, whose decision was based on the belief that competitors did the same thing. Unlike its competitors, Hertz didn't notify its customers that they would be paying "prevailing retail rates."

Company chairman Frank A. Olson ended the policy as soon as it was made public, and the company has so far refunded more than $3 million to customers. What of the future? Olson insists that if he catches "one guy billing at something other than cost, I'll throw him out the window myself." Well, maybe not literally, but Hertz is now likely to be a lot tougher on employees who don't uphold the company's values.

In the mid-'80s, Boeing found itself in a similar predicament. The aircraft manufacturer has had an ethics committee in place reporting directly to the board since 1964. Ethics training is done by line managers, not consultants, and the company has a corporate ethics office through which employees can report infractions. "Yet in 1984, a Boeing unit illegally used inside information to gain a government contract."

Another corporate beacon of ethical light also took a fall. Recognized as a pioneer in corporate ethics, Dow Corning was among the first corporations to establish an ethics program. Believed to be the most elaborate in corporate America, it was touted as a "brilliant process," and a model for others to emulate. Yet Dow has been accused of selling faulty breast implants and of silencing the engineer who brought the information to light. When it became public, Dow announced it would stop making implants.

Right vs. Right

If companies are doing the right thing, than why do things sometimes turn out so wrong? Part of the problem is that "real-life" managers face ethical challenges that are not necessarily what Harvard Business School lecturer Joseph L. Badaracco, Jr., refers to as "right vs. wrong," but rather "right vs. right." Managers need help in navigating situations in which the right path is clear but "real-world competitive and institutional pressures lead even well-intentioned managers astray," wrote Andrew Stark in a recent *Harvard Business Review*.

"The problem is that the discipline of business ethics has yet to provide much concrete help to managers in either of these areas," continues Stark, "and even business ethicists sense it. One can't help but notice how often articles in the field lament a lack of direction or poor fit with the real ethical problems of real managers."

Or maybe it's that actions speak louder than words. Increasingly, executives with companies large and small believe that active civic involvement is a critical part of a corporate ethics campaign. As one General Mills executive told a researcher with the Business Roundtable: "It's hard to imagine that a person who reads to the blind at night would cheat on his expense account."

Professor Henk van Luijk, chairman of the European Business Ethics Network (EBEN), articulates an even broader perspective. "Ethical competence . . . is not a matter of imposing something on somebody, but of enlarging the scope of our social attention. . . . Ethics in business, as in public administration, is a dimension of reflective management and policy.

"Participants in a market society have distinct, legitimate, but often not easily compatible interests. They have rights that are perfectly justified, but sometimes overtly conflicting. To find a mutually and morally acceptable balance of rights and interests, ethics can be specifically supportive. Not by imposing rules and regulations, but by explicitly raising the moral point of view."

In an address to the Fifth European Business Conference in Paris, van Luijk related a third function of ethics, "encouraging new projects and initiatives." Referencing public-private partnerships in Britain, France, and the Netherlands, van Luijk observed that "many recent city innovation projects could not have been realized if there had not been a joint venture of local government and local businesses, willing to cooperate in a common effort in view of a common good."

Public-private partnerships have been a mainstay of U.S. programs designed to address some of society's most pressing concerns. Today, such programs are increasingly coming about as a result of private companies pressing public agencies to participate in programs initiated by corporate citizens.

Ethics officers, codes of conduct, national and international organizations established to encourage businesses and their employees to behave more ethically all have their place, but actions do speak louder than words. And a growing number of companies are taking action.

European Companies

The trend toward greater corporate social responsibility is by no means a U.S. phenomenon. "A survey published by the Prince of Wales Business Leaders Forum shows that Europe's multinational corporations are finding new ways to promote health and welfare. . . . " A network of international business leaders, the Business Leaders Forum was established to promote the concept that "good corporate citizenship helps sustain the global environment and the quality of life." In its report, "Corporate Community Involvement," the forum highlights emerging trends.

According to the report, European companies are moving away

from the old-style corporate philanthropy of writing checks for selective causes and toward market-led sponsorship. At Volkswagen's German headquarters in Wolfsburg, recycling has been institutionalized. "The ultimate aim of the giant Wolfsburg headquarters is to roll new cars out at one end of the plant for use until they wear out, and then wheel them back in at the other end to have their components recycled."

While they aren't likely to achieve that goal anytime soon, every effort is made to work toward it. Evidencing their commitment to recycling, the water pumped into the plant "is recycled to a higher standard than legally required, then reused up to seven times."

According to the report, continental Europe lags behind both the United States and Britain in developing a sense of social responsibility. Its argument sounds plausible: "urban unrest and rioting hit Britain and the United States much earlier than in continental Europe" and consequently companies in both countries were forced to "rethink corporate involvement in the community. . . . It is taking time to fashion appropriate political and corporate responses to the growing—but comparatively recent—social unrest in France and Germany caused by immigration, unemployment, and in the German case, reunification."

CORPORATE INTEGRITY AND FOREIGN FACTORIES

A series of articles published in the Portland *Oregonian* in late 1992 claimed that Oregon-based Nike, Inc., exploited Indonesian laborers by paying them less than poverty wages to work in unsafe factories. Nike chairman and CEO Philip Knight was so distressed by the accusations that he sent a letter to every newspaper in the country that had picked up the earlier story.

Insisting that the story contained many inaccuracies and distortions, Knight wrote: "We do accept responsibility for working conditions in factories we contract with to make our products, and we have tried to upgrade both the quality of life and the skills of employees working in our factory.

"Nike's foreign factories generally offer the highest pay and the best working conditions of any athletic shoe factories in the particular country. In China, a worker in a Nike factory makes higher wages than a professor at Beijing University.''

Another article, this time in the *Far Eastern Economic Review*, reported that Indonesians who make Nikes earn far more than most workers lucky enough to get factory jobs in that low-wage country. Prompting company spokesperson, Dusty Kidd, to comment: ''Americans focus on wages paid, not what standard of living those wages relate to.''

That may well be true. Or it may be true that when Nike insists that factory workers ''just do it,'' the intent is a lot more serious than is the intent of its popular advertisements.

The point is that as companies become more global, with factories, sales and marketing, and back-office operations in far-flung places, convincing socially conscious customers that they are not exploiting the disadvantaged, disturbing the environment, or destroying a country's cultural heritage will become critical to the success of their product.

In the last week of December 1992, NBC aired a program asserting that Little Rock, Arkansas–based Wal-Mart's ''Buy American'' program was misleading. NBC maintained that not only are clothes sold at Wal-Mart not made in America, but that children as young as nine years old manufacture the clothing in Bangladesh sweatshops. Exposed by an official with the AFL-CIO, which has long taken issue with Wal-Mart for relying on imports, Wal-Mart insists the charges are false. However, when questioned by NBC, it was the union official who looked authoritative while Wal-Mart CEO David Glass seemed to be uncertain as to where the company gets its products.

Donna Katzin of the Interfaith Center on Corporate Responsibility says, ''Just because companies don't make a product themselves doesn't relieve them of all obligations.''

Pittsburgh-based H. J. Heinz doesn't catch its own tuna, but mail from youthful consumers regarding fishing techniques that trap and kill large numbers of dolphins prompted Heinz to say its Star-Kist brand of tuna would buy only from fishing boats that use ''approved'' tuna-catching methods.

An article in *Newsweek* posed the question: "Is it fair to hold Third World suppliers to U.S. standards of conduct?" That same article quoted Northwestern University business ethicist David Messick: "It's easy to take cynical views of American corporations, but what gives us the right to decide at what age people in Bangladesh should work?"

Fair or not, companies are no longer willing to take the chance that their manufacturing, importing, or processing can be construed as coercive, unethical, or exploitive of people or the environment. Name-brand companies like Sears and Levi Strauss, as well as lesser-known companies like New Hampshire–based Timberland Co., now refuse to import products from China, for fear that those products might have been manufactured by prison laborers. Philips-Van Heusen asserts it will "terminate orders to apparel suppliers that violate its broad ethical, environmental, and human-rights codes."

Demands on Suppliers

Some companies are going beyond simply drafting codes of conduct and are soliciting information from suppliers and conducting on-site investigations. In January 1993, Atlanta-based Home Depot sent all of its suppliers of home-improvement products a questionnaire asking whether any supplier in its worldwide chain employed children or prison convicts. To demonstrate just how serious it was about the inquiry, Home Depot gave companies 72 hours to respond or lose contracts.

Levi Strauss took a similar mandate several steps further. Strauss inspected each one of its 600 suppliers worldwide. When the inspection process had been completed, 30 suppliers were dropped and reform pledges were obtained from another 120. The company also pulled out of Myanmar (Burma) after determining that the government was responsible for pervasive human-rights violations.

Not insensitive to the impact of its decisions, Levi Strauss made a bargain with factories in Bangladesh, where children under the legal working age of 14 are routinely employed. In at least one factory, Strauss agreed to educate 40 under-age child laborers while the factory continued to pay them regular wages.

What these and other companies are discovering the hard way is that "going global" is fraught with hazards not discussed in business school. Activists of all stripes, from environmentalists, unions, human-rights advocates, and socially conscious investors, are rediscovering the press. Not terribly imaginative, advocacy groups have always known that public awareness and response affects social change; however, today the power of the press translates into instantaneous global exposure. Importers and others are being forced to monitor not just their own behavior and that of their foreign suppliers but that of their suppliers' suppliers as well.

FROM AD HOC RULES TO GLOBAL STANDARDS

According to Professor Gary Clark, comparative culture teacher at Sophia University in Tokyo, Japan is a "sophisticated tribal society" where people tend to make up rules as they go along rather than rely on a consistent moral code. "The tribal ethic has precedence. But it can't cope with all situations," says Clark. "The problem [for the Japanese] is deciding what is a scandal. And usually, he adds, they'll wait for someone else to decide for them.

The same could be said for all of us. Hence the emergence in the last decade of such institutions and organizations as the Center for Business Ethics at Bentley College in Waltham, Massachusetts, The Business Enterprise Trust, based in Stanford, California, Emory University's Center for Ethics in Public Policy and the Professions, Businesses for Social Responsibility, the Brussels-based European Business Ethics Network, and the latest entrant, Transparency International, a coalition of senior government, business, and development-agency officials. Modeled after Amnesty International, this group will concentrate on battling what officials termed "grand corruption" in global business transactions. Among the founders are Robert S. McNamara, former head of the World Bank, Oscar Arias Sánchez, former president of Costa Rica and Nobel Peace Prize winner, former U.N. ambassador Andrew Young, and Paul Batchelor, Chairman of Coopers & Lybrand International Consulting.

These, and the hundreds of other organizations and associations established in an effort to define ethical behavior and encourage their colleagues and cohorts to do the same, are certainly to be applauded.

But can values be defined and, once defined, can they be institutionalized? Business schools are grappling with a similar question. Can ethics be taught? Unethical conduct continues despite the fact that over 500 business-ethics courses are currently taught on American campuses.

According to the *Harvard Business Review,* "fully 90 percent of the nation's business schools now provide some kind of training in the area. There are more than 25 textbooks in the field and three academic journals dedicated to the topic. At least 16 business ethics research centers are now in operation, and endowed chairs in business ethics have been established at Georgetown, Virginia, Minnesota, and a number of other prominent business schools."

Stewardship Is a Human Rights Concept, Too

Just as companies are beginning to view their environmental responsibility as a stewardship of the earth, so too are companies beginning to accept their responsibilities toward humankind. Writes Edith Weiner, president of Weiner, Edrich, Brown, Inc., "Dominion is an industrial model which implies that mankind is at the top of a hierarchy and entitled to exploit all of nature, even other humans, for its own ends. Stewardship, however, says that there is no hierarchy, that humanity is given the task of caring for and preserving the earth and all its resources, to return them in as good or better shape to each succeeding generation."

It is, says Weiner, stewardship, not Marxism, socialism, or communism, that will provide the future counterpoint to capitalism. If we want to know which of the millions of businesses being created today will survive into the 21st century, then we need to look first at how they are structured and secondly at how they treat their employees, their customers, and society at large. Companies that embrace the small-is-efficient model will prosper. Companies that are configured as confederations of entrepreneurs, and that take seriously their responsibilities as stewards of the planet and of their community, will flourish.

The fact is that most individuals are basically ethical—and I suspect that's true everywhere. Most of us don't steal from our neighbors or embezzle money from our employers. We give to charity and live by a code of conduct that lets us sleep peacefully at night. So if we're not lying, cheating, and stealing, who is? More important, why? Because it is tolerated. Because in many cases institutional cultures do not discourage small lapses in ethical standards if the payoff is big enough. The bigger and more impenetrable the institution—business or government—the greater the size of the "ethical lapses."

That, however, is about to change. In the 21st century, the component parts of large corporations will get smaller and smaller. Business units will behave as individual operating divisions, each responsible for profits and losses. Individuals will carry a far greater share of the responsibility for their organization's performance.

When the onus is on the individual, individuals will reach decisions based on the same ethical standards they live by.

As individual responsibility increases in business and in politics, a universal code of conduct will evolve; we will all hold ourselves and each other to higher standards of behavior.

5

The Dragon Century: The Chinese Commonwealth—Gaining Power from Its Parts

I have never seen anything like it in my life. One hundred miles of uninterrupted construction.

On an early morning in September of 1993 I arranged for a car and driver to take me from the Garden Hotel in Quangzhou (we used to call it Canton) to the railroad station in Shenzhen on the border of the New Territories of Hong Kong. Along this 160-kilometer corridor thousands of small and medium-sized factories, warehouses, and residental buildings are in various stages of construction, all being created by entrepreneurs. Because the traffic is so heavy (mostly trucks), the trip took more than four hours. Four hours of witnessing the largest construction project in the world.

Another paradox:

The last great Communist country becomes the world's biggest market economy.

If China can sustain its current economic momentum, and there is little reason to believe that it cannot, by the year 2000 it will be the world's biggest economy. Bigger than the United States, bigger than Japan. In time, China's economy could be bigger than the combined economies of all of today's rich industrial economies.

Now the World's Third-Largest Economy

Skeptical? Skepticism is understandable considering how the world has viewed China (and how China has viewed itself) since 1949 when Mao Zedong declared the country the People's Republic of China and claimed it for communism. Skepticism is understandable but not warranted. China is already the world's third-largest economy, surpassing Germany, trailing only the United States and Japan. And by some measures, it already has surpassed Japan.

Traditionally, a country's economy is measured by determining a per capita income which is calculated by converting the value of its gross domestic product into U.S. dollars at the official exchange rate. A big problem with this method is that if a country's currency weakens against the dollar, its economy automatically shrinks, which can be very misleading. But that is precisely what happened in the case of China. Between 1978 and 1992, the yuan (China's currency) fell from 1.7 to the dollar to 5.5 to the dollar. But to use this traditional measurement effectively negates China's real economic growth during the same period. By this calculation, China's economy is the 10th largest, and its people among the poorest.

Even keepers of the world's ledger know the numbers make no sense, and so in 1993 the International Monetary Fund (IMF) used a different methodology, and came up with dramatically different results. The IMF calculated each country's national output by what goods and services its currency will buy *at home* compared with the purchasing power of other countries' currencies. By using the purchasing power parity (PPP) method, the IMF found that China had produced $1.7 trillion in goods and services in 1992, far greater than the $400 billion previously estimated, and that in 1992 its per capita income was $1,600, not $370.

Predictably, the IMF's use of the PPP method engendered considerable controversy among traditional economists, most of whom said the method lacked credible statistical data. When the IMF began the process it used price data from the United Nations International Comparison Program provided by Robert Summers and Alan Heston, both economics professors at the University of Pennsylvania, recognized as among the world's authorities on the subject. Using data and interpretive analysis provided by Summers and Heston, the IMF first came up with a per capita income for China of $2,598, or $2.9 trillion at 1990 prices. Deciding this was too high, the IMF settled on figures taken from a study published by the Center for International Research of the U.S. Bureau of the Census. Meanwhile, some economists estimate that China's real per capita income is as high as $4,000 (which would make it much bigger than Japan's economy).

The arithmetic is straightforward. If China's real per capita income is $4,000, that means it has a $4.8 trillion economy (1.2 billion × $4,000), twice Japan's 2.4 trillion, but smaller than the United States' $5.6 trillion (all based on PPP numbers). It gets even more interesting when you project China's potential growth curve. If China's per capita income rose to that of South Korea ($7,561), the size of its economy would become more than $9 trillion. If it climbed to the level of fellow Chinese in Taiwan ($10,000), its economy would hit $12 trillion, more than twice as big as the current size of the economy of the United States. In time, it probably will happen.

Size of economy should not be confused with standard of living. By no stretch of the imagination does China have—nor will it have anytime soon—a well-to-do standard of living, even after it becomes the world's largest economy.

The point is that whatever data one uses, China's economy more than triples in size when using PPP rather than more traditional means. Or as Paul Krugman, an economist with the Massachusetts Institute of Technology, so aptly pointed out: "The main importance of this is geopolitical. It's a reminder that China is a great power already, which is something many people haven't quite grasped yet."

Whether people have grasped it or not, nothing can change the fact that China, with its single-minded dedication to replacing its central economy with a "socialist market economy," or "socialism with Chinese characteristics," has unshackled its citizens, unleashing a riptide of repressed energy and enthusiasm. Napoleon warned the West to let China sleep, but Napoleon could not have imagined how the world might change when 1.2 billion people emerge from more than half a century of revolutions, war, famine, and Communist tyranny and a decade of a nihilistic repression known as the Cultural Revolution.

Hundreds of Thousands of People Take the Plunge into the Sea

Six years ago, Bai Mei was a typical Chinese worker, toiling in a state-run metals factory for $40 a month. Today, she is a real-estate developer with a net worth of somewhere around $2 million. Bai Mei is 35.

In 1987, 34-year-old Wang Yuejin opened a one-room shoe factory with 10 workers. Today, Wang employs 100 workers who turn out 500 pairs of shoes a day. The factory had revenues of almost $1 million in 1992, earning Wang a $60,000 profit. Sales are growing by 50 percent a year.

At 31, Lu Zhoukui was a happily married man with a flourishing career as a mid-level city official. His income was $46 a month. Then he took the plunge, starting a business engaged in everything from running restaurants to placing Chinese laborers in foreign jobs. His company earned a profit of $219,000 in its first four months of operation. Lu expects a profit of $1 million in 1993.

China boasts a million millionaires, almost all of whom come from the ranks of its 18 million entrepreneurs. Many insist that that figure is grossly understated as many township and village enterprises (TVEs) are actually privately owned companies. For a people who for decades looked down on commerce as demeaning and making money as politically incorrect, the Chinese have learned awfully quickly. To be sure, the vast majority of entrepreneurs are young—too young to have been greatly influenced by the Cultural Revolution—and have had greater exposure to enterprise-driven Western culture, but included in the new entrepreneurs are farmers, intellectuals, scientists, and high-ranking government officials.

Everywhere, but particularly in urban centers, young people ask the same question of each other. "Have you put out to sea?" Also referred to as "plunging into the sea," the Chinese name for this entrepreneurial phenomenon is *xaihai jingshang*—literally translated, "to the ocean to do business." Plunging into the sea . . . putting out to sea . . . to the ocean to do business, the oft-repeated phrase refers to an individual's willingness to give up the security of a government-assigned job in a state-owned enterprise and enter the risky world of private enterprise. Today, entrepreneurs are heroes and making money is honorable, maybe even noble. While their bank accounts grow and their tastes shift from government-issued Mao jackets to expensive Western designer fashions, they can rest comfortably in the knowledge that they are contributing to the Chinese economy or the greater economic good.

The entrepreneurs pretend they are doing it for the greater good; the Party pretends the country is still Communist.

PLA, Inc.

Many members of the military are jumping into the sea. Hard pressed for funds, China's People's Liberation Army (PLA) has established thousands of businesses—from arms exporting and airlines to pig farms—to raise extra money. Military units can't get enough money from the government's budget so they are raising their own, with the funds raised through business dealings now equaling or surpassing those they get from Beijing.

Some observers say that there could be as many as 20,000 PLA-backed businesses up and running today, but the number is increasing so fast it is hard to know. The PLA's main businesses are in construction, transportation, medical services, hotels, and farming. Their factories produce three quarters of all the pharmaceuticals that China makes. They run several hundred hotels and guest houses. Seven years ago the PLA started China United Airlines, which uses air force transport planes and military airports for commercial passengers.

There is concern that all this activity may distract the PLA from its supposed primary mission of defending the Communist party, but it is a little late in the day. The PLA is very much a part of the economy and the economy is very much a part of the PLA.

The Chinese economy is being decentralized dramatically, from centrally planned and run, down to townships, villages, and individual entrepreneurs. That is resulting in the economy becoming larger and larger. It is a manifestation of the Global Paradox:

The larger the Chinese economy becomes, the smaller and more powerful the parts.

A survey of young people found that their top job preference is now to be an entrepreneur. Working for the national government ranked 8th out of 16 choices. By some estimates, almost one third of China's 103 million government employees have given up their positions to start their own businesses, or have taken a second job in the private sector.

Money, not power, is what motivates this burgeoning group. Says Chen Wei, a 26-year-old businesswoman who, with her twin brother, owns a Beijing-based computer company: "We don't have power, but we have money. With money, you can get power."

While they may not have a great deal of political power, they are beginning to attain at least some. In March 1993, 20 entrepreneurs were elected as delegates to China's nominal parliament and to a prestigious political advisory group. More important, Rong Yiren, one of China's most prominent entrepreneurs, was elected the country's vice president.

What these entrepreneurs do have is shared values and the strength of numbers. "These people are creating a middle class, they are creating wealth, and, as elsewhere in East Asia, somewhere down the road they will be creating a demand for improved quality of life and meaningful political participation," observes David Shambaugh, teacher of Chinese politics at the University of London. Even Communist hard-liners accept that the political and social forces unleashed by economic reforms will reduce their control over society. They also know that their ability to raise living standards and maintain a healthy economy is the only way for them to retain their legitimacy as a political force. Communism—or, rather, the Communist party—and capitalism will simply have to co-exist.

Deng Xiaoping's Legacy—Let Economics, Not Dogma, Determine China's Destiny

It could not have been a less auspicious occasion that launched China's economic revolution. In December 1978, at the third plenary session of the 11th Central Committee of the Communist Party of China, party members agreed to Deng Xiaoping's economic reform proposal. Deng wanted China to abandon the Stalinist principles of central planning and state ownership in favor of a decentralized market economy. Even more startling, Deng insisted that China open itself up to the world.

In the 15 years since the 11th Central Committee meeting, the world has witnessed one of the fastest improvements in a country's welfare anywhere, at any time in history. Growth in real GNP has averaged nearly 9 percent annually, thereby doubling every eight years. In 1992, the Chinese economy grew almost 13 percent, the fastest in the world. During the first half of 1993, China's economy grew almost 15 percent, and the government began to take anti-inflation measures to cool things off a bit. China's goal is to grow 10 percent a year for the rest of the century; doubling every seven years.

By 1994, China's economy will be four times bigger than it was when Deng first made his case for economic reform. If China meets its 2002 targets, its economy will be eight times bigger than it was in 1978. If that happens, China will have matched the economic performances of Japan, Taiwan, and South Korea during the 25 years when those countries grew fastest.

But remember, Taiwan has only 20 million people; Japan has 125 million people. China has 1.2 billion. Imagine, China—now growing faster than the economic miracle rate of Japan—has almost a thousand million more people than Japan. China is rising as Japan did—and China has 10 times the population of Japan.

China's foreign trade grew to around $170 billion by 1992 (despite the economic malaise of some of its global trading partners), up from $135 billion in 1991 and from a mere $21 billion in 1978, the year the reforms began. That is not to say skyrocketing growth is uniformly distributed throughout the country: South China in particular is many years ahead of some of the northern and central provinces. Nevertheless, economic reform has touched nearly every person in China.

As *The Economist* described the situation in a comprehensive survey of the China miracle: "Trickle-down economics has little to apologize for in the case of China. Guesses vary, but 200m–270m Chinese are thought to have been living in 'absolute poverty' (basically, not even enough food) in 1978. The number of absolutely poor in 1985, when the farming reforms had largely been accomplished, was 100m. A Japan, two Britains, or half an America: about that many people were lifted out of poverty in China by the first six years of economic reform."

If well-being can be measured by the ability to purchase consumer products, then many Chinese people are doing very well. In 1981, urban Chinese averaged fewer than one color television set for every 100 households. By 1991 it was 70 sets for every 100 households. In 1981, there were six washing machines for each 100 city households; a decade later, more than 80. Construction is booming everywhere. Factories, offices, homes, mixed-used facilities are being built just as fast as twenty-four-hour construction crews can build them, and there are plenty of people waiting to occupy them once completed.

It can be said that never before have so many people risen from poverty so rapidly. When visiting China, I asked scores of people how the market reforms had impacted on their personal lives. Almost every one of them said they had raised their standard of living.

Gordon Wu's Barometer

Gordon Wu, one of the major Hong Kong players in mainland China projects, says he has been using his own yardstick to measure China's dazzling economy—the "Wu Economic Barometer." It works exclusively in developing countries and is split into five phases. As a developing country begins to experience real economic growth:

Step 1: People start to eat out.
Step 2: They buy new clothes.
Step 3: Consumers start accumulating new appliances.
(A number of people in China told me: "We now have refrigerators.")
Step 4: They buy a motorcycle, car, or apartment.
Step 5: Consumers start traveling overseas.

Much of China is in Steps 2 and 3, with many moving to Step 4. The Wu Economic Barometer is a good way to gauge the economic takeoff of poor countries moving toward rich. If you are in the appliance business and see Steps 1 and 2 being played out, you had better be positioning yourself to take advantage of moving target Step 3 coming up.

Secrets of Deng's Success

Economic reform in China started with the farmer.

In the beginning there was Deng, who personally directed the first three waves of reform. Deng's first critical steps turned out to be just the right ones. He created a market economy in food, first by freeing prices for all food, except grain, and second by abolishing agricultural communes in favor of what became, essentially, family farms. Output improved dramatically. Having remained stagnant from the mid-1950s to 1978, real value added rose by 7 percent in the early 1980s while the number of people working the land declined. Everyone, food producer and food consumer, became better off.

In the decade of the '80s the productivity of the Chinese peasant increased more than that of any other workers in the world.

What was most remarkable was that these first two steps ran completely counter to traditional Stalinist-industrialization drives in which the countryside was milked dry to support growth in the industrial sector. **By turning farmers into entrepreneurs, Deng was able to ensure a source of capital for future industrial development by generating a surplus of rural savings.** At the same time Deng wooed and won a political constituency that encompassed three quarters of China's population.

Deng's second step (which was considered less significant at the time but now has proved to be equally or perhaps more important) was to eliminate the central government's monopoly over foreign trade. His "open door policy" included establishing four experimental "special economic zones." Guangdong province, Hong Kong's neighbor, was granted three zones. Fujian province, which lies across the strait from Taiwan, was home to the third. Deng intended the zones to bring in foreign capital, companies, and expertise, primarily from ethnic Chinese businesspeople operating out of Hong Kong and Taiwan. They were more successful than even Deng could have imagined, paving the way for an infusion of foreign capital, joint ventures, and technological and managerial expertise not just from Hong Kong and Taiwan, as the location of the zones would suggest, but from every corner of the globe.

By the mid-1980s, flush with the success of agricultural reforms, Deng went to the third step, turning his attention to the industrial sector. As Harvard economist Dwight Perkins points out, for a centrally planned economy to be successfully transformed to a market economy, four conditions must be met. "(1) Goods must be made available through the market rather than through administrative allocation. (2) Prices must reflect long-run relative scarcities rather than the dictates of the plan. (3) Competition must exist; no monopolists, otherwise no productivity gains. (4) Managers must behave according to the rules of the market, rather than those of the state bureaucracy."

China has met or is meeting all four criteria, and is especially strong, at this early date in the reforms, in the first two.

Increasingly, goods are distributed through market mechanisms. In 1978, approximately 700 products passed through the central planning system. By 1991, that number had dropped to 20. In the nonstate sector, almost nothing is allocated through central planning and even state-owned firms distribute much of their goods through market channels.

By 1992, the market, not a central plan, distributed almost 60 percent of coal, 55 percent of steel, and 90 percent of cement.

Consequently, prices are much more reflective of supply and demand.

Increased competition is being propelled by two significant trends. The first is an increase in foreign trade and investments. In 1992, the government approved the establishment of 47,000 new enterprises based on foreign investment, more than the total of the past decade. Foreign business agreed to invest $57.5 billion. The second is that China's provinces are very competitive and now see themselves as economic rivals. The decentralization of economic power paved the way for every province to attempt to mimic the dizzying pace of growth in southern China's Guangdong province, whose GDP has grown by 13 percent every year for the last 15 years. It is generally accepted that the influence and investments from neighboring Hong Kong had much to do with Guangdong's phenomenal success, but Hong Kong's interest was because the percentage of state-owned firms in the province was very low. Guangdong's strong pro-business environment did not hurt. Now the rest of the provinces all over China have a role model and are eager to beat each other out in following it.

Township and Village Enterprises

Making reformation possible, particularly in rural China, is the curious hybrid firm that is not truly private, but not state-owned either. Controlled by units of local government, township and village enterprises are introducing cutthroat competition to communities once dedicated to socialist precepts. TVE (township and village enterprise) managers are answerable to local officials and to the householders who have started the business or invested in it. In some areas, TVEs are merely thinly disguised private companies; in others they are, in fact, owned by local governments. In any case, it doesn't seem to change their performance or their fierce dedication to the bottom line. There are now almost 20 million TVEs.

Local governments show no mercy: TVEs contribute a great deal to a local area's economy, including roads, schools, and hospitals. So managers have been forced to behave like businesspeople, not bureaucrats. Bankruptcies, unheard of during the Communist era, are a fact of life for poorly managed TVEs. During the difficult days of 1989, losses of state-owned companies reached astronomical levels. None went bankrupt. At the same time, 3 million TVEs failed or were absorbed by others.

A famous ancient Chinese saying goes "The mountain is high and the emperor is far away." This represents the typical Chinese attitude toward central authority. "When you succesfully cross the ocean, you will ascend to heaven" is another famous Chinese saying—explaining the risk-taking attitude of the Chinese people. With these two combined, and powered by a strong profit/money motive, it would be difficult to imagine the central government had any real grip on the way grassroots enterprises operate. Also, the sheer size of the country, the enormous number of people and business units are too numerous and formidable for the state to effectively control them. Besides the state has limited resources.

There are no laws or regulations governing TVEs, so local governments and private owners are free to make them up as they go along. If TVE managers don't like the rules set forth by Beijing, they simply ignore them or find a creative way to get around them. Much of the TVE market growth comes from *exporting,* forcing them to compete not just with one another but with the rest of the world.

For example, Xiao Shan, a county seat half an hour from Hangzou, capital of Zhejiang province, is one of the ten wealthiest of China's 2,200 counties. In the last decade, Xiao Shan's economy has been transformed from largely agrarian to a thriving industrial center. Since the early 1980s, industrial output has risen by 30 percent a year. In 1992, growth was 35 percent and total output was 14 billion yuan, only 1 billion of which came from agriculture. Exports are growing by 30 percent a year, reaching 80 countries, and are valued at greater than $200 million. Seventy percent of the township's industrial output comes from TVEs, 10 percent from state-owned firms.

Xiao Shan is a great example of how the provinces go their own way with or without Beijing's approval. At present, there is about $50 million worth of foreign investment in the community; county planners would like to see investments increase to $400 million; however, the central government has rules about where foreign investments can and cannot be made and has established trade zones for such activity. No matter. Xaio Shan is setting up a zone anyway; they simply won't call it a zone, and as likely as not Beijing won't blink an eye. In fact, unsanctioned special-investment zones are popping up all over China, and Beijing is either powerless to stop them or simply won't, despite concerns about the economy overheating.

A Successful State Enterprise

This is not to suggest that it is not possible for state-owned companies to be competitive. Some are. Beijing-based Shougang Corp., a $1.8 billion iron and steel maker, has been given sweeping government authority to take over weak competitors and to diversify its operations. With the state's blessing, Shougang will double its steel capacity to 10 million tons by 1995. In the first quarter of 1993, the company paid $120 million for a Peruvian iron mine and spent an undisclosed sum to purchase a Fontana, California, steel plant, which the company plans to dismantle and ship back to the mainland. Shougang also is the first industrial group granted permission to launch its own commercial bank with capital of $175 million.

However, it is more often the case that companies controlled at the local or regional level, or by the private sector, win hands down when competing with state-owned enterprises. One such example, cited in an article in *Business Week*, is the competing firms of Rongsheng Refrigerator Factory and the Shenyang Medical Instrument Factory in Liaoning province, which despite its name until recently manufactured refrigerators.

Rongsheng is a model of the TVEs that are reaching Western standards of quality. Rongsheng's 3,500 workers are struggling to fill orders for China's most popular brand of refrigerator, which is expected to turn a profit of $32 million in 1993. Meanwhile, 300 of state-owned Shenyang's 2,400 employees have no jobs but stay on the payroll, contributing to a $5.3-million loss in 1992, and its warehouse is full of Great Wall refrigerators awaiting repairs. Repaired or not, nobody wants them. The factory has given up trying to compete with Rongsheng, turning to new products like pruning shears and X-ray equipment. Although it isn't likely it will be any more competitive or profitable with its new ventures.

In China, I heard it said that Deng's 15-year economic revolution was in many ways more profound than Mao's revolution of 1949. That will certainly soon become clear to the rest of the world, now it is becoming clear to the Chinese.

Leading China steadily toward a socialist market economy, which is looking more and more like an unvarnished capitalist economy, is the rising tide of Chinese citizens eager to ''plunge into the sea.''

BUILDING AN INFRASTRUCTURE FOR THE ECONOMY

In 1993, China started negotiations to buy billions of dollars' worth of equipment from America's AT&T, including switching and transmission systems, cellular telephones, and business phones and computer networks. AT&T also will enter into an agreement with China to train local telephone operators. China currently has 30 million phone lines. Its goal is to reach 100 million lines by the year 2000, or 10 million switches a year. They average $120 each, so sales revenues from the switches alone will reach $1.2 billion.

China's explosive growth is making phenomenal demands on its infrastructure but the Chinese are attacking the issue with the same fervor and single-minded determination with which they approached economic reform. Not unexpectedly, China is again turning to foreigners for the expertise and the capital needed to bring the provinces' infrastructure into the 21st century.

Motorola is laying the groundwork for what will be Corporate America's biggest manufacturing venture in China. The company is completing a $120-million plant in the Tianjin Economic & Technology Development Area which will make pagers, simple integrated circuits, and cellular phones. This is the first step in planning stages that will include automotive electronics, advanced microprocessors, and walkie-talkie systems. At the same time, Motorola is spending millions on in-house training programs in preparation for its start-up of design centers for integrated circuits and telecommunications projects.

China's Civil Aviation Authority (CAAC) has approached several Western airline companies, including British Airways, for help with the modernization of its airline industry. Although China is currently seeking advice, BA and others are hopeful that establishing a consultant relationship with CAAC will ultimately lead to market access. It is a huge and growing market. Passenger traffic is growing 35 percent a year. (And demand is still overwhelming supply. All of the flights I have recently taken in China were full and there were somewhere between 100 and 200 standbys for each flight.) There are at least 40 airline carriers in China today. It's hard to keep track; they are popping up everywhere.

By the year 2000, some 500 new or renovated airports will be operating.

Airport construction, aircraft maintenance, and the setting up of airlines will be opened to Sino-foreign joint ventures, while construction of airport concourses can be granted entirely to foreign firms. There is a booming market for aircraft as China struggles to accommodate the millions of people eager to travel for business and pleasure. In 1993, China Southern Airlines alone ordered six Boeing 777s, 14 737s and four 757s. Boeing expects more big orders, as the company calculates that China will need to purchase $45 billion worth of commercial jets from U.S. and Western European manufacturers over the next 20 years.

China's first highway was built just five years ago in Shanghai. Only 16 kilometers long, it carries 7,000 vehicles a day.

As badly as China needs to get its air-service house in order, it cannot afford to pay any less attention to its ground-transportation network. China has put its highway development on the fast track with plans to build 35,000 kilometers (25,000 miles) of highway over the next 25 years. China's longest highway, completed two years ago, starts in Shenyang, capital of Laioning Province, and extends 375 kilometers southwest to Dalian. Because of its importance to the local economy, the highway was given the lofty name "Wings of the Economic Takeoff."

The nation's new economic artery is a 2,400-kilometer (1,500-mile) superhighway—the longest in China—stretching from Beijing in the north to Shenzhen in the south.

Ambitious as Beijing's highway plans are, lack of funds is putting the brakes on some. Enter Gordon Wu, Hong Kong magnate, managing director of Hopewell Holdings Ltd. and financier of a $1.2-billion, six-lane toll road, bringing high-speed travel to southern China for the first time. Toll collections over the next 20 years will return Wu's investment, after which Wu will turn the highway over to China. Another Hong Kong property developer, New World Development Co., is investing $86 million in a highway in Wuhan, linking the city's new international airport to the downtown area.

Serious energy shortages have prompted China for the first time to allow 100 percent foreign ownership of power stations. Zhou Heliang of the Ministry of Machinery and Electronics Industry said that China would need a least 50 billion yuan at 1993 prices to invest in power plants up to the year 2000. ABB Asea Brown Boveri now has a $400-million slice of a coal-fired power station under construction in Guangdong, while Total of France has a 20 percent share in a $450-million refinery that will open in 1994.

Megawatts for Mega-Growth

In its 1986–1990 Five-Year Plan, China set the goal of increasing power capacity by 35,000 megawatts. The country's power output increased by 57 percent—not nearly enough. The current five-year plan targets another 45 percent increase by the year 2000, but China's three energy-equipment manufacturers can't do it alone; that means great opportunity for global firms like Bechtel, GEC-Alsthon, Asea Brown Boveri, Westinghouse Electric Co., Wing Merrill and Mitsubishi Heavy Industries, and a host of others eager to win a piece of this billion-dollar market.

Clearly, the Chinese have seen the light. They know that if they want to keep pace with the rest of the world, after more than half a century of isolationism, they are going to have to open their doors just as wide as they can. They may need the expertise of foreign companies, but foreign companies need their 1.2-billion consumer market. A huge win-win situation.

GLOBAL GOLD RUSH—CHINA'S CONSUMERS COVETED

The Americans are coming . . . and the Europeans . . . and the Japanese . . . everyone wants in on the action. Companies are flooding into China with a fervor that might be compared to America's gold rush in the 1840s. "The Chinese market has virtually limitless long-term potential," says Coca-Cola Company chairman Robert C. Goizueta.

Levi Strauss may have captured headlines when it pulled out of China saying the country's violation of human rights caused its withdrawal, but thousands of other companies are passing Levi Strauss going the other way.

- Coca-Cola plans to spend $150 million to build 10 more bottling plants in central China.
- Procter & Gamble, the U.S. consumer-products giant, is firmly ensconced in Guangdong province, and its detergent commercials are being watched on Beijing television.
- 7-Eleven, America's mini-mart franchise, has taken root in Shenzhen, a special economic zone north of Hong Kong.
- In addition to Motorola and AT&T, Eastman Kodak, Heinz, and the "Big Three" U.S. auto manufacturers are making significant investments in China.

R. J. Reynolds has signed a deal with a Chinese company to create the first joint-venture cigarette factory, which will turn out 2.5 billion smokes per year. "That's enough to give R. J. Reynolds Tobacco Inc. a toehold in the country that produces and consumes more cigarettes than any other nation."

Meanwhile, Rotorex, a U.S. compressor manufacturer that boasts 35 percent of the American air-conditioning market, is preparing to set up a $40 million joint-venture plant in southern China.

From elsewhere around the globe has come Siemens, with plans to double its investments in China, and luxury-car maker Mercedes-Benz. Sweden's Ericsson already has $600 million worth of orders to export and manufacture AXE-10 switchboard systems and mobile telephones.

Australia's Melbourne-based Foster's Brewing Group Ltd. is joining the long line of companies waiting for the opportunity to tap into China's market. Foster's joins international brewers Heineken, Beck's, San Miguel, Suntory, BSN, and Spaten Brewers in establishing joint ventures in China.

The world's fashion designers are beating a path to China's wide-open door. Giorgio Armani, Chanel, Donna Karan, Calvin Klein, and Louis Vuitton all have retail outlets in China, and more are planned. Shopping has become one of the Chinese people's favorite leisure activities. Shoppers revel in the colors, excitement, and variety offered by Western fashion designers.

So strong is the passion for designer fashions that Hong Kong luxury-goods entrepreneur Dickson Poon opened a store to sell women's suits that had Charles Jourdan labels sewn on the sleeves. In Guangzhou, tailors make shirts with the left sleeves an inch shorter than the right—the better to show off one's Rolex.

Retailing Boom

Guangzhou (Canton), in the province of Guangdong, is eager to be seen as an international metropolis. Toward that end, the city is spending a great deal of money to turn itself into a shoppers' paradise. Before 1995, 10 large-scale shopping centers will be built, along with another 10 specialized markets. Together, the projects will cost 3.8 billion yuan ($655 million) and will cover 1.2-million square meters of floor space.

Some of the projects will be undertaken in cooperation with overseas partners, all of whom are anxious to cash in on the city's booming retail market. Despite a double-digit increase in the price index in the first three months of 1993, sales volumes increased by 35 percent to 6.927 billion yuan, or 1.19 billion U.S. dollars.

Prosperity is flowing from the coastal cities inland. Hong Kong-based Sincere Co., the first foreign retailer to open a department store in Shanghai, became the first to commit to opening one in an inland province in April 1993. Sincere forged a joint-venture agreement with a Chinese company to redevelop a 35,000-square-foot site in Chengdu, the capital of Sichuan province. Situated in the southwest and known as China's breadbasket, Sichuan has the country's largest provincial population at about 110 million. Chengdu, population 3 million, is one of the most densely populated cities in China.

Other retailers casting about for inland cities with money to spend are Wing On Co. International Ltd. and luxury retailer and wholesaler Dickson Concepts (International) Ltd. Both plan to invest in Chengdu. SHK Hong Kong Industries Ltd., an investment company, is in discussions with Chinese partners about establishing a chain of department stores throughout the country. Wing On has opened a 50,000-square-foot children's-wear shop in Wuhan, the capital of central China's Hubei province, and is considering opening stores in Dalian, on the coast of Liaoning province in northern China, and at Liaoning's capital, Shenyang. In southern China, Tiger Enterprises Ltd. is the clear leader. Closely held by Jimmy Lai, a Hong Kong retailer, Tiger owns Giordano, which is moving aggressively into Shenzhen and Quangzhou.

Don't Leave Home Without It

Where there is money to be spent, there will be credit-card companies to help you spend it. American Express came to China 10 years ago after reaching an agreement with the Bank of China, which included appointing the bank as its agent for the American Express Card business in China. Now American Express has plans to expand its reach in the world's largest consumer market. With an office already in Beijing, AmEx plans to open two more, one in Shanghai and another in Guangzhou.

When American Express succeeds in issuing credit cards to the Chinese people, it will be a true symbol of capitalism. Traditionally, Chinese do only cash transactions. This is still true even in many parts of Taiwan, where checks are unheard of and people carry stacks of money with them every day.

Nearly 3,000 establishments in 130 cities currently accept American Express cards. The amount of money charged to its cards has increased by an average of 40 percent a year since 1988. The company has maintained a 50 percent share of total foreign credit-card purchasing since 1986.

In addition to providing high-quality customer service, American Express plans to invest in telecommunications facilities, including point-of-sale terminals and automatic teller machines.

Patience Is a Virtue, Creativity a Must

It is not by chance that some 75 to 80 percent of all foreign investment in China has come from within the Asia-Pacific region. More than one Western investor has explained frustration with the market in China in one word: *guanxi*. *Guanxi* is the Chinese word that describes special relationships with influential people that help grease the wheels of success when doing business in China. While these relationships certainly don't hurt, China is much more open to doing business with Westerners than Japan, which has its own network of special relationships.

While it's true that the Chinese market poses challenges to foreign investors, many companies are learning the secret to success in China. They start with small investments, learn the market, develop relationships with Chinese partners, let each experience make them a little stronger. They have to rely on the ingenuity that made them successful in the first place.

Mars Candy Company, makers of M&Ms, sells its candies directly to consumers through two different distribution channels. Mars is not involved in a joint venture, but it uses East Asiatic Company, a Hong Kong–based company, to distribute its product in three major markets—Beijing, Shanghai, and Guangzhou. The "normal" Chinese distribution channels require that retailers call on wholesalers to obtain the product and then figure out a way to transport it to the store. Mars's distributor turned the practice upside down. M&Ms wholesalers sell and transport their goods directly to the retailers.

Mars is also relying on a host of marketing tools common to the American market, but unfamiliar in China. The company sponsors sporting events, advertises heavily, and emblazons its logo on anything that might attract children and other chocoholics. Now the company's biggest challenge is battling a local company for copyright infringement. Sanlian Food Co. in Zhejiang province is attempting to sell its W&W candies in the same markets as M&Ms.

Avon Calling

When the direct-to-consumer market fell flat in the United States—these days when Avon comes calling in America more likely than not there won't be anyone at home—the company set its sights on mainland China. Unlike many companies setting up operations in China, Avon had the distinct advantage of long-term business dealings with China from which the company had bought gift and decorative items to sell in the United States.

But even with its previous experience Avon had some hurdles to overcome. Presenting Beijing with a carefully laid-out development plan, it was met with reluctance. The concept of direct marketing was alien to government officials and they ultimately rejected the project. Undaunted, Avon sought partnerships with officials in some of China's larger cities. Ultimately, the company entered into a joint-venture agreement with the Bureau of Light Industry in Guangzhou. Since marketing began in November 1990, the joint venture has launched more than eighty products, sales revenues reached 4 million yuan in four months, the joint venture is establishing its own retail outlets, and Avon has increased its investment by $1.2 million.

Through trial and error, Avon learned that the market approach it used in the Philippines would work in China. Salespeople do not go door to door but make presentations to friends, neighbors, relatives, and co-workers. They offer seminars on skin care and other beauty secrets as part of their marketing effort. Merchandise is not delivered to customers but is distributed at special depots to avoid problems with communications and transportation.

Any concern that Chinese Avon Ladies might not grasp the concept of direct sales has faded away: Avon's top part-time salesperson after four months had earned $5,600 (U.S.) in commission alone—200 times the average income of a Chinese worker. "These people are not only beauty oriented, they understand business. This is the first place in the world where the local representative told us to double our prices. And here we were worried about teaching them how to calculate commissions," observed John Novosad, Avon's vice president for business.

First-year sales for the venture were $4 million. By 1995, Avon projects sales of $50 to $60 million. Two additional cities in the province will see sales networks within the next couple of years. Despite Avon's success, some public officials accuse the company of distracting its sales force from their regular jobs. Avon sales reps, officials say, are putting themselves and their desire to make money ahead of the needs of their work units. Underlying this hostility is the fear that the venture is polluting people's minds with Western-style values.

Some of China's people may well be adopting Western-style values but it can't all be attributed to Avon, or Giorgio Armani, or any other single foreign investor. China has opened its doors to the world, the world is exploiting the opportunity, and China's people are being exposed to a new way of life.

If Western-style values are a concern to public officials, perhaps they should take a look at the "Western-style" capitalist frenzy promulgated by their very own stock market.

FROM COMMUNISM TO CAPITALISM—STOCK MARKETS AND BANKS

Two years ago, China shocked the world by becoming the first Communist country with stock exchanges—two of them, located in Shanghai and Shenzhen. In 1992, China's markets outperformed all others except Jamaica and Peru. Today, China has 2 million shareholders, and their ranks are growing by about 50,000 a week. On any given day, $350 million worth of shares are traded, more

than on a low-quantity day in Hong Kong. Furthermore, growth
has been impressive. In the first quarter of 1993 alone, volume at
the Shanghai Stock Exchange registered 2.2 times that for all of
1992.

In the first quarter of 1993, the price of China "B" shares—the
ones that foreigners can buy—rose 49 percent. The price of "A"
shares, which are restricted to domestic buyers, rose 67 percent. By
comparison, prices in Taiwan, the region's next-best performer,
rose less than 19 percent during the same period.

Activity on the Shanghai exchange has surpassed Shenzhen and
it is to Shanghai that thousands of Chinese flock to pay several
weeks' salary for an application form that will give them a 10
percent chance of being allowed to buy shares.

"The rise of the market legitimizes the kind of quasi-capitalism
that has been around for a dozen years," says *The New York Times,*
"but is steadily becoming less quasi and more capitalism."

At least a half-dozen Chinese cities want a piece of the action,
seeking government permission to set up a stock exchange. So far,
none has managed to convince Beijing officials. Meanwhile, Shanghai is clearly positioning itself to become a national exchange. Fifty
cities, in every province but Tibet, are now hooked up to the Shanghai computer system. In April 1993, the exchange began to broadcast share information by satellite to a network of 600 receiving
stations all over the country. Two-way trading by satellite began in
November 1993.

Shanghai's stock exchange is located in a former ballroom in the
Pu Jiang Hotel, where several hundred red-jacketed traders work at
individual computers. The new Shanghai Securities Building, designed by WZMH of Canada, will be located in Pudong Development Area across the Huangpu River and will open in 1995.

Eager to position itself to take advantage of growing financial
markets, Merrill Lynch in 1993 opened an office in Shanghai (the
first American brokerage invited to open an office in China), just
as it did 32 years ago in Tokyo. William A. Schreyer, then chairman of Merrill Lynch & Co., was so impressed with China's move
to a basic capitalist mechanism that he declared, "The modernization of China's economy, I think, is one of the most exciting

endeavors in this century.'' He also added that if he were 25 years younger, he would ''study Chinese and ask Merrill Lynch to post me here.''

China's stock market *officially* lists only 94 companies. But Hong Kong investment analysts speak of a booming unsanctioned trade in shares of cash-starved companies from as far away as Mongolia. These are companies that have been denied bank loans or listings on stock exchanges but nevertheless ''sell shares'' in their firms to successfully raise funds. No one really knows for sure just how large the market for shares in China is, legal or illegal. It is totally legal, however, to buy shares in TVEs, which are privately traded.

Four of China's most prosperous farmers-turned-entrepreneurs (two from the booming south, two from the underdeveloped northeast) have become well known for their knack for high-tech production and for selling shares to individuals. None is relying on the state for funds, and although all four are considered TVEs, they are also not relying on their local government for financing. All four have lifted their town's annual per capita income way above the national average.

Doudian Group Corporation in the Fangshan District of Beijing also is focusing on production of much-sought-after pharmaceuticals. As Wu Renbao, president of the Huaxi Industrial Corporation, an umbrella group that controls several factories in Huaxi Village in Jiangsu Province, explains: ''Although the government is encouraging township enterprises, it is still difficult for us to get bank loans or credit.'' Wu turned to villagers for capital. More than 10 percent of his corporation's fixed assets, valued at 230 million yuan ($39.7 million) are in the hands of individual farmers. ''We are actually pioneering the country's shareholding system, and the prospects are even better,'' Wu adds.

Huaxi Village's 320 residents, who bought 200 Jetta cars (Volkswagen) at one time, now enjoy bank deposits ranging from 20,000 yuan ($3,458) to 200,000 yuan ($34,580)—a princely sum by China's standards.

Other private trading mechanisms seem to be part of a bizarre trading web. But there are two sophisticated national over-the-counter trading systems, both based in Beijing: the Securities Trading Automatic Quotation System (Stags) developed in 1989 to trade bonds, which now lists eight shares, and the National Electronic Trading System (Nets), which lists four shares. Shares listed on both are supposed to be traded only between companies as long-term investments, but industry analysts are convinced that wealthy individuals in China are now eschewing the official stock exchanges in favor of cheaper Stags and Nets.

Today the people of China are getting a taste of speculation, risk taking and money-making—and they're responding with great enthusiasm. A lot of it is chaotic, but it is a rich chaos that signals China's economy has entered a new age. A new Securities Regulatory Commission has been established, although nobody seems to pay much attention to it. Meanwhile, Shanghai has ambitions to become the financial capital of the Far East, and may just realize that goal.

Making It into the Big Time

China's steady march toward capitalism took a giant leap forward when four state-owned companies were listed on the Hong Kong Stock Exchange. Those listings are a milestone for both the Communist party and for Hong Kong. It sends the clear message that the Communist party is committed to economic reform and has no intentions of backsliding.

Investment-hungry industries in China now have a crack at foreign funds to help fuel continued growth. For Hong Kong, China's entry into its exchange lends credibility to its claim that the colony is the place from which to invest in China. It also eases concern that Beijing might crack down on the boldly capitalistic Hong Kong in 1997.

If these flotations are successful, more will follow. Investors already have demonstrated a taste for China-related new issues. In February 1993, an initial public offering by Denway Investment Ltd., which makes Peugeot cars and other vehicles with French and Chinese partners in Quangdong province, was oversubscribed 657 times. Stated in U.S. dollars, the offer was for $52 million; $31 billion was put up; 657 times the offering is a record so far, but these amazing oversubscriptions are becoming routine.

A week earlier Tack Hsin Holdings set an oversubscription record of 553 times its offering to raise funds to expand its hotpot restaurants into China. Late in 1992, China Travel Services, a unit of China's state-owned tourist monopoly, was oversubscribed 411 times.

During the latter part of 1993, nine large Chinese state enterprises were scheduled to be brought to the Hong Kong market. These businesses include petrochemicals, steel, shipbuilding, brewing, and machine tools. Unlike Hong Kong's Denway, they are to be incorporated under Chinese law. Fifty more mainland companies are lining up to get a Hong Kong listing should these first nine be successful, as they are expected to be.

This is tantamount to a decision by the Chinese government to make Hong Kong the main market for raising foreign capital for corporate China. One fund manager, Robert Lloyd George, believes that by the end of the decade, China-related listings in the Hong Kong market will account for 45 percent of its capitalization, which he estimates will have grown to US$900 billion—almost a trillion dollars. Now you know what all the excitement is about.

Relaxing Rules on Private Banking

Until the mid-'80s China's financial institutions had no legal competitors. They didn't have to worry about technicalities—like making bad loans. Money was simply distributed to those with connections. The rest had to make their own way. Obviously this system was in no shape to finance the economic boom of the Dragon Century. But change has been evolutionary rather than revolutionary. Hundreds of small credit cooperatives—run like retail banks—have sprung up around the countryside. The number of unofficial banks and financial institutions is growing by leaps and bounds—there are 45 in Wenzhou alone.

China has one central bank—People's Bank of China—and five specialized banks: Agricultural Bank of China, Bank of China, Industrial and Commercial Bank of China, People's Construction Bank of China, and China Investment Bank. There also are nine national commercial banks. All specialized banks are owned by the Center State Council, all commercial banks by state-owned enterprises and local governments.

Among those who have paved the way for private banking is Yang Jiaxing, manager and founder of the Wenzhou-Lucheng Credit Cooperative. Starting with $86,000 in capital (his own and funds borrowed from friends), Yang quietly revolutionized the banking world. To attract deposits, Yang offered interest rates one-fifth higher than those offered by state banks. His bank is open seven days a week, and in a country where courtesy is sometimes considered a weakness in business dealings, the banks tellers are friendly and polite. Service with a smile, and sometimes cash deliveries to important customers.

Even more revolutionary, however, the bank lends money based on creditworthiness. What a concept. ''At state banks, it's the state's money, so if you have good connections or if you send the loan officers a gift, then you can get a loan, even if your credit isn't so good,'' explained Yang.

Not at Mr. Yang's bank. Making loans to private merchants and small factories, Yang reduces his risks by lending only where there is real estate available as collateral and only for up to 60 percent of the value of the property. Typically he lends money for just four months at a time (although loans can be rolled over) to finance trade or the purchase of raw materials that will be quickly turned into finished merchandise.

Predictably, the state-owned banks have tried to smother the private institutions by pushing through regulations that drown them in red tape and prevent them from expanding or paying higher interest rates than state banks. Nonetheless, Yang and his fellow private bankers are optimistic that Beijing will slowly relax the rules on private banking to maintain the momentum of economic reform.

In a move that will also keep the ball rolling, China's Ministry of Foreign Economic Relation and Trade (MOFERT) announced the formation of an export financing bank, the first of its kind in the country. Designated a ''special purpose bank,'' MOFERT will set up three or four branches of the new bank in commercial hubs, likely Shanghai, Guangzhou, Shenshen, and Dalian.

One banking source said that the bank would be much like the Export-Import Bank in the United States, providing credit guarantees for mainland exporters on large and medium-size shipments. Faced with resistance from the Bank of China, which is concerned that the bank will expand its scope into general trade-financing business such as letters of credit, a MOFERT spokesperson hastened to assure the financial community that it would not compete with them. They won't, for now. But the announcement sends a clear message that economic reform will bring with it the reform of China's banking system. There is no other way.

CHINA'S GROWTH HUBS

Few have not read or heard about China's showcase Guangdong province. Neighboring Hong Kong, it was the first area to benefit from an infusion of foreign investment when Deng opened the doors of China to the rest of the world in 1978. Fifteen years later, Guangdong has a population of more than 60 million of the country's most affluent people.

Guangzhou is earning a reputation as "the city of lights," as shopping centers, entertainment complexes, cultural events, and the excitement of a thriving metropolis bring domestic and foreign tourists in droves. Shenzhen, Hong Kong's border city and a designated "special economic zone," is home to one of China's two stock exchanges, has a population of 2 million, and the average household owns more than one color television set.

So integrated are Shenzhen and Hong Kong's economies already that in Shenzhen all commercial places ask visitors to pay in Hong Kong dollars. In 1997 Hong Kong and Shenzhen will merge into one city.

But it is the less well-known city of Dongguan that in many respects is becoming a symbol of the success Deng's policies engendered. A city of nearly 1 million people, Dongguan is situated in the western reaches of the Pearl River estuary between Hong Kong to the south and Guangzhou to the north.

Since that most auspicious of moments in China's history fifteen years ago, foreigners have invested nearly $1.5 billion in textiles, consumer electronics, food products, and many other operations. The city has achieved an average annual rate of growth of 20 percent—comfortably outpacing the average provincial and national growth rates. As in Guangzhou, many investors are from Hong Kong and can trace their ancestral homes to one of the 29 towns and 582 administrative districts in the city. Indeed, it is estimated that 70 percent of overseas Chinese are from Quangdong Province.

But when investors come to Dongguan they bring more than capital and expertise. They are often accompanied by other investors without familial or cultural ties, and they succeed in convincing the newcomers that the government means business and success can be achieved. One such investor is Vtechm, a London-listed but Hong Kong–based manufacturer of consumer electronics, computers, and mobile telephones.

Vtechm first invested in Shenzhen in the early 1980s but came up against the Communist party. The government wanted too much control of its operations. Later, it moved to Dongguan, and today, with a cumulative investment of HK $700 million, it is employing 8,000 workers. "We told them that we wanted to run the factory ourselves and we wanted to do the administration," says Mr. Joseph Tam, the Hong Kong manager. "They agreed. We are also free to recruit any person we like and fire them if they do not meet our requirements."

Hunan Hinges Hopes on Proximity to Guangdong

Just north of Guangdong, and bisected by the Guangzhou-Beijing railroad, Hunan province would appear to be a natural choice for investors looking for cheaper inland alternatives to China's southern province. In fact, investments have risen rapidly; however, infrastructure restraints, a shortage of capital, and the conservatism of government officials make doing business in Hunan a challenge.

"Hunan officials talk about reform and openness, but in their bones they're still central planners. In terms of their thinking, they're 10 to 15 years behind the coastal areas," says one frustrated foreign investor.

That's all about to change. Rumor has it that when Deng Xiaoping made his now famous sweep through southern China in early 1992, he refused to detrain at Hunan, saying the government had done too little to encourage economic reform. Since then, the province has launched an aggressive campaign to attract foreign investments. Among activities undertaken was a trade fair held in Hong Kong. Plans are now under way to host three annual festivals promoting tourism and trade.

Already, these efforts have paid off. Hunan has approved 867 projects, involving $567 million in foreign investment, three times the number and double the value of approvals in 1991. In the first quarter of 1993 alone, the provincial government approved 488 projects with $380 million of foreign investment. Although foreign investments in Guangdong, which reached the $15 billion mark by 1991, dwarf those of Hunan, the people there have a few more tricks up their sleeves.

Some 20 major projects are planned, valued at $2.1 billion and designed to bring technology and capital into the province. These projects will address pressing infrastructure needs, including a highway project involving Hong Kong's New World Development Co., and several power plants, including a project in which Germany's Siemens will play a role.

At the same time Hunan is pressing to maintain the 12 percent growth rate in its gross economic product realized in 1992, after average growth rates of 7 percent between 1985 and 1991. Hunan is promoting the availability of raw materials, especially in agriculture and mining, and the fact that it offers some of the best rail and road networks around. Further, proximity to Guangdong is being advertised as an asset, as is the province's relatively well-educated workforce and the availability of affordable land.

Lastly, officials point out that because Hunan is still in the early stages of development there is little speculation and consequently little danger of the market overheating. At least for now.

The Paris of the Orient Rises Up

Perhaps nowhere is the envy of Guangdong more palpable than it is in Shanghai, which in the mid-1980s lost to Guangdong its ranking as China's number-one exporter and lost to Jiangsu its long-held status as having the highest industrial output. For a city once lauded as the "Paris of the Orient," that was a bitter pill to swallow.

"Wild, exuberant, lusty, sinful, fabulously rich and disgustingly poor, Shanghai was the preeminent Western gateway to China. The greatest financial center of East Asia—and the birthplace of the Chinese Communist party—it was fabled as an adventurer's paradise," said the *Los Angeles Times*.

"The 1949 Communist revolution seemed to end all that. The foreigners were expelled. Prostitutes were rounded up and assigned factory jobs. Opium dealers faced execution, and capitalists lost their fortunes. The neon lights came down. Night life died. Shanghai's history was pilloried as one of unmitigated decadence and corruption."

Now Shanghai is back and it is better than ever. And while dazzle and decadence are back as well, its emphasis is on reaping the fruits of communism turned upside down.

In Shanghai on October 1, 1993, on the occasion of the 44th anniversary of the founding of the People's Republic of China, I saw four 10-story-high, freshly painted banners on Nanjing Road which read: "Continue to push for reforms"; "Strengthen macro controls" (inflation was beginning to be a problem); "Accelerate the pace of reforms"; and, "Expand opening to the outside world."

Shanghai has become the "Dragon Head" of the whole Yangtze River region, and boasts ambitions to become a finance and trade powerhouse in Asia and the Pacific by 2010. Says Huang Ju, the city's mayor, "Between 2000 and 2010 we want to turn Shanghai into a financial and trading centre of the Asian and Pacific region. Our objective is to achieve complementarity with other regional financial and trade centers."

That's the public voice; the private voices of city officials speak of overtaking Hong Kong as a financial service and trading giant. Few in the city have any doubts that their lofty goals can be reached, because, explains Huang, "We are at the crossroads of the golden highway and golden coastline. We stand at the gateway to the world outside."

Although careful not to criticize Beijing or speak disparagingly of the southern provinces, the mayor of Shanghai is clearly unhappy with the central government for keeping the city on a short string during the first decade of economic reform. But now that Beijing has given the city its blessing, officials plan to make up for lost time.

Last year, Shanghai's economy grew by 14.8 percent, compared with national growth rates of 13 percent. The city's target is to maintain an annual growth rate of 10 percent until the year 2000, but the mayor is confident it will exceed that rate. According to the *Los Angeles Times*, development will focus on banking, trade, real estate, tourism, telecommunications, steel, petrochemicals, cars, and household electrical appliances. Foreign investment is actively being sought to build these industries with 1,912 foreign-funded projects valued at $3.3 billion being approved in 1992 alone, more than eight times the previous year.

Despite living with economic stagnation for the past 40 years, many industries, in fact, grew during those decades. Shanghai built a heavy industrial and high-technology base that in some ways is stronger than Hong Kong and south China combined. "Shanghai can produce rockets that can put satellites in orbit," notes Zhang Puxian, spokesman for the Pudong Development Office. "Outside Shanghai there's a nuclear power plant that we built ourselves. The technological conditions for Shanghai's development are very good. There are more than 1,500 research institutes, and 450,000 scientific and technical workers. Its work force is first in the country."

Tourism is one of Shanghai's engines of recovery. Revenue from tourism surged to $580 million in 1992—up 107 percent from 1991. In 1992, the city welcomed 1.253 million foreign visitors, a 27.6 percent increase over the previous year. By the year 2000, China's tourism industry will reach an estimated $10 billion (excluding domestic tourism, which also is booming). Shanghai will account for half those gains.

Look for Shanghai and Quangdong to be the two great hubs of Chinese economic development.

How Are You Going to Keep Them Down on the Farm?

For seven years now, farmer turned entrepreneur Yang YuFu has made shoes, fixed appliances, and sold glasses and plastic buckets to eke out a living in the city. When he is doing well he earns $100 month, which goes to pay rent on two rooms and to support his mother and two sisters. Only his father remains in Zhejiang province to tend the tiny family farm.

Unable to live on the family's meager farm income, Yang joins millions of poor people from rural China no better able to live on equally meager wages earned in the big city. Yet the migration continues, and it evidences a much larger trend—the ultimate breakdown of central control over individuals' lives, the point at which communism will have been completely replaced by, if not democracy, then something very close to it.

In China's inland, rural provinces there is growing discontent. Although Beijing has long promised that economic reforms will catch up to them, and many former pockets of poverty are now enjoying much higher standards of living, nonetheless, China's rural population fears that it is being left behind and expresses anger over the disproportionate share of taxes paid by the agricultural sector to support high-growth industrial activities in the coastal cities. In frustration, and in hopes of finding a better life, people are flocking to China's urban centers. Disparity between urban and rural makes reform all the more urgent for China, and it is only through accelerated economic development that this disparity can be reduced.

FROM ECONOMIC REFORM TO POLITICAL REFORM

These days the question is on lips of every journalist, government official, or corporate investment decision maker: What happens after Deng's death? Can the reform movement maintain its momentum when its driving force is no longer leading the parade? The answer has to be yes. Once people have glimpsed what the rest of the world has to offer and have had even a taste of the good life that capitalist fortunes make possible, there is no going back.

Deng knew that when he put the wheels in motion. Others are not too sure, so it is with bated breath that they watch and wait to learn whether Deng will anoint a like-minded successor. In fact, political positions have recently been filled by younger, more open-minded party members, but that doesn't even matter. Money, not politics, is on everybody's mind. If people don't like the central government's policies, they circumvent them. It's a poorly kept secret that few in China take the Communist party all that seriously, other than being eager to maintain political stability so as not to disrupt the flow of capital.

Improvements in the country's telecommunications infrastructure have given millions of people in China a window on the world. They like what they see. Western fashion, Western music, Western food, Western television. At least 25 million people receive China Star, a satellite television station broadcasting TV programs from the United States, sports from around the world, news from Britain, and general entertainment from Australia—all have an allure to people grown weary of drab Mao jackets and correct political thought.

Art and religion, banished during the inappropriately named Cultural Revolution, are once again a part of China's life-style.

One of the paradoxes of contemporary China is that Christianity is growing more rapidly today under a Communist government than it ever did earlier in this century when missionaries were free to proselytize at will.

Despite a quiet but extensive crackdown on Christianity in 1989, unofficial figures are that 80 million people in China have joined either a Catholic or Protestant church. Scholars are of the opinion that the popularity of religion is due to the fact that the Church is an important power base and source of moral values outside the Communist party. That may be true, but it is also a manifestation of people's desire to choose their own life-style after decades of being told what to do.

Relaxation of controls over the media has spawned a plethora of newpapers, magazines, television studios, and talk radio, where people uninhibitedly (more or less) discuss business, religion, family life, and the trials and tribulations of city life. Politics is carefully avoided by talk-radio hosts. No reason to challenge the powers that be now. That too will come.

Automobiles, expensive watches, designer fashions, and other obvious symbols of wealth and prestige are being snapped up by Chinese yuppies. Men and women both flaunt their success by buying luxury goods; the more they paid for it, the more comforting the purchase—discount outlets won't make it in China for a while. Even the government now is anxious to compete in fashion design.

While such conspicuous consumption might seem slightly declassé to more sophisticated Western cultures, we've all been there in one way or another. One can be sure that once people have satiated their pent-up desire for what the capitalist world has always had available to it, they will turn their attention to social concerns. That's when the real political reforms will begin. Socialism with Chinese characteristics will increasingly look like capitalism. Democracy waits in the wings—to a point.

Democracy in China will have to evolve and take on a very different form from the way it is understood by the West. The concept of democracy is alien to the Chinese people. Take Singapore, for example. The West may not regard it as a true democracy, but many Chinese agree that it is the best (some contend the most suitable) form of government for the Chinese people. The argument rests on the unique characteristics of the Chinese people. They have a poor sense of the rule of law, where individual self-discipline forms the foundation of liberty and the legal system. For centuries the Chinese have been used to command from the top. (The Emperor being the source of power; the Emperor regarded as the Son of Heaven.) There is a famous Chinese proverb that says "Once rules are relaxed, chaos will follow"—this strengthens the belief of most Chinese that government must retain an iron fist and remain authoritarian. Confucianism essentially preaches the same philosophy—central authority, hierarchy, respect for status and position. The Emperor, superiors, and parents (as heads of the household) are the source of power and governmence.

If China, Then Why Not Russia?

If China is on its way to successfully reforming its economy and growing it faster than anyone else, why is Russia stumbling so badly?

Because China had some distinct advantages.

China enjoys the synergy that comes with being in close proximity to other fast-growing and emerging markets, but more important, there exists an extensive network of Chinese businesspeople who no longer live in China. Living in Indonesia, Malaysia, India, Taiwan, Hong Kong, and elsewhere, they are part of the world's largest tribe and they have strong emotional ties to the motherland.

Additionally, China's economy has always been decentralized—distributed widely. The Chinese Communists centralized political control, but their fear of neighboring Japan prompted China to place manufacturing plants throughout the country so that if part of China was lost in war, it would not in the process lose a key or sole manufacturer of strategic goods. Stalin, on the other hand, divided the Soviet Union into manufacturing sectors: Tanks were made in one place, tractors in another. Where Russia now has only a few enormous industrial operations in each manufacturing sector, China has many small manufacturing plants scattered throughout the country. In the shift to a market economy China's thousands and thousands of small operations easily lent themselves to entrepreneurism and privatization. Russia is stuck with huge, clumsy, inefficient plants.

China also has a great entrepreneurial edge. China's farmers eagerly embraced the opportunity to be in charge of their economic future and to make a profit. Russian farmers, on the other hand, reacted to even talk of liberalization with a mixture of cynicism and fear.

In much of Southeast Asia, ethnic Chinese already run the show. Perhaps the single most significant factor in China's success is the power and pride of the Chinese diaspora. There are an estimated 55 million Chinese living outside the People's Republic. "They include a disproportionate number of successful businesspeople who have now decided that it's safe to invest on the mainland. They jump-started the boom,'' says the *Singapore Business Times*.

Russians have no memory or history of entrepreneurism or free markets, and no tribe of ethnic Russian entrepreneurs to tutor them in creating a new economy.

China's switch from communism to capitalism has been occurring gradually; Russia has tried to do it all at once. The Russians mismanaged their monetary affairs so badly they now have hyperinflation. The ruble is virtually worthless. China, on the other hand, took a more cautious approach, the result of which has been that while they are experiencing double-digit inflation, the gains of 1 percent to 2 percent per month don't even approach hyperinflationary rates—50 percent or more a month. Additionally, the yuan remains convertible at about 5.9 to the dollar and has depreciated only 5 percent a year for the past two years—better than Italy's record, for example.

Lastly, Deng Xiaoping is the undisputed leader of China. He is charismatic, single-minded, and certain of his leadership. When Deng speaks, people listen, and they will continue to listen even after his death, because it has been proved that his path to economic reform was the right direction at the right time. Leadership in Russia, meanwhile, is the target of suspicion and hostility.

The only market in Russia that works is the black market. A viable de facto strategy is to let the black market take over the whole market; then market forces over time will shape and refine it. That's about what will happen in Russia, and that will take a very long time. Meanwhile, China continues its march to becoming the world's biggest economy.

GREATER CHINA AND THE GLOBAL CHINESE TRIBE

Even as the China miracle unfolds, there are many who insist that it is not possible to reform a communist economy gradually. Pointing to the failed attempts in Hungary and Yugoslavia in the 1970s and 1980s, some economists maintain that the only way to ensure long-term success is to plunge headlong into privatization and free trade. Since no other country has successfully escaped from Third World poverty and communism at the same time, there is a strong voice of negativity that says it can't be done. China is proving otherwise.

Not given to sweeping gestures or recklessness, China refers to its slow but steady progress toward reform as "crossing the river by feeling the stones underfoot." What advocates of a more radical approach fail to take into account when considering China is that in its rise from poverty the country has learned from its East Asian cousins. Escaping communism is not part of the plan. The communists very much want to stay in power, but are well aware that to maintain power they must also maintain the country's economic momentum. If in doing so communism takes on capitalist overtones, so be it. The Chinese Communist party is interested in political power, not market management.

Even more significant, but often ignored in communist vs. capitalist ideological debates, is the extraordinary size of the global Chinese tribe and their economic influence in the region. Of the four Asian "tigers," only Korea is not predominantly Chinese.

Explains Harvard professor John Kao: "Most experts still divide the global economy into three major powers: North America, Europe, and Japan. Countries with Chinese-based economies are usually defined as the small, industrialized 'dragons' of South Korea, Taiwan, Hong Kong, and Singapore or the monolithic, but underdeveloped, People's Republic of China. Yet for generations, emigrant Chinese entrepreneurs have operated comfortably in a network of family and clan across many national borders."

Chinese business in Asia Pacific now constitutes the world's third economic power.

The Chinese Commonwealth

Kao calls this global network the "Chinese Commonwealth." Primarily a network of entrepreneurial relationships that extends around the globe, it is a model of economic efficiency that many Western multinationals have been trying to create in their own organizations. It is *the* organizational model for the 21st century.

And although this network still involves few outsiders, that, too, is changing. Citizens of the Chinese Commonwealth are abandoning political dogma and growth-limiting clannishness in favor of economic self-interest. Unlike the Japanese, who continue to rely heavily on interlocking keiretsu relationships, the Chinese already have demonstrated a talent for forming partnerships and joint ventures with outsiders based on bottom-line benefits, not long-standing relationships. Although that too is part of the mix, particularly for Chinese entrepreneurs, expatriates and citizens alike.

The rest of the world should take heed. Concludes Kao: "The central strategic question for all current multinationals—be they Chinese, Japanese, or Western—is how to gather and integrate power through many small units. The evolution of a worldwide web of relatively small Chinese businesses, bound by undeniably strong cultural links, offers a working model for the future." That, of course, very much fits the Global Paradox.

There are more than 50 million overseas Chinese. Many have lots of money, long entrepreneurial experience, and strong emotional ties to the motherland. Now, members of the biggest tribe in the world are helping each other. Investment from Asian cousins is fueling China's breathtaking economic transformation. More than 85 percent of foreign investment in China stems from Hong Kong, Taiwan, Singapore, and Japan. Some 80 percent of Vietnam's foreign investment comes from these four economies, with Taiwan emerging as the single largest investor with about $1.2 billion in commitments. And as much as 70 percent of the private sectors in Chinese Singapore, Malaysia, Thailand, Indonesia, and the Philippines are controlled by minorities of Chinese descent.

From November 22 to 24, 1993, Hong Kong played host to the Second World Chinese Entrepreneurs Convention, where 1,000 delegates from all over the world assembled in the Convention Centre. The convention discussed the changing economic trends in the new global order, and the role of Chinese enterprises and entrepreneurs in contributing to the new world order. The convention also strengthened economic and cultural cooperation and exchange among them. The slogan of the Convention: "Overseas Chinese entrepreneurs hail from the four seas, building prosperity in five continents."

Nowhere is the influence of the global Chinese tribe more apparent than in the fast-emerging economic region of "Greater China." A report released by the World Bank in the first quarter of 1993 announced that this triad was "arguably becoming the fourth growth pole of the global economy." It isn't arguable.

China, Hong Kong and Taiwan—Economics Overcome Leftover Political Squabbles

Inextricably intertwined, the three economies of China, Hong Kong, and Taiwan—frequently referred to as Greater China—are all but indistinguishable from one another. When China opened its doors in 1978, Hong Kong was the first to walk through. Today, some 25,000 enterprises in Guangdong produce goods for Hong Kong companies. Combined, these businesses employ 4 million workers, which is four times the size of Hong Kong's manufacturing work force. Estimates are that as much as 20 percent of Hong Kong's currency circulation occurs in Guangdong.

Success breeds success and Hong Kong businesses have begun to work in Shanghai, Beijing, and many other Chinese cities. Mainland China also has surpassed the United States as the colony's largest trading partner. The reverse also is true. China's investments in the colony now surpass Japan's investments as well.

Hong Kong's extensive global business ties, its financial savvy, sophisticated telecommunications infrastructure, and transportation facilities make it an ideal entrepôt for China. Chinese corporations have major holdings in Hong Kong's telecommunications market, aviation sector, and property development. Mainland buyers may well control as much as one fifth of Hong Kong's real estate market by 1997. And the Bank of China group is the second-largest banking conglomerate in the colony, with one fifth of all Hong Kong dollar deposits.

But what will happen in 1997 when Hong Kong becomes once

again a part of China? In a word, nothing. Or more accurately, more of the same.

By then, the economies of Hong Kong and southern China will be wholly integrated. In newspaper after newspaper, political and economic pundits have been bandying about the question of who needs whom more, China or Hong Kong. The answer is, they need each other. The Chinese government and the Chinese people know this. That's why no one is waiting. While speculation is that prices might be lower once the colony belongs to China, and opportunities greater, the general feeling is that Hong Kong is as good an investment now as it will be in 1997. The mainland Chinese certainly think so, as vouched for by their huge current investments in the colony.

China has its own history with Taiwan. Officially, there still exists a ban on direct commercial relations with the mainland. That, however, has done little to restrain the tide of investments. Trade between Hong Kong and Taiwan is increasingly dramatically, and much of that is indirect trade between Taiwan and China.

According to official figures, 3,000 Taiwanese firms have invested an estimated $3 billion in projects in China. Unofficial estimates place the figure at closer to $10 billion. Nearly half of those investments have been in the coastal province of Fujian, which is just across the strait that separates Taiwan from the mainland. Like Hong Kong with Guangdong, there are strong cultural, family, and linguistic ties between Taiwan and Fujian. Taiwan also is investing in manufacturing operations in southern China, frequently as part of a joint venture with a Hong Kong firm.

In 1992, exports to China from Taiwan were 35 percent above 1991 levels. Meanwhile, exports from Taiwan to Japan fell 3.3 percent. China now takes 8 percent of Taiwan's total exports, up from virtually nothing six years ago. "Before 1980, the most important market to Taiwan was America, but for the 1990s we know the most critical factor in the success of Taiwan's economy is the mainland," says Yen Shiang Shih, director general of Taiwan's Medium and Small Business Administration.

While it's true that Taiwan and China have some differences to settle, it can be said with certainty that resolution will be reached in 1994 or 1995. The timing is almost irrelevant. Carefully orchestrated (and much ballyhooed) talks between business representatives of the two countries were held in Singapore in early 1993. Great emphasis was placed on the "unofficial" status of the parties and both sides went to great lengths to avoid any hint of political posturing.

Said a senior adviser to the government on mainland policy: "We are being very pragmatic, sitting down and talking business. . . . It's a very good thing, a very good start."

The last time representatives of the two factions sat down to discuss their relationship, Harry S. Truman was president of the United States and China "was an impoverished country mired in civil war and on the brink of a socialist revolution. Today, the parties meet on an equal footing, representing increasingly prosperous and self-assured nations drawn inexorably together by common economic interests."

Evidencing the certainty that the differences between China and Taiwan will be resolved and direct business relations will be reestablished was the announcement in the spring of 1993 of a joint venture between Taiwan's ruling Kuomintang's (KMT) China Development Corp. and Beijing's Great Wall Industrial Corp. The two former antagonists plan to launch a Hong Kong–based partnership to design and build a regional telecommunications satellite. Although details remain to be worked out, it is the first known example of direct business links between the two countries. More are certain to follow.

Greater China's Network Extends Throughout Asia

While China, Hong Kong, and Taiwan are the heart of Greater China, and the Greater China network is concentrated in Asia—including Singapore, Malaysia, Thailand, Indonesia, and the Philippines—its reach extends across the globe. In 1992, the exports of Hong Kong, China, Taiwan, and Singapore were worth US $350 billion, about equal to Japan's and not far behind those of the United States.

The rapid growth and integration of the economies of Greater

China are now being recognized as only the first stage of its development. Stage two already is under way as the less-developed Asian countries increase their investments in China, and as ethnic Chinese businesspeople in America and Europe follow the same path back to the mainland.

"The emergence of Greater China will provide a counterbalance in the Asia-Pacific region to the economic might of Japan. The ultimate challenge is whether Japan and China can share leadership in the Asia-Pacific Century with an increasingly introspective America," writes Paul M. F. Cheng, chairman of Inchcape Pacific Ltd. and the Hong Kong General Chamber of Commerce.

Japan didn't get to be the economic superpower it is by not playing the odds. No foreign government endorsed Deng Xaioping's economic reforms more enthusiastically than Japan. History is history; this is a marriage of convenience. As with Taiwan and Hong Kong, pragmatism will prevail.

According to Japanese industry estimates, Japanese investment in China doubled to about $1 billion in the year ending March 31, 1993, while Sino-Japanese trade increased 27 percent to $29 billion. Rarely does a day go by without another announcement by a Japanese company of planned investments in China. In just the first two weeks of May 1993, Nissan Motor Co. and Suzuki Motor Co. agreed to build vehicles in China, Kurabo announced its intentions to make men's suits in Hubei province, Mitsubishi Heavy Industries Ltd. said it will build a polyethylene plant in Jilian province, and the Mos Burger fast-food franchise revealed plans to open 3,000 restaurants in China.

In 1992, Japanese companies announced 1,800 investment projects in China, almost equal to that of the previous 13 years combined. Also in the past 13 years, the Japanese government made or committed to 3.3 trillion yen (US $30 billion) in loans to China, and Japan provides half of all development aid to China from individuals.

Investments also are flowing in the other direction. In the first quarter of 1993, two Chinese companies took a 15 percent stake in the Japanese retail giant Yaohan International Co. Other Chinese companies are considering buying parts of a factory Nissan is closing in Japan. More Chinese companies will follow.

The next frontier for Japan, and for the rest of the developed world, will be selling directly to China's 1.2 billion people. And it isn't just the sheer number of people that is attracting foreign investors. It is that the Chinese people are spending as never before. Having risen out of poverty they are ready to enjoy many of the same consumer products Westerners take for granted, and they have the cash to spend. China's savings rate is one of the highest in the world and the percentage of disposable income is going up.

SOME CONSIDERATIONS

For China the shift from a command economy to a market economy will not be a smooth turn of the wheel. There inevitably will be many ups and downs and some setbacks. Here is a list of some important considerations in contemplating China's future:

Increased efficiency and productivity in the Chinese economy is causing a rise in unemployment. Some 100 million people in the urban work force are employed by state-run enterprises. In the past these have been lifelong jobs, which also provided housing and medical benefits. Now the employment system is to be gradually reformed so that employment is not automatic and people can more freely be both hired and fired. Wuhan Iron and Steel Works cut its work force by two thirds in its drive for increased efficiency. In the process it shifted 50,000 of 120,000 workers to newly affiliated companies and will in the coming months reassign 30,000 more.

More than 200 million people are unemployed in China today, hundreds of thousands of them farmers who migrated to urban areas in hopes of finding a job.

China's rapid growth has been accompanied a huge increase in corruption. The corruption in China is as great as in any other country in Asia. Collusion between local governments and businesses to avoid regulations and taxes is widespread. Tax evasion is threatening to bankrupt the central government.

China's serious inflation problem worries many investors. In the last half of 1993 economic growth was running at almost 14 percent. There is widespread concern that this seeming overheating of the economy will bring it down. The government finally decided something had to be done to avoid a hard landing. In July 1993, the government unveiled a tough, 16-point austerity plan, widely believed to have been put together by Executive Vice Premier Zhu Rongji, China's economic supremo. The plan includes: Call in loans diverted to speculative schemes, force workers within two weeks to buy all government bonds that had failed to sell, raise interest rates, impose a 20-percent cut in government spending and a ban on new imports of cars, suspend price-reform measures, reduce the scale of infrastructure projects, and send inspection teams to ensure that provinces obey orders.

There continues to be a shortage of reliable economic information. Chinese economic figures tend to underplay inflation and ignore the off-the-books economy, which is considerable. One of the largest question marks is per capita income figures. Because of the new way the IMF calculates the size of economies, this is additionally important to remedy.

There is a lack of attention to the training of human resources. While China is building the much-needed physical infrastructure to power economic development, little attention and few resources are being put behind the training and transforming of human resources. More and more young people are going into the private sector instead of continuing their education. Also, there doesn't seem to be a lot of interest in programs to help people shift from bureaucratic work habits to become competitive and cooperative. In many instances it will be left to foreign enterprises to help some Chinese change their attitudes toward work. (In the Bank of China in Guangzhou it took 20 minutes and two approvals to change my Malaysian ringgits into Chinese yuan. They say that in China it takes an average of 40 "chops" to get an application through the bureaucracy, each chop being a stamp of authority or completion of a process. I've suggested that someone should develop a "Chop Index" so as to measure any decrease or increase in Chinese bureaucracy.) In summary, China's labor minister, Li Boyong, says, "China now faces the difficult problem of the labor-force quantity exceeding demand and the quality not meeting demand.''

China needs a legal system. The development of a legal system is urgently needed for the conduct of business. Unless a good legal system is in place, China will remain a risky place for enterprises to operate.

There is a widespread disregard for the environment. China's headlong rush for growth could lead to a lot of environmental damage, and the fallout could harm the whole region. In June of 1993 China's official watchdog, the National Environmental Protection Agency, reported annual increases of 4 to 9 percent in air pollution, waste water, and solid waste. The government also said pollution had fouled more than 10 percent of China's arable farmland. The World Bank has agreed to lend $50 million to help China address its environmental problems.

There is an urgent need to restructure the financial and taxation relationship between the government and the provinces. Beijing is losing its grip on the provinces. This fits with the Global Paradox, but it could be trouble for China. The provinces are not remitting to Beijing the taxes they have collected. Executive Vice Premier Zhu Rongji said that in the summer of 1993 the central government was on the verge of bankruptcy before he launched an offensive to reimpose economic order. Zhu said that at the worst moment, the central coffers had only tens of millions of yuan left, and he didn't know if they could pay wages.

Whether China can continue to surge ahead in its economic reforms and development largely hinges on how rapidly and successfully the government restructures the financial system. The relationship between Beijing and the provinces will be based on economic considerations, and a mutually acceptable formula in the deployment of tax revenues. In general, what is unfolding now is an unspoken agreement that ''we will pretend to rule if you pretend to be ruled.''

Nevertheless, for all the reasons given in the first 33 pages of this chapter, while it will not be a smooth turn of the wheel, China seems destined to develop into a powerful economic presence, its economy performing as well in the next decade as in the last.

Next century, looking back, it should be clear that the emergence of China was the most important economic force shaping the world in the latter part of the 20th century.

6

Asia and Latin America: New Areas of Opportunity

In the new Global Paradox you can measure the economic viability of a country by gauging the extent to which the leaders are allowing the parts to contribute to the whole. In the metaphor, is it a country led by a central government mainframe, or are the PCs allowed on their own to create or revitalize an economy?

Judged by these lights, if you're looking to invest in a solid-growth area that will carry you profitably into the 21st century, you can forget Europe. You can certainly forget the Europe of three-year media hype about the EC's single market's economic domination.

For the balance of the decade the world's economic profile will look something like this:

- Europe in recession for a long time.
- Flat to modest growth in Japan.
- Modest to solid growth in the United States.
- Asia booming, led by China.
- Booming growth in Latin America.

To these generalizations must be added a large caveat. As economies of the world continue to integrate, it is increasingly difficult to isolate and measure the economic size of any country. And in countries that are in general doing poorly there are many individual companies, industries, and market niches that are doing very well, just as in very well-off countries, there are many companies doing poorly. Although Europe's economic prospects are not exciting, a sharp entrepreneur just might be on the verge of making millions in Portuguese tiles. The United States economy is already so interlaced with other economies that to precisely measure its size is impossible. And imagine the lack of precision in keeping track of all the economic activity of the entrepreneurs of Greater China.

There are opportunities in all parts of the world—including Europe. But in some countries, in general, the economic environment is more favorable than in others, and there is a constant shifting of this favorability. For the rest of the '90s and beyond, the new areas of great economic favorability are in Asia and Latin America. But again:

The more the economies of the world integrate, the less important are the economies of countries and the more important are the economic contributions of individuals and individual companies.

As we turn the corner on the millennium, investment-generating economic growth is occurring in some surprising places. Like Vietnam and India; Argentina and Chile; Brazil, Uruguay and Paraguay, Bolivia, Colombia, Ecuador, Peru, and Venezuela; and Mexico, whose net private investment inflow soared from $3.8 billion in 1990 to $15.3 billion in 1992, and which has had a budget surplus for the past three years.

What these countries—and the other countries of Asia and the Americas—have in common is a new and unwavering commitment to the principles and practices of a free-market economy. Each also has demonstrated the political will to implement the structural reforms necessary to promote free markets, such as privatization, trade liberalization, and tax reform, as well as the creation of capital markets and the necessary financial intermediation systems.

Where there is economic growth, there are also emerging more free-market forms of governance—an acceptance of the fact that people, not political fiat, create economic opportunity.

In the Americas democracies are everywhere. They sort of sneaked up on us. Allowing a special tentative category for Peru, where voters are threatened with a hefty fine if they don't vote— preferably for one of the two parties openly supported by President Alberto Fujimori—today all the countries of Latin America are democracies except French Guiana.

Virtually every Latin American country now encourages citizen participation in the reform process, including the more or less free and open election of political leaders. Even in Venezuela, where two attempted coups in 12 months might be expected to dampen enthusiasm for the electoral process, President Carlos Andres Pérez insisted that the elections for state governorships and over 5,000 local posts proceed as planned in December 1992. Many heralded the administration's actions as evidence that democracy is being strengthened in this sometimes politically troubled country. Then in the spring of 1993 Pérez was forced out in high scandal, but a peaceful, democratic change in governments ensued.

It is generally accepted in these countries that the benefits of a free-market economy must be extended to all citizens—not just a privileged few. Even leaders of the Communist party in Vietnam understand that to hold on to political power they must ensure continued economic growth, and that opportunities to participate in that growth must be available to all.

Global investors are tantalized by consumer markets numbering in the hundreds of millions. Vietnam offers an untapped consumer market of 71 million, India, 800 million plus, and Latin America, collectively, 400 million. Each of these areas also boasts a burgeoning middle class whose disposable income continues to grow, and who, through exposure to Western (mostly American) television, are developing a taste for the "finer things in life." (Of Mexico's 84 million residents, 24 million are classified by Mexico's

Census Bureau as "economically active," that is, wage earners with growing consumer appetites and money to spend).

These regions also offer a relatively young population, whose prime spending years are still ahead of them, as opposed to Japan, Europe, and the United States, where the graying of the population already has had an impact on consumer spending habits, including the type of products bought and a growing sensitivity to costs. Producers and retailers of products that appeal to the young, like Coca-Cola, Pepsi-Cola, M&Ms candies, Benetton, Esprit, makers of the internationally popular denim jeans, and entertainment are powerfully motivated to overcome whatever barriers (real or perceived) might exist in entering these markets. At the same time, across the board, efforts are being made to reduce the numbers of families living below the poverty line.

Europe Has a Long Way to Go

For the past two or three years, most observers were telling us that the newly unified Germany was an economic superpower about to lead the EC into world economic dominance.

Of course that is not happening. And it is not about to happen. Don't look to Europe for economic growth in anything like the near future. Europe is in a serious recession. Meanwhile, in 1992 the countries of Latin America taken together were growing at a healthy 3 percent, led by Chile with 10 percent and Argentina and Venezuela, each with 9 percent growth. Chile and Mexico were running budget surpluses, and Argentina had successfully overcome hyperinflation. While consumer price increases in Argentina are still high by U.S. standards (25 percent as compared to 6 percent), shopkeepers now affix prices in ink, something they wouldn't have done three years ago, or even two years ago.

The real domestic product of Germany in 1991 was only 28 percent of the output of the United States. Germany is not even in a class with Japan. Japan's economy is almost twice the size of Germany's. Germany is now in a recession, and won't be out of it anytime soon. Figures released in June 1993 showed that Germany's

GDP dropped 3.2 percent during the first quarter of 1993, the sharpest drop since 1975.

The unplanned costs of reunification are overwhelming: West Germany will have to cough up more than $1 trillion over the next decade and a half to subsidize unification.

If Germany is to be the engine of Europe it is going to be a slow EC train to the next century. Germany is fast becoming the sick old man of Europe.

The European Community—for now, at least—is a declining player in the global economy. The European recession has really shaken up companies that rushed to establish a presence in the much-hyped single-market Europe.

The high cost of Europe's welfare burden will continue to put it at a disadvantage with its competitors in Asia and the Americas.

And now Jacques Delors, the president of the EC, has called for legislation to compel large companies to consult workers on important strategic decisions, further burdening their competitiveness. Europe is sick and distracted by its sluggish economies, by mass migration and the surge of ethnic tension, by corruption and by big scandals in Italy, France, Spain, and Belgium.

Europe in the years just ahead will see no growth or negative growth. For Eastern Europeans—four years after the fall of the wall—the prospect of entering the EC seems as distant as ever—and less attractive.

Of course, Europe's no growth or negative growth is an average; and when you average out, you lose much of the intelligence. Obviously, some sectors and many companies will do well. Les Alberthal, chairman of EDS, the world's biggest computer services company, for example, thinks that Europe is just warming to the idea of outsourcing, and is the marketplace for EDS in the '90s.

But on average, most of 1994 and into 1995, and probably beyond, Europe will be engaged in limiting the damage.

Unemployment in the EC is reaching levels not seen since the 1930s. Nearly 18 million people—more than 10 percent of the work force—is without a job, 50 percent higher than jobless rates in the United States and almost five times higher than in Japan. By all accounts, the EC is losing its competitiveness in the global economy. In 1980, its members accounted for 21 percent of the world exports; today they account for 16 percent. In 1992, the EC ran a trade deficit of $90 billion with the rest of the world, three times the 1985–1990 average.

What's more, the leadership vacuum apparent throughout the industrialized world is even more keenly felt in the EC. Says David Howell, a respected member of the British Parliament, ''A sense pervades that communities are falling apart, values are collapsing, institutions are crumbling, nation-states are weakening. High expectations after the end of the Cold War have given way to bitter disappointments. People feel misled.''

In a sense, they have been. While the global economy was forcing others to ''trim the fat,'' the EC continued to dole out extraordinary sums of money to maintain its very generous welfare programs.

If Europe does not reform its welfare-burdened economy in an increasingly competitive world, it is in danger of becoming a history theme park for well-off customers from Asia and the Americas.

Because the media tend to report the virtues of economic reform only after countries have demonstrated a degree of success, the world comes to view the experience of economic growth as some sort of miracle. Other countries look to the success of their neighbors and wonder why they can't be as fortunate. They can be. But all the pieces have to be in place. Unfortunately, there is no one right way to implement a successful economic-reform program, and looking for a pattern is a bit like trying to answer the question, which came first: the chicken or the egg?

Does democracy lead to economic growth? Not necessarily. Bolivia has had a more or less democratic government for more than a decade, yet Bolivia lags behind some of the more dynamic Latin American countries like Chile and Argentina. Although recently Bolivia has managed to push inflation rates to levels lower than that of either Chile or Mexico. And the government of Vietnam is still committed to Communist party rule, yet Vietnam is one of the fastest-growing ''tiger cubs'' in Asia.

Or privatization? Not by itself. Argentina led the world in the pace at which its state-owned enterprises were privatized yet certainly has had its share of setbacks along the road to reform. Singapore, on the other hand, was slower to privatize industry but is the undisputed world leader in developing a state-of-the-art telecommunications infrastructure that is certain to turn that tiny city-state into a hub of international economic activity for the 21st century.

Trade liberalization is a key component of economic reform. Both Mexico and Argentina, which for decades had endeavored to create closed, self-sustaining economies, went from two of the most closed economies in the world to two of the most open economies.

It is all of these things, and it is strong leadership, too. Not strong leadership to direct an economy (to command an economy), but strong leadership to allow an economy to be grown bottom-up by entrepreneurs.

In Latin America, there is a new generation of just that kind of leader.

In Mexico it is President Carlos Salinas de Gortari and finance minister Pedro Aspe. Argentina's economic renaissance is being led by President Carlos Menem and finance minister Domingo Cavallo. Alejandro Foxley, Chile's minister of finance, is another standout. And Brazil, whose economic rebirth was jeopardized by the scandal-ridden presidency of Fernando Collor de Mello, now is back on track with Itamar Franco at the helm, and Planning Minister Paulo Haddad, a former economics professor, crafting the country's plans for economic reform.

Throughout Latin America, the "old guard" is being replaced by young, talented, in many cases American-educated businessmen, bankers, and economists whose focus is on making deals, facilitating economic growth, and managing change. Observes Ronald Maclean, Bolivia's 43-year-old, Harvard-educated foreign minister, "Cabinet meetings tend to be like management meetings in the States."

In Asia the places to be are Vietnam, led by Prime Minister Vo Van Kiet, and Singapore, where Goh Chok Tong recently took over as prime minister from the legendary Lee Kuan Yew, who is credited with moving the country from a colonial backwater to a thriving city-state with one of the best standards of living in Asia. India's impressive record of economic reform over the past two years was crafted by Prime Minister Narasimha Rao, and his minister of finance, Manmohan Singh, though Rao has recently been hurt by scandal which could, but probably will not, derail reform.

All of these leaders—and the others who are facilitating the shaping of the world economy—share one thing in common: They know absolutely that to survive and prosper they must tear down all barriers, real and artificial, that prevent their country's participation in the growing global economy. Economics, not political ideology, drives these heads of state.

FROM TRADING BLOCS TO BUILDING BLOCS

In 1991, then President George Bush articulated the vision of a free-trade area stretching from Anchorage to Tierra del Fuego. Bush lost the election, but nothing will alter the course that already had been set. Before the 1990s are over there will exist a pan-Americas free-trade zone from the North Pole to the South Pole. The building blocks were being put in place before Bush became president and the momentum of the global economy is such that the movement toward freer and freer trade among all countries everywhere will continue long after President Clinton leaves the White House.

What is evolving around the world is not protectionist trading blocs designed to isolate any given region from the rest of the international players, but economic alliances that promote development within regions, while making all borders more porous.

The pace and pattern of barrier-free trade will, of course, not always occur in a straight line. There will be fits and starts and setbacks. Protectionist chatter will continue to create confusion, but in the end pragmatism will overrule parochialism because it must. Observes Arthur Dunkel, former director-general, General Agreement on Tariffs and Trade (GATT): "Asia's growth validates two foundations underlying the General Agreement on Tariffs and Trade: that trade is a major engine of economic progress, and that exposing domestic industries to the rigors of international competition promotes efficiency.''

In 1992, Asia's growth rate was 7 percent, substantially higher than performance worldwide. Import and export trade growth for six Asian countries—China, Taiwan, Hong Kong, South Korea, Singapore, and Thailand—was a very impressive 11 percent. Seven of the world's 25 leading exporters in 1992 were Asian. And if one counts the EC as a single entity and excludes intra-EC trade, six of the top exporters in 1992 were Asian: Japan (third), Hong Kong (fifth), China (seventh), Chinese Taipei (eighth), and South Korea (tenth).

Many observers insist that there will never be a NAFTA (North American Free Trade Agreement)-like regional trade pact in Asia, that the diversity of cultures, language, history, and ethnic affiliation precludes the creation of a single regional market. But in many ways Asia has already accomplished what NAFTA is designed to create—a cooperative regional market in which trade is encouraged through lowered tariffs, removal of quotas, and shared resources.

The countries of Asia may not have formalized trade agreements, but intraregional trade is a significant share of each country's gross national product. Throughout Asia the more developed countries are now investing in the less developed countries, creating economic ties that are stronger than any lingering intraregional disagreements over politics, policies, and even historic grievances over war crimes and territorial disputes. Notes Barry Wain, editor at large for *The Asia Wall Street Journal:* ''In the spirit of pragmatism and a desire to succeed, political, historical, and ethnic barriers, responsible for so much grief and violence in Europe, are being largely ignored in Asia.''

Hanoi and Beijing Speaking Again

In 1991, after decades of hostility and war, Vietnam shook hands with its traditional enemy, China, announcing that Hanoi would resume diplomatic relations with Beijing. Beijing and Taipei don't even have diplomatic relations, yet trade and investment in both directions are on the rise—albeit funneled through Hong Kong. And Beijing and Tokyo are anxious to put to rest old territorial disputes to get on with more pressing economic matters.

Attempts to establish regional trading alliances have met with some interesting results. Early in 1993, Brunei, Indonesia, Malaysia, the Philippines, Singapore, and Thailand formed the ASEAN Free Trade Area (AFTA). Meant as a modest attempt to lower trade barriers among the six countries, and despite the fact that it will take 15 years to fully implement the agreement, the pact met with resistance from both within and outside the group. Many Asian countries would rather lobby for global free trade under the auspices of the Asia-Pacific Economic Cooperation (APEC) forum. Founded in 1989 as an informal discussion group, the organization now has 15 member countries, including the United States, Canada, Japan, Australia, and China, and a permanent secretariat in Singapore.

Although some economists insist that Asia is within reach of becoming a completely self-sufficient region, others maintain that any attempt to establish a protectionist regional trading bloc would send the wrong signal to the world. No country in Asia is interested in closing its borders. All are interested in keeping their options and borders open, and some envision the formation of a Pacific Area Free Trade Agreement, which would marry NAFTA to APEC (creating Pacific Area Free Trade Area).

That's much more in keeping with the direction the world is going. Within a PAFTA-like trading bloc each member country would be free to concentrate on those components of its economy that offer the greatest growth potential. An example of what would be possible on a much larger scale is the relationship currently evolving between Singapore, Malaysia, and the Indonesian Island of Batam.

Singapore has emerged as a world leader in the electronics industry. Singapore increased its level of foreign investment in 1992 by 21 percent over 1991. Some 40 percent of those investments were in the electronics sector. But Singapore has a problem. It is running out of space to build manufacturing plants and it long ago ran out of people to employ in them. (Singapore encourages older workers to stay in the work force and actively seeks foreign laborers.)

GROWTH TRIANGLE

Demand is so great, and investment interest so high, Singapore had to come up with a more ambitious plan. What is emerging is a "growth triangle" formed by Singapore, southern Malaysia, and portions of the Indonesian archipelago. The three have created a win-win-win situation and complement one another. Singapore has the technology, the telecommunications, and the transportation infrastructure while Malaysia and Indonesia offer much-needed land, low-cost labor, water, and electric power.

Results of Singapore's attempts to push multinationals' low-cost, lower-skill operations offshore have been astounding. In 1990, the Indonesian island of Batam was a jungle. Today, 30 companies operate out of its newly built industrial park, with more ready to sign on. Exports from those plants already operational are growing fast. Another Indonesian island, Bintan, twice the size of Singapore, is likely to be added to the plan.

There cannot be too many examples of a country actively encouraging foreign investors to go elsewhere. Doing so evidences Singapore's confidence both in its own increasingly sophisticated economy and in the prospects for growth in the wider region. This is a model for economic growth into the 21st century. Creating win-win situations in which countries assume the economic tasks for which they are best suited.

It is a model Malaysia and Indonesia felt was suitable enough to repeat. In August 1993, the two countries, along with Thailand, agreed to create another growth triangle. Encompassing five provinces in southern Thailand, four northern provinces in Malaysia, and two Indonesian provinces in Sumatra, across the strait of Malacca, the triangle has a market of 21 million people.

Although the synergy of this alliance is not as apparent as that created by Singapore, Malaysia, and Indonesia, and the infrastructure necessary to attract business less well developed, the three believe that together they can accomplish more than they can by going it alone. All three countries insist that bureaucracy will be kept to a minimum, any two countries can proceed with a project without approval of the third, and the private sector will drive decision making in the zone. In fact, the only mechanism governing the triangle will be a two-tier body comprised of a trilateral council of businessmen and a nine-member intergovernmental committee.

The formation of this northern triangle also underscores a broader interest in creating subregional growth areas as an engine of free trade. That's it. Government paves the way and then gets out of the way to let the private sector and the marketplace decide.

Some variation of this model is also being developed in Latin America, which is raising the practice of strategic trade alliances to a fine art.

LATIN AMERICA—A MODEL OF REGIONAL COOPERATION

The idea that Latin America might be a positive model of anything might raise some eyebrows, particularly if one hasn't been paying attention lately to all those Latin American countries the world was prepared to write off as lost causes a decade ago. While the United States, Canada, and Mexico quibble about NAFTA's fine print, the rest of the Americas have gone about the business of strengthening local economies by bringing down barriers to international trade as they wait their turn to negotiate to become part of NAFTA.

Chile will be the next Latin American country to sign on with

NAFTA, unless Argentina gets there first. Meanwhile, Chile has signed a raft of trade agreements as it pursues its plans for economic rejuvenation through exports. By some accounts it is setting the economic pace for the rest of Latin America. Its treaty with Mexico doubled trade between the two. Chile has also signed mutual trade agreements with Argentina, thereby doubling its exports to that country, and with Bolivia, increasing its exports by one third.

Colombia, which historically has isolated itself through the imposition of extraordinarily high tariffs, is now opening its doors. In 1992, it broadened its trade agreements with Venezuela and Ecuador. Formerly, these countries welcomed goods only from one another; imports from nonmembers were discouraged. Now, any product can be bought or sold, whatever its origin. The only existing barrier is the imposition of a common external tariff ranging between 5 percent and 20 percent.

The result has been an increase in trade between Colombia and Venezuela of more than $400 million between 1991 and 1992. Within four months of signing the agreement, trade between Colombia and Ecuador increased by about 30 percent. Freer trade is bringing the three countries closer together. Early in 1993, Venezuela issued $100 million worth of government bonds in the Colombian stock market. They were sold in minutes. Colombia and Venezuela are together negotiating a free-trade agreement with the three Central American countries and also are negotiating with Mexico. Once an arrangement is finalized among the three, Ecuador will be given consideration.

Diplomatic rifts between Venezuela and Peru aside, all five members of the 23-year-old Andean Pact are anxious to rekindle relationships. Even Peru, which suspended its membership in the five-nation pact, is nonetheless negotiating bilateral free-trade agreements. One was recently signed with Ecuador.

From Nationalism to Economic Realities

Everywhere in Latin America, nationalist sentiments are giving way to economic realities. Chile and Argentina have a long history of conflict. In 1902, Britain's King Edward VII stepped in to mediate between the two to prevent them from going to war. In 1979, it was Pope John Paul II who averted armed conflict over the Beagle Channel. Today, both have come to realize that together they are stronger economically than either of them could hope to be separately.

Argentina needs capital and know-how to help it recover from the hyperinflation of the 1980s. Chile, with its impressive recovery record, offers both. On the other hand, Chile's home market is small—13 million people and a GDP of $38 billion compared to Argentina's population of 32 million and $72 billion GDP. Chilean President Patricio Aylwyn is encouraging his country's businesspeople to grasp Argentina's outstretched hand.

In the spirit of cooperation, Chile and Argentina together are working on a pipeline that will carry oil fifteen miles from Argentina's oil fields at Neuquén to San Vicente in Chile. The pipeline will supply 40 percent of Chile's oil needs. They also are jointly developing oil deposits on the Argentine side of the Magellan Strait. A $1 billion joint venture will provide Chile with 8 million cubic meters of natural gas a day. Meanwhile, Chilean firms have bought a privatized Argentine utility company, which will provide Buenos Aires with much of its electricity.

Cooperative arrangements are not limited to energy. Having perfected the art of transforming unwieldy state firms into profitable, market-driven enterprises, Chilean managers are now applying that experience to Argentine firms. Using customized computer software, Chile's managers are trimming overstaffed work forces and modernizing billing in some of Argentina's most troubled companies.

Chilean retailers now operate high-tech supermarkets next to Argentina's corner shops. Several Chilean credit-risk agencies are joining with their Argentine counterparts to funnel information back and forth across the Andes. When Argentina's parliament offered tax breaks to attract foreign investors to the country's mining industry, Chilean companies lined up to take advantage of the offer.

So far, the relationship has been somewhat lopsided. Which

makes sense—Chile was well ahead of Argentina in rebuilding its economy. Chilean investment in Argentina has increased ten-fold, to $500 million, since the two joined forces; Argentina's investment in Chile is not even a tenth of that. Argentina's long-running surplus with its neighbor has been eroded, as Chile's exports have risen more than twice as fast as Argentina's. But there is little concern on either side. Both countries are certain that as Argentina's privatization continues and state-owned firms become more competitive, the relationship will become a more equal one.

More important than the present imbalance is that both have realized that they gain more from working closely with each other. More strategic alliances. Argentina needs capital inflows from Chile, and Chile needs to demonstrate to the world that it can be a major player in the global economy. Chile can't do it without Argentina.

Mercorsor—South America's Richest Market

That same realization prompted the signing of the four-nation Mercorsor agreement, which created South America's richest market. Its purpose is to accelerate economic growth by linking Argentina, Brazil, Paraguay, and Uruguay in a common market of 190 million people, with a $427 billion total gross regional product and intraregional trade valued at $4.9 billion. The region also is Latin America's biggest industrial base.

Under the March 1991 Asunción Treaty, Mercorsor members will cut import duties every six months, with the goal of eliminating tariff barriers completely by December 31, 1994. Meeting the demands of the treaty requires that each country continue to deregulate its economy. Says Carlos Floria of Argentina's University of San Andrés, "It's a form of regional collective discipline."

Regional collective discipline is the force behind all successful trade agreements, that and the fact that none of these pacts is protectionist. Capitalizing on the strengths of each country, these regional alliances make all members stronger international players.

Most of the expansion resulting from Mercorsor will be concentrated in South America's economic powerhouse—the 1,200-mile stretch of industries, farms, and urban centers on the east coast from São Paulo to Buenos Aires. As barriers fall, the pact will also accelerate the shift from state intervention to free markets throughout the hemisphere.

As described in an article in *Business Week*, already the impact of Mercorsor is evident. In the small town of Puán, 300 miles southwest of Buenos Aires, Brazil's green-and-yellow flag and the blue-and-white colors of Argentina flutter side by side from the rooftop of the Maltaria Pampa factory. Built by Brazil's largest brewer, with Argentine partners, the factory supplies malt to Brazil's brewers. Brazil's largest auto-parts manufacturer, Cofap, bought a 50 percent stake in its counterpart in Argentina to share distribution networks. And the Brazilian agribusiness giant, Sadia Concórdia Indústria e Comércio, extended its market to include Argentina. Sadia is selling processed chicken and turkey in Argentina, and buying from them wheat, meat, and plastic margarine containers.

Multinationals with a presence in numerous South American markets are now looking for ways to consolidate operations, to cut costs and increase profits. Monsanto, for example, has two plants making ingredients for its Roundup herbicide—one in Brazil, one in Argentina. One plant could supply both countries. Eastman Kodak do Brasil is establishing a distribution center near São Paulo. Kodak products will be imported from around the world for sale within the region. And Volt Information Sciences Inc., a New York–based maker of digital typesetting systems, is expanding its regional service center and printing plant in Montevideo, Uruguay.

For these multinationals, and others, including a Ford Motor Co. and Volkswagen joint venture, which even before the Mercorsor agreement were looking for ways to combine production in Brazil and Argentina, the easing of restrictions will change the way they do business in the region. Apparel maker Benetton bought a 1-million-acre sheep ranch in Argentina which will supply wool to Benetton factories in Brazil and Argentina.

Local businesses, keen on establishing joint ventures with foreign giants to help them meet rising competition, also will benefit. This easing of trade barriers will make local companies more attractive to foreign companies, international venture capitalists, and adventurous entrepreneurs alike.

Regional Alliances

And that's just the point. In articulating the intent of establishing regional cooperative trade alliances, Malaysia's prime minister, Dr. Mahathir bin Mohamad, expressed sentiments that could have been spoken by a representative of any one of these newly allied countries.

Said Mahathir: "Our economic integration is a clear example of market-driven open regionalism. Our achievements are the fruits of market-driven open regionalism. In the years ahead, I am sure that our comprehensive economic integration will continue to be driven by market regionalism. We will, I am sure, continue to welcome the other great economic players of the world in the process of enriching our market-driven open regionalism. Indeed we must welcome all nations to join us in the making of our great market-driven East Asian regionalism."

A bit repetitive perhaps, but maybe that's what it takes for people to catch on. It is imperative that politicians, corporate decision makers, and people in general understand that strong regional alliances do not inhibit economic growth worldwide; that the economic well-being of one country does not depend on the economy of another declining.

The global economy is not a zero-sum game, but an expanding universe.

Regional Markets Create Greater Opportunities Worldwide

Apparently influenced by NAFTA's vociferous critics, public opinion in the United States was, at one point, running two to one against ratification of the treaty, according to *The Wall Street Journal*. Why? An abiding fear that liberalizing trade will result in U.S. companies stampeding southward to take advantage of Mexico's $2 hourly wage and more relaxed environmental standards. That fear exists despite the fact that virtually every serious effort by economists to model the effects of NAFTA comes to the same conclusion: Freer trade among the United States, Canada, and Mexico will energize all three economies. For the United States, specifically, that translates into a GDP increase of roughly $30 billion a year once the treaty is fully implemented.

And what about those lower wages? Well, as an article in *Fortune* magazine explained, they aren't always the bargain people believe them to be. In some maquiladors—plants built along the U.S.-Mexico border, which import finished products to the United States courtesy of preferential trade treatment—employee turnover is as high as 20 percent. Replacing and retraining for these positions, along with nonwage expenses, can raise the total cost of employment to $10 an hour, well above the touted $2 an hour. Besides, American workers are five times more productive than Mexican workers.

But even that's not the point. American markets, 20 times larger than Mexico's, already are fairly open to Mexican goods. Tariffs on Mexican imports average 4 percent, and many enter duty-free. It is estimated the removal of trade barriers will help sustain Mexico's GNP growth at average annual rates of 4 to 5 percent for the next 25 years. Faster growth in Mexico will ensure continued expansion in U.S.-Mexican trade, which has doubled to $76 billion annually since 1988. Growth in U.S. exports accounts for much of this trade. In 1991, the United States ran a trade surplus with Mexico for the first time in nearly ten years. In 1992, that surplus swelled to $5.5 billion.

No other consumers in the world have a greater propensity to buy American products than Mexicans. The average Mexican purchases $380 worth of U.S. products annually as compared to Koreans who, with twice the annual income, purchase only $20 in American goods. The payoff for America is more jobs, and better paying jobs.

The U.S. Commerce Department's rule of thumb is that for every $1 billion in exports, another 19,000 net new jobs are created. Extrapolated out through the end of the '90s, that's an increase of 60,000 jobs. To be sure, some U.S. jobs will be lost, and for those affected it will be painful, but the creation of new jobs will more than offset the losses.

This will be most apparent in the telecommunications industry. NAFTA will allow companies producing everything from network switches to satellite networks and the software that makes it all work to widen their already sizable lead, thereby creating the high-tech, high-wage jobs the Clinton administration and others insist are needed for the United States to grow.

NAFTA also will strengthen the U.S. textile and apparel industry. Over the past five years, U.S. textile and apparel makers have developed a strategy called "quick response" (QR). Electronic data exchanges now allow retailers to send design and order specifications to garment makers, who in turn communicate electronically with fabric suppliers. The result has been improved quality, lower inventory costs, and higher sales volume. Using QR, Pennsylvania-based VF Corp., maker of Lee and Wrangler jeans, reduced the time it takes to produce and ship an order from two weeks to one day. The company regained five percentage points of market share in 1992, much of that from imports, and hired 4,500 new employees.

Under NAFTA, Mexico will eliminate its 17 percent tariff on American-made clothing, which will allow U.S. companies to spread the benefits of QR over a much larger market. Retailing giants Wal-Mart, JC Penney, and Dillards are leading the way. At present, Mexico has only 550 square feet of retail space for every 1,000 shoppers—the United States, on the other hand, has approximately 19,000 square feet per 1,000 people. Penney plans to open five Mexican superstores, each with between 150,000 to 180,000 square feet of space. Penney executives insist that lower tariffs will mean that 60 percent of the clothing on their racks in Mexico will carry the "Made in the USA" label.

Greater demand for American-made fabric will benefit U.S. textile workers. Low Mexican wages mean little in this capital-intensive industry, as the 25 percent higher energy costs in Mexico more than outweigh the benefits of cheaper labor. Walter Elisha, CEO of Spring Industries in Fort Hill, South Carolina, anticipates that increased business from south of the border will increase his

20,000-employee work force by 900. Says Elisha, "NAFTA is one of those rare times in life when what makes sense for the business is also the right thing to do."

Because the region created by NAFTA is so large, the benefits are more obvious and more dramatic than the benefits of some of the regional alliances being created in Asia and Latin America, but they are no less important. These trading blocs, as many insist on calling them, inclusive of all the negative, protectionist connotations of the phrase, are not trading blocs at all but building blocks toward a truly integrated world economy.

It is also important to emphasize that it didn't matter all that much that NAFTA was ratified by the U.S. Congress. Driven by economics and businesspeople, the integration of the U.S. and Mexican economies is continuing and inevitable. As with the drive toward a single-market Europe, the politicians were scrambling to keep up with the businesses of Europe and single-market Europe is in place. Symbolically it was nice that the U.S. Congress signaled that it was in touch with the 21st century, but it was not all that critical economically. Symbolically, of course, it was hugely important.

Opening trade creates economic opportunity, including much-needed foreign direct investment. This, then, is the formula that is proving itself successful over and over again. Lowering trade barriers, encouraging foreign direct investment, and implementing the structural reforms necessary to ensure continued movement of capital and goods in both directions.

NEW BUSINESS STRATEGIES

Removal of trade barriers worldwide will create business opportunities everywhere. Obviously, some regions and some individual countries offer more immediate payoffs in the short term, but savvy investors scout around for areas that will pay off in the long term.

That's what brought the United States' Texas Instruments and Europe's SGS-Thomson, two companies in the electronics field, to Singapore nearly twenty years ago. Germany's BMW plans to assemble cars in Vietnam and IBM has set up offices there, despite the fact that U.S. companies are still embargoed from doing business there. Corning is ready to give India a second try, investing $210 million over the next decade in a plant that will manufacture glass bulbs for television picture tubes. (An earlier joint venture was abandoned after Corning ran into difficulties with Indian subcontractors.)

And such corporations as AT&T and Pepsico are in India and Singapore and all over Latin America, where Pepsico plans to invest $750 million over the next five years. Joining Pepsico and AT&T in Latin America is Colgate-Palmolive, which has experienced strong growth in the area since 1985 and is now shopping around for acquisitions. Hewlett Packard is teaming up with Brazil's Edisa Informatica to cash in on the country's soon-to-be-open computer market. From Venezuela to Argentina, Spain's Iberia Airlines is snapping up state carriers in preparation for an anticipated battle with U.S. carriers as Latin America makes its skies a whole lot friendlier. And Pizza Hut International now has 110 franchises from Chile to Mexico, and is aiming for 500.

The world is a much-changing place, and these countries that were once all but written off by international investors are hot. What happened? The evolution of each is slightly different, but each now presents global players with extraordinary prospects for new business development.

Vietnam's Policy of Doi Moi

Keep an eye on Vietnam. In 1986, the Communist regime realized that the country's battered economy and decaying infrastructure could not be rebuilt without an infusion of foreign capital; that to avert disaster they, like their traditional enemy, the Chinese, would have to embrace capitalism. Vietnam adopted a policy of doi moi, or economic rejuvenation.

The National Assembly approved revisions to the country's foreign-investment laws, which made them one of the most, if not the most, liberal in the world. Foreign companies can have 100 percent ownership of their facilities. Profits can be repatriated in hard currency. Companies enjoy tax holidays, the terms of which are highly negotiable. Employers can hire and fire at will, and while land is still owned by the state, investors can get leases for up to 70 years for offices and factories.

Other economic reforms have been very successful. Agrarian reforms have transformed Vietnam from an importer of rice to the world's third-largest exporter of rice after the United States and Thailand. A trade deficit has become a trade surplus. By increasing exports and slowing down the money-printing presses, the government has pushed inflation down from 900 percent a year to about 15 percent. In 1992, Vietnam's economy grew by 8.3 percent, a sharp increase from the 4.7 percent in 1991.

Not bad for a country that lost $1 billion of annual Soviet non-military aid, and with the U.S. embargo still in place.

Everyone Except the United States

The United States may not be ready to do business in Vietnam (although this could change any moment), but everybody else is. Taiwanese companies are leading the parade, with investments totaling about $790 million through December 1992.

In July 1993, Taiwan's state-run China Petroleum Corp. and Total SA of France announced intentions to form a joint venture with Petroleum Vietnam to build a $1 billion refinery, which would process 130,000 barrels of oil a day. If approved by the Vietnam government, the project would be the largest-ever foreign investment in Vietnam. Each company would own 30 percent of the venture, with a Taiwanese investment company owning the remaining 10 percent.

Hong Kong follows with $606 million in investments; then come France ($475 million), Australia ($404 million), and Britain ($305 million). Japan is holding back somewhat, partly in deference to the U.S. embargo. Nonetheless, as of December 1992, Japan was tied with Britain in total dollars invested. However, a flurry of activity in the first quarter of 1993 probably put Japan in third place ahead of France, or possibly first place.

Fortune magazine listed these foreign investments in Vietnam in its April 5, 1993, issue:

- A Japanese group has built an assembly plant in Saigon, turning out four-wheel drives that closely resemble Chrysler Jeeps.
- Australian companies have a big hold on telecommunications, including cellular phones.
- Taiwan's Ching Fong Co., the biggest single corporate investor in Vietnam, with a string of deals, has now formed a $290-million joint venture with the government to build a cement factory near Hanoi.
- The Netherlands' Heineken and Singapore's Tiger are jointly building a $5-million brewery in Saigon.
- South Korea's Daewoo has a $170-million project to assemble television tubes with Hanoi Electric Corp., a state-run money-maker that already puts together TVs and cassette players for Japan's JVC.
- National airlines from Singapore, Taiwan, and Thailand feed Hanoi and Saigon, while Vietnam Airlines flies to those countries in reciprocal arrangements. Lufthansa now serves Vietnam, as Air France has for years.
- Oil companies from 13 countries, including Canada and Mexico, continue to buy the rights to search for oil in the Big Bear area and other oil fields off Vietnam's coast. The shelf is believed to contain between one billion and 2.5 billion barrels, which would top Brunei's reserves.

THE VIETNAM WAR IS OVER FOR ALL BUT THE UNITED STATES

In Vietnam they have a saying: "The buffalo that is too slow to reach the watering hole must drink from the muddy water." If the United States doesn't lift the embargo, it's the muddy water for the Yankee dollar. The Vietnamese seem to have forgiven Americans for the war long before we forgave ourselves; and in any case, more than half the population of Vietnam has no memory of the war, but they have a strong appetite for all things American.

So certain are the Vietnamese people that America will soon join the rest of the world in its stampede to rebuild and rejuvenate Vietnam that learning English, considered the international language of business, has become a national passion.

They're undoubtedly right. As president, George Bush took a few tentative steps in that direction in the spring of 1992 by clearing the way for AT&T, Sprint, and MCI to provide long-distance phone service. U.S. tourists are now free to visit Vietnam but they cannot get a visa in the United States (I got mine in Kuala Lumpur). In December 1992, the embargo was loosened another notch when U.S. business were given permission to apply for exemptions from the Trading with the Enemy Act to open offices in Vietnam and to draw up contracts. Although they can't actually do business there, some 160 companies have obtained licenses enabling them to open offices and hire employees. In September President Clinton opened things up just a crack. U.S. companies can now bid for Vietnamese construction and development projects financed by the World Bank and other international lending institutions.

The Vietnamese are understandably baffled by the United States' apparent lack of interest in tapping into one of the world's hottest growth markets. Says Nguyen Son, head of cultural affairs at the Ho Chi Minh City People's Committee, a group that has overall authority in the metropolis of eight million people: "You must let bygones be bygones. It's time to leave the past and look to the future."

There is a long list of U.S. corporate executives who would agree with him. Included among the many companies that have sent representatives to Vietnam to scout around—sometimes posing as tourists—are a veritable who's who in corporate America. Boeing, Chrysler, Citicorp, Coca-Cola, General Electric, Holiday Inn, Mobil, and a host of airlines, including Delta, Northwest, and United.

The MIA issue won't go away. Nor should it. Although there are many credible experts on the Vietnam War who insist that there are not, and could not possibly be, any MIAs still in the country, that is small comfort to the families of those still unaccounted for. But even some former prisoners of war advocate a release of the embargo, insisting that with closer and closer economic ties will come stronger confidence in each other on the part of both governments; that if the United States is ever to get a full accounting, it will be as a result of improved economic relations, not badgering or embargoes.

In fact, Americans are divided about reestablishing ties with Vietnam. In response to a poll conducted by *USA Today*/CNN and Gallup, slightly half the respondents—48 percent—said they supported the idea of better relations with Vietnam; 42 percent remained opposed. John Wheeler, a Vietnam veteran who headed fund-raising efforts for the Vietnam Memorial, insisted the poll "confirms what I thought: Most Americans want to improve relations with Vietnam." And added, "The way to get answers to questions (about MIAs) is to have lots of Americans in Bermuda shorts walking all over Vietnam."

Vietnam and the United States need each other, although Vietnam's most pressing need was resolved on July 2, 1993, when the United States announced that it would permit Vietnam to pay off its debt to the International Monetary Fund. Once that debt has been paid—and there are a number of companies and consortia more than willing to pay the Fund off for Vietnam—international lending organizations like the Fund, the World Bank, and the Asian Development Bank can once again turn on the tap. None too soon. The greatest threat to Vietnam's continued growth is its decaying infrastructure. Now, the country can begin to make the necessary repairs and improvements.

For most Americans Vietnam was a political war. We now need to think of it as a country—as an economic opportunity.

James Rockwell is the only American doing business in Vietnam. He has created a consulting firm, headquartered in Hanoi, to help companies get started there. I asked him to summarize his advice to clients. This is what he said:

"Stay flexible and personable and you'll succeed in Vietnam; be rigid and aloof and expect to fail. This is the first and most important advice we give our clients. Massive positive changes have rocked Vietnam for the past five years, freeing the individual while clogging the machinery. All things are subject to change. Take it in stride. But don't count on an arm's-length relationship with the bureaucracy; count on personal relationships with those who make up the bureaucracy. Go with it, work through it, stay flexible.''

Singapore, in a Class by Itself

Singapore is the smallest of what are often referred to as Asia's four ''Little Dragons''—South Korea, Taiwan, and Hong Kong are the other three—but in many ways it is the most successful. Singapore is Asia's dream country. This small island-city at the tip of the Malay Peninsula achieved full independence from Britain in 1965. Today, the country boasts the world's biggest container port. It is the third-largest oil-refining center and the major exporter of disc drives.

Its manufacturing base is composed of multinational corporations, and some 3,000 foreign companies have been attracted to the city-state by generous tax breaks, ultramodern telecommunications, an efficient airport, and tame labor unions. The country's industrial policy is straightforward: Discourage declining industries; bring in high-growth industries like electronics and biotechnology with investments, grants, and worker-retraining programs.

For a country some call Singapore Inc., because it is run like a business, not a country, it is interesting to note that the government still owns scores of firms, including electricity and airline companies, banks, supermarkets, and taxis, but they all run on a competitive, profit-making basis. Observes one Western analyst: ''Fortune 500 executives love it here because the government runs the country the way AT&T would.''

Strategy for Success

Singapore's success says a great deal about how a country with virtually no natural resources can create economic advantages with influence far beyond its region. What the government did, under the leadership of former prime minister, now senior minister, Lee Kuan Yew, ''was leverage its single natural advantage of strategic location by establishing world-class transportation and materials-handling facilities [and then] extending such 'hubbing'

into the financial and other service domains by establishing a sophisticated communications and information technology infrastructure.''

And what an infrastructure. Singapore is poised to become the
first fully networked society—one in which all homes, schools,
businesses, and government agencies will be interconnected in an
electronic grid. A comprehensive National Information Technology
Plan was issued in 1986 by the National Computer Board, established in 1980 to set and implement Singapore's information technology policies.

Writes Rajendra S. Sisodia, assistant professor of marketing at
George Mason University in Virginia: "The plan included specific
objectives and deadlines for training people; creating an IT [infor-
mation technology] culture; enhancing the communications infrastructure; generating and supporting IT applications; fostering a
world-class indigenous IT industry that includes software, hardware,
and computer services; and pioneering new information technology
applications through R&D. In most of these objectives, the National
Computer Board has either achieved or surpassed its goals."

Additionally, Singapore's commitment to technological research
and development has attracted virtually every company in the electronics industry. Some came in the early years to take advantage
of Singapore's low-wage, pliant work force but stayed to take advantage of Singapore's knowledge base and extraordinary infrastructure. Among the industry leaders ensconced in the city are
Apple, AT&T, Black & Decker, Digital Equipment Corp., Grum-
man Data Systems, Hewlett Packard, IBM, Matsushita, NEC, and
Philips.

Is Singapore a Model?

Although widely criticized for its somewhat paternalistic (some
would say repressive) politics, Singapore has steadfastly adhered to
its goal of investing heavily in technological and human capabilities
toward the goal of creating an economy where both individuals and
organizations would be more likely to flourish.

And flourish they have. Citizens of Singapore enjoy the highest living standard in Asia, after Japan, with an average per capita income of $15,000, and have the highest per capita foreign reserves in the world. In sharp contrast to other booming Asian cities, Singapore has no pollution and virtually no street crime. Although Singapore has minimal public assistance, and no unemployment benefits, less than 0.3 percent of its families live in poverty. Moreover, all citizens have access to affordable health care, and 82 percent own their apartments.

So why shouldn't the rest of us model ourselves after Singapore? Well, for one thing, it wouldn't work. Not in the United States certainly, and probably not in most of the Western world. Singapore takes a dim view of political dissenters. The government has vast powers to stifle dissent: An Internal Security Act allows for detention without trial, sharp restrictions on any statement that has the potential to stir racial or religious tensions, and extremely tough libel and slander laws. Strict fines are imposed on any who break the unwritten code of public conduct.

Such paternalism wouldn't wash in the United States, but the consensus in Singapore is that that's the price they pay for security. A nation of immigrants, many Singaporeans came from countries torn by chaos and poverty; apparently many feel that given a choice between rich and poor, rich is better.

It is also a question of manageable scale. Singapore has a population of only 2.7 million. When Lee Kuan Yew started his economic reforms the population was only 1.4 million. But it certainly is an example of an extraordinarily successful small country in a big world. The 1,000 countries in the world will not be 1,000 Singapores, but Singapore shows us how powerful very small countries can be in the global economy.

Paternalism may not be attractive to folks in the United States, but to some in the newly formed countries emerging out of the breakup of the Soviet Union, the Singapore model is preferable to the violence and disorder that is convulsing parts of Russia and others who have attempted free-market economies by ''shock therapy.'' Although long borders with Afghanistan and Iran threaten President Saparamuryad Niyazov's vision of a peaceful and profitable move toward a free-market economy, Turkmenistan, thus far, has managed to maintain order in the tidal wave of disorder surrounding it.

Just as Singapore is developing its economy based on its strategic location as a gateway to Southeast Asia, Turkmenistan is using its large reserves of natural gas to pave the way to economic reform. Estimates put the country's "stabilization fund" from sales of natural gas at $1 billion—all held in Western bank accounts. Niyazov has announced that he will share the wealth with Turkmenistan's four million citizens. Already, he has promised free gas, water, and electricity for every household and promises to keep prices for food staples at prereform levels.

And, like Singapore, one-party rule is the order of the day, strenuously opposed by Helsinki Watch, the New York–based human-rights group, and press censorship is justified as necessary to suppress ethnic animosities. When asked to explain the need for press censorship and the lack of political freedom, Niyazov responds, "We don't want any conflicts in society that could hinder the transition to market relations."

He also adds that controls are necessary during this period of transition and that in three to five years, when the population is prosperous, controls will be loosened as people will be less vulnerable to religious or ethnic demogoguery. Many of Turkmenistan's citizens apparently agree with him. He is extraordinarily popular despite heavy censorship and a rather lax definition of human rights.

Of course, it remains to be seen whether he can pull off a Singapore-like economic coup, but don't count Turkmenistan out. In the cycle of economic favorability, this small desert country may well be next in line for growth.

Can Singapore Maintain Its Momentum?

The country isn't resting on its laurels. Satisfied that its internal house is more or less in order, Singapore is now turning its attention outward. Encouraged by Lee Kuan Yew, Singapore businesses are looking for new opportunities, especially in China.

Many have come down with a case of "China fever." According

to Zhu Zhen-Yuan of the Chinese Embassy in Singapore, Singapore's investments in China in the first six months of 1992 were $494 million, as compared to a total of $896 million for the entire period between 1979 and 1991.

Singapore businesspeople also are busy in Vietnam. And this aggressive, outward-looking approach to business is now being embraced by the country's cash-rich banks. Traditionally conservative, Singapore's four main banks are now big lenders in the region and are encouraging more international loan syndication business. Singapore's banks have now surpassed Hong Kong as Thailand's primary lender. While Hong Kong still has the lion's share of loans to China, Singapore is moving into this territory as well.

Maybe others can't do what Singapore has done, but economies and opportunities are growing in other corners of the world.

ASIA PACIFIC REGION—THE RISING SON OF THE NEW GLOBAL ORDER

The three most important considerations shaping the new global order are (1) the worldwide collapse of communism, (2) the revolution in telecommunications, and (3) the rise of the Asia Pacific region.

Asia with its spending power, the spread of new technology, growing capital resources, and the increase in intra-Asian trade has reached the critical mass needed for self-sustained economic growth and influence.

Asia Pacific is destined to lead the global economy into the next century.

While Europe is self-absorbed with its single market, and the United States is preoccupied with Europe, the real economic action has shifted to the Asia Pacific region.

The Asia Pacific Rim—bounded by Tokyo, Shanghai, Hong Kong, and Singapore—is taking over from the formerly dominant Atlantic—with its New York-Paris-London industrial culture. Five hundred years ago the world's economic center moved from the

Mediterranean to the Atlantic. Today, it has shifted from the Atlantic to the Pacific.

The United States and the European Community are mature economies with modest growth rates. Asia's manufacturing strength makes it a booming market, and its consumer sector, compared to the United States and the EC, is just opening up.

Steel consumption in Asia (excluding Japan) is already greater than in the United States or the EC.

Semiconductor demand in Asia Pacific exceeds that of the EC.

Container and air-freight traffic in Asia already exceeds that of the United States or EC.

Asian firms already have 25 percent of the world PC market.

Asia Pacific will probably grow by more than $5 trillion by the year 2000, more than one-third the forecast growth for the whole world.

Although Japan is the region's undisputed leader today, the rest of the East Asia region—China, Taiwan, Hong Kong, Singapore, and Korea—will eventually dominate, with strong backup from Malaysia, Thailand, and Indonesia.

One of the elements in achieving critical mass for self-sustained growth in Asia Pacific is the development of regional capital for growth. The United States, and to a lesser extent Europe, have been the engines of growth by providing markets for Asia's exports. They also provided most of the capital and technology in the initial phase. Now the region's four economic tigers—South Korea, Taiwan, Singapore, and Hong Kong—are investing in the next group: Malaysia, Thailand, Indonesia, and the Philippines. The four tigers now account for 35 percent of all foreign investments in those countries: more than the Japanese, the Americans, or the Europeans. The countries that have prospered are reinvesting in the next big growth areas. The new tier is financing the next tier.

Growth in the Asia Pacific region is as close as we can get to a textbook example of the global paradox—the bigger the world economy, the more powerful its smallest players. Not only are the more prosperous countries now investing in the less developed countries, but throughout the region entrepreneurs are fueling the

economy of their home country as well as the economies of the
rest of the region.

As mentioned in the previous chapter, there are an estimated 55
million Chinese living outside the People's Republic. Literally millions of them have become successful entrepreneurs in their
adopted countries, and are now reinvesting in China and elsewhere,
spreading both their wealth and their entrepreneurial know-how. In
Indonesia, the Liem Sioe Liong's Salin group—a multinational
business conglomerate owned by a Chinese family—alone is estimated to account for 5 percent of Indonesia's GDP. Other Chinese
families run 17 of Indonesia's biggest 25 conglomerates. Chinese-
Thai business families have dominated the economy of Thailand
for decades, as have Malaysian-Chinese families. In Singapore, ethnic Chinese are the majority of the population and hold the majority
of family wealth.

A New Role for Asia

Today, the countries of Asia Pacific are rushing toward a wholly
new role in the family of nations, and other nations will be required
to make room for Asia on center stage. Including Japan, Asia's
economic output could overtake North America's as early as 1996,
according to David O'Rear, senior consultant and regional economist at the Economist Intelligence Unit in Hong Kong.

Excluding Japan, O'Rear anticipates that Asia will overtake North
America in 2018 and the European Community in 2022. Gus
Hooke, an Australian economist, believes Asia, excluding Japan,
will account for 57 percent of the world's economy by 2050. The
24 OECD countries, including the United States, Japan and most
of Europe, will among them account for only 12 percent. In 1990,
the OECD countries boasted 74 percent of the world's economy,
Asia only 9 percent.

Despite the raised voices and dire warnings emanating from the
U.S. Congress and assorted European governing bodies, there is
no immediate danger of a single Asian economic bloc turning
into a power-hungry club. Each country has too much work yet
to do in getting its own economic house in order, and there are

too many leftover political disputes among them yet to be resolved.

While it is not likely that the ever-pragmatic Asian countries will compromise hard-won global relationships by threatening enforcement of regionally aligned trading alliances, there is emerging an economic behemoth that will hold sway over world markets by virtue of its size and entrepreneurial savvy.

Beyond economics, Asia doesn't yet know what new, larger, and more important role it should play in the world. The rest of the world doesn't know what Asia's role should be either. That vacuum holds great potential opportunity.

There is an opportunity for Asia to profoundly help shape the new global order, to assert leadership. But the countries of Asia Pacific—now the driving force of the global economy—must have a vision of what their role in the new global order should be. First articulating a vision, and then reaching consensus among culturally and economically disparate Asian countries on how to realize the vision, is some years away.

From Chile to China, keep an eye on growth in Asia Pacific and the Americas.

Latin America Offers Economic Growth Opportunities for the '90s and Beyond

After three years of slowdown, world trade growth accelerated in 1992. The value of world trade grew by a healthy 5.5 percent, as compared to 1.5 percent in 1991. The main stimulus came from North America and Asia. And the greatest rise in imports came in Latin America, where imports jumped 18.5 percent in 1992.

What this signals is that economic growth and opportunity in the '90s will be found in the Americas as well as in Asia Pacific. In its annual report, the Inter-American Development Bank painted a bright picture for Latin America as it entered the first quarter of 1993 in a stronger position than it has ever been. "In 1992, capital flooded back into the region, inflation was reined in, most governments pushed forward free-market policies and some struck debt-reduction deals." Under such circumstances, trumpeted the report, "the outlook for sustained recovery in 1993 and beyond remains favorable."

This same report noted that Chile had grown by an outstanding 10 percent in 1992. Others that performed well were Argentina and Venezuela, each with 9 percent growth, and Panama, with 6.2 percent. Net capital inflows in the region reached a record $48 billion, Argentina negotiated debt-reduction deals with private creditor banks, and Brazil reached similar agreements in principle.

Furthermore, privatization and economic restructuring policies attracted massive amounts of foreign capital. Many of those dollars were money repatriation and some were attracted by the area's vigorous stock markets. The continued sale of state-owned industries also was a major contributor. Additionally, inflation was brought under control in several countries, including Nicaragua where it fell from 1,400 percent in 1991 to 20 percent in 1992.

Overall, the economies grew by 2.6 percent in 1992, the second consecutive year of growth after a decade of stagnation—the so-called "lost decade."

The Crisis That Wasn't

These are impressive accomplishments for a region that a little over a decade ago was a pariah in international capital markets. Mexico started it all on August 20, 1982, when the government said it would not be repaying its international bankers for a while. Brazil and Argentina quickly followed suit. Media headlines predicted the collapse of the international financial system. The outlook, all agreed, was dismal. The standing joke at the IMF/World Bank meeting in Toronto in September 1982 was that "any effort to contain the crisis amounted to no more than rearranging the deck chairs on the *Titanic*."

This *Titanic,* however, didn't go down. There were real threats to New York's money-center banks, to be sure. Their exposure to troubled debtor countries exceeded their capital. And there existed the possibility that a major bank would encounter funding problems in the markets, which in turn would have set off a chain reaction that most certainly would have shaken the international financial system.

But that didn't happen. The banks were given the time they needed to raise capital and increase reserves, and the debtor countries began to reform their economies. Furthermore, all the major players temporarily put aside their own interests for the good of the whole. And lastly, the long-term response to the problem didn't just help Latin Americans cope with their debt, it gave them time to put in place the necessary structural adjustments that resulted in sustained improvements in their economies.

There existed no blueprint to show the international financial community how to undo the mess it was in. That was probably for the best. Instead of trying to find a solution that served everyone equally, each debtor country was given the opportunity to figure out for itself the best way to make repairs.

Investments Flood Back In

Private investors are pouring money back into Latin America. From net outflows of $13 billion in 1990, they recorded net inflows of almost $26 billion in 1992. Mexico's net outflow of $3.8 billion in 1990 is now a net inflow of $15.3 billion. Argentina has gone from a net outflow of $4.9 billion to an inflow of $5 billion. Meanwhile, Venezuela, which experienced a drain of $4.2 billion in 1992, enjoyed a net inflow of $344 million in 1992. Even Brazil, the region's biggest debtor, has seen a net outflow of $7.4 billion reversed to an inflow of $1.4 billion.

These remarkable turnarounds prompted economists meeting at the London-based Overseas Development Institute to declare that for Latin America the '90s would be "the decade of equity investment."

Still, economists at the London conference argued that this surge in private investments is a mixed blessing. Warning that private investments are notoriously volatile and that any signs of economic improvement in the United States, Japan, and Europe could reverse Latin America's fortunes, World Bank officials discussed the situation with their usual cautious optimism. However, they did also point out the many irreversible benefits of current investment flows which bring to these developing economies new technology, management know-how, and worker retraining. Additionally, export capacity improves as does access to markets. What's more, portfolio investment can lower the cost local companies face in raising capital.

It's their job to be cautious, but the upward trend in Latin American economies is not likely to lose momentum anytime in this decade. And maybe not for decades to come.

Writes Roland Dallas, editor of *The Economist*'s Foreign Report: "The pattern is now unmistakable. In election after election, free-marketeers win office. Privatization starts. Ignoring the example of the 'Giant of the North,' budgets are frequently balanced. Inflation falls to still-imperfect, but reasonable, levels. Flight capital flies back. Exports flourish. Growth resumes."

Predictably, some countries are doing better than others, but most are showing solid, sustainable improvements. Chile, which became the region's standard-bearer as it steadily reduced inflation, privatized industry, and built a trade surplus, is on a continued course toward prosperity. Mexico is also a bright light on the world economic horizon. There is still work to be done there. The country still has a trade deficit to overcome, jobs to create, and inflation to get under control, but foreign direct investment continues apace and the ratification of NAFTA will turn this steady rain into a downpour.

Look for continued high-speed privatization in Argentina, where flight capital is returning in huge quantities to Buenos Aires, mostly from Miami and New York. In 1992, the country's gross domestic product grew at a lusty 9 percent and indications are that 1993 will be even better. For its part, Venezuela has a ways to go in privatizing the state sector, which is an enormous drain on this oil-rich country, and much needs to be done to improve public services—the impetus behind two coup attempts and continued rumblings of discontent. Nonetheless, expect GDP growth of about 5 percent in 1993.

Colombia recently discovered huge oil reserves and the world's multinationals are lining up to help with the extraction. The government has a trade agreement with Venezuela and is opening itself up to foreign competition by slashing import tariffs.

And Bolivia is keeping the faith. One of the first converts to economic reform, it has had many internal pressures to overcome, not the least of which was inflation, which peaked at 23,000 percent in 1985 but is now at an annual rate of only 10 percent. Slowly Bolivia is beginning to attract foreign investments.

Expect some economic surprises in the volatile Central American region starting this year.

Guatemala, El Salvador, Honduras, Nicaragua, Costa Rica, and Panama are enjoying relative peace for the first time since breaking away from Spain in the early 19th century. Although still poor, except Costa Rica and Panama, they are showing early signs of economic recovery. All six countries now have sound monetary policies, and have brought inflation under control. Following in the footsteps of their northern and southern neighbors, Guatemala, El Salvador, and Honduras are forming a common market with a combined population of 20 million. They also are working cooperatively on such structural problems as inflation, interest rates, and fiscal deficits.

Businesses Develop New Regional Strategies

Business Week described how business strategies have changed in the wake of lowered trade barriers. After decades of organizing Latin American operations to accommodate small national markets separated by protectionist trade barriers, foreign companies are now able to consolidate operations and to make long-term business decisions from a regional rather than a small-market perspective.

In the past, for some companies trade barriers meant setting up copycat plants in a dozen countries. Now companies are free to match markets and manufacturing capacity and certainly in some situations are shutting down plants. Dow Chemical, for example, has long had a factory in Brazil and one in Argentina; both made latex and emulsions. Both markets are growing. Formerly, Dow would have had to expand the capacity of each plant to serve separate markets. Today, Dow is trading products between the two plants and won't expand either until both run out of capacity. It also is trading products between plants in Venezuela and Colombia.

Xerox do Brasil has lowered its costs dramatically. As tariffs fell, Xerox was able to replace local materials and components with cheaper imports. In the past, Brazil required the company to make copiers with as much as 90 percent local content. Now local content can be as little as 40 percent, and Xerox has slashed costs by 30 percent, translating into a competitive gain for the company worldwide. Copiers manufactured in Brazil are now exported.

Computer markets also are heating up and IBM is positioning itself to take advantage of this newest growth market. IBM has entered into a joint venture with Villares Group, a Brazilian conglomerate, to get a head start in the rapidly expanding PC market which is now open to foreigners. This same strategy is being pursued by a number of Brazilian computer companies.

For oil and mining companies, it is not so much the lifting of trade restrictions that is making Latin America an attractive investment, but the elimination of government regulation and hostility toward foreign investors. Mineral-rich Peru is privatizing all state-owned companies, including mining operations expropriated from U.S. companies years ago. That times have changed is evidenced by the return of Exxon to Venezuela. When its operations were nationalized in 1975, Exxon lost oil-production capacity of one million barrels a day. Two years ago, the company opened a Caracas office to pursue joint ventures with companies in the region.

Look for that pattern to be repeated over and over again as the United States specifically, but also companies from around the globe, move to take advantage of one of the hottest growth areas in the global economy.

SHARING THE OPPORTUNITIES—PART OF THE REFORM PROCESS

If the momentum of economic reform is to be sustained, then its benefits must be available to all citizens. The Communist government of China understood this basic tenet, and so launched its economic recovery program by first reforming its agricultural sector. Millions of peasant farmers lifted themselves out of poverty as the state encouraged farmers to profit from their labors. Vietnam pursued a similar strategy. And while neither country has eliminated poverty, the overall standard of living for many has greatly improved.

Poverty also plagues Latin America. According to a report issued by the World Bank, income is more concentrated in the hands of the rich in Latin America than in any other region of the world. In the 1980s, inequalities worsened significantly and poverty increased. Unlike that in China and Vietnam, poverty in Latin America is more an urban than a rural problem, requiring very different solutions. Fortunately, it is widely accepted by government officials that social issues must be given high priority. That if the poor are not able to benefit from growth, then all their hard work could be undone.

Antipoverty programs are on the political agendas of virtually every Latin American country. Chile, Mexico, and Argentina are leading the way.

Chile's Antipoverty Program Doesn't Count on Trickle-Down Effect

Adán Ramírez and his wife, Gladys Fuentes, once subsisted on the $170-month income from his electrician's job. They had to choose between eating and paying the bills. Then, in 1980, Ms. Fuentes borrowed $350 through a government program created to help small (tiny) businesses. Fuentes bought an industrial sewing machine with which to do piecework for clothing manufacturers. Today she has five machines, Ramírez has quit his job to join his wife in the sewing business, and together they are making more than $1,000 a month.

Fuentes and Ramírez are two of a growing legion of microentrepreneurs who are making clothing, shoes, and furniture, running fish farms and managing small mining operations, which in turn sell their products to larger manufacturers or traders for exports. Employing fewer than five people, these tiny companies are critical to the economy since they employ 40 percent of the work force and 80 percent of the country's poorest citizens.

They also are the beneficiaries of President Patricio Aylwin's far-reaching antipoverty campaign. When Aylwin took office he imposed a tax increase equivalent to 2 percent of gross domestic product—about $700 million—all revenues from which were to be dedicated to social programs. By all accounts, he has done just that.

Aylwin's strategy for social spending was twofold: Chip away at structural poverty, which is manifested in poor housing, education, and health care, and create programs that increase the earnings of the young and owners of small businesses.

In education, attention was given to the 1,500 primary schools in the poorest districts, raising the salaries of teachers and offering them special training courses. New books were bought, and buildings were repaired. In health, some funds were dedicated to refurbishing hospitals, but more was spent on improving medical treatment centers around the country, keeping them open longer and paying workers better salaries.

All agree, however, that the innovations with the greatest long-term benefits were efforts to create a work force not dependent on a higher minimum wage or higher union wages, but capable of earning more because of their greater skills.

Some 300,000 students a year dropped out of school because their families couldn't afford to keep them there or the students needed to earn extra income for the family. Scholarships were established that paid for books, transportation, and meals. Prizes were given to students who excelled. Official estimates are that the program has kept 100,000 students in school. For students who had no choice but to work, work-study programs were created.

The success of these programs, which rely on tax increases, heavy social spending, and vigorous free-market economic growth, defied the dire predictions of many economists who were certain that they would result in increased unemployment, would bring on a recession and fuel inflation. Instead, the economy grew, unemployment has fallen from 25 percent to 4.4 percent since 1990, and inflation is down from 26 percent in 1989 to 12.7 percent in the first quarter of 1993.

Francisco León, a population expert at the United Nations Economic Commission for Latin America and the Caribbean, says, "While economic growth lifts a lot of people out of poverty, the Chilean experiment shows a government can do more than wait for the trickle-down effect of macroeconomic policies. This means you can target policies to alleviate poverty."

Mexico Moves to Integrate Its Poorest into the Mainstream Economy

According to the World Bank, 20 percent of Mexicans—17 million people—are extremely poor, that is, they do not have enough money to meet minimum nutritional levels. They also have the lowest levels of education. To integrate this group into Mexico's mainstream economy, President Carlos Salinas de Gortari created Solidarity, a $2.7-billion-a-year antipoverty program. Unlike many poverty plans, Solidarity does not pour money into depressed areas in the hopes that funds will find their way into useful programs.

Communities wishing to participate in the program must first form a Solidarity committee, which can then request funds for specific programs. The federal or state government provides basic materials and technical help. The local committee builds its own roads, school, or clinic. Since the community shares the cost of a project, and identifies its own needs, Salinas and his supporters believe it is unlikely that they would choose projects from which they would not benefit.

At present, there are about 100,000 Solidarity committees around the country, providing 10 million people with electricity and water, and eight million people with drainage facilities. Half a million school scholarships have been granted through the program and 2,400 small businesses have been created.

Solidarity provides food for the undernourished, free credit for farmers, risk capital for small businesses, scholarships for children, land titles for squatters, and funds for urgent infrastructure needs such as roads, electricity, and hospitals.

The program is not without its critics, who see it as little more than political grandstanding, a pork-barrel program to ensure Salinas's continued popularity. Carlos Flores Rico, the social development delegate for the state of Mexico, insists that Solidarity has given citizens a stake in their community that will encourage greater productivity in the future. Says Rico, "Now people own their houses, electricity, and water whereas before they were outcasts. Their view of the system has changed."

Menem's Social Plan Improves Quality of Life for Argentina's Poor

Even before Carlos Menem went before the television cameras on January 7, 1993, to announce his new Social Plan, which would spend $1.8 billion on the country's have-nots, life was getting better for the 25 percent of the population who live below the poverty line.

Critics dismiss the Social Plan as a lot of political showmanship; supporters point to programs already in place and insist that this is just what is needed to extend the benefits of economic reform to all Argentineans.

Menem's government already has created programs to help child nutrition, vaccination, AIDS awareness, and flood prevention. Other programs are being created to help bring down the high infant-mortality rate. And his latest promises 22,000 new jobs through health care and work-creation projects.

These programs may well have the result critics say Menem is after—a constitutional amendment lifting the ban on presidential succession, allowing him to run for reelection in 1995—but they also are likely to push the benefits of economic reform down to the country's poorest. Menem is popular because he brought the country back from the brink of disaster. If lifting millions out of poverty ensures reelection, few would argue that that's not a good thing for the country.

Continued economic growth depends on greater democracy; democracy depends on greater citizen participation. When people's basic needs are met, they are more likely to promote the greater good of the community. The more involved they become, the more productive they become. The more productive each individual becomes, the more productive the overall economy. Sharing the wealth, lifting people out of poverty, whether or not the motivation is political, can only improve a country's overall economic performance. That's the lesson that China learned, that Vietnam is learning, and that Latin America also now embraces.

Conclusion

A revolutionary confluence of technological change has set the stage for a new environment that will empower individuals as never before.

Today a person's business card might list a phone number for office and home, a fax number, an E-mail number, an Internet number, and car phone number. But in the not too distant future each person will have a lifelong number that goes with him wherever he goes. His personal computer assistant (which is always with him) will sort out what messages go where. Individuals will phone other individuals wherever they are in the world—without knowing where they are. Heretofore we have always called a place and asked for a person (currently only one third of all calls actually connect on the first try with the person being called). In the new world we will call a person's unique number and the computer in the sky will ring him wherever he is.

This zeroing in on the individual as the locus of this new telecommunications revolution is a metaphor for the Global Paradox:

The larger system in service to the smallest player.

When Bell Atlantic merged with TeleCommunications Inc. and

271

announced the $33 billion merger—the biggest ever—the media focused on its huge size. But the purpose of the merger was to position the new entity to better serve individuals, one by one. Bell Atlantic and TCI coming together was a marriage of great complementarity: Cable networks can carry hundreds of channels of information and entertainment, but they are not very good at allowing people to talk back; telephones, on the other hand, can handle only limited amounts of information, but they are fantastic at switching everyone to anyone else. The new entity combines bulk with traffic control, creating almost unlimited possibilities.

Everything is finally coming together. That is what will create the telecommunications revolution we have heard about for so long.

Here is a list of the ideas and media that are in the process of coming together:

fiber optics	entertainment	cellular
interactive	television	global
digital	computer software	pagers
wireless	telephone	virtual reality
computer	multimedia	networks

Over the next years and decades these ideas and media will be put together in thousands of combinations by thousands of alliances and entrepreneurs. The interplay will create products and services we can't even imagine today. That's why, while we know the telecommunications revolution is upon us, we don't know what it will produce. John C. Malone, the chief executive of TCI, at the news conference announcing the merger with Bell Atlantic, said, ''The overwhelming majority of revenues we get by the end of the decade will be from services and products that have not yet been invented.''

One thing we do know is that the telecommunications revolution will enlarge the role of the individual with more access to information, greater speed in execution, and greater ability to communicate to anyone or to great numbers anywhere, anytime. All trends are in the direction of making the smallest player in the global economy more and more powerful.

The telecommunications revolution is the driving force that is at once creating the world economy and making its parts smaller and more powerful. It is the new technology that is allowing companies to deconstruct, to radically decentralize, to push power and decision making down to the lowest possible point.

The world's smallest companies and the larger ones that have reconstituted themselves as a collection of small companies will survive and flourish.

This radical decentralization applies to the political arena as well. Before the liberating technology was available, companies were hierarchical organizations, and democratic societies were organized through representation. Now citizens who live in representative democracies have the power to radically decentralize and to evolve into direct democracies—a model for this kind of direct democracy is Telluride on Internet—or, as I have suggested, free-market democracies. Centralized governments—in the metaphor, mainframe governments—must now yield to the periphery, to the PCs.

If we have true subsidiarity in our large corporations, why not in our societies? In both instances, we now have the technology to facilitate the necessary communications and computers to keep track of the complexity. Technology now allows for widely and finely distributed activity. Power, activity, and resources are moving from the center to the periphery. The small will flourish in this new environment because they have always been at the periphery and they have economies of scope and the ability to make quick decisions. They have speed. In the old economy speed was not so critical. Today it is everything.

Now that the Cold War is over citizens seem to feel it is safe to seek new and different brands of leadership. The new political leader has not as yet been definitively described, but the old mainframe head of state is obsolete. The voters intuitively know what the pollsters and pundits are only beginning to grasp. In 1993 in France a sitting government lost more than three quarters of its seats in parliament; in Canada the ruling government lost all but two seats. Politicians don't know that the party is over.

And the more democracy there is the more countries, smaller and smaller units, or parts, of the global economy. The spread of self-rule will characterize the decade in front of us. There are almost 200 countries now; there will be 300 or so by the year 2000, heading for 1,000. Somewhere along the way it will become apparent that the idea of countries and borders are irrelevant ideas—as we move toward linking millions of host computer networks, with perhaps 2 billion people all interconnected on a network of networks. The in-place Internet already linking more than 15 million people suggests that 2 billion is not so far-fetched, particularly with the technology we will have in the first decade of the 21st century.

The Global Paradox is a sturdy framework for understanding the world of today. The new rules of business and political conduct that are becoming universal are derived from expectations of local and family practices and relationships. Individual decisions are driving the biggest industry in the world, travel and tourism. Tourism is the face-to-face corollary of the communications revolution. In the context of the Global Paradox you can measure the economic viability of a country by gauging the extent to which the leaders are facilitating the contribution of the parts to the whole. In this regard, China is the test case. With a central, command economy China got nowhere. Now that the leadership is allowing the small parts—in this case, family-based entrepreneurism—to contribute to the whole, China has become the fastest-growing economy in the world and is moving in the direction of becoming the world's largest economy not long after the turn of the decade.

For the years just ahead, the areas of economic growth will be the Americas, from the North Pole to the South Pole, and Asia Pacific. It is in the economic interests of the United States to concentrate on forming economic alliances with the countries of Latin America and with China, Japan, and the four tigers, and Malaysia, Indonesia, Thailand, and Vietnam. In short, the United States should give up the old U.S.-Europe-Japan triangle for a new Americas-Japan-China alliance.

The new leadership required in the world is to facilitate entrepreneurship, the contributions of individuals, to facilitate the sorting out of what will remain local and what will be global, what will remain tribal and what will be universal.

With the end of communism, the decline of the nation-state, the building of a single-market world economy, the spread of democracy throughout the world, and the new revolution in telecommunications, the opportunities, the possibilities, for individuals, families, companies, and institutions are far, far greater than they have even been in any of our lifetimes. The Global Paradox tells us that the opportunities for each of us as individuals are far greater than at any time in human history.

Notes

CHAPTER 1: GLOBAL PARADOX

9–10 Heineken information and quote from "The United States of Europe," privately circulated pamphlet, Amsterdam, June 1992.

12 *Coming of Age in the Milky Way* was published by William Morrow and Company, New York, 1988.

13 Export percentages from Cognetics, Cambridge, Mass.

14 Barnevik quote from "Librarians at the Gate," *Rocky Mountain News*, March 23, 1993.

14 Welch quoted in "Welch Thinks Small, Acts Big," *USA Today*, February 2, 1993.

14 Allaire quote from "Settling Down to Small Talk," *The Financial Times*, March 12, 1993.

15 Galvin quote from "Balancing Corporate Power: A New Federalist Paper," by Charles Handy, *Harvard Business Review*, November–December 1992.

15 Gerstner quote from "Notebooks May Hold Key to IBM's Revival," *The New York Times*, June 23, 1993.

15 IBM quote from "The Shake-up of Big Blue's Army," *The Financial Times,* July 7, 1993.

16 Williams quote from interview with author.

16–17 Gilder quotes and information from "Into the Telecosm," *Harvard Business Review,* March–April 1991.

19 Friedman quote from "Cooperation, Competition Go Hand in Hand," *The Nikkei Weekly,* May 31, 1993.

22 *The Economist,* July 6, 1991.

23–24 Luca Pacioli story drawn from "Father of Accounting Is Bit of a Stranger to His Own Progeny," *The Wall Street Journal,* January 29, 1993.

27–28 Indonesian information on banning English from "Indonesia to Expunge English Ads," *Media,* Asia's media and marketing newspaper.

28 Colonna d'Istria quote from *Publishers Weekly,* March 8, 1993.

29 Archbishop Carey quote from "Archbishop Offers Vision of Europe," *The Financial Times,* February 18, 1993.

29 "Monetary Chernobyl" from "Krygyzstan Is Out from Under the Ruble," *The Wall Street Journal,* May 18, 1993.

29 Fyodorov quote, ibid.

31 Perrin quote from "Cartier: Snobbery with Mass Appeal," *International Herald Tribune,* April 22, 1993.

31 All quotes and information in Name That Country section from *The Sunday Times* (London), August 1, 1993.

38 Tatarstan's constitution quote from "Regions Wrest Powers from Kremlin," *The Washington Post,* May 25, 1993.

47 Projections of the number of Internet users from "Internetworking and the Internet," by Vinton G. Cerf, Internet Society, Reston, Va., 1993.

47–48 Information on Community Computer Networks from "Community Computer Networks," by Steve Cisler, privately circulated.

48 Valéry quote from "Today in History," *Rocky Mountain News,* December 19, 1992.

CHAPTER 2: POWERING THE PARADOX

57 Scully quote from "Beyond the PC: Apple's Promised Land," *The New York Times,* November 15, 1992.

58 Information on personal computer systems from various articles including "Era of the Tiny PC," *The New York Times,* March 23, 1992.

59 Caraso quote from "General Magic Got Quite a Start," *Digital Media,* March 29, 1993, Vol. 2, No. 10–11.

60 Hoffman quote from "Rebels Turned Diplomats," *The Financial Times,* February 8, 1993.

61–63 Kravner statement and Wheeler, McCaw, Martin, and Fisher quotes from "Building a Wireless Future," *Business Week,* April 5, 1993.

63 Dougherty quote from "Era of the Tiny PC Is Nearly at Hand," *The New York Times,* March 23, 1992.

64 Saffo quote from "Your Digital Future," *Business Week,* September 7, 1992.

65 Leibowitz quote and cable companies information and Southwestern Bell data from "Phone Company Breaks Ground by Buying into Cable Television," *The New York Times,* February 10, 1993.

65–67 Stage Is Set for Alliances—and Raids, and Cable Companies Fight Back sections from various sources including *New York Times* article directly above and "Telephone Service Seems on the Brink of Huge Innovations," *The New York Times,* February 10, 1993.

68 Bullets on cooperation between cable and phone companies reported in "Cable, Phone Firms Wrangle over Future," *USA Today,* February 11, 1993.

68–70 Bullets from various sources including "Merger Activity Is Up," *The Wall Street Journal,* June 16, 1993.

71 Argentina and its phone system described in "Privatisation Programmes, Momentum Remains Strong," *The Financial Times*, October 15, 1992.

73 Hungary information from "For Emerging Countries," *Business Week*, April 5, 1993.

74–77 Telecommunications activity in China reported in "Long March from Chaos"; Taiwan happenings from "Still Room at the Top"; Philippine action from "Home Before Abroad"; and Pakistan and Bangladesh described in "Radio vs. Fiber As Way to Go." All articles appeared in the June 4, 1992, issue of the *Far Eastern Economic Review*.

78 Morelli quote from "Developing Cross-Border European Communications," Northern Telecom Advertisement Feature on the 4th Economist Telecommunications Conference.

80 Tobias quote from "In Today Walks Tomorrow," *Vital Speeches of the Day*, delivered to the McDonough Caperton Lecture Series, University of West Virginia, October 1, 1992.

81 Dertouzos quote from "Communications, Computers and Networks," *Scientific American*, September 1991, Vol. 265, No. 3.

81 Hall quote from "Road to the Future: Computers and the Information Highway," *Harvard Gazette*, July 9, 1993.

81 Tobias quote from *Vital Speeches of the Day*, listed above.

82 Dertouzos quote from *Scientific American*, listed above.

82 Data on fiber-optic bits and 70 million simultaneous conversations from Tobias article listed above.

84 Motorola research reported in "Building a Wireless Future," *Business Week*, April 5, 1993.

85 Dertouzos quote from *Scientific American*, listed above.

86–88 Kapor quote and information from "Where Is the Digital Highway Really Heading?," *Wired*, July–August 1993.

87 Smoot and Bushkin quotes from "Ring in the New: Telephone Service Seems on the Brink of Huge Innovations," *The Wall Street Journal*, February 10, 1993.

87–88 Lawrence quote from "ADSL: A High-Bandwidth Hope for Copper," *Telephony,* October 5, 1992, Vol. 223, No. 14.

90 Kapor quote from *Wired,* listed above.

93 Grove quote and Sculley estimate from "Your Digital Future," *Business Week,* September 7, 1992.

93 Kagan Associates estimate from "Boob Tube No More," *Business Week,* June 7, 1993.

94 Johnson quote from "What Multimedia Means to PCs," *Advertising Age,* November 4, 1991.

95 Quote from "A Far-out Ride to the Future: Multimedia Age Is at Hand," *The Washington Post,* February 14, 1993.

95 Kessler quote, ibid.

101–102 All Weiser quotes from "The Computer for the 21st Century," *Scientific American,* September 1991, Vol. 265, No.3.

CHAPTER 3: TRAVEL

103–104 Survey of 400 policy and opinion makers reported in "Travel and Tourism Is Top Employer," *Travel Weekly,* August 1992.

104 Bullets on tourism, taxes generated, and jobs worldwide from the WTTC's 1993 report *Travel and Tourism.*

104 Global tourism growth and employment between 1990 and 1993 reported in "Travel & Tourism Is Top Employer," *Travel Weekly,* April 6, 1992.

104–105 Lipman quote from "World Council Forecasts Boom in Industry Jobs," *The Asian Wall Street Journal Weekly,* July 12, 1993.

105–106 The survey appeared in *The Economist,* March 23, 1991.

107 Business travelers data and industry analyst information from "Fierce Battle for Hearts and Wallets," *The Financial Times,* April 19, 1993. IATA survey information appeared in the same paper in "A Time for Fresh Ideas."

108 Conway quote from *Airport Cities 21,* Conway Data, Inc., Atlanta, p. 75.

109–110 Airline losses reported in "Bitter Fruits of Deregulation," *The Wall Street Journal,* April 8, 1993.

111 *International Herald Tribune* quote appeared in "International Air Travel: 1990s Outlook," March 3, 1990.

113 GAO report described in "Shift Urged on Foreign Stakes in Airlines," *The New York Times,* January 9, 1993.

114 Crandall information from "Strong Head Wind," *The Economist,* October 10, 1992.

114 U.S. carriers and their percentage of international travel reported in "U.S. Airlines Are Challenged Abroad," *The Washington Post,* April 19, 1993.

115 Increase in international travel reported in "Flights Overseas to Soar," *USA Today,* March 20, 1990.

115–116 Bunya-ananta quote from "Dogfight over Asia," *Far Eastern Economic Review,* March 11, 1993.

116 Air travel growth in Asia and the Pacific from "International Air Travel: 1990s Outlook," *International Herald Tribune,* March 3, 1990.

116 Scott quote from "Dogfight over Asia," *Far Eastern Economic Review,* March 11, 1993.

116 *The Economist* quote appeared in "Too Many Airlines," October 19, 1991.

117 Mesa Airlines was described in "The Little Carrier That Could," *The New York Times,* August 23, 1992.

117 Amount required to meet the needs of passengers and Cahill quote from "Operators: Airports Need $50B," *USA Today,* March 2, 1990.

118 Hoyt quote, Japanese airport data, and *Asia Technology* quote from "Airports for the 21st Century," which appeared in the March 1990 issue.

119 Conway quote from *Airport Cities 21,* p. 29.

120 *Travel Industry World Yearbook* quote appeared on p. 4. The *1992 Yearbook* was published by Child & Waters, Inc., Rye, N.Y.

120–121 American Express office openings reported in "Amexco Opens 5 Slovak Offices," *Travel Weekly,* January 25, 1993.

121 Paine quote reported in *Travel Industry World Yearbook 1992,* p. 5.

122–124 Statistics on people over fifty-five and travel data between America and Europe reported in "Broaden the Mind," *The Economist,* March 23, 1991.

124 Coates quote appeared in "The Future of Tourism," *Vital Speeches of the Day,* October, 1, 1992.

124 *Travel & Leisure* quote appeared in "Adventures of a Lifetime," May 1992.

125 Williams quote is from "Green Cathedrals," *Maclean's,* August 24, 1992.

125 Loeks information reported in "Honing the Arctic Edge," *Alaska Business Monthly,* March 1992.

126 *International Herald Tribune* quote appeared in "New Destinations from an Oasis to the Arctic," March 3, 1990.

126 *Parks and Recreation* quote appeared in "Research on Adventure [Risk] Recreation," May 1991.

126 Danner quote from "Thrill-Seekers Proliferate," *Industry Week,* November 16, 1992.

127 The *USA Today* section "Leisure Travel" appeared in the February 11, 1993, issue.

127 *World Travel & Tourism Review,* Vol. 1, 1991, CAB International, Wallingford, United Kingdom, p. 152.

128 Galápagos Islands information from "Wide Horizons," *The Futurist,* September–October 1992.

128 Hawkins quote from "Eco-tourism Gets a Collective Voice," *The Financial Times,* October 14, 1992.

128–130 Some of the advantages of ecotourism were drawn from "Market Approach to Conservation," *Rocky Mountain News*, August 11, 1992.

130–131 Kurent quote from *World Travel & Tourism Review*, Vol. 1, 1991, p. 81.

131 Tourism earnings in 1991 in developing countries from the WTTC.

131 Natureland Brazil campaign described in "Reopening the Road to Rio," *Financial Times*, December 10, 1992.

132 Caribbean tourism statistics from *Travel Industry World Yearbook 1992*, p. 80, and the WTTC's 1993 report *Travel and Tourism*.

133 Davidoff quote from "Against the Tide," *Time*, February 17, 1992.

133–134 Cruise statistics and information, ibid., and "Choose a Cruise," *Travel Holiday*, October 1991.

134 Singapore information reported in "Singapore Strives to Position Itself as Industry's Gateway to Far East," *Travel Weekly Cruise Guide*, January 7, 1993.

135 Dickinson quote from "Against the Tide," *Time*, February 17, 1992.

136 Portugal data from *Tourism Policy and International Tourism in OECD Member Countries*, published by the OECD, 1992.

138 Tourism statistics from WTTC's 1993 report *Travel and Tourism*.

140–141 Ritchie quote from *World Travel & Tourism Review*, Vol. 1, 1991, p. 150.

142 Budapest World's Fair figures from "Budapest to Be 1996 site of World's Fair," *The New York Times*, April 26, 1992. World Cup data from "USTTA Chief: World Cup Will Lure," *Travel Weekly*, April 2, 1993.

143–144 FAST described in *WTTC Review*, Vol. 2, No. 2, September–October 1992.

144 Quote about ODAPS from "An Air Traffic System Goes Off Course," *Condé Nast Traveler*, March 1993.

CHAPTER 4: NEW RULES

147 Wilson quote from *The Moral Sense* (New York: The Free Press: 1993).

150–151 Capriles and Escovar Salom quotes from "Venezuelans Undergoing a Political Awakening," *The Washington Post*, May 21, 1993.

152 Quotes from "Throwing the Bums Out," *Newsweek*, March 15, 1993, and *The Financial Times*, February 27, 1993.

152 Engholm quote from "German Opposition Leader Quits in Scandal, Kohl Stands to Gain," *The Washington Post*, May 4, 1993.

152 Möllemann report from "Minister Quits," *The European*, January 7–10, 1993. Russ-Mohl quote from "Germans Revel in Scandal-Watching," *The Washington Post*, April 1, 1993.

152 *Newsweek* quote from "Rebels with a Cause," February 8, 1993.

153 Japanese section from "Japan: The Fall of the Don," *Newsweek*, October 6, 1992. Whitson quote from "A Matter of Ethics," *Industry Week*, March 16, 1992.

155 U.S. investment in China reported in "China Presents Dilemma for Clinton's Policy," *The Washington Post*, May 1993.

155 State Department report quotes from "Human Rights Improve Globally, State Department Says," *Los Angeles Times*, January 20, 1993.

156 U.N. actions in Cambodia and Akashi warning reported in "U.N. Official Warns Cambodians," *The Washington Post*, May 19, 1993.

156 Sri Lanka information and Udagama quote from "Sri Lankans Address World's Worst Human Rights Record," *The Christian Science Monitor*, May 4, 1993.

159 Viederman quote from "Sustainable Development: What It Is and How Do We Get There," presented at Stanford University, November 1991.

159 Bowie quote from "Business Ethics: Highlights of Bentley College's Eighth National Conference on Business Ethics," October 26 and 27, 1989, p. 6.

159–160 Mahoney quote and bullets on business leaders' actions from "Executives of the World Unite," *Business Ethics*, September–October 1992.

161 L'Eggs action reported in "Plastic Out, 'Green' L'Eggs the Plan," *USA Today*, July 10, 1991.

161 Sizer quote from "No Waste Here," *Business Ethics*, November–December 1992.

161–162 Wellman Inc. description from "Darling, You Look Stunning," *Business Week*, May 3, 1993.

162 Martin quote from "Executives of the World Unite," *Business Ethics*, September–October 1992.

162 *Business Week* quote from "How Corporate America Would Go About Being Green," May 3, 1993.

162–163 Cox and Power quotes from "Executives of the World Unite," *Business Ethics*, September–October 1992.

163 *Industry Week* quote from "Business Integrity, an Oxymoron?," April 6, 1992.

163–164 O'Neill quotes from "True Innovation, True Values, True Leadership," *Industry Week*, April 19, 1993.

164–165 *Industry Week* survey, quotes, and data on bias in the hiring process from "Torn Between Halos and Horns," March 15, 1993.

165 Josephson statement from "The New Crisis in Business Ethics," *Fortune*, April 20, 1992.

166 Corporations building ethics programs reported in "More Big Businesses Set Up Ethics Offices," *The Wall Street Journal*, May 7, 1993.

166 Hoffman quote, ibid.

166–167 NatWest data and quote from "NatWest Publishes Its Principles," *The Financial Times*, May 26, 1993.

167 Spokesperson quote from "Laying Down a Code of Honor," *The Financial Times*, May 26, 1993.

168 Burke quote and J&J information from "Businesses Are Signing Up for Ethics 101," *Business Week*, February 15, 1988.

168–169 Textron data, federal regulations, and Neary quote from "More Big Businesses Set Up Ethics Offices," *The Wall Street Journal*, May 7, 1993.

169 Hertz information and Olson quote from "Hertz Is Doing Some Bodywork—on Itself," *Business Week*, February 15, 1988.

169 Boeing described in "Businesses Are Signing Up for Ethics 101," *Business Week*, February 15, 1988.

170 Badaracco and Stark quotes from "What's the Matter with Business Ethics?," *Harvard Business Review*, May–June 1993.

170 General Mills executive quote from "Businesses Are Signing Up for Ethics 101," *Business Week*, February 15, 1988.

170–171 van Luijk quotes from "A Threefold Function of Ethics," *European Business Ethics Newsletter*, Vol. 6, December 1992.

171–172 Business Leaders Forum information and quote and Volkswagen data from "Green the Color, and Caring the Name of the Game," *The European*, January 7–10, 1993.

172–173 Nike information and Knight quote from "If the Shoe Fits," *Business Ethics*, November–December 1992.

173–175 *Far Eastern Economic Review* statement, Kidd, Kazin, and Messick quotes, and information on Wal-Mart, Heinz, Home Depot, and Levi Strauss from "The Supply Police," *Newsweek*, February 15, 1993.

175 Clark quote from "A Matter of Ethics: Why Japan Is Not Like the U.S.," *Industry Week*, March 16, 1992.

176 Number of business ethics courses and *Harvard Business*

Review quote from "What's the Matter with Business Ethics?," May–June 1993.

176–177 Weiner quotes from "Business in the 21st Century," *The Futurist*, March–April 1992.

CHAPTER 5: THE DRAGON CENTURY

180 Purchasing power parity methodology from "Agency Ranks China's Economy No. 3 in World, but Some Analysts Question Validity of Figures," *The Asian Wall Street Journal Weekly*, May 31, 1993.

181 Krugman quote from "New Tally of World's Economies Catapults China into Third Place," *The New York Times*, May 20, 1993.

182 Source for "million millionaires": *China Digest*, excerpted in *China Watch*, March 1993.

183 Information about the PLA's role in the economy from "China's Military Launches Profit Offensive," *Far Eastern Economic Review*, October 14, 1993.

184 Chen quote from "China's Young Capitalists Choose Dollars over Doctrine," *The Washington Post*, April 11, 1993.

184 Shambaugh quote, ibid.

185 Source of statistics re China's growth: "When China Wakes," *The Economist*, November 28, 1992.

186 "China Titan Stirs," *The Economist*, November 28, 1992.

188 Perkins quote from "When China Wakes," *The Economist*, November 28, 1992.

190 Source of statistics re Xiao Shan's economy, ibid.

191 Rongsheng information from *Business Week*, May 17, 1993.

192 Source for data re Motorola: "Motorola in China: A Great Leap Forward," *Business Week*, May 17, 1993.

193 Source for CAAC data: "China Turns to BA for Advice," *The Financial Times*, June 6, 1993.

193 Source for airport and airplane sales data: "Aircraft Orders to Take Off," *China Daily,* May 3, 1993.

195 Goizueta quote from "Corporate America's Infatuation," *Singapore Business Times,* April 28, 1993.

195 Quote about RJ Reynolds from "China Land of Opportunity for U.S. Tobacco Industry," *Telluride Daily Planet,* June 21, 1993.

200 Novosad quote from *China Business Strategies for the '90s,* by Arne J. De Keijzer (Berkeley, Calif.: Pacific View Press, 1992).

201 Quote from "Don't Joke About This Stock Market," *The New York Times,* May 9, 1993.

201 Source of stock market statistics: ibid.

201 Schreyer quote, ibid.

202 Wu quote from "Shareholding Leads to a Pot of Gold for Farmers," *China Daily,* April 12, 1993.

205 Yang success story and quote from "Entrepreneurs Banking on Loans in the Private Sector," *Hong Kong Sunday Morning Post,* February 28, 1993.

207 Tam quote and Dongguan information from "The Rush Through China's Most Open Door," *International Herald Tribune,* June 2, 1992.

207 Quote from "China's Hunan Province Hopes to Match Neighbors," *The Asian Wall Street Journal,* June 1, 1993.

208 Information on Hunan, ibid.

209 Quote from "The New Religion Is Money; Shanghai Flamboyance Returns," *Los Angeles Times,* January 15, 1993.

209 Huang quote from "Centrist at a Golden Crossroads," *The Financial Times,* May 17, 1993.

209 Huang quote, ibid.

210 Zhang quote from "The New Religion Is Money; Shanghai Flamboyance Returns," *Los Angeles Times,* January 15, 1993.

210 Source of data re tourism: ibid.

214 Quote from "Why the Chinese Are Making It While the Russians Aren't," *Singapore Business Times*, April 7, 1993.

216 Kao quote from "The Worldwide Web of Chinese Business," *Harvard Business Review*, March–April 1993.

217 Kao quote, ibid.

218 World Bank report quote from "The Next Economic Giant? Watch Greater China," *International Herald Tribune*, April 27, 1993.

219 Shih quote from "Asia Investments Make China Competitor, As Well As Consumer," *The Wall Street Journal*, May 17, 1993.

220 Adviser quote from "Beijing and Taipei Prepare to Open Historic Dialogue," *The Asian Wall Street Journal*, April 26, 1993.

220 Quote, ibid.

221 Cheng quote from "Here Comes Greater China, Getting Richer by the Day," *International Herald Tribune*, May 27, 1993.

CHAPTER 6: ASIA AND LATIN AMERICA

232 Howell quote from "Push Comes to Shove: Western Europe Is Ailing, Angry and Afraid of the Future," *U.S. News & World Report*, June 14, 1993.

233 Maclean quote from "Bolivia's New Generation Takes the Helm," *The Wall Street Journal*, June 11, 1993.

234 Dunkel quote from "GATT to Be Good," *Far Eastern Economic Review*, May 1993.

235 Source of statistics on Asian growth: ibid.

235 Wain quote from "Asia's New World Order Strut," *The Asian Wall Street Journal*, May 25, 1993.

241 Floria quote from "The New World's Newest Trading Bloc," *Business Week*, May 4, 1992.

243 Mahathir quote from "PM: Asia Will Be Home to Economic Miracles," *The Star*, May 1, 1993.

244–245 NAFTA-related statistics and information from "How NAFTA Will Help America," *Fortune*, April 19, 1993.

246 Elisha quote, ibid.

248–249 List of foreign investments from "Vietnam: Business Rushes to Get In," *Fortune*, April 5, 1993.

250 Nguyen quote, ibid.

251 Wheeler quote from "Poll: Renewed Vietnam Ties Favored," *USA Today*, July 13, 1993.

252 Analyst quote about government strategy from "Is Singapore a Model for the West?," *Time*, January 18, 1993.

252 Quote about government's strategy from "Singapore Invests in Nation-Corporation," *Harvard Business Review*, May–June, 1992.

253 Sisodia quote, ibid.

255 Niyazov quote from "New State Untouched by Chaos," *The Washington Post*, March 23, 1993.

258 O'Rear and Hooke statistics cited in "Asian Economic Growth May Change World Order," *The Asian Wall Street Journal*, May 17, 1993.

259 Report quoted in "Outlook Brightens for Latin Economies," *International Herald Tribune*, March 29, 1993.

260 Quote from "The Disaster That Didn't Happen," *The Economist*, September 12, 1992.

261 Statistics and quote from "Investment Pours Back into Latin America," *The Financial Times*, February 12, 1993.

262 Dallas quote from "Latin America Prepares to Sprint," "The World in 1993," *The Economist*'s Foreign Report.

263 *Business Week*'s description of changing business strategies from "Latin America to Be Home to Free Markets," July 15, 1992.

267 Leon quote from "Chile Advances in a War on Poverty and One Million Mouths Say Amen," *The New York Times*, April 4, 1993.

267 Information on Solidarity programs from "Mexico: Salinas Leads the Attack on Poverty," *The Financial Times*, March 26, 1993.

268 Rico quote, ibid.

268 Information on Menem's health programs from "New for the Poor," *The Economist*, January 16, 1993.

CONCLUSION

272 Malone quote from "When We Build It, Will They Come?," *The New York Times*, October 17, 1993.

Acknowledgments

The first person to be acknowledged is the godfather of this book, my agent, Bill Leigh. He knew I was to write what turned out to be *Global Paradox* long before I had any idea I was going to do it. He slowly and gently allowed me to understand what I had to do, all the while arranging for the publishing contract and editor. Now that it is over and I've delivered the manuscript, I thank him for it, and I thank him for his contributions to the concept of the book and to the book itself. I now thank the editor, too, who turned out to be Adrian Zackheim, who is editorial director at William Morrow. I've known Adrian for some time. He was our editor on *Megatrends 2000*. Besides being a wonderful and extremely intelligent human being, Adrian could not have been more supportive of this project. At one point he journeyed to my home in Telluride, Colorado, to spend a couple of days helping me conceptualize the book.

My deeply felt thanks go to my primary researcher and collaborator Corinne Kuypers-Denlinger, without whose support and contributions this book would not have been completed, certainly not anywhere near the time it was. Her devotion to this project was heartwarming and her memos were the foundation for a good part of the book.

Steve Rhinesmith, who read several versions of the manuscript, was extremely important in helping me conceptualize many of the ideas in the book, and, indeed, the book itself.

I owe a great debt to Foong Wai Fong, the managing director of the Transforma Group of Companies out of Hong Kong and Malaysia, who provided an endless stream of information and counsel regarding the extraordinary transformation of China, and who read and commented on several versions of the chapter on China.

Peter Lert read the entire first draft of the manuscript and made many helpful suggestions and corrections. Phil Burgess read the penultimate version; one could have no more penetrating, interesting, and creative reader than he. From both Peter and Phil I learned a lot, and from each I pinched some comments for the book.

Launny Steffens was another who read the manuscript and gave warm support and incisive comments. Kyle Roth and Richard Lowenberg read the chapter on telecommunications and did their best to keep me out of trouble on that complex subject.

Pamela Zoline read early versons of several chapters. Her keen intelligence pushed me onward in desired directions. Several people read the title chapter: Wendy Brooks, Bill Ury, Oscar Motomura in Brazil, Bill Brock, Kyoko Nagai, Elizabeth Sherwood, and in Sweden, those great foresighters Sven Atterhed, Gustaf Delin, and Lennart Boksjö. I thank them for their thoughtful and useful comments.

I give very special thanks to our longtime researcher Joy Van Elderen and the head of our office, Linda McLean Harned. Both read and commented on various versions of the manuscript, in addition to providing the support structure needed for such a project. My thanks also to a young graduate student, Matt Moseley, who helped me during the summer of 1993 go through the stacks of newspapers I get every day at my home in Telluride.

Lastly, and most importantly, I want to thank my wife, Patricia Aburdene, my children, and my grandchildren, who put up with my neglecting them so much during 1993 while I was obsessively cobbling this book together, and to whom I now return.

Index

295